MAR1 6 1994

Accounting

Accounting

a book of readings

Edited by

GERHARD G. MUELLER
University of Washington

CHARLES H. SMITH
University of Texas

HOLT, RINEHART AND WINSTON, INC.
New York   Chicago   San Francisco   Atlanta
Dallas   Montreal   Toronto   London   Sydney

To our wives,
Coralie
and
Anjoe.

Preface

The title of this book is *Accounting: A Book of Readings,* and the emphasis is on introduction *to* accounting. We have carefully avoided giving any space to topics which traditionally have fallen into the realm of *fundamentals* of accounting, *elements* of accounting, *introductory* accounting, *essentials* of accounting, and all the rest of similar titles. Books carrying these titles are designed to serve as a first step in learning something about the techniques, procedures, and concepts underlying actual accounting processes.

Our introduction to accounting has a liberal arts flavor—it is not a traditional approach with a particular bent. Thus we have not limited ourselves to a particular direction of accounting thought—be it behavioral, financial, quantitative, managerial, or information theory/computer science oriented. Rather, we have attempted to paint as nontechnical a picture as we could of what accounting is, how it relates to the affairs of modern men, how and why it comes into play at all levels of organized society, and how it manifests itself in its day-to-day applications for a highly differentiated variety of purposes.

It is our view that the contents of this book has significance for any citizen of a modern industrial state. Thus it is not a book designed only for prospective business administration majors, and much less one only for prospective accounting majors. At the same time, we feel strongly that the business administration student, as well as the future accounting specialist, will benefit as much from studying the material in this book as will the student in forestry who plans a career as a national park ranger, the future hospital or public school administrator, or individuals working as industrial engineers or as professional architects. In fact, this book might well be used as a framework for a financial citizenship course useful for college and university students in general. While we recognize that our goal for this book is ambitious, we are convinced that it will fill a need already demonstrated on many campuses.

We believe firmly that the bare structure of double-entry book-keeping is inappropriate to introduce students to that which constitutes the discipline of accounting. We feel that both procedural and conceptual aspects of the accounting process can be taught more efficiently *after* a student has been introduced *to* accounting. Technical processes make more sense if one understands how they operate in a larger setting, whom they affect, and why they are important. Moreover, the whole process of learning is more enjoyable if one has prior awareness of the potential consequences and general implications of the material being studied.

Depending upon individual curricula and course sequences, we submit that *Accounting: A Book of Readings* can be used effectively in conjunction with most existing introductory accounting texts. It can also be used by itself if it is supplemented with appropriate lecture notes and selected problems and case materials. The book should be useful in undergraduate curricula as well as for non-business administration students entering graduate work in schools and colleges of business administration. Moreover, continuing education programs and professional development activities for practicing accountants or financial management and personnel should find good use for a large portion of the material in this book.

Collection of materials for the type of book at hand entailed considerably greater difficulty than was first anticipated. The vast majority of existing accounting literature is written by accountants for accountants. Accounting literature seems singularly replete with technical jargon, narrow in its subject orientation, and typically pitched at a level that appears unintelligible to the uninitiated. In order to find simple, concise, and yet relatively broadly based expressions of the various aspects comprising the accounting discipline, we had to turn to a number of articles published either by American authors in foreign journals or by foreign authors published in both foreign and American journals. In the end this proved to be an ideal solution to our dilemma. We not only found material of the type we desired, but were able to portray some insights on the accounting scene in the United States which only a person from without could achieve by using distance and perspective. Furthermore, our rather international collection of sources implies that accounting is really not as nationally oriented as some textbooks and much of the literature would lead one to believe at first blush.

Without the kind consideration of the original publishers and authors and their respective permissions to reproduce the material found in this book, we would have been stalemated at the start. We recognize our indebtedness to these individuals and organizations, and express our thanks to them. We also acknowledge the stimulation and encouragement received from our colleagues at our two respective universities. Finally, we are not reluctant to concede that the initial conceptualization of the content for this book would not have taken place at this time without the support from the Price Waterhouse Foundation for an educational project in the subject matter area.

Seattle, Washington G. G. M.
Austin, Texas C. H. S.
May 1970

Contents

PART SIX
EDUCATION AND CAREERS   383

PART SEVEN
EPILOGUE—THE DYNAMISM OF ACCOUNTING   411

Part One

Accounting Influences and Is Influenced by Its Environment

The cause and effect between the organisms, institutions, and total structure of society and the practice of accounting run in both directions. Accounting must look to its environment for what society recognizes as value, what property rights society protects, what organizations and institutions are used to carry on economic exchange, and what legal and political procedures and instruments are involved in economic transactions and organizational operations. The environment thus shapes accounting.

On the other hand, accounting functions as part of the information-communication-feedback networks that bind a society and that members of society use to control and reshape the environment. Accounting provides an important part of the information base for the constant reevaluation of social, political, and economic objectives and the relative costs and benefits of the alternative means of achieving these objectives. In short, the societal role of accounting is a supportive function—an information

1

service among the various microorganisms in the total social system. This instrumental role is essential to the individual functioning of each part of the total social system insofar as each part must deal with other parts in the system.

The first group of readings introduces the reciprocal environmental effects of accounting (Capon and Ma). All elements of society should have an interest in this—from the collection of tax revenues to the reporting of financial affairs of large corporations, and on to the management of large-scale government-directed enterprises like the new social programs for economic opportunity. The shorter selections in this section illustrate how virtually all societal processes depend in some measure on information produced by various accounting systems. These selections also show that accountants are found in many interesting administrative positions throughout society.

Environmental influences and effects upon accounting are illustrated in a forceful fashion by the history of accounting development (Newgarden). Throughout its existence accounting has responded sharply to new concerns of society. These have included the profit motive of early Italian seafaring traders and early British mercantilists, the factory-cost problems of the age of the industrial revolution, and the financial stewardship reporting problems to absentee business owners in the modern corporate enterprise system (Fesmire). Responsive change has been particularly pronounced in the last few decades within which accountants have become concerned over a myriad of innovations ranging from the use of electronic computers to behavioral elements of management control systems, and economic concentration ushered in by a wholesale business merger movement. The selection from Storey illustrates the cycles in "The Search for Accounting Principles" that have occurred in the United States since about 1930. Details of more recent accounting responses are explored further in subsequent sections of this book.

The final group of selections in this initial part of the book sets the stage for an appreciation of the fact that the accounting function plays an important role in every known social and economic system. The massive mobilization of industry in recent totalitarian systems like Nazi Germany and her Axis allies could not have been accomplished without planning and control devices facilitated by accounting systems. Today's Soviet system requires efficient accounting systems just as much as any market-oriented economic system does. The well-known political economist, Werner Sombart, asserts that large-scale economic enterprise could never have developed in the absence of double-entry bookkeeping—or at least a comparable system of rigorous and precise record-keeping. Central administration and control of large enterprises simply cannot occur without the systematic information provided by accounting. Thus the reader is introduced to the notion that the dimensions of accounting reach across all socioeconomic systems, even though the particulars (Hoover and Fischer) might be fashioned by the environment of a given type of system. On a very general level, accounting may well play the same role in any system. This is explored further in Part Four.

In concluding the introduction of environmental accounting relationships, one might recognize that a direct relationship may exist between accounting development and economic development, which would in turn give accounting a special significance in the affairs of the newly developing nations. This likelihood is raised in Ross' article. Similar to most selections offered throughout the book, Ross' article merely introduces the subject without extensive development of it or exhaustive references to the literature on the subject.

Chapter I

The Role of Accounting in Societal Processes

1. Accounting in an Expanding Environment*

Frank S. Capon**

Like all types of men through the ages, the accountant of tomorrow will be a creature of his environment. Thus, to get any feel for his opportunities, his responsibilities, or his problems, it is necessary first to consider the environment in which he will operate. Since accountants collect, analyze, evaluate, interpret, and report on the myriad transactions that take place daily between individuals, corporations, and institutions, the environment in which we are interested is that of the total economy—its basic nature, its fiscal policies and tools, its political orientation, and even the economic relationships between nations.

It would be both easy and reassuring to assume that we shall continue to follow the comfortable gradual economic development of the past, with the free enterprise system secure in the developed nations and rapidly spreading its proven blessings into the underdeveloped nations. But in a world of constant change, the one thing we can be sure of is that the environment of tomorrow will be vastly different from that of today. The very speed of change itself is increasing on an exponential curve. The discernible trends which will determine our economic future—population, technology, productivity, and so on—are all in the early phase of a steep upward curve after gradually gathering momentum through the ages. The challenge to our leaders—business, political, professional, and academic—will be to maintain enough control to prevent

* Reprinted from *Financial Executive*, December 1967, pages 45–54.
** Frank S. Capon is Director and Vice-president of Du Pont of Canada.

5

the entire system from disintegrating through the force of its gathering momentum. And because control will depend upon ever more accurate, ever faster information, the accountant of tomorrow will be a key figure as the increasing momentum of change brings fateful decisions within the range of our generation.

Our basic assumption is that the first objective of any community is to achieve the highest possible average living standard for its people. While there have always been differences of opinion on how this should be achieved, it seems safe to assume that it will continue to be the aim of all peoples. Regardless of its political or social system, the average living standard of any community must depend upon the amount of wealth it creates and the manner in which that wealth is distributed. If wealth generation is low, average living standards will be low. If wealth generation is high, average living standards will be high unless too much wealth is retained by a few wealthy groups.

GEOMETRIC RATE OF GROWTH

Wealth is generated by the application of man's faculties to the natural resources placed at his disposal. Apart from the limitations of raw materials, the amount of wealth generated depends both on man's ingenuity and on the degree of effort he is prepared to devote to improving his living standard.

For the earliest man, mere maintenance of life called for constant, brutally hard labor with bare hands. Such discoveries as the shovel, the axe, the wheel, and metals, spaced thousands of years apart, made possible fantastic leaps forward in man's fight to improve his way of life. And naturally one development led to another, so that progress fed upon itself.

It is, of course, this last fact which accounts for the geometric rate of growth in technology. For the great technological discoveries, which at first came painfully slowly, developed with increasing rapidity as the total body of technical knowledge accumulated. The developments of the present generation—computers, television, the jet engine, atomic power, space travel, antibiotics, lasers, masers, and so forth—have probably been greater than the sum of all prior human accomplishments in technology. This explosive increase in our ability to create wealth threatens to outpace our social ability to distribute wealth under our existing systems.

LIVING WITH AUTOMATION

Already technology exists for revolutionizing the management process and particularly the information collection and dissemination system which is at the heart of the accounting function. Since 1945 we have seen in North America a sharp drop in the proportion of workers employed directly in production and a sharp rise in the proportion of so-called white-collar workers. This phenomenon is due largely to the fact that we were able to introduce new technology very quickly into production operations, whereas sharply higher output processed by the old clerical and marketing methods resulted in huge increases in employment in these tasks. Machine systems exist for the automation of much of this work, permitting a totally new concept of management with far fewer people, more delegation of authority, and vastly improved control. The new standards of efficiency can become effective only when accountants make the fullest use of the new machine systems to collect business information automatically, to process it on predetermined programs, and to provide the figures and explanations needed for planning and control through a small but highly skilled staff backed up by the new hardware. There are, of course, frightening social and emotional problems involved in the sudden utilization of these new machines. But the machines exist, they will be used, and we will have to learn to live with them and realize to the fullest the tremendous benefits they offer us.

The accountant's responsibilities relating to the production of wealth are primarily concerned with the collection, processing, and interpretation of the information needed to ensure that optimum output and efficiency are maintained. But the distribution of wealth may be of much greater concern to accountants than its production. The accountant of tomorrow can have vast responsibilities in this area if he has the vision, the courage, and the ability to reach out for them.

NEW DEFINITION OF WEALTH

Up to the present, generation of wealth has been directly related to human effort, and it has been possible to distribute our wealth very largely in the form of wages for work done. Capital—the implements and machines used to increase human productivity—has slowly gained in importance, and some wealth has been distributed in the form of dividends and interest for the use of capital. As long as the rate of technological development was gradual, bringing rising wealth generation, we could pay increasing wages for fewer working hours and at the same time pay the slowly growing amount necessary to attract capital. Thus, there has been justification for maintaining our job-oriented social and economic structure.

But suddenly technology permits steeply rising wealth generation by machines using little or no human effort. The traditional basis of wealth distribution is no longer valid; justice will soon demand that wealth be distributed primarily as payment for the use of capital and only secondarily as wages for work done. The human effort needed to produce wealth is decreasing, the productivity of men is being replaced by productivity of machines. Labor becomes increasingly obsolete as we enter into the era of which man has dreamed through the centuries—a life of ease and luxury while machines do the work. But under such a system high average living standards are possible only if there is a wide distribution of the ownership of capital among the households. For accountants, such a total change in the economic and social structure can only mean a radical new concept of accounting, fiscal, and monetary policies affecting the measurement and distribution of national wealth. The calculation, payment, and taxation of wage income have been easy in comparison with tomorrow's complex problems of redistribution of the ownership of capital and of distribution of national income through the capital channel.

PROSPERITY DEPENDENT ON OTHERS

But there are other major environmental changes to concern our accountant of tomorrow. Most technological developments have favored very large manufacturing units supplying huge markets. This trend has had its impact on international trade and on the development of the international community. In the first place, nations are building productive capacity well beyond their domestic needs, seeking to export the surplus in order to achieve the economies of large-scale output. In the second place, as a defensive measure against the rapidly growing economic power of the great nations, smaller nations are banding together into groupings such as the European Common Market in order to achieve the large domestic markets needed to justify production units of an economical size. Thus the nations of the world are becoming rapidly more interdependent, the prosperity of each depends on that of the others, disaster in one damages the economy of the others. No longer can we cut ourselves off from one another.

That three-quarters of the people on earth have submarginal living standards can no longer be regarded with equanimity by the wealthy few. Thanks to our publicity and our tourists, they know what we have and they can be stirred to want what we have. Unless we can devise the means for them to raise their living standards, how can we hope to live at peace with them? While our technological development from their level was painfully slow, theirs can be fast because the knowledge now exists. They have the natural resources, but we must help them to develop the abilities and management skills and to accumulate the capital necessary to convert resources into wealth. And, above all, this wealth must be theirs to use for raising living standards and for new capital formation by their households. The branch-plant subsidiary-company form of exploitation of underdeveloped countries will not answer their needs.

FEARSOME LACK OF CAPITAL

Two phenomena are threatening our free enterprise way of life. In the poorer nations, which comprise three-quarters of the world's population, the fearsome lack of capital pushes men towards socialist totalitarianism because they see the state as the only institution capable of putting together the capital formations needed to finance productive enterprises. In the wealthy nations, the displacement of human effort by machines combines with the relatively narrow distribution of capital ownership to increase the pressure for socialism. Even though the incentives of the free enterprise system have proven their effectiveness in generating the highest average living standard ever known to man, the fundamental change needed in our wealth distribution system is being resisted by labor because it signifies the end of the labor-dominated wages system of wealth distribution and by capital because present owners of capital strive to maintain their tight control of equity capital. In a democracy, the majority vote counts, and present trends indicate a majority move towards socialist totalitarianism.

But let us take a quick look at the chief financial effect of these trends. The socialistic approach to wealth distribution now evidenced in a rapidly increasing variety and amount of government social security payments is in fact no different from the classical inflations which destroyed economies in the past. Initial steps in payment of old-age pensions, unemployment relief, universal medical care, and so forth are always justified on the basis of need and covered by direct taxation on those who produce the nation's wealth. But as politicians continue to follow this easy route to win elections, social security payments rise beyond the level that acceptable tax rates can bear. Governments start incurring deficits, which pushes up costs, brings on demands for higher wages, forces up prices, and increases the need for still more social security. Governments, in this process, are merely printing money to hand out to old, unemployed, or sick voters. Once the process begins it will gather momentum. The printing of money without sound backing can only cause inflation, as it has always done. While inflations of tomorrow may stem from a cause different from those of yesterday, the accountant of tomorrow will have substantially the same problems as his ancestor in trying to rebuild a sound money system out of the rubble.

EROSION OF MONEY VALUE

The almost universal trend towards socialist totalitarianism—except, of course, in the communist countries, which are now beginning the long climb back towards capitalism—brings on substantial and increasing abuse of our private corporations. Although attainment of the world's highest living standards would have been impossible without these inanimate entities, the great mass of our people seem ready to crucify them with excessive taxation, unfair labor demands enforced by crippling strikes, total refusal to understand the incentive effect of profit, and outright abuse of corporations and managements alike. A very great share of the blame for the public misunderstanding of profits, for the popular belief in the fallacy that corporations can in fact be taxed, and particularly for the totally erroneous picture of rising and excessive profits, must be laid on the accounting profession. Its willingness to deal with "profit before taxes" and even "profit before depreciation" hands to the critics of freedom a high "profit" figure to criticize, whereas in truth there can be no true profit until all costs, expenses, and taxes are paid. And then the stubborn refusal by accountants to reflect changing money values in financial statements causes even greater overstatement of profits. The accountant of today must accept the responsibility for adverse trends which are eroding our freedoms, and thus it will be up to the accountant of tomorrow to save our system by developing financial statements that are truly informative.

A challenging responsibility for the accountant of tomorrow is that of measuring the results of government operations and interpreting these results to the community. This duty is becoming significant because government operations of one type or another affect or involve a large and growing portion of the total national wealth generation and distribution. By its policies and actions, government is the greatest single determinant of living standards, even though government produces nothing. Because those who govern are politicians usually more motivated by being in power and staying in power than by the best ultimate interests of the people, it becomes imperative that the people be provided with some disinterested, objective analysis and interpretation of the immediate effects and ultimate results of government policies. As the impact of government actions on the community increases, we cannot rely solely on the reporting of accountants employed by government. Mechanisms are needed whereby the people can obtain objective and informative reports from independent sources such as the professional accounting bodies.

DISTRIBUTING WEALTH BY VOTES

Governments do not produce wealth, but through their taxation, social security, and other laws they have a major impact on the distribution of wealth. Because the incentive of politicians is to obtain the support of the largest numbers of voters, the tendency will be to redistribute income so as to give as much as possible to the largest number of voters regardless of their contribution to the generation of that wealth. Such policies invariably contravene the incentives towards the maximum generation of wealth and thus tend to be damaging to the true welfare of the community. The imposition of steeply graduated taxes upon the most productive people necessarily results in a drop in productivity. Furthermore, attempts to shift the tax burden onto inanimate corporations serves only to increase costs and to damage productivity. Only people can earn income or pay taxes, and the taxation of corporations, popular as it is politically, is merely a means of taxing people indirectly rather than directly. Recognition of the true impact of taxation and simplification of the tax structure—which requires extensive effort by the finest accounting minds—would make an immeasurable contribution to our productivity and prosperity.

Another great factor that will determine the kind of tomorrow in which accountants will find themselves is the morality, the moral standards, that will be observed by nations and by men. Casual observation indicates that moral standards and living standards may well follow opposite trends. The moral standards that will be determining are those of business and social ethics, of enactment and observance of sound laws, of honesty, of true charity, and of equity in all human relationships. It was the establishment and observance of moral standards that permitted man to develop from the animal brutality of the jungle; the present apparent tendency for moral standards to be pushed aside, particularly by youth, could quickly send us back into a kind of economic jungle in which might would be right.

The professional bodies, such as the corporations of accountants, lawyers, doctors, and scientists, are responsible for the development of moral standards as well as of knowledge in those areas in which they profess to be expert. It is to such bodies that mankind must look for the safeguarding of our future morality as well as the development of the knowledge which can ensure peace and prosperity.

And so the economic environment in which the accountant of tomorrow will work will be one of rapidly developing and fast-spreading technology, with vast increases in the production of wealth through greater reliance on capital and decreasing contribution by human effort. Population will continue to expand exponentially, and, unless very drastic and sudden action is taken to reverse present trends, the wealthy nations will become rapidly wealthier and the poor poorer. The social pressures arising from such growth curves will build up with the speed and force of an explosion. There will be ever more interdependence between nations, with a fast-growing volume of international trade and communications, resulting in complex international relationships. The economy of size will cause a growing proportion of production and distribution to be centered in giant international corporations, accompanied by conflict between those people who favor state ownership and those who favor private ownership. This world will be deeply affected by the pressures to bring about the economic development of the poor nations and the education of their people within a period infinitely shorter than that in which the developed world achieved its present position. And it will be constantly haunted by the threat of total annihilation now that man has the technical knowledge with which to destroy life on earth.

FIGURING IN THE FUTURE

So much for the environment in which the accountant of tomorrow will work. What will be his responsibilities and how will he train himself to meet them?

For ease of discussion we can divide the total work of the accountant into two parts, which I will label bookkeeping and accounting. The first is the routine recording of transactions of every type, so that information will be available. The second is the verification of the accuracy and objectivity of the information and the analysis, interpretation, and employment of that information in the management process.

The development of computers has made possible the automation of the bookkeeping system. Information must be reduced to the simplest terms for mechanization, but once fed into the computer, it can be processed in an infinite number of ways with virtually no human effort. The programming of information will call for both accounting and mathematical skills of a high order because such work can be done effectively only by those with a concept of the total operation, the total information needs of management, and the capabilities of alternative machine systems available. But the bookkeeping work will be done mainly by machines fed by workers on production lines or payroll, stores, and sales order clerks. There will always be small operations which do not justify mechanization, but we can predict a drop in the need for bookkeepers.

While the accountant will always need to have the basic knowledge of bookkeeping or information recording, he is essentially a highly skilled, and often highly specialized, professional expert. Just as the complexity of technology has caused scientists to become highly specialized, so also the complexity of economic affairs will call for new degrees of advanced specialization by accountants. They will have to understand the total economic and social system, recognize what information is necessary for its management, planning, and control, and also have a sound concept of all aspects of the collection, analysis, and interpretation of that information. They will aid in, or be responsible for, planning and implementing fiscal policies, particularly those which influence the distribution of income and the flow of international trade and payments. They will put together and report on the information needed by governments, businesses, and institutions for their operations which, in total, determine the living standards of all mankind. And they will check at all levels to ensure that policies and plans are executed properly, that honesty prevails, and that steward-ship is carried out in a trustworthy and efficient manner.

Because our businesses and our institutions primarily generate and distribute the total national wealth, all citizens are concerned with their operations, not only as employees, consumers, or suppliers, but as citizens whose way of life depends upon the most effective exploitation of the nation's total resources. Thus, those accountants recording the transactions of business and those checking and reporting on the honesty and effec-tiveness of management have a duty not only to owners of the company but also to the people as a whole. If such analysis and reporting is to be of value, it must obviously be of heroic objectivity. Any deviation from ethics, from objectivity, not only makes the accountant valueless, it actually renders him harmful to the community.

Recognizing the overpowering importance of ethics and objectivity in the complex work of the accountant of tomorrow, we cannot help but be conscious of the need for the vast degree of judgment he will have to exercise at all times. Seldom is there one right and one wrong way to record or report on any transaction. Certainly the routine transactions can be mechanized according to rigid manuals, but the analysis of information and the reporting on results calls for extensive interpretation and the exercise of a great deal of judgment. Moreover, the degree of judgment required, and thus the effect of this judgment, increases rapidly with the complexity of our economy, the changing value of money, and the grow-ing interrelationships of business and government at national and inter-national levels. As long as this judgment is exercised on the basis of expert skill and according to the strictest ethics, the community will be well served even though standardization in accounting may have to give way to great flexibility in financial statements and reports.

Our history has been that of nations slowly coming to know one another better, becoming more dependent upon one another and finally consolidating their interests. With the existence of ultimate weapons, and with the technological developments which will be fully effective only if they are allowed to serve the entire world population in one heterogeneous system, we are now emerging into an era in which all nations and all men will become so interdependent, so inextricably intertwined in their economic and social life, that national boundaries will come to lose their significance. The implications of such a course for accountants are obvious and overwhelming. The need to overcome differences between nations in monetary systems, fiscal policies, accounting practices, commercial law, and so on will become increasingly apparent if we are to avoid distortions in the production and flow of wealth and in the information needed to record, to analyze, and to plan the maximization of this production and flow.

Free enterprise corporations respond readily to market forces, and we have already seen the rapid development of huge international corporations dedicated to taking advantage of local situations anywhere. The task of the accounting officer forming part of top management of such corporations is clearly different from that of the average accountant of today, since his sphere of influence extends into many countries, each with its own laws, customs, and policies. He is the forerunner of the accountant of tomorrow, for his is the task of measuring the needs of each area and the effectiveness of its policies, the task of influencing the adoption by each nation of those fiscal and economic policies designed to bring about the optimum exploitation of its total resources. In the interdependent world of tomorrow, most accountants will be so engaged. The first real steps in this direction must surely be the establishment of internationally accepted standards of recording and reporting, an increase of international coordination and standardization of information, and rapid improvement of international information on the production and distribution of wealth.

Clearly, accountants will continue to function in two broad groupings. The first group comprises those who will form part of management in all types of operations, and who are thus actively involved in the production and distribution system. The second covers those who, as practicing professionals, will be responsible for auditing to ensure that businesses, institutions, and governments operate with honesty and efficiency. The constant development of the art or science of accounting must be a duty of all accountants of both groups, for new knowledge should come just as much from those engaged in management as from the practicing professionals.

Finally, what about the training of the accountant of tomorrow? Here we must be prepared to talk with a considerable degree of certainty, because the accountant of tomorrow must in fact be trained today.

Bookkeeping can, and should, be taught at the high school and undergraduate level in university. But each science or art has its special impact on all community life. To be fully effective, accountants must have a sound knowledge of all those basic elements which together make up the life of the community—its history, its traditions, its customs, its values, its laws, its aspirations. Thus, to be a whole man and to make his greatest contribution, the accountant must be well versed in the humanities. Such knowledge will best result from constant study of these subjects from earliest school days throughout the formal education system. Those who reach the top will as always be those who devote much personal time throughout their lives to the continual study of the humanities.

An immense challenge for accounting training comes from the new potential to employ machine systems to automate the recording, collating, and processing of financial information. Not only is it now necessary for accountants to understand how to use a totally new tool for processing information on an integrated and instant basis, but more particularly, it is necessary for us to understand how to use this information in the management process. It is now practical to produce information of types, in volumes, and at speeds hitherto undreamed of. But if we are to make our maximum contribution to management, and thus to higher living standards, we must train accountants to be highly selective in the information they produce. They must concentrate on those matters that are truly significant and avoid producing a mass of useless data just because it can be produced. This is a new area of accounting, but one which will be of increasing importance and which will require highly specialized training courses.

Training or education in data processing systems and computers is becoming so necessary for all types of employment that it is generally taught in the senior years of secondary education and throughout college or university education. Advanced training in this special field will be essential for the accountant of tomorrow since he will either have to operate or manage information systems or be expert in using their output in the management process. To a greater extent than in the past, tomorrow's accountant must be trained in mathematics, for computers have made it possible to apply mathematics to the solution of accounting or financial problems as never before. In fact, the computer potentiality for simulation of all types of management problems permits a new approach to problem solving which replaces obsolete accounting techniques and vastly increases the possible value of the accountant to management.

A vital factor in the training of the accountant of tomorrow will be the advanced education in the special fields which will make of many of them highly skilled experts in relatively narrow spheres. Just as medical men now specialize in the treatment of portions of the body and as scientists specialize in polymer chemistry, the physics of light or the electronics of sound transmission, so accounting will have to develop its highly qualified specialists in automated information processing, fiscal policy and tax law formulation, international financial reporting, money management, and so forth. The complexity of economic life can only increase. This complexity must surely result in an ever-growing need for expert skills of a depth that will call for the concentration of training of specialists in these areas, possibly—and unfortunately—to the exclusion of broader training. Special training of this order can come only after an accountant has finished basic training and has become a seasoned practitioner. There will, therefore, be a need for extensive post-graduate education in specialized accounting and financial subjects.

The accountant's horizons have broadened immeasurably. His service to the community of tomorrow will be of a new order of significance. The potentiality for contribution, for service, and for reward was never greater, and it can only increase as the world of tomorrow unfolds. But potential rewards will materialize only if the contribution is in fact made, the service actually rendered. Accounting has a right to be a profession only if it fulfills its professional responsibilities to the utmost. For only if all accountants live and work as true professionals, maintaining absolute integrity in their work at all times, insisting always on thorough competence, and keeping up-to-date the body of technical knowledge and science on which their contribution depends, can they make their greatest possible contribution to world progress.

It is, of course, always possible that our world will fall apart, that our civilization will crumble. We can only proceed, however, on the assumption that we will be able to control the forces tending to overthrow us, that we will avoid total destruction, and that we will make the best use of the vast technological gains and our natural resources to raise the living standards of all mankind. But we now know that we can survive only if nations can live and work together for common ends, overcoming their differences and distrust, probably coming eventually to common citizenship and to the surrender of national prerogatives in favor of a single world community.

Such fusion cannot happen suddenly, but it may have to happen very, very quickly if the awesome alternative is to be avoided. Economic considerations will be crucial to such decisions, and these will depend upon objective and illuminating financial information. The accountant of tomorrow will therefore be at the center of the decision-making process of mankind.

2. Accounting as a Social Force*

Ronald Ma**

Social force has been defined as:

Any effective urge or impulse that leads to social action. Specifically, a social force is a consensus on the part of a sufficient number of the members of society to bring about social action or social change of some sort. In the plural, the social forces are the typical basic drives, or motives, which lead to the fundamental types of association or group relationship.

---

* Reprinted from *The Pakistan Accountant*, December 1965, pages 13–23. Originally published in a students' journal at the University of Singapore.
** Ronald Ma is Professor of Accountancy at the University of New South Wales, Australia.

These have been variously identified, but are practically always under-stood to include hunger, sex love, and certain other desires such as the desire for recognition and response, preferably favourable, the desire to know and the desire for the good will and assistance of supernatural beings.[1]

Most accountants would understandably hesitate to classify the accounting processes as one of the basic drives of mankind, in the same category as sex love and the desire for the goodwill and assistance of supernatural beings. Nonetheless, it is the purpose of this article to investigate whether it is indeed appropriate to speak of accounting as a social force, in the widest sense of the term. By this, we mean any influence, which as a result of its interaction with the rest of society, promotes society's progress in some significant manner, or retards it or even leads society to retrogress, or maintains the well-being and continuity of the fabric of society, or leads to its destruction and disintegration. We shall see that, in fact, the influence of accounting in civilized society has both been substantial and has led, almost without exceptions, to its increased welfare and prosperity.

Accounting and Book-keeping Defined

It is implicit, then, that the accounting discipline transcends the techniques of book-keeping, for techniques in themselves are seldom revolutionary enough to cause the social structure to undergo change.[2] There is however considerable confusion as to where the boundary lines of these two interrelated professions lie.

Book-keeping has been defined as:

The procedure of analysing, classifying, and recording transactions in accordance with a preconceived plan for the purpose of (a) providing a means by which an enterprise can be conducted in an orderly fashion, and (b) establishing a basis for reporting the financial condition of the enterprise and the results of its operation.[3]

The best known definition of accounting is that proposed by the Committee on Terminology of the American Institute of Certified Public Accountants in 1941. Accounting is:

---

[1] Henry Pratt Fairchild (ed.), *Dictionary of Sociology*, published by Philosophical Library, New York City, 1944, p. 283.

[2] There have been, of course, exceptions. In recent years the technique of birth control has been a far-reaching and permanent impact on the social structure and the rate and pattern of economic growth in various countries.

[3] Eric L. Kohler, *A Dictionary for Accountants*, Englewood Cliffs, N. J.: Prentice-Hall, Inc., 1961, p. 70.

The art of recording, classifying, and summarizing in a significant manner and in terms of money, transactions and events which are, in part at least, of a financial character, and interpreting the results thereof.[4]

The question whether this definition of accounting is an adequate one will be examined at a later stage. For the present, we should note that the two authoritative definitions of book-keeping and accounting respectively given above would appear to indicate that these two fields of human endeavour are remarkably alike.

Thus the technique of book-keeping and the art of accounting have often been regarded as belonging to the same discipline. The adulation that specialists in other fields of learning have heaped on the technique of book-keeping must have at times touched the vanity of the professional accountant to the quick. A few illustrations must suffice.

An important stage in the development of book-keeping technology has been the invention of double entry, attributed to Paciolo, though he was only describing Venetian practice probably at least two centuries old at the time he wrote. This error was made by one Augspurg who, writing in 1897, "came to the romantic conclusion that 'the scientific system (double entry) based on mathematical principles could have had no other source than the genius of one individual (and he a mathematician well acquainted with commerce) from whose pen it must have flowed forth in one gush.' "[5] Later observers of the economic scene have maintained the same high regard for double entry. Thus Yamey quotes from Werner Sombart in his (Sombart's) study of modern capitalism: "Double-entry book-keeping is born of the same spirit as the systems of Galileo and Newton. . . . Using the same means as these, it orders the phenomena into an elegant system, and it may be described as the first cosmos built up on the basis of mechanistic thought."[6]

Schumpeter, too, in a discussion of the use of the monetary unit as a tool of cost-profit analysis, speaks of double-entry book-keeping as a "towering monument."[7]

Not all scholars agree, however, that double-entry in itself is of cultural significance. Littleton, for example, writes that double-entry must be considered a superficial aspect of accounting technology. The real essence of the Italian contribution to accounting methodology lies in the

[4] American Institute of Certified Public Accountants, Committee on Terminology, *Accounting Terminology Bulletin No. 1*, 1953.
[5] Quoted by B. S. Yamey, in "Introduction" to A. C. Littleton and B. S. Yamey (eds.), *Studies in the History of Accounting*, Homewood, Illinois: Richard D. Irwin, Inc., 1956, p. 2.
[6] *Ibid.*, p. 4.
[7] Joseph A. Schumpeter, *Capitalism, Socialism and Democracy*, New York: Harper and Brothers, 1943, p. 123. Quoted in George O. May, *Financial Accounting A Distillation of Experience*, New York: The Macmillan Company, 1959, p. 15.

skilful integration of real and nominal accounts. Thus the interrelation of capital in use and the income which results from management's supervision of that use is disclosed. He terms this "Italian capital-income accounting." [8]

The importance of double-entry in the accounting scheme cannot be disputed. It is an expression of exchange, and exchange is at the centre of economic life, but I find myself more in sympathy with Professor Littleton's sober appraisal.

Part of the confusion can be attributed to the limited concept that accountants have had, at least until recent years, of the responsibilities and potentialities of their profession. The oft-quoted definition of accounting propounded by the American Institute has often been criticised on these grounds.[9] Smith and Ashburne rephrase it thus:

Accounting is the science of recording and classifying business transactions and events, primarily of a financial character, and the art of making significant summaries, analyses and interpretations of those transactions and events and communicating the results to persons who must make decisions or form judgments.[10]

This revised definition does spell out the important function of financial reporting, and the role of accounting data in decision making. The emphasis in accounting in recent years is shifting from general-purpose statements to special-purpose reports. The role of the accountant in commerce and industry is increasingly concerned with the preparation of accounting and statistical data for use in the decision making process.

A particularly apt description of the function of accounting in modern society has been formulated by Moonitz:

Economic activity is carried on by human beings interacting with their environment. This type of interaction of human effort (labor) and natural resources takes place through the medium of entities which are used as organizing units for the purpose of producing goods and services In this process the existing resources must be allocated by some means among the available alternatives. To make these allocations properly, predictions as to the outcome of the available alternatives are essential. Results of the past and estimates of the future are used to form these predictions. These results, estimates and predictions are couched in part in quantitative terms so that comparisons and evaluations can be facili-

---

[8] A. C. Littleton, "Accounting Rediscovered," *Accounting Review*, Vol. XXXIII, No. 2, April 1958, pp. 246–53.

[9] See, for example, Kohler, *op. cit.*, pp. 10–11.

[10] C. A. Smith and J. G. Ashburne, *Financial and Administrative Accounting*, New York: McGraw-Hill Book Company, Inc., 1960, p. 2.

tated. *Accounting is one form of quantitative expression that is widely used.*[11]

The controversial and long disputed question as to whether accounting is an art, or science, or philosophy can hardly be settled by definition.[12] Some of the conflicting arguments might be reconciled when we remember that practice of a science constitutes an art, while the concern of science with basic presuppositions or first principles is embodied in that field of study which we call the philosophy of science. Similarly we can speak of the philosophy of accounting, for the accounting discipline, as a field of study, possesses the basic characteristics of the philosophical approach, which are (a) a return to first principles, (b) a concern with the systematic organization of knowledge, and (c) a base whereby social relationships may be moulded and understood.[13] With regard to the place of accounting in the family of the social sciences, DR. Scott has objected that the definition of accounting as an art is limited to the practice of accounting. "Accounting is also a science in the same sense that law, government and economics are sciences." [14] We might regard the learned professor's claim with a certain amount of reserve. If a scientific discipline is defined as the study of phenomena which leads to the formulation of general laws seeking to trace the relationship of effects to causes, then a concept of accounting or law as a science can hardly be accommodated within the confines of our definition. But if science is given a broad connotation so as to include any discipline based on a body of systematized knowledge then accounting can be regarded as a "scientific method, existing in the climate of logic and disciplined by orderliness and practicability." [15] Few would dispute the claim of accounting to its place among the arts. The historical development of the art of accounting is evident in the constantly improved methods of analysing and interpreting financial data and communicating them to all interested parties.

Has Accounting Been A Social Force?

The important role of accounting in society is well documented in the history of civilized nations. The author of a text on the history of accounting finds its parallel development indispensable to the growth of

[11] Maurice Moonitz, *The Basic Postulates of Accounting*, Accounting Research Study No. 1, American Institute of Certified Public Accountants, 1961.

[12] Note however the change that Smith and Ashburne have introduced into the definition of accounting given by the Committee on Terminology of the American Institute of Certified Public Accountants.

[13] R. K. Mautz and Hussein A. Sharaf, *The Philosophy of Auditing*, AAA Monograph No. 6, 1961, p. 8.

[14] DR Scott, "The Basis for Accounting Principles," *Accounting Review*, Vol. XVI, No. 4, December 1941, pp. 341–9.

[15] Smith and Ashburne, *op. cit.*, p. 1.

a sovereign state: "The development of social life and especially the formation of states or sovereignties levying any form of taxation necessitated, in addition to a knowledge of numbers, a power of holding count and reckoning. In this we find the origin of the science of accounting." [16] More recently, Professor Sewell Bray has put forward the same theme thus: "(Accounting) is indispensable to civilized society. Has there ever been economic activity in the real world which has not required the preparation of some form of account? As long as men exchange goods and services they will always want accounts to give them succinct views of their transaction." [17] Thus accounting records have been traced in the ancient civilizations of the Chaldean-Babylonian Empire and Ancient Egypt, the Indian and Chinese civilizations, as well as in Greece and Rome.

It has, however, been asserted that accounting has developed into a social force only with development of its status as a profession. Thus the concept is regarded as relevant only to events in the last hundred years.[18] The role of the profession in this process has probably been overemphasized. The development of the profession itself can be attributed to two events: firstly, the growing importance of taxation and the increasing complexities of tax legislation and, secondly, the development of the corporation into the single most important economic unit in the private sector.[19] The divorce of ownership from management in the modern economy has enhanced immeasurably the stewardship function of accounts and consequently the auditing aim of the accounting profession.

However, the development of accounting into a social force in the twentieth century must be attributed to another, though related, historical event. This is the adoption of the revolutionary changes and techniques in industry and agriculture that are characteristic of the stages of rapid economic growth. The development of large scale methods of production has demanded of the accounting profession not only new techniques for cost control and cost analysis but, what is perhaps of equal significance, a new intellectual climate in which the accountant can take his proper place in management.

Brundage in his Dickinson Lecture at Harvard University in 1951

[16] Richard Brown, *A History of Accounting and Accountants*, Edinburgh: T. C. and E. C. Jack, 1905, p. 16.

[17] F. Sewell Bray, "An Accounting Progression," *Accounting Research*, Vol. 4, No. 2, April 1953, pp. 133–43.

[18] Paul Grady, "The Increasing Emphasis on Accounting as a Social Force," *Accounting Review*, Vol. XXIII, No. 3, July 1948, pp. 266–75.

[19] On the significant role of the corporation in modern society, see, for example, Adolf A. Berle, Jr. and Gardiner C. Means, *The Modern Corporation and Private Property*, New York: The Macmillan Company, 1935 and Peter F. Drucker, *Concept of the Corporation*. New York: The John Day Co., 1946.

has summarised the interaction of accounting and the business community in the last fifty years thus:

> *During the fifty years of the twentieth century . . . the develop-*
> *ments of business and of accounting have been great and have reacted*
> *upon each other. Without the aid of accounting machines, improved*
> *methods of internal control, and adequate reporting, large-scale operations*
> *by business would have been impossible. The economies of mass buying*
> *and distribution through chain outlets might never have been realized.*
> *The statement, frequently heard, that "accounting is a tool of business"*
> *is true, but not the whole truth. Accounting is also a partner of business.*[20]

Past Developments

The failure of accounting in developing into a social force in society until recent years can be attributed to various causes. In the first place, there has been the concern of the profession with its auditing function and its role as an expert but independent party between the taxpayer and the government.[21] With the development of corporate enterprise this role was extended. The accountant became the watchdog for the shareholders and zealously reported on the performance of management. In these functions there have been known to arise, however, from time to time certain conflicts of loyalty.[22] But of far greater import is that this concern with the auditing role of the professional practitioner, important though it is, delayed for a long time the development of other and greater potentialities in accounting, the eventual recognition of which has been called "the major accounting rediscoveries of the twentieth century."[23]

It is the emphasis on this aspect of the accountant's role that has also led to the formulation of the stewardship concept and the principle that capital must be maintained intact. This in its turn led to the convention that it is the accountant's duty to account for past events. This preoccupation with the past, coupled with the pragmatic manner in which the body of rules and procedures sometimes termed accounting principles has been developed, has led to a wide dichotomy between accounting and economic principles in value determination, one of the most important areas in accounting theory and practice. Accounting concepts, such as those of conservatism, objectivity, and constancy of the monetary unit,

---

[20] Percival F. Brundage, "Milestones in the Path of Accounting," *Harvard Business Review*, Vol. XXIX, No. 4, July 1951, pp. 71–81.

[21] For a detailed account of the concept of independence of the public accountant, see John L. Carey, "Professional Ethics in Accounting," in Morton Backer (ed.), *Handbook of Modern Accounting Theory*, Englewood Cliffs, N. J.: Prentice-Hall, Inc., 1959, pp. 121–148.

[22] *R. v. Kylsant* and similar cases provide illustrations of this conflict.

[23] Littleton, *op. cit.*

which have served well in past periods where both the state of the arts and price levels were largely stable, are no longer tenable. Financial statements and asset valuations which result from the adoption of accounting conventions have failed increasingly, in this modern era of rapid technological progress and price level changes, to reflect the existing financial condition. The application of principles often diametrically opposed to the principles of economic science must be counted as a further contributory factor to the failure of accounting to develop into a social force in the past.

Indeed, certain consequences of the adoption of generally accepted accounting principles have been held to be decidedly anti-social.

The distortion in accounting profit in periods of changing prices have long been familiar to economists, and their probable effects on trade cycle fluctuations recognised. More recent analysis of this phenomenon can be found in the writings of Lacey [24] and Baxter.[25] Briefly, accounting conventions tend to distort the profit figure when prices change, through the comparison of revenue expressed in today's dollars with certain costs expressed in dollars of past periods. Such costs include the valuation of the consumption of stock and fixed assets in the revenue earning process.[26] Baxter concludes that "the depreciation error tends to make the high-price years (both before and after the peak) look better, and the low price years look worse. The stock error instead lifts profits in all years when prices are rising, and depresses profit throughout the down-grade. . . . It appears reasonable to conclude that an error so widespread and so emphatic in its rhythm must have a considerable influence on business sentiment." [27] Over-statement of the accounting profit encourages an optimistic outlook in times of inflation, while its understatement adds to the pessimistic outlook in times of depression. Thus the artificial element in accounts affects the level of employment, incomes and prices and intensifies trade cycle fluctuations.

Other deficiencies, attributed to the accountant's application of the monetary postulate, that have far reaching social effects, include (a) the charge that in periods of inflation the capital invested in industry might not be kept intact in real terms, and (b) the promotion of what is claimed by some critics an inequitable incidence of the corporate tax burden between individual firms.

[24] K. Lacey, "Profit Measurement and the Trade Cycle," *Economic Journal*, December 1947, pp. 456–74.

[25] W. T. Baxter, "Inflation and Accounting Profits," *Westminster Bank Review*, May 1952, pp. 1–8 and "The Accountant's Contribution to the Trade Cycle," *Economica*, February 1955, pp. 99–112.

[26] There may also be significant purchasing power gains and losses arising from the holding of money and money assets and liabilities.

[27] "The Accountant's Contribution to the Trade Cycle," *ibid.*, p. 112.

What Then of the Future?

There is nonetheless an impressive array of evidence which points to the growing stature of accounting.

Firstly, there is the increasing concern within the profession with fundamentals, the return to first principles, as evidenced in the post-War writings of such authorities as Sewell Bray in England,[28] Chambers in Australia,[29] and Moonitz in the United States.[30] Parallel with this development and arising out of an awareness of the large deficiencies in the existing body of theory, is the felt need for a rigorous and internally consistent body of accounting theory based on deductive reasoning rather than, as in the past, empirical convenience.[31]

Secondly, a further aspect of the growing cooperation between economists and accountants can be found in the field of national income accounting. National accounting has been described as the preparation of a comprehensive statistical statement about the economic activity of a country. National income accounts are an invaluable aid in assessing economic well-being, in particular, the rate of capital formation and growth, and the accompanying changes in the economic and social patterns of the population. They also supply the necessary statistical data on which economic planning and policies for future economic development can be based.

Littleton and others believe that the analogy of social accounting to business accounting is a tenuous one, since the integration of the balance sheet and income statement is lacking in the social accounts.[32] Nonetheless, social accounts do constitute an extension in a very real sense of the double entry principle to the totality of a nation's economic transactions as well as its individual sectors.[33] This is evident from the published models of social accounts such as the *Standardized System of National Accounts* used by the Organisation for European Economic Co-operation. The lack of sectional and national balance sheets, largely on account of conceptual as well as practical difficulties, is realized by economists to detract from the value of these accounts, and their construc-

---

[28] Bray, *op. cit.* See also *ibid., Precision and Design in Accountancy.* London: Gee and Company (Publishers) Ltd., 1947, etc.

[29] See, for example, R. J. Chambers, "Towards a General Theory of Accounting," 1961 Annual Endowed Lecture of the Australian Society of Accountants (University of Adelaide, August 2, 1961).

[30] Moonitz, *op. cit.*

[31] See *ibid.* Admittedly, this concept is not without its strong critics within the profession.

[32] Littleton, *op. cit.*

[33] See Milton Gilbert, George Jazszi, Edward F. Denison, and Charles F. Schwartz, "Objectives of National Income Measurement: A Reply to Professor Kuznets," *The Review of Economics and Statistics,* XXX, No. 3, August 1948, pp. 181–2. Quoted in Morton Backer (ed.), *Handbook of Modern Accounting Theory,* New York: Prentice-Hall, Inc., 1955, p. 58.

tion presents a challenge to the future development of social accounting.[34]

The increasing adoption by economists of accounting techniques and data is also evident in two other areas—flow of funds accounting and input-output accounting—which are being developed to assist them in the analysis and direction of the national economy. Thus accounting techniques in this instance in the hands of the economists, are fast becoming a tool of social policy.[35]

Thirdly the accounting role has been considerably widened by the complexities of corporate enterprise and the modern economy. This is emphasized in the following statement of the American Institute of Certified Public Accountants:

The committee regards corporation accounting as one phase of the working of the corporate organisation of business, which in turn it views as a machinery created by the people in the belief that, broadly speaking, it will serve a useful social purpose. The test of the corporate system and of the special phase of it represented by corporation accounting ultimately lies in the results which are produced. These results must be judged from the standpoint of society as a whole—not from that of any one group of interested parties.[36]

The accountant's use of economics as a tool to assist him in his work is seen to lie in two main fields, income determination and management accounting.[37] Income determination has remained one of the most important functions of the financial accountant.

The functions of an income measure are diverse, but there are two main functions: (a) income as a guide to consumption, and (b) income as a guide to the flow of scarce national resources into alternative fields of investment, through decisions made internally by management and, for the economy as a whole, by investors. A further aspect of the second function is that the income measure also serves as a criterion by which management performance can be judged by owners and investors. Unfortunately, there has developed a wide divergence between economic concepts of income and accounting concepts and practice. The accounting measure is generally admitted to be defective in several vital respects and the profession is aware of the many problems in this field, but in particular, the problems posed by rising prices. It is to be hoped that a

[34] See Milton Gilbert and Richard Stone, "Recent Developments in National Income and Social Accounting," *Accounting Research*, January 1954.
[35] For a description of these developments, see B. E. Goetz and F. R. Klein, *Accounting in Action*. Boston: Houghton-Mifflin Company, 1960, p. 642 *et seq.*
[36] American Institute of Certified Public Accountants' Committee on Accounting Procedure, *Accounting Research Bulletin No. 1*, New York, 1939, p. 1.
[37] John T. Wheeler, "Economics and Accounting," in Morton Backer (ed.), *op. cit.*, pp. 43–76.

rapproachment between the economist and the accountant will take place in the near future, as one of the fruits of the price level controversy. Such a development is of particular significance in view of the continuing shift of emphasis from the balance sheet to the income statement.

Lastly, the accountant has found in management accounting unexpected potentialities for control and decision making. Historically, accounts were developed to protect the proprietor's interest. Today, the emphasis is increasingly laid on the use of accounts to increase efficiency and productivity, and to optimize the corporation's profit objective. There are some leaders of the profession who believe that it is in this field of controls and systems that the most significant advances might take place in the future. At the Seventh International Congress of Accountants, held in Amsterdam in 1957, the following facts of management accounting were emphasized:

1. Cost accounting, including standard costs.

2. Material control, not limited to inventories but extending to material usage during manufacturing.

3. Budgetary control, embracing the preparation of fixed or flexible operating budgets and their use as standards of performance for interim periods.

4. Interim reporting, including monthly or quarterly profit and loss accounts, together with significant data as of the end of these periods; for example, statements of current assets and liabilities, orders on hands, etc.

5. Determination of the most efficient and economical accounting system applicable to the particular business, including the best use of mechanical and electronic devices.

6. Special cost and economic studies, such as the study of capital costs and potential profits if output is increased or additional lines are produced. This requires study of cost-volume profit relationships, mathematics of the breakeven chart, etc.

7. Assisting management in the interpretation of financial data and rendering advice in connection with pending decisions which can properly be made on the basis of such information.[38]

We may note one particular branch of management accounting which is becoming increasingly important—controllership. The controller function consists of the collection, analysis, interpretation, and presentation of management information. The broadening scope of the controller's responsibility is set out in the following statement on the purposes of the Controllers Institute of America:

[38] Quoted in Mary E. Murphy, *Managerial Accounting*. New Jersey: D. Van Nostrand Company, Inc., 1963.

1. *To develop a progressive concept of controllership, adequate to meet the requirements of modern business;*
2. *To educate business management and the public in the understanding of this concept;*
3. *To assist controllers to give full expression to this concept in their own organizations;*
4. *To provide controllers with a medium through which they may receive and exchange ideas in the field of business management;*
5. *To constitute an articulate body of management opinion on matters within the scope of the controller's responsibility;*
6. *And, by doing these things, to contribute towards soundness in business, in education, in government, and in the national economy.*[39]

An Accountant's Utopia

The best known exponent in modern times of a *Weltanschauung* concept of accounting is DR Scott.[40] Scott was much influenced by the thinking of Thorstein Veblen, a leader of the institutional school of economics. Scott believed in the evolution of human society. Concepts and institutions were tentative and relative in nature, having validity for only a particular stage in the evolution of society. He believed that the present society is in a process of change. This arises partly from its pluralistic nature and the lack of a unifying philosophy. Thus we find a faith in free enterprise and *laissez faire* co-existing with the actual control of the economy by government boards, trade unions and giant corporations.[41] This conflict leads inevitably to transition and change.

Scott further believed that in the coming society the controlling force will be a subtle but coercive one—the institution of accounting itself. Accounting would consolidate its position in three main spheres of economic activity. The first is the government sector which will extend an increasing control over all aspects of economic life through its official commissions. At the same time, the increasingly complex body of commissions will be coordinated and controlled by a central economic commission. All these controls will depend on the new accounting, which will be remoulded on a scientific base and will increasingly become a statistical methodology. The second field of accounting influence lies in the development of the super-corporations. Management, in particular the controller,

[39] Quoted in Russell H. Hassler and Neil E. Harlan, *Cases in Controllership.* Englewood Cliffs, N. J.: Prentice-Hall, Inc., 1958, pp. 1–2.
[40] The following account of DR Scott's philosophy is based on L. J. Genninger, "Accounting Related to Social Institutions—The Theoretical Formulation of Dr. Scott," *Accounting Research*, Vol. 9, 1958, pp. 17–30. See also DR Scott, *The Cultural Significance of Accounts.* New York: Henry Holt, 1931.
[41] The same theme has been analysed by other writers. See, for example, J. K. Galbraith, *American Capitalism: The Concept of Countervailing Power.* Boston: Houghton-Mifflin Company, 1952.

will become professionalized and will wield great power. The managers will rely more and more on accounting as an aid to control and decision making. The third field in which accounting influence will develop is the market place itself. Scott saw major weaknesses, even at the present time, in the ability of the market to reconcile divergent interests *within* the corporation. Accounting will become the dynamic controlling force in the business affairs of the new society, taking over many of the functions performed today by the market.

Because of the comprehensive nature of the accounting role, Scott believed that accounting principles must be tested against general social principles. Accounting principles must be based firmly on the social principles of justice, fairness and truth; the accounting principles must be revised when economic conditions change in order to reflect these basic social premises, but otherwise they must be applied consistently. Thus Scott related accounting to the wider context of ethics and morality.

Maurice Moonitz has pointed out, however: "Terms such as justice, truth and fairness designate subjective concepts which themselves need standards to be capable of application. Ultimately, the results of any purposive human activity must be judged in the light of the value judgments inherent in ethical concepts. They are not satisfactory, however, as a port of departure for an objective enquiry. . . ."[42]

Other criticisms of Scott's philosophy can be made. The relationship within a corporation is contractual or legalistic; it is, therefore, not determined at the market place. Scott has not explained, however, how accounting can replace the test of the market in promoting efficiency through the competitive activities of independent economic units, or in measuring marginal utilities, or in determining value. Further, much of this philosophy rests on an undue emphasis on the role of science in the decision making process. He ignores the role of risk-taking in a world of uncertainty, as well as non-economic motivations.

Nonetheless, we are much indebted today to Professor Scott's breadth of vision. Few will dispute that accounting has a useful, perhaps an essential, role in helping society evolve into its future form. Seen in this light, accounting is truly one of the great social institutions, charged with furthering the progress of society and, at the same time, the protection of a variety of economic interests that form its structure.

ACCOUNTANTS AS A SOCIAL FORCE

While the precise significance of the role of accounting in society may be a disputed and controversial one, few critics would deny that the manifold functions performed by the accountant have contributed immensely to social harmony and economic progress.

[42] Moonitz, *op. cit.*

Auditing

The social responsibilities of the profession are clearly evident in what was at one time its most important section—public auditing. Auditing remains one of the most remunerative and responsible careers open to members of the profession today. The task of auditing is not to measure or to communicate, but rather to review the measurements and communications of accounting. Auditing is analytical, not constructive; it is concerned with verification, proof. Above all, ". . . auditing is concerned with social responsibility and ethical conduct as well as with the collection and evaluation of evidence. . . ."[43]

In some respects, accounting development has lagged behind the evolution of economic conditions, until deficiencies have been exposed by events. Thus much advancement in accounting and auditing theory and practice followed the *McKesson and Robins* case in the United States, and the *Rex v. Kylsant* case and the *Royal Mail Steam Packet* case in the United Kingdom.

But progress has been made in other directions. For example, in the last 15 years or so the English auditor has moved from the certification of the balance sheet with hidden reserves and no responsibility for the income statement to the present position, viz., a "true and fair view" of the balance sheet with some responsibility for the income statement. It is certain that further progress will be made with each subsequent Companies Act.

Lastly, we may note that the high standards of the profession with respect to qualities such as honesty, integrity and impartiality contribute not only to a proper discharge of taxation liabilities, but also to high standards of business morality and the observance of a high ethical code in society as a whole.

Taxation

While the canons of taxation might be formulated by economists, it is the accountant who is responsible for the efficient working of the tax system. The accounting profession in this regard renders a double service to society. It enables government to obtain its revenue as efficiently and at as low cost as possible. Secondly, since large amounts of the taxation revenue represent transfer payments, the accountant is playing an important role in the promotion of a more egalitarian society.

But it is in his service to the individual client for which the accountant is best known. In matters of taxation, the accountant might be required to give such advice to his client as: At what date should a firm or company cease trading? Or, when should a private company reorganise prior to a public issue of shares? Such assistance to a client in order to

[43] Mautz and Sharaf, *op. cit.*, p. 11.

minimise his tax liability conforms to a long accepted principle of taxation, which has been formulated by a learned judge as follows:

> *Every man is entitled if he can to order his affairs so that the tax attaching under the appropriate Acts is less than it otherwise would be. If he succeeds to order them so as to secure this result, then, however unappreciative the Commissioners of Inland Revenue or his fellow tax-payers may be of his ingenuity, he cannot be compelled to pay an increased tax.*[44]

There is one further point concerning the social function of the accountant in this particular field which has been made by a past president of the English Institute: "In recent years . . . (the) Institute has adopted a policy of making representations to the Inland Revenue with a view to the removal of inequities or anomalies in existing or proposed legislation." [45]

Labour Relation

> *Permanent industrial peace may be expected only when there is understanding among ownership, management, and labor as to how the fruits of industrial production should be shared. . . . It is evident that full cooperation between employees and employers will not be attained without the aid of the accounting profession. Accountants must take the lead in devising techniques by which production and income may be measured and classified with a high degree of accuracy, and in developing methods of presenting the resulting information to employees in an intelligible manner.*[46]

More specifically, the accountant advises on and calculates "ability to pay" and other yardsticks for tying wages to profits. Another important function is the calculation of fringe benefits.[47]

A particularly vexatious aspect of the accountant's work in the field of labour relations is, as part of the management team, in meeting labour's request for information and in deciding what are reasonable or unreasonable requests. A happy example of this function is afforded by the

[44] Lord Tomlin, *Westminster (Duke of) v Commissioners of Inland Revenue,* (1953, 19 T.C., pp. 490, 520. H.L.). Quoted in Sir Donald Perrott, "What the Business Man Expects of the Practising Professional Accountant," *Accountancy,* April 1962, pp. 313–6.

[45] Gilbert D. Shepherd, "The Future Role of the Accountant," *The Accountant,* December 1949, reprinted in Mary E. Murphy (ed.), *Selected Readings in Accounting and Auditing.* New York: Prentice-Hall, Inc., 1952, p. 389.

[46] "Editorial," *Journal of Accountancy,* July 1946, pp. 1–4.

[47] See Ernest Dale, "The Accountant's Part in Labor Relations," in Morton Backer (ed.), *op. cit.,* pp. 541–60.

Caterpillar Tractor Co. Since 1937, the Caterpillar Tractor Co. has included its employees in the formal address of its report, and since 1946 has provided information of special interest to its workers, as for example, labour turnover, work training programmes, wages inducement and so on. The financial statements are presented in a form specially designed to be intelligible to employees.[48]

Educational and Other Functions

One of the most important social duties that has been accepted by the profession is that of educating the public to some degree of economic literacy. The results of a public poll taken some years ago in the United States revealed that 66% of union workers and 57% of non-union workers answered in the affirmative to the following question: "Would you say that a company that made $2,000,000 in profit could probably raise wages without having to raise prices?"[49] How could management and labour conduct their business at the bargaining table without some clear and agreed concept of what is a "fair return"?

The following quotation from *Accountancy* lends support to the urgency of the task of educating the public:

The accusation that accountants were 'to blame' for the Royal Academy's decision to sell its Leonardo cartoon—an accusation apparently based on the fact that it was accountants who, in the course of duty, pointed out what the consequences would be if it was not sold—is obviously one which is capable of much wider application by anyone sufficiently muddleheaded to make it at all.[50]

It is interesting to note that, as long ago as 1932, the American Institute of Accountants in correspondence with the New York Stock Exchange gave its opinion that the education of the public was one of the two major tasks which faced the profession (the other being to make corporation accounts more informative and authoritative).[51]

There are other social functions in which the profession has played a commendable part. For example, the United Kingdom Government has recently accepted in principle the introduction of decimal currency. Views strongly supporting such a change were submitted to the government by the Council of the Institute of Chartered Accountants in England

[48] Mary E. Murphy, *Accounting A Social Force in the Community*. Melbourne University Press, 1956, pp. 23–4.
[49] "What is Reasonable Profit." *Modern Industry*, June 1948, quoted in James Don Edwards, "Contemporary Concepts of Business Net Income—The Shares of Capital and Labour and the Influence of Public Opinion," *Accounting Research*, Vol. 5, pp. 121–32.
[50] "Accountants under Fire," *Accountancy*, October 1962, pp. 826–8.
[51] Quoted in Brundage, *op. cit.*, p. 75.

and Wales,[52] and a similar memorandum was submitted by the Association of Certified and Corporate Accountants. Views, which include the desirability of increased disclosure in accounts and the introduction of no par value shares, among other matters, were submitted by the two professional bodies to a committee set up a few years ago to consider revisions in company legislation.

Accountants also serve industry by serving on its boards of directors. It has been claimed by some that "when an accountant enters the board room, initiative flies out of the window." Such an attitude is less than fair. It has been pointed out that the accountant is often appointed to the board because of his integrity, and experience and knowledge of financial and business matters. In any case, the accountant does not run industry, he is part of a team.[53]

Conclusion

Perhaps, like Professor Vatter, we should conclude our survey of the social role of the accountant with the following words of Canning:

It ought never to be forgotten that those who are capable of profiting by all the information that the accountant is capable of giving are a very small number indeed. Nor should it be forgotten that the number who looks to the accountant for help is very great. The accountant forgets neither of these things.[54]

[52] *Accountancy*, February 1961, pp. 76–77.
[53] See F. M. Wilkinson, "The Influence of the Chartered Accountant in England," *Accountancy*, February 1963, pp. 105–9.
[54] John B. Canning, *The Economics of Accountancy*. New York: Ronald Press Co., 1929, p. 140, quoted in William J. Vatter, *The Fund Theory of Accounting and Its Implications for Financial Reports*. Chicago: University of Chicago Press, 1947, p. 123.

3. How Government Makes Expenditures through Tax System*

Many special tax deductions, credits, exclusions, exemptions, and preferential rates now contained in our tax system serve the same ends as budget expenditures. Thus, instead of making direct outlays or loans, granting subsidies, or insuring or guaranteeing private loans, the govern-

* Reprinted from *Standard Federal Tax Reports*, January 22, 1969, page 2.
Published and copyrighted 1969 by Commerce Clearing House, Inc., and reproduced with permission from the *CCH Standard Federal Tax Reports*.

ment can be said to be making expenditures through the tax system. There is, in effect, a revenue loss to the extent of tax preferences, and it is in the neighborhood of $50 billion per year.

This is the substance of an analysis presented recently by outgoing Treasury Secretary Joseph W. Barr to the Joint Economic Committee.

The analysis is based on Assistant Treasury Secretary Stanley S. Surrey's "tax expenditures" theory. It sets out the revenue cost of such items as charitable contributions deductions, the percentage depletion allowance, special exemptions, as for multiple corporations, and the preferential tax rate for capital gains, especially those on which no tax has been paid before a property owner's death.

4. Total Revenue Climbed $5.3 Billion in Fiscal 1968*

Internal revenue collections for the fiscal year ended June 30, 1968 have been made public by the IRS. Here is a summary (in millions of dollars, rounded off):

Source	1967	1968
Corporation income taxes	34,918	29,897
Individual income taxes, total	69,371	78,125
Withheld	50,521	57,214
Other	18,850	20,910
Employment taxes, total	26,958	28,213
Old-age and disability insurance	25,563	26,748
Unemployment insurance	603	607
Railroad retirement	793	858
Estate and gift taxes	3,014	3,082
Excise taxes	14,114	14,320
Total	148,375	153,637

* Reprinted from *Standard Federal Tax Reports*, January 8, 1969, page 4.
Published and copyrighted 1969 by Commerce Clearing House, Inc., and reproduced with permission from the CCH *Standard Federal Tax Reports*.

5. Nixon Seen Naming an Accountant to SEC in Move That Could Trigger Controversy*

President Nixon is expected to announce shortly the appointment of a young New York accounting executive to fill a vacancy on the Securities and Exchange Commission. And the move could stir controversy.

Sources say the President will name James Needham, a partner in A. M. Pullen & Co., a public accounting firm based in Greensboro, N. C. Mr. Needham, a 42-year-old certified public accountant, works in the company's New York office.

Mr. Needham would fill a vacancy left on the commission when Manuel F. Cohen, former SEC chairman, resigned in February. Hamer H. Budge, already an SEC member, was named to replace Mr. Cohen as chairman, and the fifth commission seat has been vacant ever since.

The appointment of Mr. Needham would swing the balance of the five-man commission to the Republicans for the first time since the Eisenhower Administration. Mr. Budge and Commissioner Richard B. Smith are Republicans, and the other two members, Francis M. Wheat and Hugh F. Owens, are Democrats.

Mr. Needham also would be the first member in several years who isn't a lawyer. All four of the current commissioners are attorneys as is Mr. Cohen, the former chairman. The appointment of Mr. Needham, who received a business administration degree from St. John's University in New York, could stir controversy among those who believe securities law has become too complicated to be dealt with by anyone but attorneys.

FINANCIAL DISCLOSURE CITED

However, the appointment may draw support from others who note that financial disclosure, a major concern of the commission, is ready made for an accounting expert.

Clearly, financial reporting is a hot topic at the SEC these days. The recent merger trend has caused the commission to consider the need for more detailed reporting from so-called conglomerate companies that have a number of diversified operations. Too many of these companies

* Reprinted from *The Wall Street Journal*, May 26, 1969.

tend to lump their operations into one financial total rather than breaking them down by, say, product lines and services, the SEC believes.

Recently, the commission proposed to require companies registering shares with the SEC to disclose for specified periods the contribution of separate product lines and services to earnings. The commission still is considering the possibility of requiring such disclosure in regular shareholder reports.

A number of other accounting-related issues also are getting the SEC's attention. The agency is concerned, for example, about variations in reporting corporate per-share earnings, especially where the reporting company has acquired other companies since the last time it reported earnings. Some companies take those acquisitions into account in their reports; others don't.

BACKED BY PROFESSION

Mr. Needham is relatively unknown outside of accounting circles. However, sources say he was the candidate for SEC commissioner of the American Institute of Certified Public Accountants, an influential professional association that establishes accounting standards. One accounting official describes Mr. Needham as "bright and aggressive, a coming leader of the (accounting) profession."

Besides being a member of that organization, Mr. Needham also is treasurer of the New York Society of Certified Public Accountants, the largest such state group. He has served on committees for both organizations, written for various accounting journals and is a frequent speaker on accounting subjects, associates say.

Mr. Needham is married and has five children. He lives in Plainview, N. C., where he's treasurer of the Plainview Republican Club. Mr. Needham was unavailable for comment.

6. External Influences on Accounting*

Dudley E. Browne**

The financial accounting and reporting of any corporation are subject to a variety of external influences. A larger number of common approaches to accounting and reporting problems can be found in a given industry or other relatively homogeneous group of corporations than in all of industry, but the internal relationship of its operations and programs with external influences will continue to make each corporation different from every other.

The necessity that corporate financial accounting and reporting be sufficiently unrestricted to respond readily to change should be kept in mind . . . the principle of full and fair disclosure must remain the keystone of successful corporation-stockholder and corporate-society relationships.

* Reprinted from a review of *Corporate Financial Reporting in a Competitive Economy* (Herman W. Bevis) by Dudley E. Browne, *Financial Executive*, January 1966, page 50.
** Dudley E. Browne is Director and Group Vice President of Finance and Administration of Lockheed Corporation.

Chapter II

Historical Development— Chronology of Major Influences

7. Accounting and Accountants: An Anthology*

Albert Newgarden**

Systems of accounting are believed to have existed as early as 4500 B.C., in the ancient civilizations of Babylonia and Assyria, and some historians have traced the origins of auditing almost as far back. Thus Richard Brown, in *A History of Accounting and Accountants*, published in Edinburgh in 1905, observes:

> *Whenever the advance of civilisation brought about the necessity of one man being entrusted to some extent with the property of another the advisability of some kind of check upon the fidelity of the former would become apparent. As we have seen, the ancient Egyptians imposed such a check by arranging that the fiscal receipts should be recorded separately by two officials. In later times, the Greeks instituted a system of checking public accounts by means of checking-clerks, every public official having his accounts scrutinised at the expiring of his term of office. The Romans, too, as early as the time of the Republic, recognised the salutary distinction between the official who authorises or orders*

* Reprinted, by special permission, from *The Arthur Young Journal*, Spring-Summer 1969, pages 47–62. Copyright © 1969 by Arthur Young & Company.
** Albert Newgarden is the Editor of *The Arthur Young Journal* and partner of Arthur Young & Company.

revenue and expenditure and the official who has the duty of handling cash, and they developed an elaborate system of checks and counter-checks among the various financial officials.

Although the accounting methods followed prior to the development of double-entry bookkeeping in the Middle Ages bear little resemblance to present-day accounting practices, the following quotations from early Egyptian, Roman, and Arabic sources may strike some sparks of recognition:

> *You should know that an inspector of temple finances has arrived in these parts and intends to review your accounts also. Do not be unduly disturbed, however, for I will get you off. As quickly as you can, write up your books and bring them here to me, for he is a very strict fellow. If you cannot bring the books yourself, at any rate send them to me and I will see you through, for I have become friendly with him. . . .*
>
> Letter from an Egyptian priest to another,
> second century B.C.

> *I have also reviewed the unlimited power of accountants, because they are accused by everyone of making very many illegal entries at their own pleasure. Hence it has come about that they grow wealthy while Egypt is laid waste.*
>
> Edict of Tiberius Julius Alexander,
> Governor of Egypt, 68 A.D.

> *In each man's account book, Fortune makes out two pages.*
>
> Pliny the Elder (c. 23–79 A.D.),
> *Historia Naturalis*

> *Expenditures ought not to equal income but should be smaller, so that a surplus will remain for unforeseen contingencies, such as losses that may occur at sea, or, if you are a food-merchant, having to sell a certain commodity at a loss because it threatens to spoil. None of this permits the expenses of one day to be measured by the expenses of another day; instead, you must use as a basis of comparison a long period, preferably an entire year. Bad times may follow directly on the heels of good, for receipts which one day are very small may be much larger (or even smaller!) on another day in the same period. And so it is with expenditures; they, too, vary with changing circumstances. Take this advice to heart, and may the Almighty see that you prosper!*
>
> Abu Al-Fadl, *The Delights of Commerce*,
> Damascus, ninth century A.D.

BIRTH OF THE BALANCE SHEET

Italy, the birthplace of modern commerce, was also the birthplace of the double-entry bookkeeping system, upon which many of today's accounting practices are based. The double-entry system is first met with in Genoa, in the year 1340, in the accounts rendered by the stewards of that city to the governing authorities. Other early examples of the double-entry system are two ledgers of the firm of Donado and Soranzo & Brothers, merchants of Venice, covering the period 1406–1434. In these ledgers, every debit has its corresponding credit, and the "goods accounts" are closed with a balance of profit or loss. In the later of the two ledgers, the items of profit and loss are combined and transferred to a capital account.

Although a few particularly well-kept books such as these indicate that the art of double-entry bookkeeping was well developed by the early fifteenth century, the system was still incomplete and its use still the exception rather than the rule. It was not until Fra Luca Pacioli wrote the first treatise on bookkeeping in 1494 that the "Venice method," as it came to be known, began to spread, not only throughout the trading centers of Italy but to England, Germany, and elsewhere in Europe as well.

Pacioli (or Paciolo, as the name is sometimes spelled) described himself modestly as "Brother Luke of the Borough of San Sepolcro [a small town in Tuscany], of the order of St. Francis, and of sacred theology a humble professor." In actuality, however, he was one of the brilliant "all-purpose" men for whom the Renaissance is noted. A friend of the artists Piero della Francesca and Leonardo da Vinci (who illustrated one of Pacioli's works), the Franciscan monk was highly esteemed in his time as a writer, a teacher, and an expert in such diverse fields as mathematics, theology, architecture, sports and games, military strategy, and the world of commerce. Although most of Pacioli's writings are on the subjects of arithmetic and geometry . . . he is best remembered today for his treatise on double-entry bookkeeping, published in his *Summa de Arithmetica, Geometria, Proportioni et Proportionalita.* Most of the accounting methods described in this treatise are considered to be as applicable today as they were in the fifteenth century, as are Pacioli's many practical hints on "how to succeed in business."

A fascinating account of Pacioli and his times is Robert Emmett Taylor's *No Royal Road*, published by the University of North Carolina Press in 1942. More recently, Professors R. G. Brown and K. S. Johnston have published a modern translation of the treatise on bookkeeping in *Paciolo on Accounting* (McGraw-Hill Book Company, 1963). The following brief excerpt from that translation will give some idea of the clarity and practicality of Pacioli's treatise:

After all the transactions in the Journal have been entered in an orderly manner, you must post them to the third book called the Ledger. The Ledger usually contains twice as many pages as the Journal. It should

contain an Alphabet or Repertory, or as some call it, an Index (the Floren-
tines call it Stratto). Enter in the Index all debits and credits in alpha-
betical order, together with the numbers of their respective pages: Those
names that begin with the letter A, on the page marked A, and so on.
It will be best to assign the marks to the pages of the Ledger that corre-
spond to those that appear on the Journal and Memorandum.

Having numbered the pages of the Ledger and placed the date at
the top at the right and left margin, enter Cash as a debit on the first
page, as it is in the Journal. Reserve the entire first page for Cash; do not
enter anything else as a debit or credit, because cash entries are more
numerous than all others. This is because money is almost continuously
being received or withdrawn, therefore it needs much space. The Ledger
must be ruled with as many lines as there are kinds of money which you
intend to enter. If you enter lire, soldi, denari, and picioli, draw four
lines. In front of the lire draw another line in order to record the page
number of the related debit and credit entries. In front of all these lines
draw two more wherein the dates may be entered for each entry. As was
seen in the other books, this will assist in finding the entries quickly.
This book shall also bear the Sign of the Cross.

"THE RICH-MAKING ART"

Less than 25 years after Pacioli published his *Summa*, a German
accountant, Matthäus Schwartz, published two works which, in their
time, had almost as great an impact as Pacioli's. The works were *Model
Accounts*, published in 1516, and *Model of Accounting*, published in
1518. The popularity of these works derived only partly from their content; undoubtedly of equal interest to aspiring accountants of the time
was the fact that Schwartz was the chief accountant of Jacob Fugger
of Augsburg, the richest man in Europe. Fugger, the grandson of a weaver
and the son of a successful merchant, parlayed a modest inheritance into
a financial empire that included banks, mines, factories, and farmlands.
Earning an average profit of 54 percent for 16 years, he was held in awe
by the Pope and Luther alike, and was the chief creditor of Charles V
of the Holy Roman Empire.

Schwartz's *Model Accounts* consisted of literal extracts from the
books of his employer, designed to serve as a model for students of
accountancy. The later work, *Model of Accounting*, presented Schwartz's
opinions and advice on accounting and business in general. In it he refers
to accounting as "the rich-making art," and it is clear from the portrait
of himself and Jacob Fugger, which he painted in 1516, that he did not
refer only to the fortunes of his employer.

The following quotations are principally from the *Model of
Accounting*:

The real money-dealers know each other by their faces, their crooked figures and gestures. They would not hurt their equals more than necessary, for one snappish dog does not bite the other. But when a simpleton comes along who thinks he can hear the grass grow, who doesn't know the customs and is ashamed to ask: such a man is soon caught and laughed at and taken for a good fellow. They are well aware of that at the Stock Exchange of Antwerp. "May God give him long life," they will say behind his back, "he gave us a good bargain."

The good merchant usually divides his assets into three parts: one-third ready money, one-third accounts receivable, and one-third goods. For when his creditor comes he can pay him in cash without having to sell his goods at a loss, so that even when his debtors do not hold to their terms he can still keep faith and goodwill.

Some merchants are lazy and negligent, want to keep everything in their heads and trust themselves too much. They make a note of their transactions on writing pads and scraps of paper, stick them on the wall and keep their accounts by writing on the window-sill. Rather than use a little diligence and effort they let their business go to ruin and cannot understand why in the end they are forced to abscond. . . .

When the book lies open in front of you and you look at the book (not the book at you) then the side where you have your heart is the left or Debit side. The side away from your heart is the right side and is called Credit.

[Internal control in a business employing three clerks:] If the three of them wanted to be rogues and thieves they could cause much loss and damage to a merchant with a substantial trade. But the reason why three clerks are employed is that rarely will three people reveal to each other their evil intentions. So none of them knows the mind of the other two and they all stay with their job. If one of them falls down on his duties, the others will find him out. In this way the principal is not cheated and the servants remain faithful against their own will.

IN PLAIN ENGLISH

Accountancy may have been born and bred in Italy, but it was in England, Ireland, and particularly in Scotland that it grew to full stature as a mature and respected profession. In the seventeenth, eighteenth, and nineteenth centuries, hundreds of treatises on bookkeeping and accounting were published in English. Although none of these books—including E. T. Jones's famous work of 1796, *The English System of*

Bookkeeping, which attempted (unsuccessfully) to discredit the Italian double-entry system—had an impact comparable to that of Pacioli's or Schwartz's treatises, together they were responsible for developing the wide interest in accounting that has prevailed ever since in the English-speaking countries of the world.

The following excerpts from some of these early English works have been selected as much for their literary interest and flavor as for their historical significance:

Take the generality of Accountants. First, they all differ in their Forms: The best of them are confused, the others so blotted and blurr'd . . . that neither Head nor tail can be discovered: And how many of these, distrusting or disregarding their own Books, leave them imperfect even in their own spurious wayes, and trust for the most part to their mortal Memories, or loose Papers.

> S. Montague,
> *Debtor and Creditor*, 1675

Arithmetick is indeed necessary, and a Dexterity in the Use of it is to be made a Postulatum here, as being presupposed, but in Practice, Accompting is an Art of it self distinct, and Arithmetick to Book-keeping, is as Language to Oratory, or as setting one Foot before another to the Skill of a Dancing-Master.

> Roger North,
> *The Gentleman Accomptant*, 1715

I do not know that any Art practised among Men is come up to a positive ne plus ultra, but that of Accompting.

> Roger North,
> *The Gentleman Accomptant*, 1715

It is usual with Merchants, when they make a general Balance of their Books, to value the Goods that they have by them at the Market Price they then go at, at the time of their balancing, but some do not so.

> R. Hayes,
> *The Gentleman's Complete Book-keeper*, 1741

The inimitable method of accounts being founded on the principles of reason, will prove a kind of practical logick to young people, when it is rationally and methodically communicated, not mechanically and by rules depending on the memory only, which latter does not merit the name of instruction at all.

> Malachy Postlethwayt,
> *The Merchants Public Counting House*, 1750

A Book-keeper who hath the principal Care of a Merchant or Tradesman's Books of Accounts, may be esteemed as a Person of some

Consequence to his Employer, and expect Encouragement suitable to his capacity, Fidelity and Care; a Return which he generally receives, and it would not be reasonable otherwise, seeing the Pleasure and Satisfaction a Merchant or Trader receives from the good Conduct of a faithful and able Book-keeper in whom he confides and in whom may meet all the good Qualities which duly qualify a Man for such a Station and Trust.

S. Dunn,
The New Method of Book-keeping, 1760

Hence also no general Rules for Book-keeping can be applied with equal Elegance and Utility upon all Occasions. For Book-keeping, considered as a Science with all its Appendages, and in all its various Forms or Modes, in its present State is incomplete, and not arrived at that degree of Perfection and Elegance in all its Cases to which it may be brought by the Industry of succeeding Times.

S. Dunn,
The New Method of Book-keeping, 1760

I think it will very evidently appear to any considerate Person that all this [i.e., the study of accounting] can't be done in six Weeks, much less in twenty-four hours. Such hasty Performances in Book-keeping or in any other Branch of Literature, being more likely to produce a crazy and tottering Building, subject to fall at every Blast, if not wholly undermine it, rather than make it firm and lasting.

Thomas Dillworth,
The Young Book-keeper's Assistant, 1785

It frequently occurs, that Books kept by Double Entry do not balance, and several months in each year are spent in some compting-houses to discover the cause: Some I have known to undergo seven or eight examinations before they were found to balance; and others I have seen in use fifteen or twenty years, which were never balanced, although great pains had been taken to make them correct.

Edward Thomas Jones,
English System of Book-keeping, etc., 1796

It is not without reason that most people of business and ingenuity are desirous to be master of this art [of double-entry]; for if we consider the satisfaction that naturally arises from an account well kept, the pleasure that accrues to a person on seeing what he gains . . . the acquirement of this knowledge must surely be desirable.

E. N. Marks,
The Young Man's Best Companion, 1862

CROSSING THE ATLANTIC

The history of the accounting profession in the United States dates back no further than the 1880s and 1890s, when accountants from Scotland, England, and Ireland began to emigrate to these shores. By 1905, the American Association of Public Accountants, predecessor of today's American Institute of CPAs, numbered 146 members, and the twenty state societies then in existence boasted a total of 397 members—more than half of them in the states of New York, Illinois, New Jersey, and Pennsylvania. In his *History of Accounting and Accountants,* published in Edinburgh that year, Richard Brown devotes a mere ten pages (out of a total of 460) to the profession in the United States, and describes it as follows:

The work of an Accountant in the United States is carried on under conditions which differ considerably from those prevailing in Great Britain. The scope of business is more limited, being confined chiefly to audits and investigations. Little of the nature of liquidations or adminis-tration of trust estates comes the way of the [American] accountant. The commercial spirit is more in evidence. . . . Large pieces of work have often to be carried through at high pressure, and as a consequence there is a floating population of accountants' assistants who are only taken into temporary employment by the different firms as they may require extra help. Those are not the safest kinds of persons on whom to rely for efficient work. There is also a tendency among practitioners, perhaps the outcome of necessity, to employ too large a number of unqualified assistants in proportion to principals, with consequences hurtful to the profession. It can hardly be doubted too that the growing practice of forming auditing or accounting companies, in which the element of per-sonal responsibility is completely obscured, is an unhealthy manifestation likely to prove injurious. . . .

Withal a good deal may be learned from our American cousins in matters of Accounting, more especially in the working of costing systems and in the devising of methods of book-keeping by which the results of the trading of huge concerns are shown with a frequency and a rapidity which would astonish accountants or book-keepers of the old-fashioned school. In most of the larger commercial undertakings systems are found in operation which have been perfected by specialists in that particular business, which are wonderfully successful in attaining the objects aimed at.

Fourteen years later, in 1919, the American Institute of Accountants published a small booklet, *Duties of the Junior Accountant,* which, to judge from its contents, was designed to discourage all but the very brave of heart and strong of back from pursuing a career in accounting. The following excerpts from this document provide an interesting contrast to the "career literature" published by the Institute, and by large accounting firms, today:

> *This series of articles, written in response to many inquiries from persons who are considering the desirability of public accounting as a means of livelihood, or who, having studied therefor, are about to commence practical work, does not aim to add anything to the sum of human knowledge. Its object is to set forth just what work is expected of the beginner and of the more experienced junior accountants. . . .*
>
> *We hope to set forth herein the drudgery, and sometimes the pettiness, that is inseparable from accounting, so that those contemplating taking up the work may do so with open eyes.*
>
> *Here we would point out that the several examinations for the degree of C.P.A. are necessarily artificial, in that during a very few hours the applicant must show his knowledge of those branches of accounting that demand special technical training. In actual work the accountant does not pass in rapid succession on important matters of principle. Such matters occur only at intervals—sandwiched between them being long periods of plain, ordinary hard work. . . .*
>
> *In the practical examination for the C.P.A. degree there are usually five or six difficult decisions to be made and worked out within as many hours, without possibility of obtaining additional information as to circumstances. It is probable that if, in actual business, any reputable public accountant were asked to render an opinion or give a certificate upon information as limited and as vague as that contained in an examination question, he would decline to consider it.*
>
> *The person contemplating entry into the profession should not, therefore, derive his impressions of the nature of the work to be done from the books containing the questions asked at these examinations nor from the periodicals in which such questions are discussed and solved.*
>
> W. B. Reynolds and F. W. Thornton,
> *Duties of the Junior Accountant,*
> New York, American Institute of Accountants,
> 1919

A somewhat more attractive picture of the U.S. accounting profession was provided in 1932 by an anonymous journalist, writing in *Fortune* magazine:

> *. . . Today it is no overstatement to say that there are pre-eminently three professions upon whose ethics as well as upon whose skill modern society depends: law, medicine, and Certified Public Accounting. Yet this third profession, which is no heritage but a creation of our*

necessity, is so little known that certainly 100,000 of our . . . American contemporaries will die in A.D. *1932 without ever having the vaguest notion of what manner of men Certified Public Accountants are. They walk in the shadow of virtual anonymity. So discreet are they that at times it seems as though their aim were to become a disembodied function, almost without proper name. Yet upon the expert opinion of these abstract beings—who pit their judgment against the unbelievably subtle economic forces of this generation—the financial structure of our greatest industries is founded. . . .*

Certified Public Accountants (who call themselves C.P.A.'s) may descend like a swarm of locusts upon a manufacturer, explode his delusion that he is solvent. C.P.A.'s charge by the day—regardless of the amount of money involved. C.P.A.'s sometimes become millionaires—usually because they perform other services as well. C.P.A.'s practice in partnerships, almost never corporations. C.P.A.'s fly in large flocks, in huge offices with branches, as many as fifty-four, all over the U.S., employing up to 1,200 men. One mistake and a C.P.A.'s career is ended. C.P.A.'s as a rule do not think they ought to own stock in, or become directors of, the companies of their clients. It was C.P.A.'s—and their $46,000,000 disagreements—who figured so largely in the failure of the Bethlehem-Youngstown merger. C.P.A.'s have gone beyond their functions as auditors and accountants and are turning up as advisers to business and as management experts. C.P.A.'s are by nature skeptical, cool, cautious, and conservative; to them understatement is a golden virtue and overstatement almost the equivalent of fraud. C.P.A.'s spend years at their apprenticeship and are still learning.

"Certified Public Accountants,"
Fortune, June 1932

GOODBYE, MR. HUBBARD

One attribute of CPAs which that *Fortune* writer overlooked—or perhaps it was not so evident in the 1930s—is their tendency to worry a good deal about their "image." CPAs, it seems, are not satisfied with being one of the "three professions . . . upon whose skill modern society depends"; nor, apparently do they find sufficient solace in the fact that "CPAs sometimes become millionaires" (possibly because not even CPAs are finding that so easy to manage in the face of constantly rising taxes). No; it appears that CPAs want also to be liked—and not merely liked but, as Willy Loman put it, well liked.

In the past ten years particularly, there has been a virtual flood of articles by CPAs (and articles *about* CPAs by public relations advisers and other well-wishers) lamenting what has come to be known as "the green eyeshade image" and proposing to eliminate it and substitute a better image in its place. Inevitably, when this lamenting and proposing take place, somebody quotes the following description of a "typical auditor," by Elbert Hubbard, the American author, publisher, and handicraft enthusiast who is perhaps best known for his *Message to Garcia* (1899) and his *Little Journeys to the Homes of Great Philosophers (Statesmen, Businessmen,* etc.):

. . . a man past middle life, tall, spare, wrinkled, intelligent, cold, passive, noncommittal, with eyes like a codfish; polite in contact but at the same time unresponsive, cool, calm, and as damnably composed as a concrete post or a plaster-of-paris cat; a human petrifaction with a heart of feldspar, and without charm or the friendly germ; minus bowels, passion, or a sense of humor. Happily, they never reproduce, and all of them finally go to Hell.

As an exercise in the art of diatribe, this is really quite a little masterpiece—worthy of a W. C. Fields or a Westbrook Pegler. It has been quoted in a number of articles and brochures published by the American Institute of CPAs—most recently, in a brief essay entitled "Getting Rid of the Green Eyeshade," which appeared in the February 1968 issue of *The Journal of Accountancy.*

Possibly there are some CPAs who have not grown so fond of this particular piece of self-abuse that they will not be disappointed to learn that Mr. Hubbard did not write or say it of an auditor at all, nor of any sort of accountant, bookkeeper, or clerk. It is extracted from a brief essay entitled "The Buyer," which appears in Volume VIII of the *Selected Writings of Elbert Hubbard,* published by his own Roycrofters Press in 1922. The relevant parts of the essay are as follows (emphasis supplied):

Not long ago I called on a great corporation president, who is also the president of a great corporation. "You are a student of human nature," he said, *"the pergola of pellucidity, and I want to show you a curiosity."* He pressed a button, and in about a minute a man entered. This man was past middle life, tall, spare, wrinkled, intelligent, cold, passive, non-committal, with eyes like a codfish. *The president introduced us. . . . He was as cool, calm and damnably composed as a concrete post or a plaster-of-paris cat. I tried a pleasantry, but it fell flat. "What can I do for you?"* asked the Human Petrifaction.

Just then I glanced at the president, and I saw he was laughing behind a newspaper. . . . When the man had gone, he asked, "What do you think of him?" "Well, he is not exactly effusive," I answered. "Why should he be? He is a buyer. Been here forty years and has worked at the one job until he has lost his soul. His brain is a mass of mathematics, and his heart is feldspar . . . charm *of manner doesn't count. Salesmen are decent, but buyers don't have to be. Buyers are unhuman,* without bowels, passions or sense of humor. Happily they never reproduce. *They are minus the* friendly germ. . . . *This man . . . is valuable, but if he went on the road to sell goods he would divert trade from the house to our competitors. We couldn't do without him—but all buyers* go to hell!"

While it is hoped that this little piece of literary detective work will put an end to further use of the Hubbard "quotation" as Exhibit A for the prosecution in the apparently never-ending *Green Eyeshade* case, determined image-improvers should have no difficulty in finding equally derogatory substitutes in other literary sources.

ACCOUNTING AND ACCOUNTANTS IN LITERATURE AND THE PRESS

Many of the same accountants who worry about their image complain that, whereas lawyers, doctors, ministers, teachers, and other professionals have frequently been portrayed or discussed in novels, stories, essays, plays, and movies, very little attention of that sort has been paid to professional accountants. Possibly if those who express this complaint were more familiar with the kind of attention that *has* been paid to accountants in novels, stories, essays, etc., they might be less anxious to see more of it.

From the several dozen novels, stories, essays, etc. dealing with accounting or accountants with which this writer is familiar, the following selection of quotations is offered here for no purpose more profound than pleasure:

> . . . *His promises fly so beyond his state*
> *That what he speaks is all in debt; he owes*
> *For every word: he is so kind that he now*
> *Pays interest for 't; his land's put to their books.*

> . . . *Take the bonds along with you*
> *And have the dates in compt.*

> *O my good lord!*
> *At many times I brought in my accounts,*
> *Laid them before you; you would throw them off,*
> *And say you found them in mine honesty.*

> *If you suspect my husbandry of falsehood,*
> *Call me before the exactest auditors,*
> *And set me on the proof . . .*

Thou has painfully discovered: are his files
As full as thy report?

William Shakespeare,
Timon of Athens, c. 1605

And indeed what is the whole business of the Trader's Accompt,
but to overreach him who trusts his Memory?

Sir Roger De Coverley,
The Spectator, 1713

If he is steady, cautious, proficient in arithmetic and with a dis-
position towards the prosecution of its higher branches, he cannot follow
a better line than that of an accountant.

Sir Walter Scott,
letter to Thomas Scott, his brother,
on July 23, 1820

Of quite another stamp was the then accountant, John Tipp. . . .
With Tipp form was everything. His life was formal. His actions seemed
ruled with a ruler. His pen was not less erring than his heart. . . . With
all this there was about him a sort of timidity—(his few enemies used
to give it a worse name)—a something which, in reverence to the dead,
we will place, if you please, a little on this side of the heroic. . . . Tipp
never mounted the box of a stagecoach in his life; or leaned against the
rails of a balcony; or walked upon the ridge of a parapet; or looked down
a precipice; or let off a gun; or went upon a water-party; or would will-
ingly let you go, if he could have helped it. . . .

Charles Lamb,
"The South-Sea House," 1820

He's an articled clerk. He seems to know his job. He can't get over
the way our accounts are kept. He told me he never expected a theatre
to be run on such business-like lines. He says the way some of these firms
in the City keep their accounts is enough to turn your hair grey.

W. Somerset Maugham,
Theatre, 1937

Grayson was a long stooped yellow-faced man with high shoulders,
bristly eyebrows and almost no chin. The upper part of his face meant
business. The lower part was just saying goodbye. He wore bifocals and
he had been gnawing fretfully at the evening paper. I had looked him
up in the city directory. He was a CPA and looked it every inch. He even
had ink on his fingers and there were four pencils in the pocket of his
open vest.

Raymond Chandler,
The Lady in the Lake, 1943

Sir Eric maintained his habitual icy, semi-military, semi-priestly accountant's expression . . .

Tarbolton was the managing clerk, overworked, intelligent and industrious, and Sir Eric had heard about him; but he knew nothing about the audit clerks who worked under Tarbolton. In the accountancy profession big fleas had little fleas upon their backs, not to bite them, but to do their biting for them, and it was not to the interest of the local partners to let the London partners know too much about the excellence of their subordinates.

All in all, he looked the typical youngish chartered accountant of ability whose intelligence was so absorbed by his work that there was none left over for anything else.

Syme had become a chartered accountant as a gambler played for safety by backing two horses in the same race: he had wanted to accumulate experience to write about and to be sure of earning his living should he fail as a novelist. As he stood waiting for his bus to come along he was wondering whether he had not fallen between two stools: he had to work so hard to attain competence in a profession in which he was not naturally expert that he generally came home at night too tired to write, and his distress about this impeded his industry on audits.
    Bruce Marshall, The Accounting, 1958
    (Published in England as The Bank Audit)

Auditors are like St. Thomas; they require to see before they believe.
    Bruce Marshall,
    The Divided Lady, 1960

He was only a CPA, although of course Louise's family always had loads of money, so that couldn't have mattered less.
    Frederick Buechner,
    The Return of Ansel Gibbs, 1958

Owen stood at the window, smoking a cigarette and watching for the occasional flash of the dog's body when the sun caught it. The colour of a new penny. What was wrong with a dog being the colour of a new penny? Nothing, but only an accountant would notice it. Why was he an accountant anyway? He had never wanted to be an accountant. He had never wanted to be anything much but he had particularly not wanted to be an accountant. He hated the job. Of course he knew why he had taken it up. His father had made him. Owen drew the cigarette smoke into his lungs and thought that if his father had been there at that moment

*he would have gone out into that copse and played with [the dog]. Father
was a great man for dogs.*

P. H. Newby,
The Barbary Light, 1962

*Aggressive-looking young woman to studious-looking young man
at a cocktail party: "You certainly have a wonderful way of expressing
yourself, for a certified public accountant."*

Cartoon by F. B. Modell,
The New Yorker, May 19, 1962

*Little more is known of Parson Weems' publishing career, but he
died happy, full of years and presumably remembered by the friends he
made at Court houses and among throngs of Country People. Of his
employer I know nothing, but can surmise that he came to a bad end,
selling shares in his firm to the public and spending his last days sur-
rounded by accountants, management consultants, and public-relations
men . . .*

William Jovanovitch,
Now, Barabbas, 1964

*To the generation that succeeded mine, stories about the Lower
East Side are like stories about the moon. The 40-year-olds have been to
Princeton or to the University of Bridgeport. They have advanced degrees
and they are accountants. They live in the suburbs and invest their energies in perpetual wars with the Board of Education. They are different,
no doubt about it . . .*

Harry Golden, explaining the closing down of
his newspaper, *The Carolina Israelite*, in an
interview reported in *The New York Times*,
February 22, 1968

8. A Peripatetic History of Accounting*

Walker Fesmire** and the Editors of
Cost and Management

Accounting as we know it today began with the trading partnerships of the Italian city-states. Before that, accounting was for individuals, mostly for the landed gentry as a means of preventing loss due to carelessness, embezzlement or the like. Accounting's great growth commenced with the development of institutions of national government, trade, commerce and industry. The development of institutions is a relatively modern phenomenon. It was practically unknown in the ancient and medieval world. Even the Romans, considered masters of organization, had only very primitive notions of institutional management.

Our peripatetic history tends to demonstrate the link between accounting and institutional growth. The centres of accounting development perpetually move to where the action is. After its slow and primitive beginnings in Greece (money), Egypt (tabular accounts), and Arabia (numbers), our accounting history travels to Florence, Genoa and Venice where it gains its first momentum from the practice of the great international merchant traders and banking institutions. With quick visits to Germany and France, our itinerant accounting history arrives in England to prosper on the growth of empirical trade. After reaching maturity with the power of the English purse, the centre of accounting development migrates, with hardly more than a cryptic nod of thanks to its Italian and British parents, to that western land where the streets were reputed to be paved with gold (always a most interesting proposition for accountants). And there the centre of accounting development has resided ever since.

If our little history lesson, with due apologies to historians everywhere for our conceit in calling it that, teaches us anything, it would seem to be that accounting thrives wherever man is concerned with maximizing his profits and the size of his institutions in politically stable societies. We detect no trend of decline in either category. Peripatetic or not, accounting history seems to bode well for the future of accountants everywhere.

Our history begins, with profound logic, where it should, in the beginning of recorded time, some 5000 years ago. But, because we are

* Reprinted by permission from *Cost and Management*, official journal of The Society of Industrial Accountants of Canada, July-August 1967, pages 33–38.
** Walker Fesmire is at Ferris State College.

accountants, we will simply dismiss the first half of history with apologies to the Babylonians, Chinese and early Egyptians. Even though it seems fair to assume that something of accounting significance may have happened then, we know nothing of it. The records, if there were any, are lost. Such carelessness suggests that the people in those days did not have a very professional attitude, anyway.

The first ray of light to brighten the dark ages of accounting might seem, to some, of dubious merit. The introduction of stamped coinage by the Lydian Greeks around 630 B.C. was not apparently welcomed by the rest of the world with much rejoicing. Even the Romans were not entirely sold on the idea.

Money, and the Hindu-Arabic numeral system, were the two developments upon which accounting had to wait to make its true beginning, in the early 14th century, with the advent of double-entry bookkeeping, in Genoa and Florence.

Table 8.1   Major Events in the History of Accounting

The Accounting Event		Its Environment
Introduction of coined money by the Lydian Greeks.	Circa 630BC	Western civilization dawns in Ancient Greece.†
Earliest known tabular accounts from Ancient Greece—record in stone of the receipts and expenditures of the 14th Board of Overseers in the erection of the temple Athena (The Parthenon).	Circa 430BC	
The Zenon archive, earliest comprehensive accounts on Papyrus, of the private estate of the chief finance minister of Ptolemy II, Appollonius, in Egypt, as recorded by his agent Zenon, illustrating the purpose of ancient accounting to prevent loss due to carelessness, embezzlement and theft.	Circa 250BC	Egyptian and Roman conquerors introduce complex large organizations into their societies.†
Al-Khwarajmi, Persian mathematician, writes complete arithmetic treatise in Arabic on the Hindu-	Circa 825AD	

† Those expressions marked by daggers (†) are the editors' written interpretations of artwork contained in the original.

Table 8.1   Major Events in the History of Accounting (continued)

The Accounting Event		Its Environment
Arabic numeral system, the basic system of the modern recording of accounts, incorporating the zero.		Europe emerges from the Dark Ages.†
Domesday Book, earliest record of property for taxation.	1086	
Introduction of tallies in England as receipts for money transactions later evolving into a form of security until abolished in 1826.	Circa 1100	
Earliest known partnership records, of a Genoese notary Giovanni Scriba. The beginning of the recognition of the firm as a distinct entity, separate from the owners.	1157	The Roman Empire of Charles the Great begins to crumble. European kingdoms begin to assert themselves.†
The Liber Abbaci, written by Leonardo Pisano, to demonstrate the superiority of Hindu-Arabic numerals over Roman numerals and expressing the arrangement of accounts in regular columns.	1202	
Earliest medieval record of credit, in a Florentine account book.	1211	
Formalization of the accounting, organization and management system of British landed gentry—subdivision of activity, work centres, consolidated report, stewardship.	Circa 1275	By the end of the 13th century, the Normans had conquered England. The Byzantine Empire, the last vestiges of the Roman Empire, was dying in the East, the threat of Arabian conquest in Europe was passed, trade and commerce throughout much of Europe, the Levant and the Orient flourished, and European man was on the threshold of his

Table 8.1 Major Events in the History of Accounting (continued)

The Accounting Event	Its Environment
	great adventures of discovery to the west. The Roman church came to its peak of power, rights of the individual were beginning to be recognized, the Feudal concepts of noble and absolute rule were giving way to the power of the city-states and thus to nations. The Italian renaissance was soon to begin, introducing 200 years of enlightened enquiry and the stable economies upon which trade, commerce and the banks grew and flourished. It was the real beginning of modern accounting practice. 1292 Death of Kublai Khan
Earliest known evidence of double-entry bookkeeping, in the accounts of the Florentine merchant Rinieri Fini, relating to his dealings at the Fairs of Champagne (The great international money market of the period).	Circa 1296

1300—1500: Period of City-States, growth of international trade and discovery, feudal system ends, rights of individual, economy controlled by merchants and master craftsmen. Arabic numbers come into general use.

The development of agency accounting by Italian merchants to integrate various accounts into one system of classification, including receivables, sales, payables and purchases, with a balance sheet.	Circa 1325

Table 8.1   Major Events in the History of Accounting (continued)

The Accounting Event		Its Environment
Earliest example of double entry in tabular form, in the accounts of the Commune of Genoa.	Circa 1340	
		1348 Great Plague in Europe
Florentine woolen mills develop crude costing of work.	1393	

1400—1600: Italian renaissance begins period of enlightened enquiry, political and economic stability in Europe. Growth of institutions, trade, commerce and banking. Concepts of national state take shape.

Italian merchants begin using accounting for management control by developing rudiments of cost accounting, including deferred items and the audit of balance sheets. Accounts of Marco Datini & Co. demonstrate the established practice of accrual accounting, depreciation and reserves.	Circa 1400	
Medici family books. First appearance of account called "Cloth Manufactured and Sold."	1431	
Barbarigo's account books—the balance account.	1435	
		1446 First printed books (Coster in Haarlem)
		1452 Birth of Leonardo da Vinci
		1453 Constantinople falls to Ottoman Turks
		1492 Columbus crosses Atlantic

Table 8.1   Major Events in the History of Accounting (continued)

The Accounting Event		Its Environment
Paciola's "Summa." First book on accounting and mathematics.	1494	
	1498	Vasco da Gama sails round Cape to India
	1509	Henry VIII becomes King of England
	1519	Cortez enters Mexico City
	1521	Luther at the Diet of Worms
Gottlieb—the summary account.	1546	
	1547	Ivan the Terrible becomes Tsar of Russia
	1549	First Jesuit missions arrive in South America
	1563	End of Council of Trent
	1564	Birth of Shakespeare
	1566	Suleiman the Magnificent, who brought the Ottoman empire to its zenith, dies.
	1588	Spanish Armada defeated
Pietra's ledger and presentation of the summary account in the form of the modern British balance sheet.	1596	

Table 8.1   Major Events in the History of Accounting (continued)

The Accounting Event		Its Environment
1600—1800: The Rise of Nationalism, the Reformation, large trading organizations develop commercial revolutions, hold of guilds on production broken, printing spreads learning: new concepts of individual and social justice lead to political revolutions.		
		1620 Mayflower expedition founds New Plymouth.
Record keeping becomes subordinated to control function.	1633	
Pascal designs a machine to process tax data.	1640	
British trading companies concept of corporate continuity develops.	1650	
Ordinance of France "Pour le Commerce."	1673	
		1674 Nieuw Amsterdam becomes British by treaty, renamed New York.
Collins develops flow of cost concept in English style industry.	1697	
Wages owed account appears.	1712	
Malcolm publishes first text in accounting theory.	Circa 1719	
British "Bubble Act" prohibits formation of joint stock companies because of excessive speculative losses.		
French "Dictionnaire Universel de Commerce."	1723	
Allowance for "straight line depreciation" in shop accounting.	1757	

Table 8.1   Major Events in the History of Accounting (continued)

The Accounting Event	Its Environment
	1763 Peace of Paris; Canada ceded to Britain
	1776 U.S. Declaration of Independence. Watt invents steam engine.
	1789 Beginning of French Revolution—storming of the Bastille
First income tax law in Great Britain.	1799

1800—1900: The Industrial Revolution. Development of factory system. English master craftsmen develop into industrial capitalists, concept of public ownership develops along with "public-be-damned" attitude, leading to monopoly, unionism and government regulation to enforce social responsibility on corporations. Concepts of religious freedom and industrial rights grow.

The Accounting Event	Its Environment
	1804 Napoleon Bonaparte becomes emperor of France
Napoleon's "Code de Commerce."	1807
Cost accounts still not integrated in general ledger. Perpetual inventory concept developed using quantities only. Cranhelm enunciates the bookkeeping principle of "equality."	Circa 1818
	1819 First Factory Act passed in Great Britain
Babbage develops concept of cost of production for a process system.	1830

Table 8.1   Major Events in the History of Accounting (continued)

The Accounting Event		Its Environment
		1835 The word "social-ism" first comes into use
The British Companies Act. Formalization in law of the concept of managers and directors as stewards of public enterprise. Commencement of business regulatory law. Chemical industry develops concept of by-product and joint cost. Institute of Accounts, first accounting body in Great Britain.	Circa 1850	
		1854–56 Crimean War
		1861–65 American Civil War
Form of the balance sheet is prescribed by British law.	1868	
		1876 Bell obtains first telephone patent
		1882 Death of Charles Darwin
Metcalfe develops time card and time book.	1885	1883 Death of Karl Marx
Garcke and Fells publish "Factory Accounts."	1890	

1900 to present—period of international political and economic upheaval, world war, rapid advance in science, the electronic and nuclear age, collapse of tradition, the era of change, rise of socialism and the middle class, population explosion, recognition of social interest and responsibility. Rapid expansion of social law, government and corporate institutions. Beginning of space exploration.

Lewis distinguishes prime costs, factory burden recognized, perpetual inventory plans suggested,	Circa 1900	

Table 8.1   Major Events in the History of Accounting (continued)

The Accounting Event		Its Environment
FIFO advocated, concepts of normal price and average cost presented. Cost comparison used for cost control.		
		1903 Wright brothers fly
Interest as a cost debated, predetermined burden rates applied, departmentalization of costs, prime costs and imputed interest recognized. Standardized reports ordered for U.S. railroads.	Circa 1910	
U.S. Income Tax Act.	1913	
		1914–18 World War I
		1917 Russian Revolution
Scientific management movement aids development of standard cost, cost accounting principles, procedures and techniques refined. Distribution of factory overhead costs, cost variation recording, cost reports and control, flexible budgets. Use of costing for management guidance pricing. Development of budgeting.	Circa 1920 1930	1920 First meeting of the League of Nations
		1930 Hitler and Nazi party emerge in Germany
		1933 Inauguration of Roosevelt's New Deal
All-inclusive income statement develops.	1936	1936–39 Spanish Civil War
		1939–45 World War II
		1945 First use of nuclear weapons
Statistical methods from World War II made available to industry. Development of interest in providing data for management planning of future economic activities. Long-range budget and forecasts, cost standards, profit margins, inventory	1946 1949	

Table 8.1   Major Events in the History of Accounting (continued)

The Accounting Event	Its Environment
turnover, return on capital systems and procedures. EDP, computer technology and use of operations research in business evolves.˙ The electronic era. Managerial economics develops, professional management systems and procedures, the development of communications as a management system, information theory. Emphasis on the behavioral sciences in management and accounting.	Circa 1950 to present

	1950 Korean conflict begins
	1956 First atomic energy plant to operate on an industrial scale—in Great Britain
	1957 Russians launch first sputnik
	1961 Russians put first man into space
	1962 Cuba crisis
	1963 Assassination of President Kennedy
	1966 U.S. land first equipment on the moon

9. The Search for Accounting Principles*

Reed K. Storey**

The first peak of interest in accounting principles was brief but productive. It began to appear around 1930 and began to blossom in late 1934 or early 1935. It was related to two landmark events in the history of accounting: the publication of the report of the special committee on co-operation with stock exchanges of the American Institute of Accountants (since 1957, the American Institute of Certified Public Accountants)[1] and the establishment of the Securities and Exchange Commission with

---

* Reprinted from *The Search for Accounting Principles*, by Reed K. Storey, the American Institute of Certified Public Accountants, 1964, copyrighted 1964 by the American Institute of CPAs, pages 3–7.

** Reed K. Storey is the Director of the Accounting Research Division of the American Institute of CPAs.

[1] *Audits of Corporate Accounts* (New York: American Institute of Certified Public Accountants, 1934).

authority to prescribe accounting procedures.[2] The upswing of interest during the late 1930's in the formulation of accounting principles ended rather abruptly with the beginning of World War II. During the war period, accountants became preoccupied with military duties, service in government agencies, or with the accounting problems caused by the mobilization program, industrial production for war, and wartime controls.

In spite of its short duration, the period of the first peak in interest produced a volume of literature on the subject of accounting principles which is unmatched by that of any other period and is probably equally unmatched in terms of progress made. During this time the accounting profession and the SEC began their harmonious working relationship. It was also during this period that the American Accounting Association was reorganized.[3] In keeping with the Association's new objective, "To develop accounting principles and standards, and to seek their endorsement or adoption by business enterprises, public and private accountants, and governmental bodies,"[4] its Executive Committee published two statements of accounting principles.[5] Furthermore, a monograph was published by two members of the Executive Committee who, as individuals, undertook to elaborate and expand the basic concepts on which the "Tentative Statement" was based.[6] Finally, this period was host to the publication of the first more or less comprehensive codification of accepted accounting principles [7] and to the birth of the expanded committee on accounting procedure of the American Institute of Certified Public Accountants which issued eleven Accounting Research Bulletins between September 1939 and September 1941. . . .

The second cyclical increase in interest in defining and codifying accounting principles began shortly after World War II and was largely a result of some serious criticism leveled at accounting and accountants. Some of this criticism was leveled, probably justifiably, at certain practices

---

[2] The Securities and Exchange Commission was created by the Securities Exchange Act of 1934. The Securities Act of 1933 was originally administered by the Federal Trade Commission.

[3] At the annual convention in 1935 the teachers of accounting changed the name of their association from the more descriptive American Association of University Instructors in Accounting to the more manageable American Accounting Association and opened the membership to anyone interested in accounting.

[4] "A Statement of Objectives of the American Accounting Association," *op. cit.*, p. 1.

[5] "A Tentative Statement of Accounting Principles Underlying Corporate Financial Statements," *Accounting Review*, Vol. XI (June 1936), pp. 187–91; "Accounting Principles Underlying Corporate Financial Statements," *Accounting Review*, Vol. XVI (June 1941), pp. 133–39.

[6] W. A. Paton and A. C. Littleton, *An Introduction to Corporate Accounting Standards* (Ann Arbor, Michigan: American Accounting Association, 1940).

[7] T. H. Sanders, H. R. Hatfield, and U. Moore, *A Statement of Accounting Principles* (New York: American Institute of Certified Public Accountants, 1938).

which developed during the war, the most notable of which was the use by some companies of profit equalization reserves. Some critics, however, concentrated on the fact that reported income and taxable income were not always the same amount or upon other similar irrelevancies. Criticisms of the latter type were symptomatic, for at the heart of much of the criticism was the basic ignorance of the public about financial statements and business operations in general. As a result of this ignorance, financial statements and the businessmen and accountants who prepared them were widely mistrusted. The matter was worsened by the lack of sophistication demonstrated by a number of commentators on the subject. There was, nevertheless, a beneficial result from this criticism. It led to substantial self-examination by accountants, and this, in turn, produced constructive steps toward the improvement of accounting practices and some improvement in public confidence in the results of accounting.

The second "boom" in interest in accounting principles differed significantly from its predecessor, although the basic problems and questions appeared much the same. The output of books and articles on accounting principles and related subjects was much smaller than that of the period immediately before the war. In addition, the publications which did appear were more concerned with the place of accounting in the postwar world than directly with the formulation of accounting principles *per se*. Consequently, no statement or code of accounting principles resulted from the activities of the period. The second revision of the American Accounting Association statement appeared in 1948, but it was no longer designated as a statement of principles.[8] Seventeen Accounting Research Bulletins (Nos. 26 through 42) were issued by the Institute's committee on accounting procedure between 1946 and 1953; the previously issued bulletins were revised and restated in 1953.[9] None of these, however, constituted the desired code of accounting principles.

The discussions about formulating accounting principles into a generally accepted code stopped as abruptly as it had begun. Although the Korean conflict may have been a factor in the decline of interest in accounting principles, another matter loomed larger in accounting thought. Accountants became concerned with a particular reporting problem, namely, accounting under conditions of changing price levels. They turned their attention almost entirely in that direction.[10] The new trough

[8] "Accounting Concepts and Standards Underlying Corporate Financial Statements, 1948 Revision," *Accounting Review*, Vol. XXXIII (October 1948), pp. 339–44.

[9] Accounting Research Bulletin No. 43, "Restatement and Revision of Accounting Research Bulletins"; Accounting Terminology Bulletin No. 1, "Review and Resume" (New York: American Institute of Certified Public Accountants, 1953).

[10] The decrease in the number of articles dealing with accounting principles is so sudden that it immediately strikes anyone working through the literature of the

in concern with accounting principles was neither as long nor as deep as the one during the war. A small number of articles on accounting principles appeared during the height of the price-level debate, and attention returned to accounting principles within three or four years.

In late 1957 a number of events occurred which returned accountants' attention to the problem of formulating accounting principles. Three of these events should be noted in particular. In August, at the annual convention of the American Accounting Association, Leonard Spacek made a proposal which was revolutionary in the view of most accountants. He suggested that an accounting court be established to hear and decide issues relating to accounting principles.[11] The second significant event was that the newly installed president of the American Institute of CPAs, Alvin R. Jennings, set accounting research as the keynote of his administration in his acceptance speech at the Institute's annual meeting in October. He called for the establishment of an expanded and independent Institute research program based on the premise that the development of accounting principles was more in the nature of basic rather than applied research.[12] Lastly, the 1957 revision of the American Accounting Association statement, which had been in progress since 1955, was published in December.[13] Although each of these events had developed independently of the others, they supported each other. The result was another burst of activity in the area of accounting principles. Much of the discussion centered on the same issues that had been the focal point of discussion in earlier periods—the need for an "authoritative, comprehensive code of accounting principles."

The suggestion which really caught the imagination of accountants at this time was Mr. Jennings' proposal for an increased research effort to re-examine the basic assumptions of accounting, to develop authoritative statements to guide accountants, and to aid in improving understanding of financial statements by those who relied upon them. This suggestion, after study by a special committee, led to the Institute's present research program and to the establishment of the Accounting Principles Board.

---

period. This happened about the time the Study Group on Business Income published its report, *Changing Concepts of Business Income* (New York: Macmillan Company, 1952).

[11] Leonard Spacek, "The Need for an Accounting Court," *Accounting Review,* Vol. XXXIII (July 1958), pp. 368–79.

[12] "Present-Day Challenges in Financial Reporting," *The Journal of Accountancy,* Vol. CV (January 1958), pp. 28–34.

[13] *Accounting and Reporting Standards for Corporate Financial Statements, 1957 Revision and Preceding Statements and Supplements* (Columbus, Ohio: American Accounting Association, 1957), pp. 1–12.

Chapter III

The Accounting Function in Different Economic Systems

10. Accounting as an Instrument for Achieving National Goals*

Editorial

With Russia becoming a formidable competitor for global markets, its current economic emphasis is significant. Russia is trying to improve its industrial position by a technique it calls cost accounting.

The Russians say it is a means not only for controlling material, labor and financial resources, but also for choosing the most profitable among alternative investments. Since Russia is the second-ranking world power—and obviously aspires to be first—its range of alternative investments has widened to where comparison of costs and returns is vital.

Accounting in Russia is now given high priority. Kosygin recently said: "It is certainly society's concern by what effort and what price results are obtained and also the efficiency of each enterprise. . . ." Kosygin also noted flaws in Russia's accounting techniques, especially the failure to include cost of capital, when he said, "We cannot speak of genuine cost accounting if the enterprise is not responsible for utilizing capital." The admission that there *is* such a thing as capital, and that it is vital, is quite a step forward for the Soviets.

* Reprinted from the *Lybrand Journal*, Vol. 49, No. 3, 1968, page 2.

This stance emphasizes the stake that every country, whatever its political environment, has in accounting. It is basic to a nation's attainment of high economic standards and may also be the key to competition with other countries for a position in the world market. For accounting can make the difference in how a nation mobilizes its resources.

The U.S., of course, has been in the vanguard of accounting progress, its interest being both broadly and historically based. The 1933 Securities Act, which set up the SEC's authority over reporting practices of publicly owned companies, began a new era. The SEC relies upon the accounting profession for accounting principles and auditing standards and it has given the profession the necessary backing to upgrade reporting practices dramatically. The role of this upgrading in expanding our capital market since 1933 is a matter of record.

The U.S. and Russian emphasis points up the importance of accounting techniques of all types, whether for external reporting or for internal efficiency purposes. Similar emphasis is seen in such developed nations as the U.K. and Germany. Others, like France and Italy, still seem mired down despite their progress elsewhere. And developing countries are, of course, new to the complexities of industrialization.

The Common Market has also been concerned about financial reporting. An EEC committee studying European capital markets has urged more information in financial reports because *investor confidence* is "particularly important." Fuller disclosure was also urged by 60 major industrialists in an OECD-sponsored meeting.

National aspirations are obviously expanding. As in the past, economic achievement is the key to all worthwhile goals. Important now is that the times be read correctly. We are in an age of striking technological advance and broad democratic participation. The means for accommodating these trends must be established. To create what we in the U.S. regard as a workable economy, the development of capital markets with broad participation and of methods to make industry run effectively must assume priority. Indeed, from the viewpoint of world competition, accounting may well become the next economic battleground.

11. Accounting in a Free Economy*

J. M. Yang**

Since the beginning men have been engaged in producing things necessary for subsistence and have been confronted with the problem as to what things to produce and how to produce them. As soon as several persons combined their efforts in production, there has been the problem as to what each should do and how the product should be distributed among them. The order or condition under which men decide and carry on their activities with reference to production and distribution characterizes an economy. An economy is said to be free when the members of a community, each according to his ability and situation, freely make decisions and carry on economic activities, with little or no interference from the government.

In the early days of economic life, when each individual constituted a unit of economic activities by himself, there was no problem of distribution and his own choice of consumption determined the character of his production. Later, as the household became the economic unit, and still in a state of self-sufficiency, the consumption of the household determined its production; work was assigned and product was distributed among its members largely according to the wish of the head of the family. After a further period of development, the household economy was gradually broken up and in its place a social economy emerged.

In a social economy production is undertaken mostly by separately organized business enterprises which constitute the cells of the entire economic organism of society. Individuals take part in these business enterprises in various specialized capacities as landowners, workers, capitalists, and enterprisers supplying respectively land, labor, capital, and enterprise, the four basic factors of production. Production is no longer for the direct consumption of persons participating in each business enterprise, but for sale to consumers or to other business enterprises which in turn produce for final consumption. The underlying reason for this development is the efficiency resulting from specialization and cooperation. Men produce more and better things when they concentrate their effort on particular tasks and they can do so by cooperating with

* Reprinted from *The Accounting Review*, July 1959, pages 442–451.
** J. M. Yang is a Professor at the New Asia College, Hong Kong.

others in a business enterprise; and a business enterprise in turn gains efficiency by devoting itself to one kind of production and selling its product on the market rather than producing what its participants need for consumption. In other words, the present economy is a market economy in which production is disposed of in the market and it is the money realized from the sale of the product that is distributed among those participating in production rather than the product they themselves produce. With the money thus obtained each individual decides for himself what things he wants to buy for consumption. In these circumstances the problem of production becomes more complicated and some equitable basis of distribution has to be found.

While all productive factors cooperate in carrying on production in a business enterprise, it should not be inferred that the business enterprise comes into being through their joint initiative; rather, the initiative for its organization comes from the enterpriser who sees the possibility of success for a certain line and method of production and risks his money and effort over it. The enterpriser plans and coordinates the work of production and engages the services of the other factors. The problem of production, therefore, is primarily one for the enterpriser who alone is responsible for the success of the business undertaking. As a matter of fact, not all the factors taking part in the business wait for the sale of its product to secure their share of production: each factor is generally paid remuneration according to a predetermined rate, except the enterpriser who gets what is left after the claims of other factors are met. There is always the possibility that the proceeds of sale will be insufficient to meet even the prior claims, in which case the enterpriser suffers a loss. Thus the position of the enterpriser seems a precarious one and that of the other factors more secure but subject to the whim of the employer. However, aside from personal aptitude and condition every individual is free to decide what part he wants to play in production; whether to be an enterpriser, start a business of his own and earn profit, or to take part as a land-owner, worker, or capitalist in the business of others and receive rent, wage, or interest. Moreover, as an enterpriser, every person is free to decide on his line and method of production; and as any of the other factors, every person is free to choose the specific business enterprise with which he wants to be associated.

ECONOMIC ACTIVITIES GUIDED BY PRICES

In an economy in which every individual is free to do what he likes, without a set of rules to govern economic activities or a central agency to direct them, confusion would seem inevitable, with production out of gear with consumption and distribution largely on an arbitrary basis. One may indeed wonder, with various alternatives open to him, how is the enterpriser to know whether he should produce one thing rather than another? What should be his method of production? Similarly, among the different business enterprises, how is the supplier of each of the other factors to decide whether he should join any particular enterprise rather than another? Decisions in this regard affect not only the interest of the individuals concerned, but also that of the society as a whole, because erroneous decisions would mean a waste of economic resources which could be devoted to more useful production, and social interest requires that all economic resources be used in such a manner as to yield the maximum economic well-being. In economic considerations every person is predominantly self-seeking and his economic activities are motivated by the prospect of maximum advantage to himself. Such being the case, what is the assurance that the decisions of individuals will be in line with the interest of society? What is the guide to decisions which will be beneficial to both individuals and society?

In a completely individualistic economy in which, it is assumed, production is for direct consumption, every individual with limited resources at his disposal, must apply them in the production of things essential to life in order of their relative importance so as to insure that nothing of greater importance will be sacrificed for something of lesser importance. He considers, that is, the various products to which his resources can be applied and sees that none of the resources which are needed for a more important product are used for a less important one. In other words, he compares each time the importance of his contemplated product with the importance of the resources in the production of an alternative product. A process of comparative evaluation is always going on. In the present economy in which all members of society cooperate in carrying on production, essentially the same process of evaluation is in effect; only the evaluation is made more definite through an expression of value in money terms, that is, through price. Economic decisions and activities are now guided by price. There is a price for everything—every product as well as every factor used in production; and price is determined by demand and supply over the whole field. Hence it may be said that price represents social evaluation; and it tends to be set always at a point at which demand and supply are equalized. At this point maximum economic well-being is achieved, because factors will have flown into the production of various products according to their relative importance, and products will have been used for the satisfaction of various wants according to their relative urgency. Let us see how this works out in an economy composed of business enterprises.

Every business enterprise also takes price as the sole guide for its economic activities. Being self-seeking, each enterpriser chooses the line of production which yields him the highest profit, but profit results from the difference between the price that can be realized from his product and the price he has to pay for the services of the factors employed for production, in the form of rent, wages, and interest. In so far as price represents social evaluation, the enterpriser in making his calculation of revenue and cost is in effect also comparing the social value of his product and the social value of the factors necessary for its production. The price of each factor indicates its social value in other lines of production, and unless the contemplated product will bring a price which is high enough to pay the cost of all the factors, the enterprise had better switch to another line of production. In addition, the method of production which the enterpriser adopts affects the proportion of factors to be employed— whether more capital or labor is used, for instance—and this naturally influences his cost also, and attempt is generally made to improve the method of production so that cost may be reduced to a minimum. In this way the enterpriser will not only be improving his prospect of profit, but also acting in conformity to social need. It should be observed, further, that the price of each factor in the form of rent, wage, and interest, besides expressing its social importance in production, represents also the rate at which each factor shares in the product, and in so far as the rate is determined by the demand and supply of each factor over the whole field rather than in any specific business enterprise, it is based on social decision. The owner of each factor will work for a business enterprise that pays this rate, or he will work for some other enterprise that does; while at the same time he cannot expect to receive more or he will not be employed.

In a free economy, therefore, price is the all powerful factor which guides economic decisions and activities as regards production and distribution. It has made possible the preservation of individual freedom on the one hand and of an orderly economic organism on the other. To be sure, it has not been possible to avoid the waste of resources altogether, but broadly speaking, the increase in production with general improvement in economic well-being has been noteworthy and no serious problem of distribution has been experienced.

BUSINESS COMPETITION AND ECONOMIC PROGRESS

The foregoing outline of the operation of the free economy should not give one the impression that economic activities tend to settle down to a set pattern according to which business enterprises become established. On the contrary, demand and supply on the basis of which price is determined are dynamic facts and are subject to change at all times. Population increases, human tastes change, substitutes are found, inventions and discoveries are made; these and other occurrences cause disturbance to the established relation of demand and supply, and as a result price is altered. An economy must be flexible enough to permit adjustments of its production to changed conditions of needs and resources so that the most effective utilization of resources may be constantly kept up. Business enterprises through which production is carried on must be able to adapt themselves quickly to changes in social evaluation; and as variations in prices of product and of productive factors invariably affect revenue and cost, they must be taken into account by business enterprisers in determining their future course of production. Further, development in industrial art brings new techniques of production, by which productive factors can be employed more effectively; and as a result more abundant supply is made possible at lower unit cost. Gradually price is lowered and more demand is satisfied. Business enterprises which are quick in adopting new industrial techniques are benefited by reduced cost while those that lag behind are confronted with the possibility of loss.

One characteristic fact of the free economy is that there is no restriction as to the kind of business which an individual may enter, or the manner in which the business may be conducted; both are left completely to individual initiative. In general, therefore, a large number of business enterprises are engaged in the same line of production, and there is no effective agreement possible among them as to how much each should produce to satisfy the total demand. Moreover, new enterprises keep on coming into the field. This complicates the calculation for each of them, especially in view of the fact that in a modern enterprise with large overhead costs, cost per unit of product varies considerably with volume of production. What actually happens in the business world is that every enterprise tries to increase its production and capture as much of the market as possible, and this means competition. Competition is as old as business history. But when market was limited in scope and production was simple, supply could be easily adjusted to demand. In the modern economy, however, with improved transportation, the market has been considerably enlarged, and with increased use of machinery production has been greatly increased in scale, with the result that production in many lines is for world demand. Competition has become keener and many-sided, and forecast of demand has become more difficult. Of course competition is not necessarily carried on blindly; there are statistics inside and outside each business enterprise which can be used as references for making forecasts and decisions. However, no business acts on statistics alone nor is it satisfied with past achievements; it forever wants to push ahead even in the face of uncertainties.

From the standpoint of the community, economic progress, like progress along other lines in human life, is hastened in an environment of uncertainty and change. In a dynamic economy every business enterprise has to keep up its struggle for existence; not only does it adapt itself to changes, but it also initiates changes wherever possible so as to bring itself to the fore in the company of its competitors. Will it ever make a mistake? Doesn't a mistake by any business enterprise mean a loss of resources? How about over-production? These are all possibilities in a free economy, but progress is made only through trial and error, and through the survival of the fittest. In fact, many of the conveniences and luxuries of life enjoyed today would have been largely impossible had it not been for the foresight and indomitable spirit of the business enterprisers. The gain in quantity and variety of production has been so great that the loss of resources due to error and adaptation has proved to be but a small price to pay.

ACCOUNTING AND BUSINESS MANAGEMENT

Obviously, in an economy in which business enterprises enjoy complete freedom of initiative and competition, decisions made by individual enterprisers with regard to the nature, method, and quantity of production have a direct effect on the soundness and progress of the economy as a whole. Rational decisions will guide production into socially desirable channels, promote efficiency, and prevent waste of resources. From the standpoint of each business enterprise, the making of these decisions and of efforts for their implementation constitutes the problem of management. The management of a modern business enterprise, with its complex operations and extended market, is no longer by rule of thumb but requires ability and experience of high order. In addition, adequate information concerning the general economic condition and what is going on inside the enterprise itself must be available so that sound judgments may be formed. In this connection government research and publications are helpful, but every enterprise must know specifically the result of its past production and the condition of its present resources in order to decide rationally on the line of action to be taken with reference to the general economic climate.

This latter information is supplied by accounting records, which are built essentially on price data, as price constitutes the all-important guide to production in every business enterprise. With production understood in the economic sense as including all efforts made in making the product available to the purchaser, determination as to whether the result of production justifies the efforts made has to be based on the price realized from the product as compared with the price paid for the various resources or factors used in production, including both manufacturing and selling. In accounting the former is shown by the record of revenue and the latter by the record of cost or expense. Actually, with accounting on a periodic basis, the revenue and cost of any one period may not coincide with the production started during the same period due to the presence of inventories. So revenue and cost of a period show only the result of fully consummated production. The condition of resources available for further production is expressed by the record of assets, representing the price paid for the resources. The counterpart of the record of assets is the record of equities, showing the source of capital invested in the assets and coincidentally the legal claims of the various capital furnishers. Revenue and cost represent the dynamic picture of the economy of a business enterprise—what has taken place in the consummated act of production, while assets and equity show the static picture—what its present condition is during each stage of the act of production.

Profit-making being the primary purpose of every business enterprise, good management consists of putting all available resources into the line of production that promises the maximum revenue and involves the minimum cost, and at the same time obtaining the highest possible efficiency in the process of production with a view to reducing cost wherever feasible. To this end, production is planned ahead and all productive activities are coordinated and controlled. The most useful contribution of accounting in this connection is the analysis of revenue and cost in such appropriate form and detail as will facilitate comparisons and provide bases for sound conclusions. One important form of analysis for managerial purpose is that of revenue and cost by each kind of product as a basis for determining whether a specific type of production is worthwhile. Further, as a means of encouraging efficiency and economy in production, cost is analyzed by departments, processes, and operations to facilitate control and to make possible comparison with past results or comparison with budget and cost standards which have become, of late, important instruments of management. In the analysis of cost, however, the accountant is confronted with a number of complex problems, because certain costs known as overhead do not lend themselves easily to such analysis, and he has to use judgment as to how far the analysis can be carried with accuracy and where attempts at the apportionment of overhead can safely be made. It should be pointed out also that while in economic analysis cost of production includes compensation of all factors, cost as used in accounting comprises only the compensation for the *acquired* factors but not compensation for the capital and enterprise factors furnished by the creditors and owners of the particular business enterprise. That is to say, interest and profit of the producing enterprise are not considered as cost of production but rather are represented by the margin between revenue and cost in the restricted sense. So in making comparisons the cost as disclosed by the accounts must be used with this fact in mind. The reason for the accountant's narrow conception of cost lies in the fact that in keeping accounts and interpreting transactions the accountant follows the point of view of the person responsible for the management of a business enterprise who makes use of the capital entrusted to him, in whatever manner the capital may be obtained.

In emphasizing the importance of analysis of revenue and cost for purpose of management, however, we should not lose sight of the importance of assets and equities. Assets in the form of materials, plant, and machinery as well as liquid funds represent production potentialities which must as far as possible be fully utilized, and their variety and proportion are matters of no little concern for purposes of planning and control. Record of assets is needed not only for ascertaining their sufficiency but also for insuring their safe custody and for control of production cost. From the economic angle, in so far as assets of a business enterprise consist of products of other concerns, they represent congealed and accumulated cost of productive factors—land, labor, capital, and enterprise of the previous producers, to which the cost of factors employed by the present producer is added. Equities represent the claims of capital furnishers, of which there are two more or less distinct groups, liabilities and proprietorship. Liabilities are the claims of creditors or the lenders of capital and constitute the interests of pure capitalists. Proprietorship consists of the claims of owners or the investors of capital and comprises the interests of typical enterprisers. Within each of these two groups of equities, claims may further vary in scope and urgency, and accurate record must be maintained so that appropriate and prompt action may be taken to meet them accordingly. Further, sound management also requires that assets be acquired with due regard to the status of equities in order to insure that the enterprise will remain in a solvent condition. This means, for example, that durable assets should as far as possible be acquired out of the enterpriser's capital and only in case of an enterprise with relatively stable income may such assets be bought in part through long-term debt, but they should never be financed through short-term borrowing. While the problem of solvency concerns primarily the specific business enterprise, it may also be of great importance from the standpoint of general economic stability.

ACCOUNTING AND ECONOMIC PRODUCTIVITY

From the foregoing discussion it is evident that while accounting is purely an instrument of management of individual business enterprise, it has a definite contribution to make to the entire economy in that it helps to direct economic resources into the most important line of production and that it tends to increase production efficiency and lower cost. In addition, accounting helps to increase productivity by making large-scale production possible. During the past century there has been steady growth in the size of business enterprises, and the growth has been brought about largely through the development of the corporate form of business organization. The corporation has made an enormous contribution to economic progress by its large aggregation of capital, increased specialization of production, and more effective use of resources. However, the development of the corporation has been materially aided by accounting, which has helped in solving two of its fundamental problems: namely, the maintenance of an equitable relationship among its various classes of creditors and investors on the one hand, and of a satisfactory relationship between the investors and the management on the other. In order to attract capital from as wide a circle of people as possible, a corporation generally issues various classes of stocks and bonds, each carrying different rights as regards income, security, and control. It is the duty of the accountant not only to keep a detailed record for each class and individual equity, but also to give correct interpretation to terms of agreements and take prompt action relating thereto, and in particular he must be careful in his interpretation of transactions affecting the determination of income so as not to prejudice the interest of any class of equity. Further, in a corporate enterprise, although ownership resides in the stockholders, active management is usually delegated to a hired manager who has little or no ownership interest in the corporation. The manager in turn employs his hierarchy of assistants for various lines of duty, and they together constitute the body of management. This form of delegated management has become increasingly popular because the stockholders, especially those in a large corporation, are not in a position to participate directly in management, and because the management of a modern corporate enterprise requires such a high degree of competence that only persons with adequate training and experience can qualify for the task. But absentee ownership not only increases the importance of accounting as a basis for the management to render complete reports of stewardship to the owners, but also brings out sharply the sanctity of accounting procedures so that all data produced by the accounts may be fully auditable as a means of discharging trusteeship responsibility.

At present, moreover, business enterprise makes considerable use of bank credit in financing its short-term requirements, and this avoids the tying up of its own capital for temporary uses—a procedure that tends to increase the productivity of capital in the whole economy. In order that credit may be facilitated, accurate accounting and reporting of financial condition and earning power become necessary.

In another significant way accounting helps economic productivity by directing the flow of capital into more urgent and more efficient production. This is done through the publicity of production results of corporate enterprises over the security exchange. Consistent good earning reports presumably indicate that the production of certain corporations is serving a rising demand or that their production method is relatively more efficient, or both. On the other hand, consistently declining incomes suggest that production of certain corporations is faced with a falling demand or that there is inefficiency, or both. Thus investors are enabled by such information to make a more intelligent selection of enterprises for investment, and capital is thereby made to flow into the fields which promise the highest productivity.

ACCOUNTING AS A BASIS OF DISTRIBUTION

While the primary aim of revenue and cost accounting is to express the result of production, its importance as a basis of distribution also deserves emphasis. Offhand, it may seem that in so far as the economic factors used in production are paid compensation according to rates fixed by the market, there is no problem of distribution involved in each specific business enterprise except the compensation for the enterpriser which is paid out of the margin between revenue and cost, or net income. In practical situations, however, the compensation of many economic factors employed by an enterprise is conditioned, in whole or in part, upon the result of production as indicated by its income. Even for the factor of enterprise, except in unincorporated enterprises in which ownership interests are generally homogeneous and permanent, the amount of income as determined periodically is a matter of considerable importance from the standpoint of distribution.

The fact is that in determining periodic revenue and applicable cost in a modern business enterprise, a great many technical considerations are involved and careful analysis of facts and rational judgment are necessary. In a going enterprise, for example, production facilities are acquired for continued use for many accounting periods and large inventories of materials and supplies are kept to insure continuous operation; and their costs have to be assigned to the respective periods during which they render services. Further, in calculating cost applicable to each line of production during each period, there is the problem of allocation of overhead, and where sales do not coincide with production started during the same period, it becomes necessary to determine the portion of production cost applicable to the revenue of the period. Besides, in accounting for costs of current services it is often necessary to accrue certain costs and defer others, and similarly in accounting for revenue, questions of accruals and deferments are also frequently involved. All these considerations are needed to insure that revenue and cost of each period may be correctly stated. Obviously, in the exercise of personal judgment, errors of interpretation can not be completely ruled out. The fact that errors will rectify themselves in the long run will not insure equity in distribution in so far as the rights of the claimants vary from period to period. The accountant owes a duty in this connection to all those who share in the result of production on the basis of the income as determined by him. To him, objectivity and consistency constitute the two essential factors for guidance.

Of course the economic factor whose share of distribution is most commonly affected by the result of production is the enterprise factor, because ownership represents the residual interest and its compensation, including both implicit interest on capital investment as well as profit for risk-taking, is contingent on income being earned. Where ownership is relatively permanent, the effect of an understatement of income on the amount of distribution during any one period may be offset by an over-statement during some other period. However, as far as the stockholders of a corporation are concerned, they seldom represent permanent equities but frequently change through transfers of stock. It is true that the income of a corporation constitutes only the basis of declaration of dividends and does not indicate exactly the amount of dividend to be paid. Nevertheless, income earned and reported produces an important influence on the decision of stockholders with respect to their holdings. Further, certain stocks carry a right to corporate income only as it is earned during each period and the right lapses if no income is reported, as in the case of noncumulative preferred stock. Under such conditions, the accurate determination of periodic income becomes a matter of crucial importance. Contractual equities such as corporate bonds generally carry interest at a definite rate which must be paid whatever be the amount of income, but income bonds, interest on which is contingent on income earned, will suffer loss in case income is insufficient. For the labor factor, although salaries and wages are generally fixed by terms of employment, especially for the lower rank employees, there are not infrequently systems of compensation in force which are in part based on the amount of periodic income, such as profit-sharing or bonus plans. In view of the possibility of periodic change of employment, accurate determination of periodic income again assumes considerable importance from the standpoint of distribution. Land rent, while in the nature of a surplus according to economic theory, is seldom paid in proportion to the income of a specific business enterprise. However, it is not impossible for rent to be paid on the basis of revenue received or volume of business done; there are instances in which tenants on agriculture land agree to pay to the landlord a certain portion of annual produce. In business practice, royalties on mineral land are sometimes calculated on a periodic revenue basis.

ACCOUNTING AND SOCIAL COOPERATION

Finally, consideration of the significance of accounting in a free economy seems incomplete without some evaluation of its contribution to social cooperation. An outstanding characteristic of a free economy is free initiative, but initiative on the part of business enterprise is induced primarily by the prospect of economic gain. Not all activities calculated to advance human well-being, however, carry such prospect or should be made the object of economic gain. There are activities which can not be sustained by pure economic considerations but which are very essential to human life and progress, such as those relating to security, education, social welfare, etc. These in general represent governmental functions which are carried on in a democracy through elected representatives; we can therefore think of government as a form of cooperation to undertake all measures for collective well-being. A government does not render its service for a price but depends on public contribution in the form of taxes, the most important of which are taxes on income and profit. While income and profit taxes are not levied according to services received by each business enterprise or individual, they are nevertheless contributions to support activities of social cooperation in spite of the fact that contributions are largely involuntary as far as each taxpayer is concerned. Equally important as the question of equity of tax legislation is the question of equity of specific tax assessment; accounting obviously has a significant contribution to make in this connection. At the same time, the government in collecting taxes and spending the money for various activities, acts in a fiduciary capacity; complete accounting is essential for the government to render its report of stewardship to the people. Only thus can a democratic government be assured of continued support by the people and can the people maintain suitable control over the activities of the government. This is true, fundamentally, of all forms of civic organizations as well as private institutions, which carry on work for cooperative welfare.

Further, in the field of business, there are certain classes of enterprises which carry on economic production of a special character and require governmental regulation. These include such enterprises as water, electricity, gas, and other companies which are essentially monopolistic and whose rates and standards of service closely affect the interest of the public. In some countries or communities, these services are undertaken by the government, but more usually they are operated by private enterprises subject to governmental regulation. These enterprises are known as public utilities and regulation is justified on the ground of their public character. In other words, they are more or less cooperative undertakings with private investment and operation, to insure operating efficiency. But they are not to be used as sheer objects of private gain, and in order that a fair return may be earned on private investment while a good standard of service is maintained at reasonable rates, accurate accounting must be kept of investment, revenue, and cost as bases for determining whether the interests of the investors and of the public are both adequately protected.

In an important sense, moreover, accounting contributes to cooperation by increasing industrial solidarity. One of the chief problems of industrialization is the growth of a feeling of cleavage between employers and employees and an ever-present possibility of misunderstanding over questions of compensation, hours of work, and other related matters. As a result, interruption of production is often precipitated with loss to all concerned. Usually misunderstanding arises from failure on the part of employees to appreciate the real condition of the business enterprise. Consequently, in many industrial establishments today an attempt has been made to secure the representation of employees on management committees and to supply their representatives with accounting reports so that they may understand the financial position of their enterprise. This is clearly an effective way of eliminating much of the suspicion between labor and management and a step in the direction of establishing a firm basis for genuine cooperation.

12. Soviet Economic Developments and Accounting*

Robert H. Mills and Abbott L. Brown**

Accounting and control—this is the main thing that is required for the proper functioning of the first phase of communist society. . . . Be able if necessary to learn from the capitalists. Adopt whatever they have that is sensible and advantageous.
—Lenin

Professor E. Liberman, a leading Soviet economist, wrote a stimulating article on a more important role for "profits" in *Pravda* on September 9, 1962. His remarks touched off one of the most controversial, continuing debates in Soviet economic thought since the great intellectual debates of the 1920's which preceded the Soviet decision to industrialize. His principal suggestions are aimed at motivating Soviet enterprises and

* Reprinted from *The Journal of Accountancy*, June 1966; copyrighted 1966 by the American Institute of CPAs, pages 40–46.
** Robert H. Mills is Professor of Accounting at Lehigh University. Abbott L. Brown is Senior Accountant with Price Waterhouse & Co.

firms to seek higher output targets for themselves, encourage the introduction of new technology and new products, and improve the quality of
production. In order to achieve the above goals, Liberman's plan calls
for less reliance on planned targets and greater use of profit incentives
in allowing more freedom for the enterprise manager to more intelli-
gently use resources and achieve greater efficiency.

At the present time, with only a very few exceptions which will be
discussed later, planned targets for Soviet firms are handed down from
higher administrative units. The manager of the individual firm generally
seeks to have target goals set as low as possible since the firm and its
personnel are compensated according to the degree of plan fulfillment.
Firm managers are reluctant to encourage new technology, new products
and better materials and to improve quality standards, because such
changes represent uncertainty. These changes are possible barriers to
goal fulfillment in physical terms as well as exerting a direct effect on
important cost of production figures.

Liberman's plan calls for the elimination of all centrally planned
goals except targets of quantitative production, product assortment, and
destination and date of delivery. He feels the factory manager's principal
task is the efficient production of quality goods with the elimination of
as many predetermined constraints that impede this goal as possible. In
order to achieve this goal, Liberman suggests a new measuring tool, the
"profitability rate." This is defined as the total profit of the firm in relation to its stock of fixed and working capital.[1] The profitability rate would
be important to the plant manager and his subordinates since it would
be the sole measuring stick of the size of the bonus fund which the firm
and its employees will receive. The plant manager could improve the
profitability rate by either increasing the numerator, profits, or decreasing
the denominator, fixed capital and working capital, or some combination
of the two.

"Profitability norms" would be established for different industries
and firms for a period of two, three, or five years into the future. These
norms would serve as a guidepost against which to match the achieved
profitability rate in determining bonuses to be awarded to firms. An
attempt would also be made to make comparisons of performance
between comparable firms. Firms which develop new products or new
processes would have lower profitability norms to help offset initial costs
and unforeseen problems. Norms would be raised for those firms not
innovating. These actions would supposedly induce firms to experiment
with new products and new technological methods.

[1] Marshall I. Goldman, "Economic Controversy in the Soviet Union: Liberman's
Goals for Economic Reform," Foreign Affairs, April 1963, pp. 498–512.

While profits have been calculated for Soviet firms in the past, the measurement of income has been only one of several yardsticks used in determining plant efficiency. More emphasis has been placed on goal fulfillment in terms of meeting or bettering predetermined targets of physical quantities of output and unit costs of production. If Professor Liberman's proposals are widely adopted, the role of income measurement will be much more important to plant managers and higher echelons of state administration than it ever has been before.

Before examining what progress has been made in using profits as an increasingly important incentive device, a brief review of current Soviet accounting practice is in order, noting in particular those areas differing from general American methodology and procedure.

CURRENT SOVIET ACCOUNTING PRACTICE

In the Soviet economic system, accounting alone plays the major role in the whole system of prices and costs with only token assistance from market processes in a few isolated consumer goods industries. The determination of periodic income for the Soviet firm is of secondary importance. This is true because the Soviet firm is not fully independent from a financial standpoint, and few decisions to date have turned on whether the reported earnings are positive or negative. The results of operations are only a vague constraint on the firm's access to resources since resource allocation is basically the domain of the master planners attached to central administrative units.

The Soviet firm maintains one set of documentary records. The record-keeping is called *uchet* and consists of accounting, statistics and technical records. Accounting is separate from the other two types of records. Accounts are kept under the double-entry system. In general, according to Professor Robert Campbell, "Soviet accounting is virtually identical with traditional capitalist accounting." [2] One very important difference is that accounting rules and procedures are fixed and highly formalized by centralized control over accounting practices. Central administrative units gather monthly reports from all firms based upon standard forms from each industry with the information on these reports drawn from a standardized set of accounts for that industry. As a result, there exists comparatively little controversy in most areas as to the proper way of handling business transactions.

The purpose of such rigidly constructed reports is to facilitate better centralized control and planning. The reports are used in the

[2] Robert W. Campbell, *Accounting in Soviet Planning and Management* (Cambridge, Mass., Harvard University Press, 1963), p. 11.

84 *The Accounting Function in Different Economic Systems*

evaluation of the administrative organizations and resource allocation process and are an integral tool in developing regional and national economic plans.

One area of considerable interest and importance, for several reasons, is cost accounting. The virtual absence of the influence of the market mechanism on prices, except for a few consumer goods to be discussed later, necessitates the determination and fixing of prices primarily on the basis of cost accounting reports. These reports are valid only to the extent that they have been properly prepared and reflect accurate cost data. The unit cost of production has been cited as "probably the most emphasized indicator of success or failure of an enterprise in the U.S.S.R. . . ."[3]

Professor Campbell has summarized the main deficiencies of Soviet cost accounting, upon which unit cost of production figures depends, as resulting primarily from poor estimates of the costs of capital consumption (depreciation), improper allocation of current expenditures among individual kinds of output, failure to charge certain outlays to cost of product, and the use of broad aggregative accounts with the result that expense flows through the plant are poorly traced, costs of individual products or of separate processes are often not ascertainable, and so on.[4]

Problems of rapidly changing technology and the factor of obsolescence, as well as changing price levels for capital goods, plague the Soviet firm as well as its American counterpart in measuring capital consumption (depreciation) costs. The problem of depreciation measurement in the Soviet Union is complicated by the fact that an attempt is made to allocate the estimated cost of major repairs, as well as the original cost of the asset, over the life of the asset. Thus, the depreciation charge consists of two parts. One part is the amortization of original asset cost and the other is an allocation for estimated major repair costs.

These major repairs are called capital repairs; theoretically, these capital repairs are not supposed to extend the life of the asset or increase its productivity over what was anticipated at time of original acquisition. Moreover, to be classified as a capital repair, the repair preferably should occur less than once a year. An example of a capital repair is the rebuilding of an entire engine which does not increase the machine's former productivity or presumably prolong the entire machine's life beyond the original estimate. In actual practice, even though broad guidelines are highly formalized, the distinguishing between capital

[3] E. Joe DeMaris and Richard B. Purdue, "Accounting in the U.S.S.R.," *The Journal of Accountancy*, July 1959, p. 48.

[4] Robert W. Campbell, "Soviet Accounting and Economic Decisions," *Studies in Accounting Theory*, W. T. Baxter and Sidney Davidson, Editors (Homewood, Ill., Richard D. Irwin, Inc., 1962), pp. 357–358.

repairs and ordinary repairs is not clear-cut with resulting differences in the handling of borderline cases.

The apparent rationale for including estimated long-run capital repair charges as part of the depreciation charge is that actual capital repairs would tend to be bunched in time. While this reasoning might hold true for individual assets, it is hard to believe it would apply to broad aggregates of assets held by Soviet firms where a fairly uniform pattern of capital repair charges might be anticipated each period. With heavy emphasis on unit costs of production as a major criterion in evaluation of the operating efficiency of a Soviet firm, the inclusion of estimated capital repair charges as part of the depreciation charge is a device for smoothing out the impact on the cost of production over long periods of time.

All the Soviet depreciation rates are established according to the following formula: The depreciation rate (r) equals $[(V+R-S)/LV]$ 100, where V equals the original value, R equals estimated total expenditure for capital repairs, L equals the expected life of the asset and S is the estimated salvage value, if any. For example, an asset with an original cost of 5,000 rubles and estimated total capital repairs of 5,000 rubles over a ten-year life with zero salvage value would have a rate of depreciation of 20% with 10% for capital consumption and 10% for capital repairs.

While this method may smooth long-run unit costs, it may not give the best measure of periodic income depending on assumptions as to the pattern of service flows from depreciable assets. It is basically consistent with the straight-line method of depreciation as applied to original asset cost. The method may result in over- (under-) depreciating assets if actual capital repairs are less (more) than estimated capital repairs. It does add an additional complication and subjective element in the estimating of the cost of future repairs including the frequency, quantity and changes in future prices of such repairs. In addition, a decision must be reached about how much of the depreciation charge applies to capital repairs and how much to original cost expiration since the two portions of the depreciation charge are handled differently.

The portion applicable to the original cost of the asset is recognized as an expense by the Soviet firm but is remitted in cash to the central economic center. The cash remittances of all firms are pooled at the central location where decisions are made about the distribution of funds for replacement and for new investment. The portion of the depreciation charge for capital repairs is recognized as an expense, but a reserve fund is established at a state bank which is at the disposal of the Soviet firm making the deposit.

The following example is offered to clarify how the Soviet system operates in regard to capital consumption recognition. Throughout the example we will refer to the account State Equity Fund. Actually there is more than one such account. These accounts are of the proprietorship or the long-term obligation nature. We will refer to the Central Bank, meaning one of the central banks where funds are kept and distributed according to decisions made by higher administrative units. The account titles in our example will not necessarily agree with Soviet terminology but are used for clarification of concepts and similarity to American usage.

For this example, assume that a firm has fixed assets of 5,000 rubles for an opening debit balance and an opening credit balance to the State Equity Fund of 5,000 rubles. Furthermore, assume the fixed assets have an estimated life of 10 years with zero scrap value and that estimated future capital repairs are 5,000 rubles. This results in a $\left(\dfrac{5,000 + 5,000}{10 \times 5,000} \right)$ 100 = 20% depreciation rate, with one-half of the charge for capital repairs and the other half to be sent to the central pool as a result of capital consumption. The Soviet firm records 1,000 rubles (20% $\times$ 5,000) as an expense, debiting Cost of Production and crediting Allowance for Depreciation as follows:

Cost of Production	1,000	
Allowance for Depreciation		1,000

Next, the firm debits the State Equity Fund for the full 1,000 rubles and credits 500 rubles to a Reserve for Repairs Fund and credits the other 500 rubles to a Liability to Central Bank account:

State Equity Fund	1,000	
Reserve for Repairs Fund		500
Liability to Central Bank		500

At periodic intervals, cash is remitted to the Central Bank for eventual reallocation by central authorities for replacement and new assets with the following entry being made:

Liability to Central Bank	500	
Cash		500

Assuming capital repairs of 500 rubles are made this period, the firm makes the following two entries:

Capital Repairs	500	
Cash		500
Reserve for Capital Repairs	500	
State Equity Fund		500

To complete the record-keeping, the Allowance for Depreciation account is debited and Capital Repairs is credited with the interpretation being as having made good some of the depreciation on the asset:

Allowance for Depreciation	500	
Capital Repairs		500

How accurate have capital consumption charges been under the above system? According to Professor Campbell, ". . . the charges for depreciation entered in Soviet cost calculations have always been far too low as estimates of capital consumption." [5] In connection with the re-valuation of fixed assets in the U.S.S.R. in 1960, the depreciation shown on the books for all assets was only half the actual depreciation.

A strong theoretical argument can be made for the Soviet method of including estimated capital repairs cost in attempting to allocate total capital costs over estimated service lives of fixed assets. The difficulty lies in correct implementation of the concept with the additional uncertainties of forecasting both volume and price levels of capital repairs anticipated.

Another problem with Soviet capital consumption recognition is that depreciation rates are not established by individual firms but are established by higher administrative units. Since firm managers have quotas and standards to meet, physical output and cost reduction are important goals. Managers may tend to be wasteful of capital assets in order to keep both physical output high and unit cost of production low. In addition, managers are not penalized for failing to make assets serve out the estimated service lives envisaged at the time they were acquired. When assets are sold or disposed of, any retirement gain or loss is transferred directly to the State Equity Fund and does not even enter into Profit and Loss computations.[6]

In summary, the Soviet system for the recognition of depreciation is geared to an attempt to provide the best long-run average unit cost data possible. This is important since prices, in turn, are often based on reported costs. It would appear that depreciation charges in general have been understated in the past primarily because of the difficulties of estimating capital repair costs as part of the depreciation base and the failure to adequately recognize obsolescence in the establishment of depreciation rates by central authorities. All depreciation rates are calculated by one basic formula in the Soviet Union in contrast to numerous formulas available to American firms. The Soviet firm does attempt to

[5] Campbell, Accounting in Soviet Planning and Management, p. 75.
[6] For American firms following the "current operating" concept of net income reporting, material gains and losses on disposition of depreciable assets would be direct additions or deductions from cumulative retained earnings.

spread capital repair costs over the entire life of the asset, whereas American firms would basically adjust depreciation to be recognized in the future only after capital repair expenditures have been made. Retirement gains or losses do not enter into Profit and Loss computations for Soviet firms in contrast to general American practice.

All the above factors would contribute to significant differences in income measurement between Soviet and American firms where capital consumption costs were an important item. The procedure of remitting to a central bank for reassignment that portion of the depreciation charge pertaining to the original value of the asset while retaining local control of funds for capital repairs is a unique evolutionary device which the Soviets have found useful in a planned economy. Prior to 1938, funds for capital repairs were also remitted to the central bank for reassignment.

In addition to the problem of recognition of capital consumption costs, another major concern of Soviet accounting is the allocation of costs to production. The allocation of direct material and direct labor costs provides no special problem since they can be directly attributed to specific outputs. This is usually done but there are some exceptions to direct assignment of these costs.[7] For the Soviet manufacturing firm, overheads are generally accumulated in four broad accounts called shop expenses, general plant expenses, auxiliary shops (factory service centers) and nonproduction expenses including selling, maintenance of finished goods warehouses, research, etc. Shop expenses and general plant expenses are almost always distributed to output in proportion to wages of production workers. This tends to introduce errors where there is a high ratio of shop expenses to production wages, and substantial portions of the overhead are more related to machine operations than to direct labor. The expenses of auxiliary shops (factory service centers) were previously included in general plant expenses but recently there has been a tendency to keep them in a separate category and assign them to the production shops benefited. The nonproduction expenses are generally distributed among outputs in proportion to total factory cost's being treated as some type of general overhead. General plant and shop expenses are usually assigned to unfinished production only in planned amounts with the

---

[7] Campbell, *Accounting in Soviet Planning and Management*, p. 105. Apparently it is fairly common practice to distribute not only overheads but also direct expenses on a very arbitrary basis. This may be particularly true in those cases where there is a wide range of outputs where all costs may be distributed among products in accordance with some predetermined formulas. Costs may be accumulated in plant-wide accounts, such as materials, wages, shop expenses, etc., and then distributed to products for the period in accordance with superior administrative unit's norms. Any excess above norms would then be distributed according to the planned norms. As a result, there is no real ex post accounting by product line.

remainder charged off to finished production. It is felt desirable to do this for control purposes to avoid accumulation of excess expenditures in unfinished production accounts. These procedures can result in distortions in cost reports, balance sheet valuations for unfinished and finished product, and income measurement.

Attempts to allocate overhead of Soviet firms are generally fairly crude. It also must be recognized that traditional period expenses such as selling, general administration and research are allocated in some fashion to the cost of product's becoming part of the inventory accounts. Most of the expenses of the numerous higher administrative control units are not allocated to the Soviet firm but are absorbed by the national budget. Furthermore, much research that is done on behalf of firms and industries is financed out of the national budget and is not charged to the individual firms on the theory that they are of benefit to the economy in general. There are certain outlays that are not included in the cost of production but are charged directly to Profit and Loss, such as losses on canceled orders, inventory shortages and losses, expenditures on fruitless experiments, fines, penalties, forfeits, losses from production risks not envisaged in the plan, losses of subsidiary enterprises and losses from stoppages. Many of the practices described above would of necessity produce income and valuation measurements significantly different from American practice.

There are some additional weaknesses in the Soviet system of accounting if profits are to play an ever more important role and maximum efficiency is desired. Reports to higher administrative units are geared toward emphasizing the operation of the plant as a whole as well as placing too much emphasis on unit costs of production. Too little attention has been focused on looking at the internal operations of the enterprise in terms of the cost of individual processes, operations and responsibility units. The concept of flexible budgeting is apparently not employed or employed only in rare cases. Fixed budgets, drawn up in great detail by central control authorities, are alleged to be infrequently employed as a control device by plant managers.[8]

One reason for the lack of better internal accounting information is that the chief accountant of the Soviet enterprise has traditionally been the servant of higher administrative agencies and not of the enterprise manager. In addition, the low level of mechanization available for clerical functions has necessitated the accumulation of quantitative data in broad aggregates. There apparently has been some slight improvement in internal reporting recently, however.[9] The caliber of people

[8] Leon Smolinski, "What Next in Soviet Planning," *Foreign Affairs*, July 1964, p. 605.

[9] Campbell, *Accounting in Soviet Planning and Management*, p. 186.

attracted to accounting in the Soviet Union has not been very high because of low pay, long hours, excessive bureaucratic rules, controls and volume of detailed work.

Having examined in some detail differences in accounting practice and income measurement between Soviet and American firms, let us now examine those areas where "profits" are playing a more important role.

SOVIET EXPERIMENTATION WITH PROFITS AS AN INCENTIVE AND THE "MARKET" MECHANISM

In the summer of 1964 the reformers who advocate less centralized planning and more reliance on the market mechanism and the measurement tool of profits as a primary incentive device were finally given an opportunity to test their theories. The factory managers apparently had even more freedom and flexibility than originally advocated by Liberman.[10] Two large clothing factories were permitted to negotiate prices and sell suits and dresses directly to 22 retail stores. The stores placed orders directly with the factories for the kinds of goods consumers wanted. The factories were to be judged by the profits made on goods actually sold by their retail stores. Factories had a free hand in setting their production schedules and deciding on their work force.

Within six months inventories were sharply reduced and both profits and quality had improved substantially. One of the factory managers reported that the profit margin had risen to 7 per cent, that the average pay per employee had increased from $94 a month to $110 and that the factory was making better suits at a cheaper price.[11] So successful was this experiment that Premier Kosygin, shortly after assuming office late in 1964, announced that the new system would be spread in gradual stages throughout the consumer goods industry. He further asserted that eventually the reforms would be extended to all Soviet industry. In January of 1965 the first 400 clothing and shoe firms which were spread across Russia, together with 78 of their raw material suppliers, were authorized for the changeover.

IMPLICATIONS FOR THE FUTURE

It would appear that if the results of these larger field trials basically confirm the remarkable results achieved by the initial two clothing factories, the Soviet economy is taking its initial baby steps down the road

---

[10] Liberman's original proposal called for the continuance of planned targets of quantitative production, product assortment and destination and date of delivery. It may be that Liberman felt it was necessary, from a practical political standpoint, to retain the above constraints on the evolutionary road to a more market-oriented economy.

[11] Condensed from *Time* magazine, "Russia Tests the Profit System," *Reader's Digest*, May 1965, pp. 107–111.

to a more market-oriented system where prices and the profit motive are powerful tools in regulating economic behavior and resource allocation. Assuming the initial steps are successful, it would be fair to estimate that the role of centralized economic planning and control will gradually diminish in relative importance in the Soviet system.

Lenin, if he were alive, would probably approve of this change since he has been quoted as having said, "Vital work we do is sinking in a dead sea of paperwork. We get sucked in by a foul bureaucratic swamp." The problem of the growing bureaucracy in the U.S.S.R. was sharply stated by Professor Glushkov, a leading Soviet cybernetician, who estimated recently that the planning bureaucracy would increase 36-fold by 1980, requiring the services of the entire population unless there were radical reforms in planning methods.[12]

Assuming that the role of profits does attain a higher status in the Soviet economic system, what changes, if any, might be anticipated in their accounting practice? For purposes of preparing external reports that will still need to be submitted to central administrative units, accounting rules and procedures will continue to be fixed and highly formalized by means of centralized control over accounting practices. There will be little, if any, opportunity to influence reported profits by the adoption of alternative procedures other than those rigidly prescribed by the state. For example, it is not conceivable at the present time that in the same industry Soviet firms could choose one of several different valuation or amortization methods relating to depreciation, inventory, research, development costs, etc. Rigidity in terms of when and how revenues are to be recognized as well as cost classifications and valuations are to be expected. This is true because the Soviet state is the owner of Soviet enterprises. It quite properly will continue to insist on centralized review of operating reports and statements of financial condition in order to make comparisons with other firms.

Allocations of resources for new investments will probably continue to be made by central authorities. However, profit performance and demonstrated demand-supply relationships may continue to be more important in making these allocations than they have been in the past. It would seem that major improvements might be expected in the areas of budgeting, internal reporting and overhead allocations. If plant managers are to be given more freedom to operate in response to market demands, it would make sense that operating budgets might be prepared first at the local level and then reviewed by higher authorities. Both fixed and flexible budgets should become more important control tools in local management's hands than they have been.

[12] Smolinski, *op. cit.*, p. 602.

In order to maximize profits, better internal reports are also a necessity. The reporting of costs by processes, cost centers and responsibility units as well as the principle of "exception" reporting to higher management should increase. More effort needs to be devoted to estimating as carefully as possible at the local level the probable costs of new products before they are introduced. Better methods of allocating overhead must also be developed.

Greater emphasis on profits with greater local autonomy might be accompanied by less emphasis on the broad unit cost of production than heretofore. In other words it is assumed prices might be more flexible in general in response to market conditions and much less emphasis placed on broad, stable, long-run unit cost of production figures on which to base the overall price structure. This might result in the treatment of general administrative, selling and research expenses as period costs with no attempt made to allocate them to cost of production through broad overhead accounts.

If profits do assume a role of primary importance in Soviet reckoning, it seems imperative that better financial control systems be developed. This means that higher caliber people must be attracted to the Soviet accounting profession and that the responsibility of the accounting staff of the Soviet enterprise be given primarily to the local firm managers. Furthermore, the need for mechanization of the handling of quantitative data is great.

There still would be a need for good external auditors to render reports to higher administrative units. These auditors would probably function in basically the same role as independent accountants in this country. The internal audit function would become recognized as an important tool of control by the Soviet enterprise managers to see that the firm's policies and procedures are being carried out.

In summary, a more prominent role for profits and reliance on the marketplace should lead to greater flexibility in the hands of Soviet firm managers. These managers, in turn, will look increasingly to sound financial reporting and control systems to assist them in their responsibilities. Lenin's advice "to learn from the capitalists" applies not only to the role of profits and the market mechanism but also to the proper accumulation and use of accounting data.

13. Marx as a Management Accountant*

Kenneth S. Most**

Investment comes from savings, said Marx, and savings can only come from profits. Thus, the capitalist must pay as low wages as possible in order to maintain profits, and this leads to low purchasing power in relation to output and, eventually, to economic crises. We can see from this how it came about that Marx thought he could foresee capitalism destroying itself. We can also see some of the reasons why it has not done so.

Is it too fanciful, then, to see in Karl Marx the first management accountant, who lost his way by becoming a political economist instead of taking a job in a counting house? His method was basically sound and not entirely dissimilar from modern concepts of standard costing, value analysis and ratio analysis.

Perhaps if he had gone to work for one of Engels' customers, in one of those dark, satanic mills which awoke in him such strong feelings and opinions, he would have been able to test his hypotheses against the hard realities of business economics, and refine them into a form in which they would have helped to improve the efficiency and material prosperity of the society against which he railed. If so, we should perhaps be a generation of accountants nurtured on 'Karl Marx's management accounting' instead of citizens of a world divided by the Iron Curtain.

* Reprinted from "Marx and Management Accounting," in *The Accountant,* August 17, 1963, pages 177–178.
** Kenneth Most is Professor and Chairman, Department of Accounting, Texas A. & M. University.

14. Accounting in Newly Developed Nations*

J. W. Ross**

What are the prime factors that generate a nation's progress? Since the days of the early economists studies have been made and theories formulated to determine these. Many have subscribed to the "laissez-faire" doctrine of Adam Smith; some, of more recent vintage, have adopted the other extreme of a completely planned economy.

Everyone seems to agree that an underdeveloped nation should not receive a sentence of eternal poverty. There is also general agreement that economic progress can be stimulated by conscious action. History tells us, however, that economic progress can be a painful, slow, erratic process regardless of whether a country emerges under a free enterprise system or under the aegis of state planning.

History has also shown that economic development is inextricably interwoven with the development of government and other social institutions. Indeed, it is difficult to visualize any degree of sophistication in economic development that is not accompanied by a corresponding development of informal social organizations.

Emerging countries usually have several characteristics in common: a high percentage of illiterates; a brand new constitution, but a lack of stability in government; few people knowledgeable or experienced enough to handle the public affairs of a modern nation; a lack of capital; and a lack of exports by which to obtain or import the equipment needed to build public transportation systems and basic industries. To these seemingly insurmountable difficulties can be added the grave problem of burgeoning and starving populations.

Despite these obstacles, plans must be devised to build social and financial institutions as well as industrial complexes.

One wise observer of the human race has commented that institutions are grown rather than imposed. What many people, and even some governments, fail to understand is that one cannot place a modern complex

* Reprinted by permission from *Cost and Management*, official journal of The Society of Industrial Accountants of Canada, July-August 1967, pages 43–44.
** J. W. Ross is a Contributing Editor of *Cost and Management*.

organization in the midst of a primitive country and expect it to blossom immediately. Most people in emerging nations have neither the experience nor the understanding to make it work. That is why a country must go through the first painful stages of government and economic growth before it reaches stability. True, this growth can sometimes be accelerated but, generally, experience in different levels of sophistication is needed first.

WHERE ACCOUNTING COMES IN

What does accounting have to do with all of this? It is difficult to think of any significant institution or organization that does not need financing to launch and sustain it through the years. Let us look at some of the major segments of a developing country in which progress is virtually impossible without the direct involvement of accounting.

First, government plays a major role in the development process. It must provide a stable climate for progress. It must provide the infrastructure, such as power and transportation facilities, for the growth of both private and public businesses. It must also provide the schools to remedy the severe drawback of an illiterate population.

It is obvious that no government could perform these services without a corps of knowledgeable accountants to do the government accounting and manage the country's finances.

Moreover, every developing nation today depends for loans and capital equipment on the more advanced nations and on the international financial institutions such as the International Monetary Fund or the International Bank for Reconstruction and Development. While some of this aid is gratuitous, much of it is in the form of loans that have to be repaid. Obviously, the lenders want to be sure that the new countries have proper methods of accounting and financial control over the use of their borrowed funds. The lending institutions find, in fact, that it is very difficult to advance aid where it is most needed and can do the most good. While many of the developing countries have great natural resources and good potential for economic development, the lack of reliable data and proper accounting procedures discourages the lenders.

A second large area requiring trained accounting personnel is that involving feasibility and priority studies for capital formation. Regardless of whether capital projects are being undertaken by a government or by private industry, the appraisal studies for capital expenditure and the control of finances during construction call for a high degree of accounting knowledge and managerial skill. All industrial enterprises must keep accounting records and provide financial information to operating management and, as this capital formation begins to produce, the need for accountants grows.

Finally, all nations belong to an international community that involves trade, balance of payments, capital movements, and imports and exports of a great variety of items. Before a country can gain the respect and confidence of other nations, its accounting records on each aspect of these international affairs must be in good order. They must be capable of being analyzed, interpreted, and compared within the international monetary and financial communities. For this, the developing countries again need well qualified accountants.

HOW WE CAN HELP

In the past few years, some universities and accounting bodies have taken a hand in the training and education of accountants for newly developing countries. Nevertheless, there are still many countries with only a handful of qualified accountants in a population of several millions. There is still a drastic shortage of financial people capable of helping these new governments to get their economies off the ground.

There is a big challenge here for the accounting profession and the universities of the advanced nations; not only must they find people to serve in developing countries, but they must also plant the foundations of the profession there so that the nationals can "grow" and develop accountants to serve the particular needs of their countries. One would have to place the importance of accountants to the newly developing countries high on the scale of their priorities.

15. Accounting Investigations of the FBI*

John Edgar Hoover**

The work of an FBI Agent is not all the glamour of chasing down bank robbers, engaging in gun battles with desperate criminals or tracking down hijackers, kidnapers and car thieves. While he necessarily conducts such investigations, the Special Agent Accountant may just as likely find himself auditing the records of a subject in connection with a suspected violation of the Federal Reserve Act, the National Bankruptcy Act, the Labor-Management Reporting and Disclosure Act of 1959, Fraud Against the Government or various other criminal and civil matters.

To be considered for the position of Special Agent with the FBI,

* Reprinted from *Management Accounting*, (U.S.A.) August 1968, pages 11–14.
** John Edgar Hoover is Director of the Federal Bureau of Investigation.

the applicant must, among other requirements, be a graduate of a state-accredited resident law school or a graduate from a resident four-year college with a major in accounting with at least three years of practical accounting and/or auditing experience. As of the end of the last fiscal year, 10.8 percent of the more than 6,600 Special Agents in the FBI were accountants.

The accountant-investigator must be thoroughly familiar with accounting systems and procedures. Many times he is confronted with the problem of incomplete, missing or altered records and he must use his investigative ingenuity, together with outside sources as well as secondary supporting records such as bank statements, financial statements and the like in order to reconstruct devious or unexplained transactions.

As of possible interest to the readers of *Management Accounting*, I should like to relate some of the experiences of our Special Agents as they pertain to the field of accounting.

FEDERAL RESERVE ACT

The Federal Reserve Act provides criminal penalties for embezzlement and related offenses by officers and employees of banks and certain other financial institutions, the deposits of which are insured by designated Federal insurance agencies.

Bank embezzlement and similar offenses pose a major problem to this Nation's financial industry. Those who specialize in such fraudulent practices can greatly undermine the financial stability of these institutions and seriously hamper their functions. Coping with these culprits requires trained, expert auditors and comptrollers who can readily detect irregularities.

Among the many cases in this category successfully concluded during the past year was an investigation involving a detailed review of records and books of several banks and corporations controlled by two West Coast businessmen. These two men acquired control of the First National Bank of Marlin, Marlin, Texas, and Mainland Bank and Trust Company, Texas City, Texas, and the FBI's inquiries related to the purchase of approximately $1,000,000 in questionable mortgage and real estate notes by these banks. The payment of commissions in connection therewith was made to corporations controlled by the two businessmen. As a result of the investigation, both men were convicted of violations of the Federal Reserve Act and Conspiracy Statute, and received 3-year prison sentences.

NATIONAL BANKRUPTCY ACT

Investigations of violations of the criminal provisions of the National Bankruptcy Act are conducted by the FBI. These investigations are, in many instances, directed at ascertaining whether or not the bankrupt fraudulently concealed assets of the bankrupt estate from the bankruptcy court. Concealed assets are often uncovered during our investigations and this discovery results in a larger distribution to the creditors of the bankrupt.

In order to prove criminal acts on the part of some bankrupts it is necessary that an experienced Special Agent Accountant examine the bankrupt's books and records. Frequently, these records are concealed or destroyed or they are incomplete, and the investigator must locate the missing records or bridge the gap by locating collateral evidence.

Briefly, during an inquiry into a bankruptcy matter, an accountant-investigator must establish a beginning inventory, the amount of purchases made over the period he selects to examine, and the sales made during this same period. He then is able to determine the amount of inventory that should be on hand at the date of bankruptcy. Comparison of this figure with the inventory reported to the bankruptcy court will reflect whether a shortage exists.

In one investigation, it was found that the bankrupt had a well-kept set of books, but the accountant-investigator became suspicious of the large number of accounts receivable upon which no payments had been made. He reviewed the sales slips and noted that in most instances sales were made to completely furnish either apartments or houses.

The investigator called at the addresses of several of the alleged debtors and found in each instance a man and a wife had rented either an apartment or a house, completely furnished it and then, within a period of thirty days, had informed neighbors that the husband had been transferred to another city. The furniture was then sold through advertisements in the newspapers. Moreover, in each instance, the description of the husband and wife tallied with that of the proprietor of the bankrupt business and his wife. When faced with the discovery made by the investigator, the bankrupt and his wife both readily admitted a scheme to defraud creditors.

In recent years, these investigations have taken on added importance due to numerous planned bankruptcies engineered by the criminal underworld in violation of the Statute. These schemes, commonly known in underworld parlance as "scam" operations, involve the acquisition or control of primarily mercantile establishments by the hoodlum element through intimidation, extortion or loan-sharking operations. The firm is then rapidly mulcted of its assets in below-cost sales of its inventory and any additional merchandise that can quickly be secured on credit. With the business laid barren, it is placed in bankruptcy while its erstwhile hoodlum owners or operators scurry to hide their ill-gotten profits.

One bankruptcy case involving a "scam artist" in which some 47 creditors lost approximately $129,000 resulted in the conviction of a notorious labor racketeer and two of his associates. The convictions stemmed from an FBI investigation involving a meat firm placed in bankruptcy within six months after being taken over by the racketeer. A necessary element of proof in the trial of this case concerned the sale of specific finished goods on certain days. To establish the use of materials and finished goods by the subjects and their corporation in manufacturing, accounting analyses were made of the raw material purchases which were compared with the sales for a one-month period.

These analyses showed that total poundage of sales far exceeded the poundage of purchases, indicating the use of raw material and finished goods not shown on the firm's books. Because there were approximately 2,000 sales invoices involved, our Automatic Data Processing Unit prepared additional accounting schedules to simplify the explanation and presentation of complicated and voluminous accounting records to the Federal Grand Jury.

LABOR-MANAGEMENT REPORTING AND DISCLOSURE ACT OF 1959

The Labor-Management Reporting and Disclosure Act of 1959 contains numerous criminal provisions under the investigative jurisdiction of the FBI. The principal type of investigation under this law pertains to embezzlement of union funds by dishonest union officials and employees of unions.

For example, one such case involved a complaint alleging embezzlement of union funds when the former business agent of a labor union refused to turn over records of the union to his successor. Our investigation was much more difficult since the ex-business agent refused to turn over any financial records of the union, including any canceled checks, check stubs, disbursement ledgers or financial statements.

To obtain some semblance of the financial transactions of the union for any one period, it became evident that the entire financial picture would have to be reconstructed from an examination of numerous microfilms maintained in local banks. This tedious and lengthy examination of microfilm by two Agent Accountants enabled them to reconstruct the activities of the bank account of the union for an entire year and evidence was obtained indicating eight violations of the ex-business agent during a three-month period of that year.

The treasuries of labor unions and other legitimate organizations provide an irresistible temptation to "hoodlums with an entree." Characteristic of FBI responsibility for certain provisions of the Labor-Management Reporting and Disclosure Act of 1959 was the investigation of an official of the International Longshoremen's Association (ILA) and a reputed La Cosa Nostra member. Following an extensive FBI investigation, the union official was convicted in Federal court during April, 1967, of embezzling $3,000 in ILA funds. He was fined $1,500 and placed on probation for two years. Even more significant, however, is the fact that this official, who for many years has been recognized as a powerful labor racketeer on the New York docks, will as a result of this conviction be prohibited from holding an official position with a labor organization for a period of five years.

FRAUD AGAINST THE GOVERNMENT

Fundamental to FBI responsibility is the protection of the vast Federal Government complex against fraud. These offenses, which are frequently complicated in nature, relate to false statements and claims made to Government agencies and their contractors, as well as to Federal lending insurance agencies, the Veterans Administration and the Federal Housing Administration. Often involving multimillion dollar contracts affecting purchases of goods and services, they may also be concerned with the truthfulness of information furnished by an applicant for Government employment. The FBI staff of expert Special Agent Accountants is often required to analyze voluminous financial records to isolate spurious claims and payments encountered in these investigations.

During the 1967 fiscal year, FBI fraud investigations resulted in savings and recoveries of more than $6,000,000. Even more important, however, FBI investigations frequently provide Government agencies necessary information for their administrators to use in correcting internal weaknesses and designing control procedures which will thwart future fraud attempts.

CIVIL INVESTIGATIONS

Important savings to the Nation's taxpayers result each year from civil investigations conducted by the FBI in matters in which the Government is a party in interest. These cases, many of which involve highly technical accounting problems, were responsible for savings and recoveries amounting to more than $143,000,000 in the 1967 fiscal year.

For example, the FBI is requested by the Civil Division of the United States Department of Justice to investigate claims against the Government brought by contractors and others who have sold goods or built facilities under Government contract. In general, these claims usually charge the United States with contributing to alleged delays in construction and resultant increases in cost, or with giving inadequate compensation for property seized under emergency proclamations.

Investigations of some of these claims require our accountants to make detailed studies of the manufacturing operations and practices of the plaintiff company for comparison with over-all practices in the particular industry. These studies may include detailed interviews with experts in the engineering, production, marketing, transportation, and other fields to obtain adequate information for assessing the soundness of the particular operations of the plaintiff which resulted in the additional costs.

Often, a company will voluntarily withdraw its suit in the Court of Claims after realizing the Government's defenses would be based on the results of FBI investigation. And, in many other instances, such claims will be settled for only a fraction of the total amount originally claimed after a thorough investigation by FBI Agent Accountants.

FBI audits—like any other audit—must be without error. In addition, our Agents must be totally impartial. Facts in the defendant's favor are reported just as meticulously as those against him. Moreover, our Agent Accountants must testify in court to their findings and, therefore, must be prepared for thorough and strenuous cross-examining.

As in all our investigations, we are frequently assisted by others in the accounting profession. On numerous occasions, certified public accountants and other independent public accountants have cooperated with the FBI, particularly in bankruptcy cases. Special examinations of bankrupt companies, made by a CPA at the request of the trustee, often disclose substantial asset shortages which are reported to the FBI. In addition, from time to time members of the accounting profession have also been of assistance in making available information needed to supplement incomplete or altered records.

We in the FBI welcome and appreciate this cooperation. We also would like to take this opportunity to assure the members of the National Association of Accountants of our own desire to be of every possible assistance in all matters of mutual interest.

16. The Uses of Accounting in Collective Bargaining*

Harry C. Fischer**

Collective bargaining has been established as the accepted means by which representatives of organized labor and of management reach agreement as to wages, fringe benefits, hours of work, and working conditions. Labor's immediate objective is an adequate return for its work and thereby improvement of the worker's standard of living. To management it is vital that the terms concluded permit the continued profitability of the enterprise and a return on the investment of stockholders.

Union representatives in a bargaining role are familiar with the desires of their members and have acquired some working knowledge of the industry. The assumption [here] however, is that they also need to make use of available and pertinent financial information as an additional tool in collective bargaining. . . .

Such financial information will not only be of interest as an indication of the employers' ability to pay, but it may also show the rate of growth of the enterprise and its standing as compared to other firms in its field. Recent emphasis by labor unions on participation of their members in the results of increased productivity requires the assembling and analysis of financial data. From time to time, the government has suggested "guidelines" or "guideposts" of percentage wage increases that would not upset the stability of the economy as a whole, another need for unions to use financial data in their attempt to equate such "guideposts" with the results to the industry of labor's increased productivity.

It may be argued that because labor negotiators may be assisted by professional advisers, they need not be proficient in understanding of financial statements and accounting terminology. However, since accounting deals with financial transactions, it is in effect the language of business, and the representatives of labor should have a knowledge of accounting terminology in order to properly communicate with manage-

---

* Reprinted by permission from *The Uses of Accounting in Collective Bargaining*, by Harry C. Fischer, from Institute of Industrial Relations, University of California, Los Angeles, 1969, pages 1–3.
** Harry C. Fischer is a practicing CPA.

ment should such references be brought up during the course of the negotiations.

Negotiations with smaller enterprises may not entail the use of professional advisers, and here the individual negotiator should indeed be conversant with accounting terminology. Furthermore, the decision-making process and the requirement to report to the union members places the burden on the negotiating committee for a clear understanding of all financial matters involved.

From management's viewpoint one would think that it would expedite negotiations and simplify communication if both sides in the negotiating process understood the meaning of any financial terms that may arise. . . .

Accountants differ in their treatment of financial data which is reflected on the "bottom line" or profit figure of the operating statement. An understanding of the makeup of the items in that statement is therefore of importance. Certain financial ratios will provide a measure of the earnings and productivity of the enterprise. Of significance too is the effect of income tax provisions on the results shown in the operating statement.

Analysis of the Balance Sheet or Statement of Financial Condition will provide significant ratios, those showing the utilization of plant and equipment and the liquidity of the organization among them.

It will be of some help to the negotiator if he has a general understanding of the structure of the business organization with which he is dealing and its accounting processes and records. This may be particularly useful should management offer to "open its books" on a claim of inability to pay. True, the union negotiating committee may call upon an accountant for this purpose, but again the committee will have a clearer understanding of what is done when it reports back to the members.

Part Two

The Nature of the Accounting Function

In Part One the reader was introduced to the general nature and evolution of the accounting function in a number of socioeconomic systems. The objective of Part Two is to describe this function in more specific terms.

Part Two is divided into two sections. The first looks at the information-type nature of the accounting function by identifying a few underlying concepts. The second introduces three possible specific segmentations, that is, social, financial and managerial accounting. The traditional manner of introducing accounting is to focus first on one area of the accounting function (usually financial), and then another (often managerial). The weakness of such an introduction is that a particular "way of thinking about accounting" is developed—often in the direction of financial accounting. The general result is (1) a desire to apply the initial "way of thinking" to all areas of accounting, and (2) an inability to discuss other accounting areas and to deal effectively with their respective problems.

By introducing the reader first to a broad framework of basic orienting concepts, we hope that the weaknesses of and the biases that result from the traditional approach can be avoided. It is to be noted that although Part Two is more specific than Part One, the approach continues to be one of working from the general to the specific.

Accounting is concerned with the collection and recording of economic information about individuals and organizations (which are assemblages of individuals), and the reporting of such information to individuals and organizations for decision-making purposes. Decisions are the single most important causal factor of behavior in a society, and, apart from information about individuals and organizations, decision making is the most basic orienting concept of the segmentations discussed in the second section of readings presented here.

The first group of articles focuses on the unity of accounting's service function by describing the information-communication-decision network in which accounting serves as an information system. In this network accounting information is the fuel of the decisions that are made by the individuals having an interest in an organization. Therefore, the information is seen as an important energizing force in the organization of all elements of a socioeconomic system. Accounting is concerned with dynamic rather than static situations and relationships.

It is an understatement to say that a "narrow focus" characterizes the history of accounting and accountants. For many, to be sure, accounting amounts to nothing more than bookkeeping. For others, accounting means reporting to stockholders, while still others think of accounting only in terms of reports to management. Smith's and Jordan's articles can be used to avoid this "narrow focus." They demonstrate that accounting is a substantive discipline, that is, that it has (1) a unique broad function in a socioeconomic system, (2) underlying concepts from which specific theories can be and are being developed, and (3) problems that require solutions.

The important question of *how formally* to integrate *which* interested parties into the information-communication-decision network is raised explicitly via the systems approach to a study of organizations and the accounting function. The Smith article discusses this issue. It also focuses on the controversy surrounding the apparent need to set a boundary for the accounting discipline by the creation of information standards or criteria. (Although this article conceptualizes the information network in a business organization, it should not be difficult to realize that it has applicability to individuals and organizations in general.)

The communication theories developed by Shannon and Weaver in telecommunications have been introduced with useful results in other disciplines, and accounting has not escaped this process of interdisciplinary borrowing. The Jordan article expands some of the earlier ideas of Bedford and Baladouni through a discussion of accounting's role in the communication process. This article can be used to illustrate how individuals and organizations (through the individuals that make up organizations) are involved in communication processes. Although the Jordan article has a financial accounting emphasis, the ideas presented and models developed can be used to describe more clearly the general nature of the accounting function.

The second group of articles pays attention to a few of the segmentations of the accounting function. In order to avoid traditional emphases, social accounting is introduced before financial and managerial accounting. It should be realized that such segmentations are made on the basis of the needs of various groups of users of accounting information and that additional segmentations are conceivable.

Social accounting is not equated here with national income accounting (dealt with in Part Four), but is initially discussed (in the Knortz article) in a broad sense. From there it is expanded with specific references to the vast sums of money that are being dedicated in many countries to a myriad of social improvement programs (the Savoie article and the item from *The Journal of Accountancy*). Economic activity within socioeconomic systems is substantially greater today than even a few years ago, and if accounting is to contribute to the goal of improved societies, then it needs to extend its formal scope beyond the information needs of individuals and organizations to the public interest at large.

The articles by May and Dombrovske discuss various important concepts and ideas relating specifically to the traditional financial and managerial accounting segmentations. The remaining shorter items relate matters of current interest concerning individual aspects of the accounting function.

Chapter IV

Accounting as an Information System

17. A Systems Approach to the Accounting Function*

Charles H. Smith**

The organization is the system to which accounting is related. A systems approach to the study of the accounting function should therefore include a study of the organization as a total system, and an identification of the role of accounting in an organization.

ACCOUNTING, ORGANIZATION, COMMUNICATION AND DECISION-MAKING

That communication plays an important role in an organization is confirmed in the following:

[Communication is the] . . . *nerve system which permits a group to function as a whole. (15, p. 212)*[1]

Communication plays a vital role in the implementation of the systems concept. It is the connecting and integrating link among the systems network. The flow of information, energy, and material . . . are coordinated via communication systems. (27, p. 380)

If communication integrates and coordinates, it seems logical to conclude that without communication there can be no organization.

---

* Adaptation from an unpublished Ph.D. dissertation entitled *Systems Theory as an Approach to Accounting Theory*, The Pennsylvania State University, March 1968, pages 173–250.
** Associate Professor of Accounting, University of Texas at Austin.
[1]References in parentheses are listed at the end of the reading.

According to Kuhn (28, p. 181) the purposes of communication are to inform, to instruct, and to motivate, that is, to influence behavior. Scott (43, p. 173) speaks of ". . . eliciting actions which will accomplish company goals effectively." He therefore links the influencing of behavior with goal achievement.

Simon goes a step further in the following:

Communication . . . [is a] . . . process whereby decisional premises are transmitted from one member of an organization to another.

. . . . the specialization of decision-making functions is largely dependent upon the possibility of developing adequate channels of communication to and from decision centers. (44, pp. 154, 171)

It may therefore be concluded that there is a distinct relationship between organization (systemization), communication, and decision making.

The function of accounting in society is emphasized by Imke in the following:

Accounting exists to serve society by recording, communicating, interpreting, and otherwise effectively utilizing financial and other economic data. (25, p. 321)

Accounting has traditionally concerned itself with information, but without communication information is useless. Communication performs an integration-type function, and the above statement emphasizes the communication of the data of a business organization[2] within society. This has led Spacek to make the following observation:

Looking at accounting as a whole, we see that it is, in effect, the principal line of communication in our economic system. (14, p. 524)

The above statement describes the nature of the total accounting function at the general level.

McDonough has made the following relevant comment:

Above the level of mechanical processing there is no justification for handling data unless there is some sort of decision being made with regard to the value of the data. (34, p. 138)

The above once again draws attention to the decision-making concept, and emphasizes the link between accounting, organization and communication. Accounting has information, and the latter is the fuel of decisions which regulate the flow of material, energy and information which, in turn, energize the business organization. Decisions become the primary

---

[2] Throughout the rest of this paper the business organization is used as a specific type of organization for discussion purposes. However, most of the ideas developed, have applicability to all types of organizations.

causal force affecting business behavior, and, seen in this light, accounting performs a most responsible function toward the business organization.

Numerous accounting scholars support the decision-making approach. Note the following:

. . . the decision-making problem . . . aims toward the center of . . . [the accounting] . . . discipline. (32, p. 14)

. . . accounting practice is essentially an analytic mechanism which seeks to expose the essence of quantified data. It is an instrument of decision making. . . . (47, p. 2)

We believe that the study of accounting should be related to the nature and objectives of business decisions—what information is necessary to make them, what data is relevant, and what the uses and limitations of this data are. (19, p. V)

. . . accounting is concerned with the provision of some of the facts on the basis of which one may act knowledgeably given one's ends or purposes. (8, p. 15)

. . . the CPA must understand accounting as an integral part of the decision-making process. (40, p. 12)

There is no need to evidence the fact that accountants have long supported the idea of "accounting information for managerial decisions." The concept of responsibility accounting has received much attention by accountants, but the direction of responsibility has been confined to management. The above statements do not limit the decision-making emphasis to any one group of interested parties.

ENERGIZING FORCES AND STABILITY

McDonough's statement above, indicating the need to handle information only when a decision needs to be made, is the starting point. There remains the need to know why the decisions have to be made.

The survival and growth objectives of a business organization are threatened by changes in the organization which can be externally induced or internally created. These changes cause variety or uncertainty in the organization, and therefore reduce the chances of being able to predict the behavior of the organization. Instead of the attainment of stability, the organization could be threatened by fluctuation and/or decline. Decisions affect business behavior, and, in the face of change, appropriate ones have to be made which would regulate the energizing flows mentioned in the previous section, and set up forces to determine tendencies toward stability. Information is the fuel of such decisions.

The problem of uncertainty needs to be faced. Uncertainty is a reality, changes do take place, and information must be communicated which will permit learning and adaptation to the changing conditions. For those who differentiate between an internal and external environment, data for purposes of achieving organization objectives of survival and growth (stability) by maintaining the internal system, and adapting to the external environment, is probably more acceptable terminology. Political scientists Snyder, Bruck, and Sapin (45, pp. 130, 133) write quite specifically with regard to the type of information that is required for the decision-making process:

1. For goal achievement.
2. For the efficient maintenance of the internal state of the system.
3. Regarding the "state of the relationship of the system to its setting."

They believe that information of the type in (1) and (3) would reduce uncertainty, but it appears conceivable to the writer that all three types would reduce uncertainty in the business organization.

A statement by Bennis calling for inferences about effectiveness of organizations, leads to a repetition of what has already been said, but it does serve to state the reasons for communicating information in different terms:

If we view organizations as adaptive, problem-solving, organic structures, then inferences about effectiveness have to be made. . . . (6, p. 273)

In order to be effective or healthy, an organization must develop the capacity to survive, adapt, maintain itself and grow. And, as stated by Wiener, "To live effectively is to live with adequate information." (46, p. 18)

It is obvious that accounting has a concern with one of the energizing inputs of the business organization system, i.e., information. Evidence has been presented to the effect that accountants recognize their responsibility in relation to the decision-making process. The question remains whether they understand the general nature and purpose of the decisions. There is evidence that they do.

The following statements by Chambers are significant:

Any . . . complex system, left to its own devices or allowed to develop without deliberately selected principles, is subject to the law of increasing entropy.

It is the function of new information to prevent this degeneration. (8, p. 160)

Entropy is a measure of variability or uncertainty in a system, and information counteracts such uncertainty. Information is therefore recognized as a factor that can increase the probabilities of predicting the behavior of the organization. Such recognition would naturally require accounting scholars to also recognize that the traditional stewardship function of accounting is being added to. This has been done, and as recently as 1966, in the report by a committee of the American Accounting Association, *A Statement of Basic Accounting Theory.* Note the following:

Accounting information is the chief means of reducing the uncertainty under which external users act as well as a primary means of reporting on stewardship. (1, p. 19)

Accountants also evidence recognition of the fact that the communication of information affects behavior, and that information performs a function in the formulation and attainment of organizational objectives. Horngren, for example, speaks of the ". . . accumulation, classification, and interpretation of information which assists individual executives to fulfill organizational objectives. . . ." (24, p. 4) The report of the American Accounting Association mentions that accounting information should be useful in the ". . . formulation of objectives, the making of decisions, or the direction and control of resources to accomplish objectives." (1, p. 8) Goldberg (20, pp. 350, 355, 361) differentiates various types of communication on the basis of purpose. Two of these types he labels activating (they influence the actions of others), and a third as informative (it does not produce action). Although he regards current accounting information as informative in that it does not in itself produce action, Goldberg suggests that accounting can play a more efficient role in influencing actions. He draws attention to the need to ". . . face up to the task of understanding the decision-making process, if only to be able to guide and educate the recipients of . . . reports to make an intelligent use of the information they contain."

The systems concepts of stability and health, and their relation to accounting have not escaped acknowledgment by accountants. Chambers emphasizes stability, and Roy and MacNeill, with reference to the quantitative information of a CPA's client's information, emphasize health in the following:

. . . homeostasis or stability of the firm . . . depends on a financial information system which is isomorphic with changes in the financial state of the firm. (8, p. 253)

Within the body of that information are the symptoms of organization illness or health, there for the diagnosis and therapy of the organization's syndromes. (40, p. 96)

At this stage attention should only be given to the recognition of a relationship between information, and stability and health. Other ideas contained in the above statements will receive attention in later sections.

The above discussion emphasizes the relationship between information, communication, organization, predictability of behavior, decision making and survival and growth (stability). Accounting is noted as having a very real function in the process of communicating its information for purposes of the decisions that affect the stability and health of the organization in the face of disequilibrating forces.

THE SOCIETAL ENVIRONMENT AND COALITION OF THE PARTICIPANTS

Manuel F. Cohen, the former chairman of the Securities and Exchange Commission, has emphasized the duties of accountants in the societal environment in the following:

Accountants owe important duties to their clients, but they also have an overriding responsibility to society to see that their efforts on behalf of their clients are not inconsistent with the public interest. (11, p. 58)

Anthony, Dearden, and Vancil (2, p. 28) noted the "limited concept of the function of accounting in corporate life," and Prince goes one step further in the following:

To understand any object or aspect of life, one must understand the interaction of the object or the aspect of life to the total surroundings or environment. (39, p. 27)

Recognition of the importance of the environment is not enough. Accountants need to realize that the accounting function is performed in the environment of society, and there is encouraging evidence that they do. The following support the conceptualization of accounting as a function in and to society:

. . . accounting operates as a service institution within society. . . . (25, p. 321)

The public accounting profession exists to provide service to society. If that service is to be maximized, public accounting practice must be adapted to our constantly changing environment. (26, p. 51)

. . . it is argued that accounting not only should be useful to the group that pays the bill but should also have its procedures appraised by reference to some quantitative scale of social usefulness. Accounting is tinged by the public interest. (16, p. 397)

Spacek, in commenting on *Accounting Research Study No. 1* of the American Institute of Certified Public Accountants, calls for ". . . fairness to all segments of the business and of the economic and political environment and the modes of thought and customs of all segments. . . ." (37, p. 57) Lewis (30, p. 241) refers to accounting as a useful device in any organized society, and, in *Horizons for a Profession*, Roy and MacNeill (40, p. 3) view CPAs as providing services to society.

A further matter needs attention. In order to perform the communication function most efficiently, accountants need to know which parties in the environment, having an interest in the organization, need to be made part of the communication network. A possible solution is to study the structure of a business organization and identify the interested parties (subsystems). Bedford and Dopuch recognize the concept of subsystems in their statement that ". . . the business enterprise is first and last a composite of individual organisms. . . ." (5, p. 63) Chambers emphasizes the concept of contributing parties in two of four propositions he has set forth, and hints of their potential influence:

(a) Certain organized activities are carried out by entities which exist by the will or with the cooperation of contributing parties.

(b) These entities are managed rationally, that is, with a view to meeting the demands of the contributing parties efficiently. (9, p. 209)

If the organization exists by the will of the contributing parties, and the latter also have demands, it is obvious that Chambers is referring to parties that can affect the behavior of the organization.

The above statements by Chambers hint of a coalition between the contributing parties. The coalition approach rejects the idea of a unique goal for the business organization on the grounds that the latter is a social organization. Because it is a social organization, recognition needs to be given to the participants (contributing or interested parties), and the interdependence between them. The participants have disparate demands, and these call for negotiation and compromise, that is, conflict resolution takes place in order to preserve system stability.

Caplan has indicated support for this approach as follows:

. . . the survival and success of the organization depends on the maintenance of a favorable balance between the contributions required of each participant and the opportunities to satisfy personal goals which must be offered as inducements. (7, p. 502)

Further support comes from Bedford and Dopuch in the following:

. . . accounting will be concerned with what should be the motives of the organization in relation to the expectations and needs of individuals. It will no longer be sufficient for accounting to assume that the income objective alone governs all organization and individual actions. (3, p. 84)

. . . the determination of the goals of a business enterprise is the province of its participants (stockholders, managers, customers, employees, suppliers). (5, p. 63)

The discussion thus far supports the recognition of all participants. There is a need to be more specific. Although stockholders are the legal owners of a corporation, there is an increasing call for accountants to recognize other interested parties in addition to stockholders. Woods confirms the fact that the participants are not to be found within a narrow, limiting legal framework:

The legal definition of a corporation is not considered to be adequate for defining the area over which an integrated system might be imposed. (48, p. 613)

Schireson, in equating the term "enterprising individual" with owner, becomes rather pointed in his criticism of the "stockholder-only" approach in the following:

. . . it is no longer adequate to view business as the private domain of an enterprising individual. Accounting statements are still organized around this concept.

Preparing accounting records from only the owner's economic interest is as unrealistic as an attempt to explain price movements by an over-simplified supply and demand theory. (42, p. 253)

Mautz and Sharaf refer to a study undertaken in 1955 which found, in general terms, the following:

. . . a majority (as indicated by a selected random sample of companies) of top managements believe that reporting to stockholders alone no longer meets the needs of business. (33, p. 193)

In his comment cited above, Spacek regards management, labor, stockholders, creditors, customers and the public as the relevant segments.

Many accountants evidence general and/or specific support for the above argument, and this should permit almost ready acceptance of the participants included in Figure 17.1. It is, in fact, not uncommon for writers to make an even longer listing than that of Figure 17.1. It might be interesting to note that as early as 1938, Littleton (31, p. 235) conceded that accounting information serves "management, owners, investors, government, and other pertinent interests."

An earlier section emphasized the relationship between accounting and decision making, and there is evidence that it is in relation to decision making that accountants accept the "widespread participant" concept. Paton and Littleton (38, p. 1) refer to the "needs of management, investors, and the public" while Bedford and Dopuch (4, p. 355) are more specific as to the nature of the needs by referring to "the basic motivational needs of a variety of decision makers." As a result of the

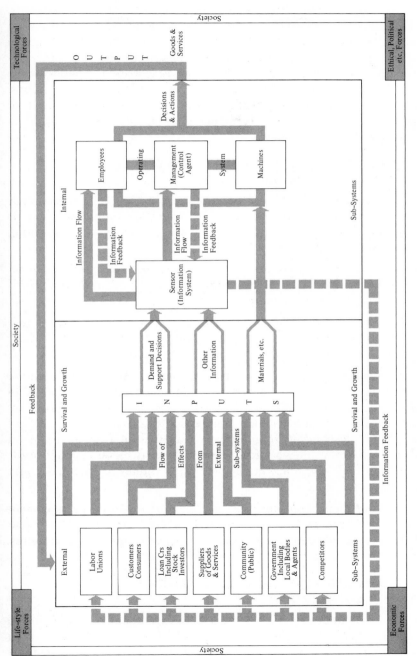

Figure 17.1　The Business Organization System as an Integrated Information-Decision Network

demands made on the organization, the various groups take action on the basis of accounting information, and the action is in the form of decisions. Hendriksen (23, p. 82) refers to the information for economic decisions of persons outside the entity such as stockholders, other investors, creditors, employees, customers, government and the public, while Roy and MacNeill (40, p. 194) identify the decisions of three groups, that is, those of present or potential investors and/or creditors, those of management, and those of government. Participants are therefore the acknowledged decision makers.

IMPLICATIONS OF A MORE INTEGRATED INFORMATION-DECISION SYSTEM

The participants make up the entity and influence its behavior. A "separate from participants" approach frustrates systemization, but it is also possible that it could continue a narrow approach for the accounting function. Note the comments of Goldberg:

[Auditors have] . . . interpreted their reporting responsibility somewhat narrowly and have not directly . . . accepted a duty towards third parties or the community generally.

. . . and if the accounting profession . . . does not shoulder these responsibilities, then it is not unlikely that others will be found . . . who will be charged with these responsibilities. (20, p. 309)

Accounting for management decisions has received much attention in recent years, and accountants have diligently applied themselves to the numerous problems relating thereto. It is submitted that this study suggests a discontinuation of the traditional "financial accounting" and "management accounting" fragmentation and that, at least at a general level, a theoretical framework for "accounting for decision making" needs to be established. The following comments by Sidney Davidson support this contention:

The notion of managerial analysis and financial reporting as separated, fragmented, and even opposing activities should, and I am confident will, be soon supplanted by the view which emphasizes the basic unity of the accounting function. (13, p. 117)

WHAT INFORMATION SHOULD BE THE CONCERN OF ACCOUNTING?

The need to answer the question "what information should be the concern of accounting?" flows automatically from the adoption of an information-decision framework. Even outside of a systems context accounting scholars have long debated this problem.

Chambers presents a reason for his argument against a certain type of information in the following:

. . . the accounting function has not hitherto been adequately defined or related to the adaptive problems of entities. (8, p. 341)

Social and physical scientists emphasize a dynamic environment, and certainly the latter concept has relevance for the business organization. It has been noted that adaptation is necessary because of the influence of the environment. However, as again stated by Chambers, if the environment is not considered ". . . effective adaptation within the entity with the object of meeting the environment beyond it will be impossible." (8, p. 368)

Information counteracts entropy, and is used in decisions which activate an organization. Rational stable behavior toward goals is the objective, and decision makers need information in order to make rational decisions. The decision makers have been identified, and their information needs appear to be the logical guide for purposes of answering the all important question of this section. With more specific reference to decisions, Chambers states that if the characteristics of the environment are ignored, then the system fails ". . . as a signalling system to those who make financial decisions in respect of the firm." (8, p. 112)

The study cited by Mautz and Sharaf in an earlier section reveals a feeling of obligation on the part of management to all parties having an interest in a business organization, and this adds to the burden of deciding what information to communicate. The framework developed herein emphasized decision making as an important influence on system behavior. Data is the fuel for a decision, and the needs or goals of the decision maker should be the guide in identifying general principles for data.

The American Accounting Association's study (1, pp. 4–12), *A Statement of Basic Accounting Theory*, emphasizes decision making in its statement of the objectives of accounting, and recommends the following four basic standards for accounting information:

1. Relevance.
2. Verifiability.
3. Freedom from bias.
4. Quantifiability.

The study makes the following general statement regarding the above:

These standards provide criteria to be used in evaluating potential accounting information. They constitute a basis for inclusion or exclusion of data as accounting information. If these criteria, taken as a whole, are not adequately met, the information is unacceptable. On the other hand, economic data which adequately fulfill these criteria represent accounting material that must be considered for reporting.

The following comment is also relevant, and is evidence of a systems approach:

Accounting information must be useful to people acting in various capacities both inside and outside of the entity concerned. It must be useful in the formulation of objectives, the making of decisions, or the direction and control of resources to accomplish objectives. The utility of information lies in its ability to reduce uncertainty about the actual state of affairs of concern to the user. The committee feels that adherence to the standards for accounting information, as proposed . . . will result in a marked reduction of this uncertainty.

The above draws attention to "people inside and outside of the entity." It emphasizes objectives, decisions, direction and control, and the reduction of uncertainty. These are all systems concepts.

Commenting on the specific standards, the study states that "the standard of relevance is primary among the four recommended standards," and that, "none of the other standards has this position of primacy." The standard of quantifiability, it would seem, sets a boundary to the information aspect of the accounting function. The study has this to say about quantifiability:

Accounting in its historical aspect is primarily a device for expressing economic activity in terms of money. Yet such expressions are not the whole of either accounting or of quantification, for quantification can be considered as the association of a number with a transaction or an activity where the numbers assigned obey prescribed arithmetic laws or procedures. There is no specification as to whether these numbers represent dollars, feet, tons, or degrees Fahrenheit.

It is important to note the lack of restriction to "monetary terms only" information.

Numerous accounting scholars have emphasized similar requirements, but often the only difference is use of terminology, and lack of one or more of the four standards. It is again interesting to note that in his 1938 article, when he spoke of service to "management, owners, investors, government, and other pertinent interests," Littleton described the function of accounting as being ". . . to supply dependable, relevant information about a business enterprise." (31, p. 235)

Daniel (12, p. 113) has categorized information as follows:

1. Environmental, i.e., regarding the social, political, and economic climate.
2. Competitive, i.e., including past performance and future plans.

3. Internal, i.e., regarding the organization's own strengths and weaknesses.

Caplan (7, pp. 496, 497) draws attention to various environmental dimensions of change, and summarizes them as follows:

1. Physical, e.g., regarding climate, availability of raw material, etc.
2. Technological, e.g., new products and processes, etc.
3. Social, e.g., attitudes of employees, customers, competitors, etc.
4. Financial, e.g., asset composition, availability of funds, etc.

The summaries of the above writers are similar but the emphasis relates to the information needs of management for planning, organizing, directing and controlling. Other participants have not been considered to the same extent as has management, although the categorization of relevant information appears to be as applicable. Chambers and Bedford state a requirement as follows:

[There is a need for financial statements] . . . which will serve as foundations for everyman's evaluations and actions. . . . (8, p. 376)

. . . there will be a need for accounting theory of the future to deal with a broader scope for the discipline where the objective of the accounting function will be to measure and communicate data on past, present, and prospective activities of all types in order to improve control methods and decision making at all levels. (3, p. 84)

Here again the emphasis is on decision making, all participants, and a lack of limitation to "transaction" and "exchange" data.

Of accounting scholars who acknowledge the participant concept, Bedford and Dopuch support the idea of goal information for ". . . individuals who might have interests in . . . various institutions . . . [so as] . . . to attempt to correlate their goals to the goals of the institutions of their interest"; (4, p. 359) Ladd (29, p. 24) and Goldberg (20, p. 292) find that reports do not provide "measurements of growth," nor do they permit judgment as to "growth potential"; the 1966 report of the American Accounting Association (1, p. 5) emphasizes the increasing demand for information on future plans, and expectations, and Prince (39, p. 179), Chambers (8, p. 371), and the report of the American Accounting Association (1, p. 7) emphasize environmental information.

The above does not exhaust the support. Information regarding competitors, to permit judgments of the future, and the position of an organization relative to others in the industry, and non-dollar information are common objectives. It is interesting to note that the information being called for by accounting scholars could quite easily be classified under the headings supplied above by management-oriented accountants.

One final point needs mentioning. Labor unions and employees are examples of participants only now being recognized. Change is continuous, and accounting will probably always be facing additional new factors requiring recognition. The basic requirements of the data remain, but the specific detail requires constant attention.

ACCOUNTING'S NEW FUNCTION IN THE BUSINESS ORGANIZATION SYSTEM

Meier, with reference to urban growth, has stated the following propositions:

Proposition 1—If a society of mortal individuals is to survive, information must be conserved.

Proposition 2—A sector of society that grows in influence, wealth or power . . . must experience a growth in information flow that occurred prior to or simultaneously with the other recorded growth. *(36, pp. 150, 151)*

Survival and growth are once again emphasized, and the importance of information cannot be ignored. If the business organization is cut off from the energizing effect of information, it will operate as a closed system and perish. Entropy must be countered, and information is the solution. Then growth and survival are possible.

The traditional emphasis in financial accounting is on transaction-cost information, while in management accounting it has been broader. Adoption of a decision emphasis would certainly mean an expansion of function for accounting, and, as Mautz and Sharaf have stated, "If over three-fourths of business managements feel they have a responsibility to keep stockholders, employees, creditors, government, and the general public informed with respect to the activities of the enterprise they manage, there certainly is an emphasis on disclosure and information not previously effective in this country." (33, p. 194) For those who would continue the argument in favor of the traditional emphases, Chambers and Dopuch answer as follows:

Censorship is not . . . one of the functions of the accountant. If his system conceals, it fails in its function. (8, p. 261)

Once it is granted that accounting is a service function . . . there can be no ground for restricting its practice by excluding estimated figures. (9, p. 210)

[The accounting function is] . . . rooted in the characteristics of change, uncertainty, peril or hazard, and the resulting condition of risk, needs, . . . choices among alternatives and the creation of values. In this respect, no limit needs to be set for the accounting function. (17, p. 261)

It should be recognized that the need for an expanded function is greater in financial accounting than in management accounting. If the business organization is considered independently of its environment, and if entropy is disregarded, then the traditional approach could be justified. However, given a dynamic environment, such an approach is unrealistic and the service less useful. To simply "account" in the literal sense of the word could conceivably relegate accounting to a relatively unimportant position in business.

The expanded function hints of a total information system, and numerous accountants support its location as part of the accounting function:

. . . *scientific developments in the field of business seem to require an extension of its information and control system; since accounting is now predominant in this area, the authors take the position that it is the logical source of the necessary expansion. (47, p. 170)*

Somebody has to manage the overall business information system. The accountant, who has long dominated quantitative information systems, is the logical candidate for the job. (24, p. 475)

Hemphill makes the following relevant observation:

One of the largest [firms] in the country has decided that . . . [the data processing function] . . . historically has resided on the financial side of the house and there it will stay. Their reasoning is that data accumulation and processing are requirements of accounting, and accounting is not restricted to dollars alone. (22, p. 22)

There is always the possibility that if the expansion is not made, others will be found to perform the function.

CONCEPTUAL MODEL OF THE BUSINESS ORGANIZATION SYSTEM

Figure 17.1[3] is an information-decision oriented model of the business organization, and reflects most of the ideas developed herein. The total system includes both outside and inside participants, that is, the descriptions, external subsystems, and internal subsystems are used instead of differentiating between an internal and external environment.

As in the case of an organism, the business organization is held together by the means to acquire, use, retain and transmit information. A sensor (information system) is an internal subsystem. It acquires information from the environment and external subsystems, supplies informa-

[3] Certain of the ideas contained in Figure 17.1 are taken from Clough (10, p. 86), McMillan and Gonzalez (35, p. 233) and Easton (18, pp. 110, 112).

tion to internal subsystems, feeds information back to external subsystems, and obtains information feedback from internal subsystems. The sensor also acts as a memory in that it stores information. The lines of communication are shown, and it becomes clear that the total organization is held together by means of this communication network. In fact, it can be seen that the organization is made up of a number of cybernetic systems in which feedback is important.

The organization is, in other terms, an input/output system in which the inputs serve to activate the system toward its goals, and where the outputs become feedback factors for purposes of continuing the behavior of the system. As the control agent, management is responsible for setting goals, and ensuring that operations go according to plan.

Cybernetic systems are concerned with the flow and communication of information. The relationship between accounting, information, and communication has already been established. As a social organization, the business organization is concerned with the content and meaning of messages (communication of information), and automatically accounting becomes involved with the related problems. As Greenlaw has stated:

[The] . . . emphasis is not solely upon the making of decisions per se, but rather upon complex information receipt-choice-information transmission networks in which "feedback and control" are core notions. (21, p. 4)

Information is communicated in order to influence behavior in favor of the health of the business organization and toward its goals, but, in order to maintain health, Schein (41, pp. 103, 104) has tabulated certain necessary conditions:

1. An ability to take in and communicate information reliably and validly.
2. Internal flexibility and creativity to make changes dictated by the information.
3. An integration and commitment to the goals.
4. Internal climate of support and freedom from factors, such as threat, which undermine communication.

References

1. American Accounting Association. *A Statement of Basic Accounting Theory.* A Report Prepared by the Committee to Prepare a Statement of Basic Accounting Theory. Evanston, Illinois: American Accounting Association, 1966.
2. Anthony, Robert N., John Dearden, and Richard F. Vancil. *Management Control Systems.* Homewood, Illinois: Richard D. Irwin, Inc., 1965.

3. Bedford, Norton M. "The Nature of Future Accounting Theory," *The Accounting Review*, 42 (January, 1967), 82–85.
4. Bedford, Norton M., and Nicholas Dopuch. "Research Methodology and Accounting Theory—Another Perspective," *The Accounting Review*, 36 (July, 1961), 351–36.
5. ———. "The Emerging Theoretical Structure of Accountancy," *Business Topics*, 9 (Autumn, 1961), 60–70.
6. Bennis, W. G. "Toward a 'Truly' Scientific Management: The Concept of Organizational Health," *General Systems*, 7 (1962), 269–282.
7. Caplan, Edwin H. "Behavioral Assumptions of Management Accounting," *The Accounting Review*, 41 (July, 1966), 496–509.
8. Chambers, Raymond J. *Accounting, Evaluation and Economic Behavior*. Englewood Cliffs, New Jersey: Prentice-Hall, Inc., 1966.
9. ———. "Detail for a Blueprint," *The Accounting Review*, 32 (April, 1957), 206–215.
10. Clough, Donald J. *Concepts in Management Science*. Englewood Cliffs, New Jersey: Prentice-Hall, Inc., 1963.
11. Cohen, Manuel F. "The SEC and Accountants: Co-Operative Efforts to Improve Financial Reporting," *Journal of Accountancy*, 122 (December, 1966), 56–60.
12. Daniel, D. Ronald. "Management Information Crisis," *Harvard Business Review*, 39 (September/October, 1961), 111–121.
13. Davidson, Sidney. "The Day of Reckoning—Managerial Analysis and Accounting Theory," *Journal of Accounting Research*, 1 (Autumn, 1963), 117–126.
14. Davidson, Sidney, David Green, Jr., Charles T. Horngren, and George T. Sorter (eds.). *An Income Approach to Accounting Theory*. Englewood Cliffs, New Jersey: Prentice-Hall, Inc., 1964.
15. Davis, Keith. "Communication Within Management," *Personnel*, 31 (November, 1954), 212–218.
16. Devine, Carl Thomas. "Research Methodology and Accounting Theory Foundation," *The Accounting Review*, 35 (July, 1960), 387–399.
17. Dopuch, Nicholas. "Metaphysics of Pragmatism and Accountancy," *The Accounting Review*, 37 (April, 1962), 251–262.
18. Easton, David. *A Framework for Political Analysis*. Englewood Cliffs, New Jersey: Prentice-Hall, Inc., 1965.
19. Fertig, Paul E., Donald G. Istvan, and Homer J. Mottice. *Using Accounting Information: An Introduction*. New York: Harcourt, Brace & World, Inc., 1965.
20. Goldberg, Louis. *An Inquiry into the Nature of Accounting*. Iowa City, Iowa: American Accounting Association, 1965.
21. Greenlaw, Paul S. "Systems Theory and Management Decision Making." Paper presented at the "General Systems Theory and Education" Sessions, Society for General Systems Research, AAAS Meetings, Berkeley, California (December 30, 1965).
22. Hemphill, Charles E. "What Is Good Systems Design?" *The Arthur Andersen Chronicle*, 26 (October, 1966), 14–23.

126   *Accounting as an Information System*

23. Hendriksen, Eldon S. *Accounting Theory.* Homewood, Illinois: Richard D. Irwin, Inc., 1965.
24. Horngren, Charles T. *Accounting for Management Controls: An Introduction.* Englewood Cliffs, New Jersey: Prentice-Hall, Inc., 1965.
25. Imke, Frank J. "Relationships in Accounting Theory," *The Accounting Review,* 41 (April, 1966), 318–322.
26. ――――. "The Future of the Attest Function," *Journal of Accountancy,* 123 (April, 1967), 51–58.
27. Johnson, Richard A., Fremont E. Kast, and James E. Rosenzweig. "Systems Theory and Management," *Management Science,* 10 (January, 1964), 367–384.
28. Kuhn, Alfred. *The Study of Society: A Unified Approach.* Homewood, Illinois: Richard D. Irwin, Inc., and The Dorsey Press, Inc., 1963.
29. Ladd, Dwight R. *Contemporary Corporate Accounting and the Public.* Homewood, Illinois: Richard D. Irwin, Inc., 1963.
30. Lewis, Charles A., Jr. "Are There Principles of Accounting?" *The Accounting Review,* 34 (April, 1959), 239–241.
31. Littleton, A. C. "The Relation of Function to Principles," *The Accounting Review,* 13 (September, 1938), 233–241.
32. Mattessich, Richard. *Accounting and Analytical Methods.* Homewood, Illinois: Richard D. Irwin, Inc., 1964.
33. Mautz, R. K., and Hussein A. Sharaf. *The Philosophy of Auditing.* Iowa City, Iowa: American Accounting Association, 1961.
34. McDonough, Adrian M. *Information Economics and Management Systems.* New York: McGraw-Hill Book Company, 1963.
35. McMillan, Claude, and Richard F. Gonzales. *Systems Analysis.* Homewood, Illinois: Richard D. Irwin, Inc., 1965.
36. Meier, Richard L. *A Communications Theory of Urban Growth.* Cambridge, Massachusetts: Massachusetts Institute of Technology Press, 1962.
37. Moonitz, Maurice. *The Basic Postulates of Accounting: Accounting Research Study No. 1.* New York: American Institute of Certified Public Accountants, 1961.
38. Paton, W. A., and A. C. Littleton. *An Introduction to Corporate Accounting Standards.* Columbus, Ohio: American Accounting Association, 1960.
39. Prince, Thomas R. *Extension of the Boundaries of Accounting Theory.* Cincinnati, Ohio: South-Western Publishing Company, 1963.
40. Roy, Robert H., and James H. MacNeill. *Horizons for a Profession.* New York: American Institute of Certified Public Accountants, 1967.
41. Schein, Edgar H. *Organizational Psychology.* Englewood Cliffs, New Jersey: Prentice-Hall, Inc., 1965.
42. Schireson, Bert. "Towards a New Accounting," *The Accounting Review,* 32 (April, 1957), 253–257.
43. Scott, William C. *Human Relations in Management.* Homewood, Illinois: Richard D. Irwin, Inc., 1962.
44. Simon, Herbert A. *Administrative Behavior,* Second Edition. New York: The Macmillan Company, 1965.

45. Snyder, Richard C., H. W. Bruck, and Burson Sapin (eds.). *Foreign Policy Decision Making.* Glencoe, Illinois: Free Press, 1962.
46. Wiener, Norbert. *The Human Use of Human Beings,* Second Edition. Garden City, New York: Doubleday & Company, Inc., 1954.
47. Williams, Thomas H., and Charles H. Griffin. *The Mathematical Dimension of Accountancy.* Cincinnati, Ohio: South-Western Publishing Co., 1964.
48. Woods, Richard S., "Some Dimensions of Integrated Systems," *The Accounting Review,* 39 (July, 1964), 598–614.

18. Financial Accounting and Communication*

John R. Jordan, Jr.**

The past few years have witnessed vigorous discussions among accountants, government officials, academicians and businessmen about accounting principles and the fundamental assumptions underlying financial statements. The quest for a set of postulates and principles upon which all interested parties could generally agree has proven futile. Yet, within these groups there is remarkably widespread agreement that the idea of *communication* is fundamental in the accounting process.

The American Institute of Certified Public Accountants has officially expressed its view of the function of accounting in Accounting Terminology Bulletin No. 1:

Accounting is the art of recording, classifying, and summarizing in a significant manner *and in terms of money, transactions and events which are, in part at least, of a financial character, and* interpreting the results thereof. *(Emphasis added)*

The Committee on Terminology went on to elaborate and emphasize that, at the highest level, accounting involves summarizing and interpreting financial (and nonfinancial) data in a significant way in reports to management, stockholders, credit grantors, and others. In other words, accounting deals with measurement, but it is measurement for *the purpose of communicating significant data to various interested parties.*

* Reprinted from *The Price Waterhouse Review,* Spring 1969, pages 12–22.
** John R. Jordan, Jr., is a Manager with Price Waterhouse & Co.

The American Accounting Association Committee on Concepts and Standards Underlying Corporate Financial Statements is more explicit:

The primary function of accounting is to accumulate and communicate information *essential to an* understanding *of the activities of an enterprise. . . .*

Accounting procedures and reports are based on the premise that quantitative data provide an effective means of description and are basic to the communication *of qualitative information about the enterprise. (Emphasis added)*

In addition to the pronouncements of the principal accounting organizations, practitioners—regardless of their considerable differences in philosophy and approach—all recognize communication as fundamental. The following statements are illustrative:

In its most elemental, as well as its most profound sense, accounting reporting is essentially a system of business and financial communication.
                                                              Leonard Spacek

. . . It is necessary to consider the fundamental nature and purpose of accounting. I start with the broad definition of accounting as the measurement and communication *of financial and other economic data. Its end product is information. The end purpose of this information is to assist someone in formulating judgments and making decisions. . . . Accounting is not an art that is practiced for its own sake.*
                                                              Herman W. Bevis

Robert Beyer refers to accounting as "the language of business"; in regard to external (custodial) reporting to investors, creditors, and the public, accounting must "tell the story of what has happened."

Our task (in financial reporting) is communication, *and our objective should be to make that communication as clear and useful as possible.*
                                                              Arthur M. Cannon

Others could be cited similarly; however, the above excerpts are typical and illustrative of the recognized fundamental significance of *communication* in the accounting process. Given the fact that accounting is a communication process, it would seem of first importance for accountants, in their "quest" for accounting postulates and principles and attempts to refine techniques and improve the reporting of financial data, to understand the nature and elements of the communication process, the limitations of communication, and the barriers to effective communication.

Even though businessmen and accountants do not tend to be inclined toward theory, theory can sometimes provide insight into some very practical problems. Communication theory offers some insight as to how communication works, and some aspects of this theory and related research findings are relevant to accounting communication. We shall then try to relate these concepts specifically to the accounting process and develop a conceptual framework for describing the accounting process in terms of its communication aspects. Then we will analyze various approaches to the accounting process in terms of their communications implications. Finally, some generalizations and conclusions relevant to the present efforts of the accounting profession will be offered.

COMMUNICATION THEORY AND THE PROCESS OF COMMUNICATION

Communication as a field of theory has developed primarily in the last two decades. Research and studies have been undertaken, processes analyzed, and principles formulated. Sociologists, anthropologists, psychologists, semanticists, and students of human relations have been particularly active in the study of communication, and the objectives and approaches of these students of various disciplines differ markedly. What will be presented here is a layman's eclectic gathering and synthetizing of the efforts of researchers from all these disciplines.

COMMUNICATION DEFINED

What is communication? Among many definitions, C. G. Browne defined it in *Personal Administration*, January 1958, as "the process of transmitting ideas or thoughts from one person to another . . . for the purpose of creating understanding in the thinking of the person receiving the communication." Communication is thus a *process*—the relationships are continuous, ever-changing, and dynamic. The process involves taking information or feelings that the communicator (which may be a group or an organization) wants to share and putting them into a form which can be transmitted. The process is not a complete act of communication, however, until the message is received and properly interpreted so that the receiver is "in tune" with the communicator (i.e., the message received corresponds closely with the message envisioned by the communicator).

THE PROCESS AND ITS ELEMENTS

The process of communication may be broken down into its components in many different ways and degrees of detail depending on the purpose at hand. For our purpose it seems useful to describe the process in terms of these elements: (1) Event(s), (2) Communicator, (3) Message, (4) Destination or Recipient, (5) Feedback.

Here is how these elements might fit together in a typical communication. An *event* occurs which is external to the communicator and recipient. The event is *perceived* and *interpreted* by the communicator. Based on his perception and interpretation, the communicator develops a *message*. At this stage there is a process of filtration. Wendell Johnson notes in this regard, ". . . to the degree that our individual filters are standardized and alike, we will agree about the world outside." Since individual filters tend to differ considerably, a great variation in messages may be developed by different individuals in response to a given event.

Once the message is developed, the communicator faces the task of selecting the symbolic representations with which to express it. The communicator, depending on the situation, may have many ways of expressing his message symbolically, or the symbol selection process may be very limited due to the existence of a precise technical language for describing the event (e.g., a chemist describing a chemical reaction in scientific symbols). It should be noted parenthetically that the existence of a very inflexible, precise language for describing events does not necessarily mean that the communication will be more meaningful. For scientific or mathematical phenomena, which may be described precisely in terms of fundamental laws and symbolic systems, such language inflexibility is desirable. In other situations, however, particularly those in which the events are unique or variable and qualitative factors and interpretation play an important role, it is desirable that the communicator have considerable flexibility in formulating his message (e.g., consider how meaningful newspaper reports of the World Series would be if the games could be described only in terms of a scorekeeper's numerical shorthand system). The message, as finally formulated, represents, as a rule, a highly condensed abstract of all that could have been spoken or written. What enters the final message depends on the communicator's available knowledge of fact and relationship, his vocabulary and his flexibility in using it, and his purposes.

The process may be represented diagramatically as shown on page 131.

The circles are a device used in a model developed by Professor Wilbur Schramm of Stamford. They represent the accumulated experience of the individuals (or groups) trying to communicate. The source can develop the message and the destination can decode (interpret) it only in terms of the experience that each has had. If the circles have a large area in common, then communication is relatively easy. If the circles do not overlap—if there is no common experience—then communication is impossible. If the circles have a small area in common—if the experiences of the source and destination are strikingly unlike—then it is relatively difficult to get an intended meaning across from one to the other. Given this analysis, Schramm concludes that it is the source's function to try to encode (formulate the message) "in such a way as to make it easy for the destination to tune in the message—to relate it to parts of his experience which are much like those of the source."

Another aspect of the diagram is *action*. Psychologists, particularly, have been interested in the effect of communication on the behavior of the recipient. For purposes of external financial accounting communications, however, we are primarily interested in achieving *understanding* of the message by the recipient; we are *not* attempting to achieve a certain type of reaction. Given the great variety of statement users, even within a given category (e.g., stockholders), if all recipients get the same basic understanding we would expect a great variety of reactions. Internal accounting, however, must not only provide understanding, it must also cause people to take certain desired action. While the internal accounting communication is just one aspect of the internal motivation system, it is a contributing factor, and the effect of internal accounting on action and motivation is an important consideration. In many instances, the action taken (or response) feeds back and alters the event(s) initially described.

Feedback to the communicator is exceedingly important in the whole process because it enables the communicator to appraise the extent to

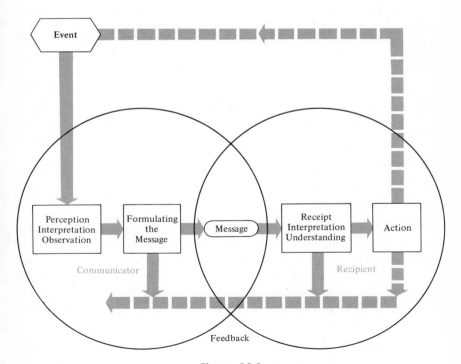

Figure 18.1

which his message is understood. When one realizes that the communication process is at best imperfect, the significance of feedback becomes clear. Feedback originates at a number of phases of the communication process. The communicator, of course, gets feedback from his own messages. The speaker who corrects his mispronunciation is immediately modifying his message in the light of feedback he receives from hearing himself. Feedback is also provided by the recipient of the message. This feedback may occur in many ways: a teacher gives an examination on a lecture he delivered; a speaker notes the puzzled expression on the face of his listener; we may observe the action taken by one to whom we have given directions. Testing, observation and direct communication from the recipient are common forms of feedback. What is important about feedback is not that it exists, but what the communicator does in light of it. The greater the sensitivity of the communicator to feedback and his skill in revising his message in light of it, the greater his chance of communicating effectively. (There are other courses of action besides *revising* his message that the communicator can take. For example, he may repeat his message or elaborate on it and/or he may educate the recipient in the language he is using.)

The difficulties involved in obtaining reliable feedback are obviously considerably increased as one proceeds across the spectrum from face-to-face communication to mass communication. Efforts to secure feedback in mass communication may produce results that are little more than inferential; some may even be misleading. Unsolicited feedback is infinitesimal in relation to the number of unanswered messages. Because of the complexity and heterogeneity of the mass, communicators direct messages to specific, concerned, and interested *segments* of the mass audience.

BARRIERS TO UNDERSTANDING

In the process outlined above, there are many links in the chain, any one of which may cause the process to go astray and frustrate efforts at understanding. Some of the more predominant causes of failure are:

(1) The *message fails to get the attention of the intended destination.* Attention is a function of the interest, the concern of the recipient, the importance of the message to him, and his familiarity with the subject of the communication and the symbolic system utilized. The communication itself, to the extent that it is interesting and intelligible, retains attention.

(2) The *message does not employ signs which refer to experience common to the source and destination.* Stated another way by John-

son, ". . . misunderstanding results when one man assumes that another uses words just as he does." As Schramm notes, little can be accomplished in achieving understanding *unless* "the communication is trimmed to fit the organization of the receiver—the way he thinks, acts, lives." As Alfred Korzybski, a founder of general semantics, puts it: "Words are used as maps of the territories that we have in our thinking. A recipient of communication also has territories in his thinking and his territories may not agree with ours when he (reads) the words which we are using. Thus it is not the words, but (the concept of) territories, that must be in agreement."

We have belabored this point because of its virtually universal recognition as the primary cause of communication failure. It is a particularly acute problem and a likely pitfall in a situation in which technicians or specialists are trying to communicate with laymen and nonspecialists (which typically occurs in accounting).

(3) *Any link in the system may be deficient.* Schramm points out that in a "linked" system of this kind, the system can be no stronger than its weakest link. There may be filter or distortion at any stage: The source may not have adequate or clear information; the message may not be encoded fully, accurately, and/or effectively in transmittable signs; the message may not be transmitted fast enough or accurately enough; the message may not be decoded properly.

So much for the basic process of communication. Let us now apply this knowledge of communication to financial accounting.

ACCOUNTING AS A COMMUNICATION PROCESS

Here, we shall try to apply communication theory to the accounting process, and develop a model for describing accounting in terms of its communication elements. The focus will be on external (financial) accounting.

THE CONCEPTUAL FRAMEWORK

The following is *a* conceptual scheme representing the financial accounting process in terms of communication theory.

The framework describes a closed-loop cycle. Each element interrelates with other elements either directly, indirectly, or in a feedback process. The principal elements and interrelationships are as follows:

The Environment   The environment is all-encompassing. All the elements of the process take place in the environmental setting and are affected by it. This would include political, social, and economic conditions and factors generally; also, it includes the industry—regulatory aspects, competitive structure, rate of innovation, customers, etc. Of course, the specific business entity is part of this *general setting in which communication takes place and observations and interpretations are made.*

Business Entity and Events   This corresponds to what we termed the "event" and represents the subject of the message (what the communicator is talking about). The business entity or enterprise is a dynamic process which is partly tangible (buildings, cash, machinery) and partly intangible (goodwill, cooperation, innovative capability). To make the process work, a continual stream of business decisions is being made and business events result. Goods are produced, expenses are incurred, financing is arranged, personnel are hired, growth and diversification objectives are set, research is undertaken, working rules or conditions are changed, and so on. Some of the resultant events are subject to direct, quantifiable (in economic measures) expression (sales, expenses, inventory purchases) and some are not susceptible to direct quantification (managerial competence, improved morale, goodwill).

Management   The management naturally is an integral part of what we have described as the business entity, and it participates in the business decision process. However, in terms of its role in financial accounting, it is useful to examine the role of management separately from the business events.

Management is the communicator, the source of the message. It records and interprets the quantifiable economic data on which the messages are based; it observes the flow of business events, interprets them, and abstracts from them. The end product of this process is a set of financial statements, which is management's message based on its interpretation and abstraction of the economic events for a period.

The Financial Statements   The financial statements represent the message which is transmitted to the users. We say represent because the financial statement is not the message, but it is the means or form of expressing the message and must be accurately interpreted ("decoded" in communication lingo) for the message to be understood.

The statements are a highly abstracted view of the business events and the business entity. They are prepared in accordance with accounting conventions that restrict their coverage to verifiable, quantitative, financial and historical data. They are prepared in accordance with varying acceptable methods and practices in some instances. They reflect judgment (e.g., materiality of lease commitments). They are interpretations. (The combining of unimportant accounts, arrangement of data, and emphasis and

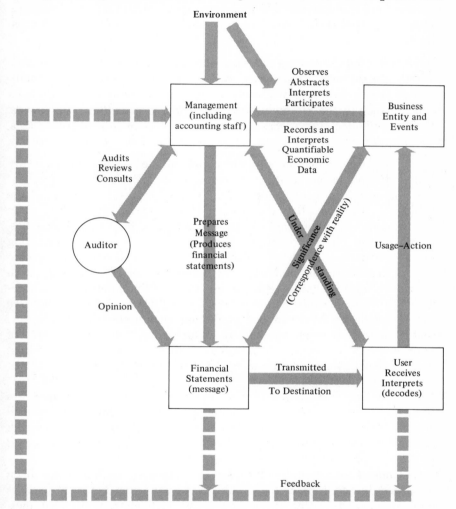

Figure 18.2
Schematic Communications Representation of the Financial Accounting Process*

* The basic framework from which the structure of this model is adapted was developed in "A Communication Theory Approach to Accountancy" by Norton Bedford and Vahe Baladouni—*Accounting Review*, October 1962; pp. 650–659.

detail on particular items all enable management to convey interpretations.)

Users   The user performs two important functions in the communication process: interpreting the financial statements and using the messages. The interpretation function has been described as follows by Norton Bedford:

Interpreting an accounting statement means reconstructing the message that the source (management) has encoded. The interpreter of an accounting statement must possess the necessary skills to be able to reconstruct and understand the message(s) contained in the accounting statements. If the destination (user) lacks the necessary skills or misuses such skills, he will fail to interpret an accounting statement with a desirable fidelity.

Given a particular message, the action (usage) of the users may vary widely depending on the attitudes, personal predispositions, group affiliation (labor, government, investor), utility preferences, and so on, of the recipients. It is clear that those engaged in financial accounting, while they cannot be oblivious to the possible reactions to their communications, are not engaged in communication designed to modify behavior according to a given pattern (such as advertising). They *must*, however, be concerned that the users' understanding (decoding of the message) is in agreement with the message in the mind of the communicating management. In regard to this, Schramm concludes, "There is (one thing) we can say with confidence about predicting communication effects . . . that a message is much more likely to succeed if it fits the patterns of understanding, attitudes, values, and goals that a receiver has; or at least if it starts with this pattern and tries to reshape it slightly."

Understanding and Significance   Understanding and significance are two concepts which are extremely important in understanding financial accounting as a communication process and in recognizing and appraising some of the major "trade-offs" involved in some of the recently proposed theories or philosophies of accounting.

Understanding (or *fidelity* as it is termed by Bedford) has been described by Bedford as: ". . . the correspondence between what is understood by the user of the accounting statements with what message(s) is, or is intended to be, expressed by the management." It reflects the extent to which there has been a "meeting of the minds" between the communicator and user. Since communication is not complete unless understanding is achieved, it measures the extent to which management and the statement users have communicated.

There is another dimension, however, to this process. *Significance* is "the degree of relevance and adequacy which the accounting statements have in relation to the world of economic events which they represent" (Bedford). This might be stated in terms of the oft-used expression "the extent to which the financial statements represent economic (and business) reality."

If statements perfectly described economic reality (if management observed, interpreted, and communicated in perfect accordance with economic reality) *and*, if messages were interpreted with perfect understanding (fidelity), the communication process would be perfect.

Feedback The role of feedback has been mentioned. In financial accounting, the communicator (management) obtains feedback from three sources: the auditor, the financial statements themselves prior to release, and the users. We shall defer the auditor's role for separate discussion. The financial statements provide feedback in that, after the statements (message) are developed, management can appraise the message to see if it presents an accurate accounting representation of the message that management wishes to convey. For example, if after the development of the income statement and the balance sheet management decides to add a funds flow statement to highlight financial results that it considers significant, then management would be modifying its message based on prerelease feedback.

Feedback is also obtained from statement users. Because statement users are diverse in their interests and interpretive capabilities and only a few are likely to articulate any direct feedback, this source of feedback has some limitations. Management is usually aware of requests for additional information or elaboration by creditors, outside directors, security analysts, and some stockholders. By systematic investigation by the accounting profession of statement users, a much more extensive and useful body of feedback could be developed.

The Auditor The role of the auditor in the communications process is currently the subject of considerable controversy within the accounting profession and in the business world. The scheme proposed incorporates the position of the Long-Range Objectives Committee of the American Institute:

The attest function results in the expression of an opinion by an independent expert that a communication of economic data from one party to another is fairly presented. Discharge of the function lends credibility to the representation and increases reliance upon it. The opinion implies (if it does not so state) that the data presented are appropriate for the representation, that there is objective evidence underlying the data, and that the judgments exercised in interpreting the data are such as to justify the opinion.

The financial statements are essentially the *representations* of management. The auditor performs some important functions:

(1) He is a source of feedback. The auditor familiarizes himself with the needs of statement users, and he can advise management as to whether the statements are adequately formulated to meet the users' needs and whether the statements convey the message that management intends.

(2) Management, as it was pointed out, participates in the business decision process, the financial results of which are presented in the financial statements. Because management is a participant and interpreter and reporter of results, it is desirable that its interpretations be appraised by an objective and independent group to assure the users that the statements are objective and unbiased and are prepared in accordance with recognized, acceptable accounting practices and principles. This adds credibility to the statements which increases the receptivity of the message by the users.

The conceptual model of the accounting process in terms of its communication elements has been developed for the following reasons:

(1) It presents simultaneously the whole communication process.

(2) It structures disjointed elements and shows their interrelationships more clearly.

(3) It may reveal otherwise unrecognized relationships.

(4) It enables us to fit various approaches to accounting into a generalized framework and thus to compare them in terms of their relationship to the communication process.

(5) It facilitates focusing on the critical aspects of the process while not losing sight of the broader picture.

(6) It enables us to focus on the strategic trade-offs and implications of various approaches to accounting.

(7) It enables us to develop the objectives of accounting.

(8) It suggests useful areas for accounting research.

Given this communications framework, let us turn to a discussion of *some* of the major controversies in accounting today in terms of their communication aspects. The approach and discussion are not meant to be exhaustive, but to illustrate that these areas can be thought of in terms of a communications perspective and to stimulate thinking in that direction.

FINANCIAL ACCOUNTING AND COMMUNICATION

As noted, there is fundamental agreement (implicit or explicit) among those of diverse philosophies of accounting that *communication* is the substance of accounting. Since *understanding* is the ultimate objective of communication, we can state the *purpose* of accounting (when it is viewed from a communications standpoint) as follows:

The purpose *of accounting is to communicate economic messages on the results of business decisions and events, insofar as they can be expressed in terms of quantifiable financial data, in such a way as to achieve maximum* understanding *by the user and correspondence of the message with economic reality (i.e.,* significance).

This statement raises several fundamental issues. It is oriented toward the users (recipients) of accounting messages and hence necessitates examination of the obviously tough question: *To whom are* financial statements addressed? or, *To whom should* financial statements be addressed?

THE ROLE OF USERS

Users, as we have seen, differ widely in their interests, predispositions, group affiliations, needs, and knowledge of accounting practices and principles. The latter differentiation is particularly important because, to a great extent, it determines the *interpretive capacity* of the user and hence the level of sophistication of messages (financial statements) which can be addressed to him with assurance that he will be capable of *understanding* the message. Needs of users also vary considerably and, as we know, the degree of interest and attention which the statements can attract and retain is a function of the extent to which the statements meet the user's particular needs. As Rex Harlow puts it, "The immediate concerns of the members of an audience must be known and given proper consideration in the preparation and distribution of messages to win their attention."

Given this situation, there appear to be several paths available. One is to differentiate from the mass of users various segments which have different levels of interpretive capacity and needs and to develop different messages for these groups (e.g., a simple summary of earnings for stockholders and more sophisticated statements for security analysts and credit grantors). Another approach is to select a particular level of interpretive capability (e.g., security analysts) and prepare statements on the assumption that users will have a sufficient level of sophistication or will seek aid (an interpreter) if they are not capable of interpreting the message. This argument, somewhat extended, has been made quite forcefully by Professor Patrick S. Kemp in his article "Controversies on the Construction of Financial Statements." Professor Kemp concludes:

Financial statements should be directed toward the informed, competent reader . . . The idea that financial statements should be comprehensible to the uninformed layman, "the man on the street," is unwarranted. Financial statements are, after all, technical reports . . . There is no more reason to expect that the uninformed layman should be able to understand these reports without competent professional assistance than that he should be able to comprehend technical reports prepared by members of any other profession.

A third approach might be to provide financial statements directed at the level of interpretive capability of the average layman stockholder. From our analysis of the communication process, it is evident that the "capacity" for communication (in terms of volume and sophistication of content) of the process is no greater than its weakest link. This last approach would direct the level of communication at an average (probably relatively low) level of sophistication, which means that the messages would be less *significant* (in communication terms). Naturally, for the more sophisticated users (creditors, analysts), this approach would be retrogressive and contrary to their expressed needs.

However these issues are approached and resolved, the thoughts of Herman W. Bevis expressed a number of years ago should become a more important part of the thinking of the accounting profession:

In tracing the role of standards for the measurement and communication of economic data, we have confined the parties at interest to two: the issuer and the user. Note that the accountant does not appear as principal at all. It may be well, then, to devote some attention to the nature of these issuers and users.

Following up on this, Bevis states: "Thus, part of the problem (of accounting standards) is: which standards, for which issuers, for which users?"

This suggests that the AICPA should direct considerably more research effort toward statement users and suggests that the participation of businessmen in the formulation of accounting principles to an increased extent is highly desirable.

UNDERSTANDING VERSUS SIGNIFICANCE

A second major issue is also raised. The above statement argues that the purpose of accounting communication is to maximize *understanding* of the message *and correspondence of the message with eco-*

nomic reality (i.e., significance). This implies a strategic balancing process in which a trade-off is made between understanding and significance. The skill with which those engaged in accounting deal with this issue will greatly influence the future role and usefulness of financial accounting. To illustrate let us examine two divergent philosophies of accounting in terms of the way that this trade-off is made.

Maurice Moonitz (in the AICPA Research Studies of "Postulates" and "Basic Principles") proposed an approach to accounting in which the financial statements would be very *significant*, that is, the statements would *correspond* very *closely* with economic reality (e.g., security price increases, as well as declines, would be recognized; leases would be reflected as debt; replacement values would be recognized; price-level changes would be recognized; etc.). Moonitz, however, did not concern himself with whether statement users would correctly interpret such statements. As we have seen, users interpret statements in terms of their experience—i.e., the way that they view things is important. Furthermore, in order to decode statements and get the desired message, the users must be able to understand the process by which the message was formulated by the communicator. For these reasons, statements which are economically "perfect" may result in confused or partial understanding, or complete misunderstanding, of the message of the communicator. Or, stated another way, statements which are in imperfect or only approximate correspondence with economic reality may be quite effective in telling users about the economic events of an enterprise simply because the message can be understood. In short, *Moonitz* has focused on *significance* in his approach; whether his approach would result in increased *understanding* (which, after all, is the purpose and justification of accounting) is debatable.

Herman W. Bevis represents a clear-cut contrast to Moonitz in his approach to the problem of striking the balance between *significance* and *understanding*. While Moonitz focuses on developing statements that reflect economic reality in a quite sophisticated manner, Bevis continually focuses on accounting as a communications process in which understanding and usefulness are of the utmost importance—"In any successful communication, a meeting of the minds must exist between issuer and user as to the meaning of terms. . . . The issuer and user must have an understanding as to standards for measurement and summarization. . . . The communication must be intelligible to the user. . . . It is important that standards used by the issuer (i.e., the method of encoding the message) be understood by the user (otherwise he cannot decode the statements). . . . Standards must result in communication of data addressed to users' informational needs and capable of being comprehended by the knowledgeable among them."

Naturally, there are all shades of approach between (and beyond)

Moonitz and Bevis. They were chosen simply to illustrate two approaches which give very different emphasis to *significance* and *understanding* in striking a balance between the two. The communications framework does not resolve this question for us. It does, however, provide a framework for appraising the various approaches in light of their communications implications.

UNIFORMITY VERSUS FLEXIBILITY

We might also say a few words about the recurring uniformity—flexibility controversy in terms of the communications implications. As Bevis points out, "The issuer and user of economic data must have an understanding as to standards for measurement, if communication is to be successful." Because of the considerable latitude in present "acceptable" accounting practices, the user may have considerable difficulty in knowing what alternatives the communicator is using, or he may assume that different managements are communicating on the same basis. In either case, incorrect interpretations may result, hence uniformity is proposed as a way of assuring the user that he is interpreting on the same basis that the message was formulated.

Imposed uniformity, however, has its perverse effects from a communications standpoint. When we discussed the communications process, it was pointed out that the communicator observes and interprets an external event, which he then *translates* into a message. The greater the range of ways that the communicator has available to formulate his message (i.e., the more alternative ways of expressing himself—the greater his vocabulary), the more precisely and accurately he can communicate his interpretation of a given event. While this is true, there is also an increased opportunity for selecting an inappropriate way for communicating—either intentionally or otherwise.

We can at least state that *ideally* from a communications standpoint, given the premise that the facts surrounding each economic entity and its economic events are virtually unique—certainly extremely diverse—it would be desirable to retain considerable latitude in accounting practices and methods so that the communicating management will not be straitjacketed in expressing economic events in different situations and perhaps based on different interpretations, *provided* that disclosure of the method or practice is clearly indicated so that the user can properly decode the message.

THE INDEPENDENT AUDITOR

Finally, let us mention the role of the auditor and the CPA profession in the communications process between managements and users. One school of thought feels that the accounting profession should take an active role in formulating accounting standards for new situations and developing and articulating present accounting methods and standards, but, in securing adoption of these standards and practices, it should primarily rely on its influential status as expert accountants, the persuasiveness of its pronouncements, and the usefulness of its proposals to management in fulfilling its communication function. Management (within limits) is responsible for developing the message.

The other group would have the accounting profession *impose* uniform standards on issuers of statements. The auditor, for them, becomes a filter in the communication network and the message now becomes the auditor's rather than management's. Management's role of observing and interpreting can become frustrated and inactive. To the extent that management's interpretations of financial events differ from the way that it has to report them, management's thinking will not be communicated to statement users, and internal accounting and decision-making will be on a different basis from external financial reporting. However this important issue is resolved, the implications of the alternatives in terms of the communications process should be given major attention.

CONCLUSION: RETHINKING ACCOUNTING RESEARCH

This article has attempted:

(1) to point out the fundamental importance of *communication* in accounting, which seems to be recognized explicitly or implicitly by most practitioners and theorists in their discussions of the accounting process.

(2) to discuss how communication works.

(3) to apply communication theory and principles to financial accounting.

(4) to examine some current issues in accounting in terms of their communication aspects.

In conclusion, it seems useful to state what the implications of this analysis are for accounting research. It was suggested initially that perhaps now is the time to do some rethinking as to the nature and direction of the research efforts. An analysis of the communication process suggests that perhaps more could be accomplished in terms of developing perspective and foundation for resolving some of the current and perennial controversial accounting issues by conducting research in the following problem areas:

(1) What are the *types of situations* in which accounting statements are issued? What are the contexts in which statements are issued and used?

(2) Who are the *issuers* of accounting communications? What differentiations exist among issuers? What implications does this have in terms of accounting standards and practices which are appropriate?

(3) Who are the *users* of accounting communications? How may they be classified? What are their informational needs? How do they perceive socio-economic reality? What are their interpretive capacities?

(4) *Content analysis*—How well understood are accounting communications? What is comparability? To what extent can it be achieved? What role can disclosure play in resolving the flexibility-comparability question?

(5) What is the appropriate *role of the auditor* and the accounting profession in the communication process?

Perspective is important in viewing and formulating judgments about any significant activity. While most practitioners and businessmen concerned with accounting have recognized the fundamental significance of communication in the accounting process, there has been virtually no attempt to study accounting as a communications process and develop a conceptual framework which would give vitally needed and useful perspective. It is hoped that this article makes a beginning in filling this need.

19. Accounting—Utilitarian, Symbolic, Selective*

A. Dean Willock**

The first broad characteristic of the accounting art and its underlying data is its utilitarian nature. It is capable of being used in a virtually unlimited variety of circumstances and purposes.

Because of this utilitarian nature of the information used in the accounting art, the possible applications of the data for managing and

---

* Reprinted from *Management Accounting* (formerly *NAA Bulletin*), March 1964, page 32.
** A. Dean Willock is a Senior Accountant with Price Waterhouse & Co.

controlling economic performance is limited only by man's ability to appraise the activities conducted by the enterprise and the ability of the accountants to measure and report upon the economic significance of these activities. Accordingly, no definition of the art is possible except by reference to the particular moment of time or history when observations of the applications of the accounting art are made.

The second broad characteristic of the accounting art is its symbolism. For example, the balance sheet and income statement are symbols of the activities of an enterprise at a point in time and over a span of years. The ledger accounts, source documents, and the multitude of other items, whether they be in the form of paper-work or electronic tape, are also symbols expressing functions or activities performed. For example, an activity, such as the receipt of goods or services, may be symbolized at the unloading platform by the preparation of a receiving report. The symbol (receiving report) travels to various places in the enterprise including the accounting department where it is interpreted and further symbolized by an entry in the inventory records. At a later date the inventory records are employed to determine income and financial position.

A further observation on the importance of a concept of symbolism in accounting data might be made. We are increasingly witnessing the introduction of high-speed electronic equipment using the symbolism principle to perform certain functions previously considered capable of performance only by accountants and within accounting departments. Now, however, the machines are not only achieving this effectively and rapidly, they are also using new mediums, i.e., punched cards, paper tape, magnetic tape, etc.

Assuming that the fundamental characteristics of the data used in the accountants' art are that it is symbolic and utilitarian, the question to be answered seems to concern the methods or techniques which the accountants use to provide meaningful information to management for control of the enterprise.

To this writer, it seems that the accountants' primary technique is one of selectivity. Broadly speaking, the accountant is continually selecting techniques and procedures which most accurately, objectively and truthfully measure and communicate the results of activities conducted by the enterprise. In some instances, the accountant selects techniques to accumulate the data representing the total activities of the enterprise over a period of time, e.g., the periodic income statement. In other instances, e.g., cost accounting and product cost analysis, the accountant is not concerned with total activities but merely with a sufficiently qualitative type of data to ascertain an activity's conformity with predetermined standards set by prior analysis. Thus, good judgment in selectivity, from symbolic information that is useful, marks the effective accountant.

20. The Accounting Model*

Editorial

Jay W. Forrester questions the central position held in a firm by accounting information (*Industrial Dynamics*, M.I.T., 1961). He takes the view that it is information flow, not money flow, which ties together the parts of a business. Furthermore, he considers that most information is non-financial in form. Financial information is not an integral part of the decision-making function. Rather it is a reporting system to measure past success. It performs a policing action to ensure honesty and acts as a basis for rewards—both to managers and to stockholders.

Forrester asks:

Does it matter whether the profit and loss statement and balance sheet for last month are available on the 5th or 25th of this month, since both reflect the result of decisions taken six months, a year, or five years ago?

A business, of course, may get into such a mess that financial inputs are the principal controllers of operating decisions. Such a state, however, is usually the result of a long earlier history in which the implications of other kinds of information have gone unheeded. Apart from these drastic situations, accounting information merely sets the general tone of optimism or pessimism, and the degree of care in authorising new expenditure.

Forrester's answer is to build a model of information flows, like the accounting model of financial flows. The type of information he refers to includes incoming and outgoing orders and incoming and outgoing shipping rates. These are all affected by delays or time-lags and result in back-logs of unfilled orders which trigger off decisions.

A major objective of Forrester's system is the elimination of fluctuations in employment rates, inventory levels, and uncollected receivables. The aim of the system analysis is to isolate critical delays in information

* Reprinted from *The Accountants' Journal* (New Zealand), October 1966, page 121.

processing and redesign the administration network. The result is expected to be an information system of automatic feedback controls, eliminating the "muddle through" approach to external changes. Forrester shows how accounting information is merely a by-product of a management control system.

Forrester is answered in part by Richard Mattesich who has compared the accountant with General Kutozov in Tolstoy's *War and Peace*. The commanding general of the Russian Army is depicted as an institution whose importance lay in representing stable authority in the midst of chaos. In the same way, accounting and its effectiveness can be understood much better from a psychological than from a logical point of view.

Like the effectiveness of General Kutozov, that of accounting lies in its authoritative character. Accounting depicts the firm's financial structure by a crude but all-embracing model which constitutes a mighty bulwark against chaos. There can be no doubt that scientific methods are better, absolutely speaking. The important question is the point at which they become profitable for a given firm.

In this major book (*Accounting and Analytical Methods*, Irwin, 1964) Mattesich asks whether accounting should be considered as one of the management sciences? His book demonstrates that some areas of management science are so closely related to the affairs of accounting that it is difficult to exclude our discipline from the new interdisciplinary movement. In addition, he shows that analytical concepts, introduced by management science, may be applied in clarifying accounting concepts in general.

Chapter V

Social, Financial and Managerial Applications

21. Bringing Accounting into Economic Measurements*

Herbert C. Knortz**

Economic progress at the national and business level has become increasingly complex and interdependent. With this increasing complexity, it is no longer possible for the various professional faculties to isolate themselves from each other and to seek improvement solely within their own self-sufficient environments. As the expanding opportunities of international activity are probed, all of the professions must join in identifying anew the resources and the goals which will characterize their mutual future. This identification must merge the investigative techniques of the various professions so that a maximum total understanding may be achieved.

Bertrand de Jouvenal,[1] the French economist and political theorist, has stated that the hostility of the intellectuals toward the businessman is the result of a clash between their value systems. Only through the development of improved factual evidence and improved analyses will it be possible to reconcile these inherent differences and thus be able to

---

* Reprinted from *Financial Executive*, November 1967, pages 26–36.
** Herbert C. Knortz is Senior Vice-president and Comptroller of the International Telephone and Telegraph Corporation.
[1] "Business—Through the Eyes of the Intellectual," *Encore*, Spring 1962, p. 13.

149

work more competently for total economic progress. In my opinion, the accounting profession is qualified to cooperate in providing this improved evidence and it has an obligation to find realistic ways to bear its share of the effort for economic development.

The progress of humanity is evidenced largely in terms of economic data. This statement does not intend to deny that the qualitative things— art, literature, music, conversation—have importance in life, but it does give recognition to the fact that these things are not yet measurable. Economic information is of importance because it can quantitatively express where we have been and how far we have come toward where we are going.

However, if economic data existed only as a measuring stick, its contribution to progress would be minimal. Of more significance is the fact that such data can become the firm basis for planning the future of national economies. The successful evolvement of national life in this modern day requires a complete understanding of general economic relationships and of inherent strengths and weaknesses.

Starting with the political economists of Adam Smith's era, governments have been continuously moving toward state-wide planning. Plannification—which was introduced by the Russian Five-Year Plans and by the early development of theory in France—has been increasingly accepted in European countries; e.g. Belgium, Netherlands, United Kingdom. As yet, it has been activated in the United States in only a fragmentary way. In 1958, the National Bureau of Economic Research submitted to the U.S. Congress and the Bureau of the Budget its proposals for an integrated accounting system covering the productive and financial operations of the American economy as a whole.[2] Then, in 1962, in recognition of the increasing American interest, the U.S. Committee for Economic Development sent a task force to Europe to find out what was being accomplished in capitalistic economies through state activities in economic planning. Since that time, there has been a marked expansion in the influence of economic situations upon American legislative programs.

It is not only at the national level that economic planning has significance. In the business world, too, there is a need for information. Essentially, management is the efficient combination of resources to achieve a desired objective at a given time. Despite this, "in the field of business management, we find men deploying resources on a large scale without any clear notion of what their strategy is, and yet a company's strategy is a vital ingredient in determining its future."[3] Since a sound

---

[2] National Bureau of Economic Research, "The National Economic Accounts of the United States," Government Printing Office, 1958.

[3] S. Tilles, "How To Evaluate Corporate Strategy," *Harvard Business Review*, Vol. 41, No. 4, p. 111.

strategy can only spring from a sound knowledge of facts, it is important that the field of personal knowledge be expanded through an interchange of economic facts to permit a wiser selection of appropriate goals and of more advantageous programs for their accomplishment.

Walter Blass, having considered the nature of the capitalistic system and the state of economic planning, wrote, "Given the prevalence of very large companies in modern capitalistic economies and their effects on production and employment, it is already clear that long-range planning has an important role to play in these large companies. It is not too far-fetched to speculate that the methods devised for European national plans might have considerable relevance for intra-company plans in the United States." [4]

Undeniably, economic information is becoming a more powerful ingredient of coordinated planning both in national and business affairs. It has important connotations for the legislator and the sociologist, for the labor leader and the business manager, and for the investor and the general public. Each of these groups wants the reassurance that can be provided by reliable economic data, but none of them is convinced that the present range of data provides a sufficiently comprehensive understanding of the total economic system nor, indeed, of such vital questions as "the extent to which the growth rate and the profit rate react on each other." [5]

ECONOMICS AND ACCOUNTING

If it is agreed—and there seems to be no question about it—that economic data and relationships are playing more important roles in national and business situations, it becomes necessary to ask how accounting as a profession can more fully participate in the new evolvement. However, before pursuing that train of thought, it is necessary to determine the nature of the linkage between the faculties of accounting and economics.

Adolf Enthoven, of the International Finance Corporation, asserts that, "Whether for an individual organization or for a nation, accounting is the coherent assembly of economic data so as to understand the past and plan for the future. The form of assembly may differ somewhat, but the principle is the same. For example, national account data may be assembled in the form of input-output tables, with production, consumption, capital formation and external transactions forming the basic economic activities. As in private accounting they are composed of and

---

[4] W. Blass, "Economic Planning—European Style," *Harvard Business Review*, Vol. 41, No. 5, p. 119.

[5] R. Speagle and H. Chace, "The Corporate Profit Equation," *Harvard Business Review*, Vol. 41, No. 2, p. 116.

interconnected through a set of debit and credit transactions."[6] The American Institute of Certified Public Accountants has stated in "The Accounting Profession—Where Is It Headed?" that "before economic data can be communicated, they must be measured. The whole process of measurement and communication constitutes the accounting function."

Under these definitions, it is through the accounting profession that the source data of economics are validated and investigation made possible. It is important to note that these definitions of accounting do not limit themselves to financial data nor to the results normally presented in financial statements. It is quite obvious that money "is the common denominator of our economy"[7] but the denominator only *represents* reality rather than constitutes actuality itself.

If the profession truly implements its own definition, it will have to take on added responsibility, for "the accountant might have to become more aware of the economic meaning and uses of accountancy than before and might have to assist in economic analysis and programming. The role of accountancy in the future might well extend itself to the whole economic sphere, and it is very conceivable that proper accounting information will greatly shape our economic thinking and policies."[8]

For example, Walter E. Heller, former chairman of the President's Council of Economic Advisors, stated in October 1965 that, while the economy is coming closer to full employment, there is still enough capacity and unemployment to justify a continuation of stimulation policies. At the same time, Arthur Burns, who held a similar position in earlier years, has remarked that the economy is already operating at or close to full employment, and he is concerned about "over-heating." What appears to be missing is an agreement on "capacity" and "full employment" and their levels. The accountant can and should supply and clarify the needed data.

The accountant should not attempt to resolve the varying interpretations of economic systems—the schools of "restraint" and "expansionism" can attend to that. But it is axiomatic that interpretations will have a better chance of being right if the underlying facts have a basic integrity and acceptance. If the facts are complete, one has some possibility of isolating causative factors and their consequences.

---

[6] A. J. H. Enthoven, "Economic Development and Accountancy," *Journal of Accountancy*, August 1965, pp. 32 and 35.

[7] R. Tyson, "The Common Denominator," *Financial Executive*, January 1964, p. 16.

[8] Enthoven, *loc. cit.*

PROVIDING ECONOMIC REALISM

Experience has demonstrated that economic information is more readily accepted when it is expressed in physical units. Because dollars are subject to inflation and because other nations use different currencies, the injection of monetary equivalents seems to limit acceptability. Although it does not seem reasonable to expect that money, the common denominator, will lose its place as the prime means of expressing diverse economic facts, there does appear to be a need for added data based on physical units.

There would be little real understanding of the economic situation if one was informed in monetary terms of the pay of an Egyptian peasant of the 1000 B.C. period, but when one is told that the peasant received "three breads and two jugs of beer each day" [9] one begins to have some appreciation of the wage scale. Similarly, if one knows that the English worker gets $1.10 per hour compared with an American's $2.40, one knows little about the true compensation until he knows what the money will buy. Even though *Fortune* magazine emphasizes sales dollar per employee, such data can have international validity only by environmental coincidence.

In the United States, a long series of basic economic units is published and analyzed according to industry and regional groupings established at the government level. Much of this data is presented in the "Survey of Current Business," published by the U.S. Department of Commerce. Another excellent tabulation of available data is printed by The National Industrial Conference Board in its "Economic Almanac." Good data is shown for units of energy consumed, population and work force, units of production, raw material produced and consumed, etc. Much of the commentary on the American economic scene is based on the data presented in these source books.

It is interesting to observe, also, that the specific data in the regular monthly publication of the "Survey" can be extrapolated into an over-all index of the expected economic future. For instance, having made certain subjective assumptions, an economist may "construct the expected gross national product for 1980 by multiplying the expected employment in that year of 94.9 million people working an average work week of 35.5 hours for 175.2 billion man-hours of work. Productivity is then assumed to grow at an annual rate of 2.75 per cent, thus raising the present GNP per man-hour from $4.65 to $6.98 in 1980. This results in a 4.1 per cent growth rate and a 1980 GNP of $1.2 trillion." [10]

[9] H. Jacobs, "Six Thousand Years of Bread," Doubleday, Doran and Company, 1955, p. 31.
[10] *Business Week*, Oct. 16, 1965.

The above illustration applies the factor of man-work input to derive an output estimate in terms of GNP. Other models using the same data can question the adequacy of metal supply, of housing, of energy units to maintain such an expectation. Applied on an industry or national level, the data can provide realism to what would otherwise be merely hopes and fears.

There has been for many years a great willingness to share the basic business data. As a rule, companies wish to keep silent on their cost of production figures, but there appears to be little reluctance to expose information on number of employees, units produced, floor space occupied, and similar facts. An investigator is more likely to be challenged by the amount of data rather than by its paucity.

Nevertheless, there is a "data gap" in the United States because the material published by individual companies and by trade associations cannot be readily integrated into national statistics. At the national level, the United States is well behind other nations in this respect. The first officially compiled input-output table in the United States covered the year 1947, but economic work along this line was largely discontinued until about 1962. Largely stimulated by the continuing work of Wassily Leontief of Harvard, "the most recent effort has brought the United States up to a level that France reached about fifteen years ago." [11] Obviously, the United States has the economic maturity to accumulate, to assemble, and to benefit from organized economic data, but it needs help in mounting a better program for validation, accumulation, and integration of the basic facts.

SOURCES OF ECONOMIC INFORMATION

As previously stated, the most authoritative source of economic publicity in the U.S. is the federal government. The Bureau of the Census has been publishing its economic census for about 150 years and adds daily to the amount of information which it makes available to the general public. Those who are interested can get "A Guide to Industrial Statistics" for a very small fee by writing to the Government Printing Office.

Customarily, the salient operating figures are supplied to the government by reports filed with various regulatory commissions (e.g. Securities and Exchange Commission, the Interstate Commerce Commission, the Federal Power Commission, Federal Communications Commission) and through such media as the "Annual Survey of Manufacturers" filed with the Bureau of the Census and the various labor reports filed with the

---

[11] W. Leontief, "Proposal for Better Business Forecasting," *Harvard Business Review*, Vol. 42, No. 6, p. 176.

Bureau of Labor Statistics. That portion of the data which deals with non-monetary facts is seldom validated, although it is subject to investigation and penalties can be assessed for capricious filing. The Survey of Current Business publishes monthly such data with some interpretation. Much of the same information is printed biennially in the "Statistical Abstract."

For many reasons, the socio-economic data accumulated by government bodies cannot satisfy the particular needs of private groups. As a consequence, trade and business associations accumulate their own specialized data, usually maintaining the confidential nature of each member's filing. Many of the more vital of these publications have become bulwarks of economic analysis. Thus, the Automotive Manufacturers Association publishes a detailed picture of car and truck distribution, the American Iron and Steel Institute comments on ferrous metals, the American Telephone and Telegraph Co. presents an analysis of world-wide telephone activity, the Engineering News Record discusses construction, and the Purchasing Agents of America provide a broad survey of purchase order backlog and activity.

In addition to the government and trade sources, the economic researcher can determine much about the environment from company annual reports, stock prospectuses and registration statements, court testimony, and the publicity releases of banks and industrial organizations. Supplementing these sources, economic information can be obtained by reference to business magazines, specialized newspapers, bank letters, and investment services.

Indeed, economic information is so readily available in America that the average businessman is conversant on a regular basis with trends affecting his economy. This does not guarantee, of course, that he truly understands the meanings and limitations of the data, but he does have an awareness of the influence and conditions which affect his economic life.

RECENT ECONOMIC PROGRAMS

During recent years there has been a stronger emphasis on economic approaches by American administrators. For instance, the wage-price productivity guideline received a great deal of publicity. Basically, the guideline attempted to regulate prices and wages without the imposition of mandatory controls. It expressed the economic truism that if increases in pay and benefits on the average do not exceed the nationwide upward trend of productivity (defined as output per man-hour), then employers' wage costs per unit of output would not rise and it should be possible to keep prices—and profits—steady. In essence, the guideline attempted to return continuously to labor a constant share of sales price at all times.

The program was subject to at least two weaknesses. First, it ignored the fact that if capital investment is added in relationship to a smaller increase in labor, then capital should get a greater share of price; this would work to the relative disadvantage of labor. Speagle and Chace state, ". . . wage increases will support a higher level of sales but not a higher level of earnings—except as a proportionate advance occurs in investment spending." [12] By failing to encourage capital investment, the program could lead toward economic stagnation.

Second, the calculation of the productivity relationship is difficult to provide with the present weapons in our statistical arsenal. "To comply with the guideline for *wages*, business would have to know the trend of increase in the over-all output of the nation per man-hour. To comply with the *price* factor would be infinitely harder because one would need to know the trend increase for productivity in his own industry and the extent to which this increase compares with the over-all productivity of the economy. Such information is not generally available nor is it readily usable." [13]

The administration in Washington also seems to be having problems with the guideline approach. The original guideline was computed on the basis of the 1960–1964 period and yielded a national index of 3.2 per cent. Inquiry into the statistical techniques revealed an error which, if corrected, would have resulted in a more proper calculation of 3.4 per cent. This, however, became unimportant when the 1961–1965 calculation yielded 3.6 per cent and the authorities chose to recommend a guideline of 3.2 per cent. Neither labor nor management was very pleased with this arbitrary approach to productivity guidelines. However, despite opposition, the technique was being sponsored as an approach to selective control, and some group should have been assigned the burden of clarifying its elements.

More recently the economic attention of the country was shifted to the balance of payments problem. The U.S. has watched its holding of gold drop from $23 billion in 1952 to $19.5 billion in 1965. The government's effort at control was officially designed as a "voluntary program," but the threat of future legislation made a myth out of the voluntary idea. The program aimed at shoring up the American balance of payments by inhibiting the investment of U.S. dollars in developed foreign areas while encouraging the speedy return of funds from abroad, including the repatriation of idle capital.

What is of interest to the accountant is the manner in which the control approach was expressed. The leaders of 900 of the largest Ameri-

[12] Speagle and Chace, *op. cit.*, p. 123.
[13] A. T. Burns, "Wages and Prices by Formula," *Harvard Business Review*, Vol. 43, No. 2, p. 60.

can firms were asked to construct "a ledger account" which would measure their firms' contributions to the balance of payments. The peculiarly accounting type of language in which the request was worded was implemented in a series of reports which were in turn the basis of discussions on financing problems. In connection with the more intense interest of the U.S. in this area, it has now begun to measure its payments situation in the same statistical manner used by other industrialized countries.

Another recent development at the federal level which has implications on the problem of accumulating economic data is the ASCII Program (American Standard Code for Information Interchange) of the Department of Commerce. This program is aimed at insuring the compatibility of the equipment being produced in the computer field. Once the appropriate interface of the processing units is insured, it can be assumed that government suppliers will be asked to submit data in a common mode. Since 20 per cent of the goods and services in the U.S. are linked to programs of the federal government, an important step is quietly being taken in making accessible a wide range of data.

DATA-ORIENTED PROFESSIONS

In the United States, economic data has traditionally been the province of the economist. For years the profession languished in government cubby holes and academic ivory towers, but more recently it has come forth into the market place of business and social policy. Traditionally, the economist has scorned the accountant as being only an historian. At the same time, he increasingly used the analytic method of the accountant in his problem solving. "The economist tends to be most useful to management in forecasting and in providing information and perspective on the principal external influences affecting the company's operations and profits." [14] He is often asked to handle the filing of accounting-like data with government agencies, to defend corporate policy in antitrust cases, to assist in price and wage determination, to interpret changes in the bank discount rate, and to set guidelines for early warning systems. "His job is that of interpretation of data rather than accumulation." [15]

The increased importance of the vast arrays of economic detail worries economists. Charles J. Hitch of the University of California says, "We really don't know much yet about projections and predictions. . . . Our analytical techniques are still quite crude, and improvements have

---

[14] W. Hoadley, "The Economist's Contribution to Management Planning," *Financial Executive*, December 1963, p. 26.
[15] "Economists in the Executive Suite," *Business Week*, February 13, 1965.

been marginal."[16] Despite this modesty, it is generally recognized that the economists have achieved their highest status since the days of John Maynard Keynes.

A new data-oriented profession is gradually evolving in the United States—the investment analyst. This professional may be employed by a bank or a credit institution, by a stock broker, or by any one of many companies interested in capital investment. In an increasingly vigorous way, this emerging group is attempting to go behind the publicity shield of business and government and to make factual determinations.

These determinations are seldom made for the purpose of improving operations. Rather, they are made in the light of taking investment advantage of a new awareness. The action which is supposed to develop is the better buying or selling of investments and such action necessarily requires economic data aimed at determining—or appearing to determine—value.

Although in some of the least sophisticated analyses, the investor is intrigued with relationships, such as the correlation of the GNP with the sale of soap, this is not to be taken as representative of the real work of the good analyst. A conscientious practitioner seeks out data from all sources, including government statistics and those garnered by personal visits to operating plants and laboratories. As a new profession, investment analysis requires exact data, and analysts would prefer presentations that yielded physical identification and industry-wide comparability.

The third profession which continuously deals with a variety of economic facts is the accounting profession. This profession emerged from obscurity in the post-Civil War era and came into high repute in the late 1920s. For the most part, the public practitioners have concerned themselves with certifying to financial statements, while the private practitioners have been involved in accumulating those financial reports and statements geared to the control of financial aspects of their companies.

It is quite true that the public accountant has customarily reviewed any economic data contained in the letter written by a company's president to accompany the financial statements. However, the review was intended only to determine that the facts mentioned therein were roughly coincident with the content of the financial statements. The review was never intended to stand as a certification nor has any attempt been made to require specific disclosure of any particular economic fact. Nevertheless, although not formalized, it has always been understood that the accounting certificate covered a professionally adequate inquiry into objective evidence.

The private accountant, on the other hand, has almost scrupulously

16 "The Slippery Path of Prosperity," Business Week, January 1, 1966.

avoided tabulating anything but dollars. He assigns units of space and capacity to the engineers; he passes personnel counts to the industrial relations people; he shares inventory data with the production control people. However, although he still does not accumulate these statistics, he has begun to use them more frequently in validating forecasts, measuring accomplishment, and reviewing plant and product performance. Where electronic data processing is widely employed, the accumulation of non-financial data tends to return to the accountant, for "a company's information system follows the same pattern as its accounting system."[17] "Today's financial function is more than ever the focal point for the facts that create correct decisions."[18]

In both public and private work, the accountant has tended to rely too greatly upon his monetarily expressed data. So great has been his emphasis that he now feels somewhat apologetic when he talks of economic realities rather than about the financial expression of such data. He must learn to take a more positive approach to basic economic data if he is going to match the challenge of the future years. Although "the postulates of accounting must . . . be based on the achievements of the science of business economics,"[19] there is a broad untouched field of endeavor waiting for appropriate cultivation.

LIMITATIONS OF THE CURRENT ACCOUNTING APPROACH

Financial executives are becoming the presidents of their companies with increasing frequency. The non-financial executives are becoming more and more skilled in the language and method of accounting usage. In addition, as already demonstrated, the government control programs are starting to employ accounting philosophies. These developments are indicative of the impact of the accounting faculty on modern activities. The contribution of the profession has already been significant, but it must now seek further opportunities to extend its area of service. I contend that this extension can lie in the area of identifying, on a more believable and comparable basis, certain basic economic facts of international importance.

Present accounting activity is limited by some of the traditional approaches taken to accounting data. These limitations have resulted in complaints which are worthy of consideration:

[17] M. Taylor, "Planning in a World-wide Business," *Harvard Business Review*, Vol. 43, No. 1, p. 132.
[18] W. Watts, "Management's View of the Financial Function," *Financial Executive*, May 1965, p. 30.
[19] I. Kleerekoper, "The Economic Approach to Accounting," *Journal of Accountancy*, March 1963, p. 39.

Accounting Information Is Not Realistic   This assertion is often made because the deferral and accrual procedure tends to alter the time of recognizing expense or income and to put it out of phase with the known time of occurrence.

Economic Use Is Obscured by Legalism   The complaint states that the same values employed under different legal circumstances yield different recordings of profit. Thus, if an owner works to accomplish a deal, the profit is different than if a corporate president does it. The devotion of an asset to manufacture yields a different cost if leased than it would if the asset were owned.

Accounting Usefulness Is Destroyed by Inflation   In countries where inflation is a strong influence, the normal price level goes out of phase with recorded accounting values. Under these conditions, many accounting procedures result in unbelievable and confusing indications of cost and worth.

Accounting Data Is Neither Timely nor Accessible   Accountants have been challenged with this complaint by corporate executives from the earliest of days. Now the government planners are asking for more immediate "recall" possibilities.

Accounting Reports Ignore Vital Factors   Formal accounting presentations have concerned themselves with the expression of special and non-operating items, but they have done nothing to reveal by requirement the productivity, wage cost, energy consumption, etc., which are basic factors of industrial activity.

Accounting Statements Do Not Provide for National Summary   The accounting profession has not established levels of minimum standardization. Thus, corporate reports often need restatement to fit into national summaries.

There are other objections which could be identified, but these are sufficient to indicate that there is room for significant professional improvement. In my opinion, the accounting profession has *chained itself* with limitations that have reduced its usefulness and lowered its stature.

STRENGTHENING THE ECONOMIC CONTRIBUTION OF ACCOUNTING

The Financial Executives Institute has stated that one of the finance man's duties (not often carried out) is "to continuously appraise economic and social forces, and government influences and to interpret their influence upon the business." This statement seems to indicate clearly an obligation to deal with more than monetary considerations. Further, since there is a growing interest and need for more information about economic facts and relationships, the accountant in government, public, and private branches of the profession must stir himself to meet the new requirement.

The following comments attempt to indicate a few of the things that can be done in meeting the new challenge:

Identification of Items   The accounting associations should be asked to join with selected government units to establish the specific new items that need identification in normal reporting. These could be—

1. Working hours paid for by each corporation and government unit.
2. Compensation (including fringe benefits) disbursed regardless of where charged.
3. Space occupied and, in manufacturing units, the machine-hours operated.
4. Production of first-use products, such as metals, fibers, leather, fish, grain, meat, lumber, petroleum.
5. Consumption of energy developed from coal, gas, oil, and electricity.
6. Production of basic building and machine capacity and the distribution thereof by industry.
7. Production of major consumer items, such as cars, TVs, radios, washing machines, etc.

Some of this identification has already been made for government reporting; other parts would need professional consideration. Obviously, the list could be extended, but it is suggested that a small immediate beginning will be of more use than a complete work on a delayed basis.

Validation of the Reported Quantities   The certification procedures of the accounting profession have resulted in a high standard of credibility for financial reports. (In general, it is their usefulness rather than their integrity which is attacked.) The application of similar approaches to basic economic data would validate the national figures to a large extent and it would make individual reports more meaningful to the users.

Herman Bevis refers to this validation as the accountant's "attest function." [20] To a large extent, it is already being carried out as the means of verifying the propriety of financial data. Certain new judgmental decisions would have to be made in providing expanded economic

[20] H. Bevis, "The CPA's Attest Function in Modern Society," *Journal of Accountancy*, February 1962, p. 28.

data but, in my opinion, these can quite properly be entrusted to professionals specializing in objective reporting.

Expanded Reporting of Economic Data   Assuming that adequate identification and validation can be provided for basic statistical data, the information should be published as a regular adjunct of the financial reports. The opinion of the public accountant should cover such information, although the profession may wish to work out some specialized phraseology.

Data-Bank Availability of Reported Data   In addition to the annual presentation of the material to the general public, the selected data would be filed monthly with an appropriate government agency. This agency would maintain a data bank which would integrate with computer-oriented information systems in business and government. The stored information, including information about competitors, would be made available to government and industrial researchers.

It is worth noting that in the U.S. there is an installed business computer network valued at $7.5 billion, with $1.5 billion having been added in 1965, according to estimates of the Business Equipment Manufacturers Association. The federal government expects to spend over $29.8 million in 1967 on labor statistical programs.[21]

Periodic Interpretation of Accumulated Data   At regular intervals the federal government would issue interpretations of the data on file. Such interpretation would be performed by economists based on integrated and validated data.

"By facing the realities of supply-demand conditions courageously and objectively, with an informed program of economic intelligence to aid in measuring and interpreting these conditions, management can improve its performance."[22]

The above program will be challenged on several points, not the least of which will concern the question of payment. If public accountants are to assume more responsibility, will the client pay? The answer is obviously that the commercial client will increase his costs only when required to furnish the data by government ruling. Fortunately, the cost will not be overwhelming. Insofar as government accounts are concerned, there is even a possibility that considerable amounts of money will be saved by a more systematic accumulation of computer-oriented data.

There will, of course, be a reluctance to provide more information

---

[21] *The Wall Street Journal*, February 1, 1966, p. 1.

[22] R. Schultz, "Profits, Prices and Excess Capacity," *Harvard Business Review*, Vol. 41, No. 4, p. 81.

to the government. But, as Herman Bevis has said, "When it is governmental policy to allow economic forces to interplay with little intervention, the flow of economic data to the government may be rather small; the more such policy is to participate in or attempt to regulate the economic forces, the more thorough must be the economic data supplied to it."[23]

The items to be reported upon will furnish much grist for professional discussion mills. The important point to remember is that a basic recommendation for economic reporting beyond the financial statements is being suggested. In an era when the U.S. has minimized unemployment and when capacity (imperfectly measured) is said to be running at a 90 per cent level, these matters are of particular current significance. As other data increase in significance or availability, they could be added to the reporting requirements. In any event, the items are only illustrative of the basic thesis that economic data need more authoritative reporting.

PROVINCE FOR ACCOUNTING PROGRESS

The eventual goal of all professional action must be the achievement of an improved society. The effective allocation of resources, the transference of skills, the avoidance of gluts and excesses, and the maximization of industrial profit and international cooperation—all demand an improved awareness of economic fact. Such information is essential to reasonable and intelligent action; thus, the accounting and economic professions must extend their present programs to encompass economic data in a more formal way.

The improved allocation of the world's resources and the strengthening of man's ability to cope with his future should be sufficient incentive to stimulate a more active professional program. However, it must be noted that, if the profession does not rise to the challenge, the governments of the world are likely to take independent action of a regulatory nature. Economic information has international significance; it is real; it is comparable. Its accumulation, validation, and reporting are properly the province of the accounting profession. Success in a program of presenting quantitative economic information will constitute a new facet of accounting progress.

[23] H. Bevis, "The Accounting Function in Economic Progress," *Journal of Accountancy*, August 1958, p. 30.

22. Social Accounting—
An Opportunity for Service*

Leonard M. Savoie**

The accounting profession faces a fascinating opportunity to serve the public by developing new and different techniques for measuring the output of social programs. There is already a need for this kind of measurement, which might be termed "social accounting," and the need is bound to grow in the future, as vast sums of money will be dedicated to programs for social improvement.

Broad social programs require the use of funds which are easily measurable in terms of dollars, but they result in attainments which are intangible and cannot be measured in monetary terms. Nevertheless, CPAs are professionals in the development and analysis of data and are well qualified to seek solutions to the measurement of social intangibles. If we wish to become involved in the measurement and interpretation of the benefits of more healthful living, maintenance of recreational space, more beautiful cities, improved education and culture and the like, we will have to move fast. The field has already been identified with others; for example, *The New York Times* has assigned this concern for social and esthetic scarcities to a new discipline of social economics. Unless it is pursued now, our profession may in the future be foreclosed from assuming this broader role in society.

The theme of social accounting and its significance in the society of the future was developed in the various speeches made at the annual meeting of the American Institute in Portland and was emphasized in the final plenary session entitled, "What Can We Expect?" A departure from more traditional technical programs, this session examined the future in terms of areas other than accounting. Dr. Simon Ramo, vice chairman of the Board and chairman of the Policy Committee of TRW, Inc., spoke on prospects in science and Joseph M. Goldsen, head of the Social Science Department of the Rand Corporation, spoke on prospects in social development.

---

* Reprinted from *The CPA*, November 1967; copyrighted 1967 by the American Institute of CPAs, page 3.
** Leonard M. Savoie is Executive Vice-president of the American Institute of CPAs.

A common thread emerging from this and other sessions of the annual meeting was that we are moving ahead so rapidly in science that technological achievements are far outrunning sociological developments. As our society becomes more complex and more capable of technical achievements, we must make choices between broad sweeping alternatives for social benefits, for it is unlikely that economic resources will ever be sufficient to accomplish all desired social programs. The direction of our resources into such major areas as air and water pollution, rebuilding of cities, transportation, retraining of people, requires decisions that can be made only through some degree of central planning and control.

The additional centralization of control of sociological developments would appear to be only the continuation of a trend which has been developing. Inevitably, centralized planning will have a limiting effect on individual freedom of action. While improved technology will provide room for individual choice as to material production, central planning will lessen the ability of the individual to influence the way in which we employ our resources for sound development. In fact, the market place will assume less importance in this major role.

This does not mean that we are coming to the end of the private enterprise system. Far from it. It implies instead that now is the time for private enterprise to establish clearer liaison with the public sector for influencing social decisions. It was Mr. Goldsen who in his address suggested—I believe for the first time publicly—that private enterprise should organize an interdisciplinary Committee for Social Development to operate in the area of social decisions in a manner parallel to the way the privately constituted Committee for Economic Development does in the area of economic problems. More specifically, Mr. Goldsen gave a direct challenge to the American Institute to form its own Committee on Social Development to work in the field of social planning.

This suggestion should be explored carefully, for a committee like this from the private sector could perform a very great public service and help assure the preservation of private enterprise in the transition to a more centrally controlled society. The CPA in this kind of development could assume a position of great importance.

23. The Horizons of Accounting*

Editorial

The horizons of accounting are expanding at a rate which is, at least in some areas, breathtaking.

If there is one thing sure about the profession, it is that the spheres of influence and effectiveness of accountants one or two decades from now will be vastly greater than they are today.

Cost accounting, which began in what now seems a rather fumbling way only a few decades ago, has flowered into an effective instrument guiding basic management decisions. Operations research, return-on-investment analysis, PERT, are only three of several important new techniques of management information and control which have a close relationship to accounting.

Another potential which may startle many accountants is proposed by Adolf A. Berle in a book just published, *The American Economic Republic*. He explains it this way (pp. 32 ff.):

I here suggest that there is no way of knowing whether any enterprise in the United States, taken by itself, makes or loses money, and that the utility or nonutility of the goods or services it produces or provides is not necessarily the factor determining the profit. I believe that the profit-and-loss statements made up at the end of the year really reflect whether the enterprise holds a favored or an unfortunate niche in the whole aggregate.

I suggest that "cost" of the operation reflects, not its real cost, but only the cost paid directly by the enterprise. All around it are services provided to it for which it does not have to pay, or, if it does, for which it pays either more or less than the full cost. The plants are located in these and these communities; to them, they pay property taxes. They may pay more than their fair share or less. They employ a community of laborers. These must be permanently available. When the plant shuts down, their savings and the Social Security allowances support those laborers and keep them available until conditions permit the plant to start up again. Part of the cost of the whole operation is then borne by the Federal Government, or by the community, or by the individuals, or

* Reprinted from *The Journal of Accountancy*, June 1963, pages 28–29; copyrighted 1963 by the American Institute of CPAs.

by all three together. The opening of a new thruway or the erection of a plant which buys their goods—neither having been brought to pass by the management—increases their market and their take, therefore their "profit." . . .

Some day we shall have true "social cost accounting," which will show not merely what it cost a producer to produce—that is, what he paid out—but also what it cost society to produce. The technique of social cost accounting has yet to be invented.

Many will disagree at least in part with Mr. Berle's analysis of the present situation, and many will object to his proposal for "social cost accounting" as having possible implications unfriendly to private enterprise. It can scarcely be denied, however, that in our present world there are costs to society—services provided at the expense of taxpayers— involved in the operations of every kind of enterprise. Sooner or later some accountant (or some economist with an understanding of accounting) will develop the techniques for figuring them out.

Whether this is "good" or "bad," or what will be done with the knowledge when it becomes available, is probably already beside the point. Once such questions are raised—and Mr. Berle has merely given explicit form to questions which have long troubled many people— somebody is going to look for and find the answers.

The applications of accounting have expanded so rapidly in recent years that accountants themselves scarcely realize what has happened. It is no accident that just in the last decade professional accountants and men with accounting training have moved into key positions in industry and government which few accountants would have dreamed of a quarter century ago.

And it seems more than probable that the most optimistic predictions anyone would dare make today about future opportunities in and applications of accounting will be exceeded by the event.

Accounting is indeed a very young profession. The "social accounting" suggested by Mr. Berle is only one of many areas in which business and government will look to accountants for more and better information about the financial facts of life. The most serious mistake members of the accounting profession could make would be to underestimate their future possibilities—or the increased education and varieties of technical ability which will be required to take advantage of them.

24. The Nature of the Financial Accounting Process*

George O. May**

Accounting has been defined by a committee of the American Institute of Accountants as "the art of recording, classifying and summarizing, in a significant manner and in terms of money, transactions and events which are, in part at least, of a financial character, and interpreting the results thereof." It is an art, not a science, but an art of wide and varied usefulness. The purely recording function of accounting, though indispensable, concerns only technicians. Its analytical and interpretive functions are of two kinds. One type of analysis is intended to afford aid to management in the conduct of business and is of interest mainly to executives. The other type leads to the presentation of statements relating to the financial position and results of operations of a business for the guidance of directors, stockholders, credit grantors, and others. This process of financial accounting, therefore, possesses a wide importance for persons who are neither accountants nor executives.

Many accountants are reluctant to admit that accounting is based on nothing of a higher order of sanctity than conventions. However, it is apparent that this is necessarily true of accounting as it is, for instance, of business law. In these fields there are no principles, in the fundamental sense of that word, on which we can build; and the distinctions among laws, rules, standards, and conventions lie not in their nature but in the kind of sanctions by which they are enforced. Accounting procedures have in the main been the result of common agreement among accountants, although they have to some extent, and particularly in recent years, been influenced by laws or regulations.

Conventions, to have authority, must be well conceived. Accounting conventions should be well conceived in relation to at least three things: first, the uses of accounts; second, the social and economic concepts of the time and place; and, third, the modes of thought of the people. It follows that as economic and social concepts or modes of thought change, accounting concepts may have to change with them.

The first point for consideration is, therefore, the major uses of financial statements. We can recognize at least ten distinguishable uses:

* Reprinted from *The Accounting Review*, July 1943, pages 189–193.
** George O. May (deceased) was Senior Partner of Price Waterhouse & Co.

1. As a report of stewardship
2. As a basis for fiscal policy
3. As a criterion of the legality of dividends
4. As a guide to wise dividend action
5. As a basis for the granting of credit
6. As information for prospective investors in an enterprise
7. As a guide to the value of investments already made
8. As an aid to government supervision
9. As a basis for price or rate regulation
10. As a basis for taxation

General-purpose statements are not suitable in all of these cases; in some instances, special-purpose statements are called for. This has become increasingly recognized in respect of rate or price control and taxation, and it should also be recognized, for reasons which I shall indicate later, in respect of information for new investors—or, in other words, for the prospectus—and also in some cases for the determination of the legality of a dividend. But even if these purposes are eliminated, there remain at least six which are expected to be served by general-purpose statements.

It is immediately apparent that any general-purpose statements cannot be expected to serve all the purposes equally well—indeed, if they are to be appropriate for the major uses, it is likely that they will not serve some other purposes even reasonably well. It becomes necessary, therefore, to consider which are to be regarded as the controlling objectives, and to view the possibility of changes therein.

Accounting conventions must take cognizance of the social and economic concepts of the time and place. Conventions which are acceptable in a pioneer, free-enterprise economy may not be equally appropriate in a more mature, free-enterprise economy, and may lose their validity entirely in a controlled economy. Some existing accounting conventions seem to assume implicitly the existence of *laissez faire* and may require reconsideration as prices, interest rates, and other vital elements become the subject of conscious government control. Under this head must be considered, also, the forms of business organization and changes either in the nature of the dominant type or types or in the laws governing them. Systems of taxation and legal decisions growing out of them also influence accounting concepts.

The third and last consideration which has been mentioned as affecting accounting conventions is the modes of thought of the people. The extent and the nature of legal influence in business affairs will affect the conventions; those developed in the atmosphere of the common law will differ from those evolved under a civil code system. So, too, a people thinking in terms of capital value and a people thinking in terms of annual value will naturally reach different conclusions on some points, as is evidenced by the American and British attitudes towards capital gains and losses in taxation and accounting.

The relevance and importance of such considerations as these have been borne in on me by the events of the forty-five years of my experience in American accounting. Within this time we have moved from what might be called the last days of a pioneer, free-enterprise economy to a period in which a large and growing segment of enterprise is under a substantial measure of government control. The major part of the development of the corporation as the typical form of business organization has occurred within the same period; there has been a marked movement toward the separation of beneficial ownership from management.

Beginning with the control over railroad accounting given to the Interstate Commerce Commission in 1907, we have seen a steady growth of accounting by prescription, and a shift from the common-law mode of thought towards that of the civil code.

The laxness of our corporation laws and the ease of reincorporation have impaired the significance of the corporation as an accounting unit. The extension of intercorporate holdings has increased the importance of accounting for interest, dividends, and other forms of transferred income; manifestly, such accounting involves different problems from those encountered in dealing with primary income, such as that from manufacturing. The creation of a wide variety of forms of capital obligations has raised questions as to the accounting significance of legal distinctions, often highly artificial, between bonds and stocks and between interest and dividends.

Perhaps the most significant change of all is the shift of emphasis from the balance sheet to the income statement, and particularly to the income statement as a guide to earning capacity rather than as an indication of accretions to disposable income.

It is appropriate, next, to consider what alternative approaches to the problem of formulating or revising the conventions of financial accounting are open to us. First of all, there is a choice between the value and the cost approach, or perhaps rather a question as to how the two can best be combined. This combination is illustrated in the custom of carrying inventories at cost or market value, whichever is lower—one of the oldest of accounting practices.

There is a choice between different concepts of income and between different theories of allocation of income to periods. We have the concept according to which income arises gradually, and the concept which treats income as arising at a moment when realization is deemed to have occurred. Here again, both concepts in practice are adopted to some, but not to an unchanging, extent. Today, the interesting question is presented whether accounting is likely to move in the direction of a more complete adherence to the realization concept of income or towards wider application of the doctrine of gradual accrual.

There is also a choice between the enterprise as the accounting unit and the legal entity that carries on the enterprise as the accounting unit. The system of consolidated accounts, freely employed in corporate reporting, is a departure from the strict separate-entity theory. In recent years, the adoption by public service commissions of the concept of cost to the first person who devoted property to the public service, as the basis of property accounting of the present owners, has created a new interest in enterprise accounting, of which it is a crude and inadequate variant, and along with it a new series of problems.

The range of possible choice of conventions might be extended if some postulates, commonly adopted, were discarded. It is, for instance, generally assumed that financial statements must be in a continuous, related series, but it may be argued that there is no absolute compulsion that they should be. The problem of continuity presents difficulties when a substantial change of conventions occurs—as, for instance, when public utility corporations are required for financial accounting purposes (and not merely for rate purposes) to account for property on the basis of the cost to the first purchaser who devoted the property to public service, instead of on the traditional basis of cost to themselves; or when straight-line depreciation accounting is substituted for other methods of dealing with property consumption which have been employed and sanctioned for decades.

Again, the monetary unit is generally assumed to be substantially constant in value, but at times this assumption of stability has to be abandoned, with the result that accounting conventions have to be modified.

The choice of conventions in financial accounting, as in cost accounting, is to some extent affected by the conflict among considerations of speed, accuracy, and expense. The accountant is called upon to produce general-purpose statements within a few weeks of the completion of the fiscal period to which they relate. These reports are expected to be final and to serve a great diversity of purposes. Delay in preparation might permit of greater refinement but might impair the usefulness of the statements; hence conventions must be such as to be capable of prompt application.

In a pioneer economy, the great opportunity for making profits is likely to lie in participating in the growth of the country and in the accompanying increase of values. At such a time capital will be relatively scarce, whereas labor—particularly if there is free immigration—may be plentiful. These causes will contribute to make capital investment relatively small; and the proportion of assets that are readily salable, and may be expected to be realized in a short time, will be comparatively high. In such circumstances, the value approach to accounting has a strong appeal. In reading American accounting literature, it is surprising to find how generally accounting has been described as a process of valuation, how this view has been maintained down to a rather recent date, and how pronounced and rapid the change of view has been. In a more mature economy, when greater capital resources, and, perhaps, changes in labor conditions also, tend to produce constantly increasing capital investment, business units become larger and enterprises more complex. Then the valuation approach becomes impracticable and resort to cost as the primary line of approach becomes almost inevitable.

The change from a value basis to a cost basis is of great importance in relation to such questions as the rate base and the "surplus assets" theory of limitation of dividends. It is undeniable, though not fully recognized outside the profession, that books of large enterprises are kept predominantly on a cost basis and do not, therefore, constitute evidence of the value of either the enterprise as a whole or of the separate assets thereof, particularly the capital assets. This might be deemed to be a serious defect of accounting procedures except for two considerations— first, that the value of the enterprise is seldom a material fact for consideration; and, second, that when it is, it can be measured only by looking ahead. For this purpose, the sole relevance of accounts of the past is as a means of throwing light on the prospects for the future. These considerations have additional force if the implicit assumption that the monetary unit remains stable is widely at variance with reality— as, for instance, in the case of property acquired before a substantial decline in the purchasing power of the monetary unit such as occurred between 1913 and 1920.

Forty-five years ago the external influence acting on accounting with the greatest effect was that of the credit grantor. In recent years there has been a marked shift of emphasis, and the use of accounting statements as a guide in the purchase or sale of securities has been more heavily stressed as a result of the efforts to impart liquidity to investments in long-term enterprises. In the early days, conservatism was the cardinal virtue of accounting; now, the virtue of conservatism is questioned, and the greater emphasis is on consistency. At that time, also, uniform classifications that were binding on particular forms of enterprises were practically unknown. Today, they are numerous and increasing in number and scope.

In this article the only objects have been to bring out the true nature of the accounting process and to advance the thought that accounting conventions are not something fixed and unalterable, but something that, like the law, should have elements of stability and of flexibility. Times are changing and accounting conventions will change with them. Today, a study of the historical development of accounting conventions and of the causes which have brought about change may be more useful than a description of present practice. It has frequently been said that the changes revealed by successive balance sheets are more significant than the individual balance sheets themselves. The same may be true of the conventions upon which balance sheets are based.

25. SEC Plan for Detailed Financial Data of Conglomerates Disputed by Accountants*

The top rule-making body of the accounting profession said it is "very much concerned" about proposals to require more-detailed financial reports from conglomerates and other diversified corporations.

The Accounting Principles Board of the American Institute of Certified Public Accountants endorsed the objective of full and fair disclosure of sales and earnings by diversified companies. But it took issue with recent proposals on this subject by the Securities and Exchange Commission. The proposals, said the board in a letter to the commission, involve "many difficult accounting problems."

Although it didn't make specific recommendations, the board indicated it would like the SEC to delay any new rules until it can complete a study under way. This analysis, said the board, "should provide a sound basis for making a definitive pronouncement on the need for, and extent of, disclosure of supplemental financial information by diversified companies."

Another blue-ribbon group, the Financial Executives Institute, criticized the SEC proposals last month and urged businessmen to communicate their views on the matter to the commission. The institute, which is made up of corporate financial executives, objected that the proposals could give competitors and customers financial information about a corporation that could be harmful to its shareholders.

PROPOSALS OF SEC

The SEC in September proposed to amend securities registration forms to require a separate breakdown for those products or services that,

* Reprinted from *The Wall Street Journal*, November 4, 1968.

during the two previous years, represented at least 10% of total sales or net income before taxes. The SEC also would require companies registering securities to report "the approximate amount of assets employed in each segment of the business." And the forms would require diversified companies to report "comparable data on revenues and earnings received from foreign sources and from government or any single customer."

The SEC has the power to require more detailed reporting in registration statements, but it issued its amendments in the form of proposals to allow time for industry comment. The registration statements the amendments would affect are those distributed in connection with the sale of new securities issues.

For several years, the SEC and some private groups, including security analysts, have urged more-detailed breakdowns of corporate results. In recent months, the pressure for such reporting has intensified in response to the wave of conglomerate mergers, which has created large corporations with highly diverse operations. At present these corporations mostly report only overall sales and earnings, although the Financial Executives Institute has found a growing number that do give shareholders a rough breakdown of results from various divisions.

VIEWS OF ANALYSTS, ACCOUNTANTS

Analyst groups argue that shareholders need detailed breakdowns of sales and earnings in order to measure a company's progress and prospects. But the subject is controversial because many companies fear they would be telling too much to their competitors. And accountants argue that requirements for detailed reporting would force them into unrealistic or arbitrary allocations of overhead expenses, not directly attributable to a particular product line.

In commenting on specific SEC proposals, the Accounting Principles Board said, "The requirement to report assets by segments creates problems of sufficient magnitude for the board to question its soundness." It noted, "In the diversified company, the various segments may have been acquired at various times and in different circumstances. As a result, the book values, even if allocated by segments, would not necessarily provide investors a sound basis for evaluating profitability of investment or efficiency of management's use of resources."

The board also took strong issue with the proposal to require sales and earnings reports from foreign sources. It said the requirement would present "definitional problems as to what constitutes outside operations, sharing with U.S. operations of costs such as research and development, and differing tax treatments among countries."

The board also questioned the 10% rule on reporting sales and earnings of a corporation's segments. It urged that the test be 15%.

26. Managerial Accounting: A Frame of Reference*

Willis J. Dombrovske**

In our increasingly complex and competitive business environment, management has an ever mounting need for pertinent information. As our business environment has grown, the rising manager has found it increasingly difficult to accumulate the necessary personal experience so needed to manage effectively. No longer can he expect to gather all of his own first-hand knowledge of situations within his firm or even to rely upon his intuition to evaluate the complex factors which affect the great majority of our business decisions.

First hand inspection of the organization is most desirable for every level of management and imperative for the operating executive. Every manager should strive to accomplish as much of it as is humanly possible. It is as Ford Bell expressed in his excellent series of memos to a rising executive, "feeling the pulse of the organization."[1] The manager's first-hand observations coupled with the factual and analytical data provided by others, serve him as a dual resource in his planning and decision making function.

Modern management is placing more and more reliance on information which is developed by others, both within and without the company. To be useful to the manager, this data must be assembled quickly and transmitted to him by means of a highly efficient information system.

This information flow is imperative for the successful manager in the performance of the basic tasks in the management cycle:

1. The establishment of his firm's objectives.
2. Formulation of plans to reach the desired objectives.
3. The implementation of these plans.
4. The appraisal of the performance of the organization in carrying out these plans.

* Reprinted from *Management Accounting* (formerly *NAA Bulletin*), August 1965, pages 46–50.
** Willis J. Dombrovske is Treasurer and Controller of the Transistor Electronics Corporation.
[1] Ford Bell, *You're in Charge*, Doubleday & Company, Inc., New York, 1964, p. 4.

5. The feeding back of revised (corrective) action and additional plans.

The information needed to accomplish this method of managing has its own requirements. First, it must contain the "right" data—necessary for effective performance of each function of the management process at all of its various levels. Second, it must be completely accurate and pertinent to the action at hand. Third, the data must be presented in a form that is clearly understandable to the person responsible for acting on it. Fourth, the information must be provided to the persons whose actions can be improved by it. Fifth, it must be received in time to influence the action which it is supposed to assist.

These considerations that lead to what Lawrence Appley describes as the "Management Factor." [2] This factor is the "something" a manager does to produce results different from those to be expected if events are left to follow their own course.

When a manager "does something about it" a planned change is in the offing. Nor does the manager stop here. Projecting past results into the future does not in itself ensure their attainment. The manager, referred to here as the managerial accountant, must possess a sensitivity to his own power to influence people and events. He must follow a process such as the following:

1. Identity of the *need* for change.
2. Develop an idea, and alternatives, that will *fill the need.*
3. *Transmit* the need and idea to the minds of others.
4. Determine the best *program* to activate the idea.
5. *Test* the economics of his program.
6. Aid in the *selection* of the individual or group qualified to carry out this idea.
7. *Follow* the program to conclusion with instruction and corrective action.
8. *Report* on the results.

The connotation for the accountant becomes increasingly apparent. The accountant today bears the tremendous responsibility of gathering data, placing them in meaningful format, interpreting them and quickly transmitting the information to the appropriate management level.

BASIC OBJECTIVES OF THE ACCOUNTING SYSTEM

In the consideration of his changing role in the management function of a company the accountant will do well to seriously concern himself with the basic objectives of his accounting system. The classification

---

[2] Lawrence P. Appley, *The Management Evolution,* American Management Association, New York, 1963, p. 36.

which follows will serve to focus one's attention on the various objectives of the accounting system. It will likewise aid in distinguishing among decisions as to what plans the business should adopt, the measurement of detailed performance against these plans, and the overall financial results of the performance.[3]

Custodial Accounting The financial accounting for the assets entrusted to the company. The basic concern here is with the preparation of the reports for groups or individuals outside of the management group: stockholders, creditors, the regulatory commissions, or the government.

Performance Accounting The quantitative matching of performance against some plan by organizational responsibility. It includes all those accounting procedures and reports which exist in order to evaluate organizational performance. Likewise, it includes the functions referred to as responsibility accounting, i.e. the collection of costs by organizational responsibility. It also deals, however, with quantitative data other than costs. It may include such items as product line revenue, physical work-load statistics, and internal net income reports. It implies the use of standards and budgets. The distinguishing characteristic here is the measurement of *actual* performance against *planned* performance by responsibility.

Decision Accounting The quantitative evaluation of alternative courses of action. This includes all the disciplined techniques for providing quantitative information in the form which can best assist a *specific* management decision at the time when the decision must be made. This area includes such things as profit planning, product pricing, make-or-buy decisions, inventory policies and the choice of alternative production methods. This is the area of accounting on which business has historically depended for special analyses and memorandum reports.

We shall refer to performance and decision accounting under the classification of *managerial accounting* and to custodial accounting as *financial accounting*. These classifications are not unrelated. The accounting structure which is established to carry out the custodial objectives will handle most of the data used in the decision-making process as well as measuring performance. The raw data on operations (cost and revenue) is recast to evaluate performance. Variance from objectives or budgets is one such example. This data is in turn rearranged to provide for decisional accounting requirements. An analysis of product profitability would involve this type of special data arrangement.

[3] Robert Beyer, *Profitability Accounting for Planning and Control*, The Ronald Press Company, New York, 1963, p. 17.

The development of accounting structures toward this objective of providing a firm's management with the highest order of quantitative information is a further advancement in the art of accounting. The accountant who can anticipate the reporting and interpreting structure tailored to his firm's need becomes a functioning participant in management rather than a producer of statistics. Further, he takes the valuable data of custodial accounting a step beyond the formal financial accounting area into the future. This step moves him from recording to forecasting. Within the realm of financial accounting the future cannot be quantified. On the positive side of this comment is the fact that the value of financial reporting is increased to those parties outside of the firm. Moreover, the precision with which financial accounting is executed provides management with the sound basis that it must have for progress.

THE NECESSITY FOR MANAGERIAL ACCOUNTING

Managerial accounting is the expansion of the accounting structure to meet the needs of management at all levels. As one progresses through these levels of management, the use of data goes further and further into the future. Consider, for example, the needs of a departmental manager, a division manager, a general manager, the president and the board of directors. The objectives may move from the short term of one week for the department manager to the long term of a five-year projection for the directors.

The managerial accountant must develop the ability to design his accounting structure so that it will produce tailored information for these levels of managerial need. The structure must provide for data that will become the basis for decision making at each level. As the level of managerial responsibility rises, economics enters with increasing impact on the data presented by the managerial accountant; this is an important consideration for him to recognize and respect. He is now well beyond the facts of purely financial accounting and into the area of projection. This is the area where the corporate manager finds himself and one in which he needs the soundest counseling he can obtain. The management accountant, with his access to the final resting place of the firm's operations expressed in monetary terms, is the logical choice to provide this counseling.

He must have at his disposal an accounting structure which is capable of providing data to meet these needs. The structure, if it is to assist, must be conceived with its function clearly defined by the managerial accountant.

The structure of this accounting system will consist of two clearly distinguishable characteristics:

1. The system must have a sound basis in accounting precision providing for reporting on a consistent basis. Supporting evidence for forecasting and projections will be well documented.
2. The management accountant designing the structure must be well versed in the .objectives of the system. The outstanding trait here must be deep understanding of business generally and of his firm's business specifically. An analytical mind working from a solid foundation of accounting is necessary to develop a structure of managerial accounting.

THE FRAME OF REFERENCE

The managerial accountant must develop a frame of reference quite in contrast to that used by the financial accountant. Consider the following data characteristics to witness what is required by managerial accounting and what is provided by financial accounting.

Description   Financial accounting is primarily concerned with the dollar consequence of operations. However, the managerial accountant is quick to recognize that not all economic events are readily convertible into the dollar terms. Consider the changes in economic values and equities. Appreciation in value of property for example may have great significance where management is contemplating a sale. Lacking some required qualifications or conversion, these data do not become processed in financial records. This distinction may be recognized profitably in classifying decisional premises as segregated from those considerations that are fixed in business events reflecting the dollar consequences of those events.

The Consideration of Time   The financial accountant is concerned with past happenings; the reporting of where the business has been and is in time. The managerial accountant has a view of the future. Historical events are useful only in retrospect. The future however is the object of managerial effort. Business decisions are forward looking; they are made to influence the future. It is the future not the past that challenges a forward looking management team. An accounting for the future demands a break-away from historical (financial) accounting characteristics —an adaptation of many available considerations to the *specific* requirements of each issue encountered. Managerial accounting here requires skill in recognizing appropriate data to apply and facility in manipulating the information to produce the needed conclusion.

The Concept of Realization   Financial accounting has its focus on actual events. Managerial accounting requires focus on potential, on opportunities. Where resources are in scarce supply their commitment to one course of action instead of others precludes the advantages that could have accrued from some other choice. These lost benefits are just as real and significant a cost as actual expenditures. The managerial accountant in this instance will take the position that it may be just as important and possibly more so to know what the organization is not doing as compared to what it is actually doing. The significance here is one of distinction— between those events rooted in accomplished fact and those which are, or were, mere possibility.

The Quantitative Unit   Monetary values are provided by financial accounting, whereas statistical data is the requirement from managerial accounting in this category. The latter is not as restricted to the double-entry system as financial accounting and hence relies on statistical evidence very frequently. Forecasting makes free use of statistics, and while monetary units may result, there is no dominance of dollar information found in financial accounting.

Rigidity of Format   The operating statements and supporting schedules of financial accounting all present great masses of data in an aggregate format. The proper choice of the titles contained in the ledger, as well as the chart of accounts, all commit one to a rigid format. These items may or may not be homogeneous. Managerial accounting often concentrates on details. A specific problem is the focal point. The data used in these circumstances is pertinent to the problem with other elements outside of the parameters of consideration. These elements may provide reference points for evaluation, but the emphasis is on specific data related directly to the issue under study.

The Concept of Reality   Those events in a business which have not yet reached the stage of completion and which will not permit reasonable identification of their consequences do not normally become a part of the financial accounting statements. Financial accounting is objective in nature while managerial accounting is subjective. Managerial decisions rely heavily upon subjective evidence. The matter of judgment as opposed to measurement is a characteristic of management.

CONCLUSION

The intent of this paper has been to demonstrate the relationship of financial and managerial accounting to the realm of decisional premises used by management. It has sought to point out the differences between the areas and the consequent limitations of each of them.

It is not intended or suggested that attempts be made in including data regarding future events within the framework of traditional financial accounting. A loss of objectivity would certainly result. The demonstrable accuracy so highly sought would likewise suffer. The usefulness of managerial accounting is in recognizing the needs of management beyond the formal statements.

The employment of accounting skills and accuracy by participating in the decision making and planning processes is the role of the managerial accountant. The shaping of the future, of planning for change—these are the marks of the managerial accountant. His final products are analysis, projection and conclusion. His tools are the observed data, statistical measurement, mathematical treatment, non-numerical evaluation and deduction. He combines these factors with a personality that is forward seeking for both himself and his company. His confidence will be well fortified by a deep understanding of his chosen field of endeavor, that of accountancy, and by a firm grasp of total management responsibility.

To perceive and meet this challenge requires one's concentration and fortitude over the span of a career. Constant alertness to self-improvement and advanced learning must be maintained. Never before in our economy has opportunity for the accountant been more widely demonstrated than at the present. Our educational institutions offer vastly improved formal preparation over that available to our predecessors. With a challenge so apparent, with the means to achieve it so much within grasp, we submit accounting will take on an even greater stature in the conduct of business.

27. The Management Role of Shell Accountants*

The role of Shell Accountants has changed, with the Controller's Organization providing interpretation of results from the basic operating unit all the way up through to the Executive Group. Improvement in controls, in measurement of earnings and costs of operations, and in analytical tools all go together to aid in making important decisions aimed at higher profit.

This expanded role of the Accountant has developed with reorganization of the Company's financial and data processing functions. With

* Reprinted from *A Current Look At Shell*, Fall 1968.

the help of advanced EDP accounting systems, accountants are spending less time recording data, and are able to devote more effort to interpreting and reporting findings to management.

The scope of the work of the Accounting Policy and Research Staff also indicates the advances being made in the Accounting function in Shell. This group of Senior Staff and Analytical Accountants was established in conjunction with regional centralization of accounting and data processing. It encompasses accounting policy and research functions previously performed in various operating and corporate accounting groups. The need to avoid duplication of effort and provide standardization of accounting practices and methods necessitated central study of corporate-wide accounting policy.

The policy and research group is responsible for interpretation, clarification and standardization of accounting policy. It plays a major role in planning avoidance of problems in accounting, helping develop analytical and reporting techniques to promote greater efficiency and profitability in financial and operating organizations, and improving communication of financial concepts and objectives. Another important part of the group's work is keeping abreast of the latest developments in the accounting profession and in petroleum industry practices.

Part Three

Accounting Roots

The growth of the so-called "scientific method" is deeply imbedded in the advances made by Western civilization over the last few centuries. Hence one finds a steady endeavor in every known field of knowledge to reach for constantly higher levels of abstraction, that is, to become more "scientific."

The field of accounting is no exception. It started in a thoroughly pragmatic manner more than 4000 years ago during the dawn of Western civilization, and then found a unique methodology during the fifteenth century in the form of the double-entry system of bookkeeping. Even though double-entry bookkeeping has been defended brilliantly by such great minds as Goethe and Cayley, it is basically a methodology only and therefore was not enough to satisfy the theoretical hunger of its eventual scholars. They soon concluded that accounting had to concern itself with issues surrounding economic events and transactions in order to satisfy the demands upon it for economic information. Thus early scholars concluded that accounting must be a close relative of economics and they proceeded to utilize various economic concepts and theories as under-pinnings for abstract reasoning in accounting. Even today in some European countries accounting is still thought of as a form of applied economics, and therefore merely as a branch of economics.

Despite many serious attempts aimed at demonstrating an alleged close theoretical relationship between economics and accounting, no real progress has been achieved toward proving the correctness of the allega-tion. Part of the explanation of this result is that economics has tended toward an emphasis on macroeconomic models and has placed increasing reliance on the abstract manipulation of asserted mathematical relation-ships. Economic theory is silent on many important social issues of our time, and the gap between economic theory and economic reality often remains wide. This situation has fostered, in turn, a growing sterility of modern economics, as expressed in the first selection of readings offered in the present part of our book.

Moreover, the goals of theoretical economics are rather different from those of present-day theoretical accounting. The economist is usually concerned with wealth in a general social sense—often in terms of aggregate measurements. Economic analysis generally disregards the specific persons or organizations who may own wealth in a society. Economists study economic activities of persons or organizations largely as types or examples. Thus, they are not interested in the fate of a particular unit as distinct from any and all other similar units.

By contrast, the accountant along with the administrator is most typically concerned with wealth in particular forms—normally owned by individual persons or organizations. Therefore, the accountant's interest runs directly to the specific units which engage in economic activity. The excerpt from the chapter from Accounting Research Study No. 1 (Moonitz) makes this abundantly clear.

Next follows the Mepham article, which brings into focus the various severe assumptions on which models of a microeconomic nature are based. While these models are useful for analytic manipulations, they are rather inaccurate portrayals of real world conditions. Thus, it is not surprising to find that even though accounting has seriously attempted over the years to find its roots in the abstract reasoning of economics, it has been unable to do so with any real degree of success.

How then did the accounting structure evolve? Since nearly all cells in an organized society came to find it useful to have certain bits of accounting information available, accounting activities flourished even without a unifying theoretical framework. Accounting growth and devel-opment were accomplished by relying heavily on convention and common, every-day business sense. In many respects the process was akin to the one which characterized the advent of common law. A few arbitrarily chosen basic conventions established themselves through repeated usage. From these conventions certain standards and technical operating procedures were derived by relying on the informed judgment of men whose authority was recognized on the basis of long and varied experiences in the affairs of men as well as convincing argumentation in the face of opposition. However rudimentary such a process may seem, it has served well for many important purposes—for instance, the growth of a widespread capital market in the United States, corporate organizations spanning worldwide operations of multi-national companies, and minute central planning activities in socialist nations.

The second set of selections in Part Three shows first what one researcher considered to be the basic concepts underlying present accounting practices as they are used in the United States (Grady). Next follow the Seidman and Powell articles, which chronicle how accounting procedures have evolved in the United States, relate the events and organizations that have helped to shape accounting as it is applied today, and finally enumerate in an abbreviated form some of the conventions and techniques known as "generally accepted accounting principles." Again we should underscore that the authority of these principles rests upon their general acceptance—which is a very pragmatic authority. These principles have not been derived through abstractions from natural or biographical laws, nor from man-made fiats or decrees.

Considering the type of background just described, the reader should not be surprised to learn that the application of traditional accounting conventions has run into a measure of difficulties in recent years. Think of the conventional orientation of "generally accepted accounting principles" in relation to the nature of the accounting function as it was projected by the readings in Part Two! The degree of incongruance should be readily apparent, as should the significant challenges (or "dilemmas") which face accounting today. The Parker article clearly brings this to the fore, and the subsequent shorter selections under it. Heavy reliance on traditional accounting conventions has not only caused difficulties with this particular root of the discipline but has also impeded progress in other directions, for example, accounting for social and other non-business purposes.

Chapter VI

Accounting in Relation to Economics

28. Sterility of Modern Economics*

Robert L. Heilbroner**

From the very beginning, economists have striven for a picture of society in which the interaction of laws of production and behavior—production and behavior *functions* is the modern term—would describe the major economic events of the social system much as if it were a branch of physics. Moreover, by reducing the complexity of the real world to the simplicity of a "model" dominated by these two great functions, economists, like physicists, have sought to predict the path of motion of their system.

How successful has been this audacious intellectual effort? On the face of it, the achievement has been astonishing. Models of the economy are now so complex that they require the facilities of a computer and the techniques of difference equations, matrix algebra, LaGrangian multipliers, and the like. Sophistication, elegance, rigor—the criteria by which mathematics has traditionally been judged—are now the standards of economic theorizing. Not least, the success of modern economics can be read in the flattery of imitation paid to it by its sister disciplines of sociology and political science which now seek to build models similar to those of the economist. Certainly, when the intellectual history of our times is finally written, the creation of the edifice of modern "neo-classical" economics will occupy a central chapter in it.

The only question is, what will that chapter say about the usefulness

* Reprinted from "Putting Marx to Work," *The New York Review of Books*, December 5, 1968, pages 8, 10, and 12.
** Robert L. Heilbroner is on the graduate faculty at the New School for Social Research.

187

and relevance of this extraordinary enterprise? Here I suspect the appraisal of the future will not be uncritically admiring. The theory of economics, magnificent to behold, is considerably less impressive to use. It is true that it has given us a rough picture of how the market system works, both in allocating its resources and in determining the level of overall output. But beyond this conception, which can be taught with ease to a college freshman, the ramifications of economics have produced singularly little. A rococo branch called welfare theory, for example, has not, to my knowledge, yet resulted in a single substantive proposal that has added significantly to the welfare of mankind. The beautifully finished portion called price theory fails to explain the pricing operations of the great corporations. International trade theory does not adequately account for the most important single fact about international trade—to wit, the failure of an international division of labor to shed its benefits on poor countries and rich countries alike. The theory of economic development does not tell underdeveloped countries how to grow.

Even the central achievement of twentieth-century economics—the elucidation of the forces that determine prosperity and recession—fails when we seek to foretell the fortunes of the economy a few months hence. No doubt economists reading these words will deem them vastly exaggerated, which perhaps they are. Yet it is surely an opinion not wholly at variance with mine that must have moved Kenneth Arrow, a well-known economist, to sum up the collected papers of Paul Samuelson, the most brilliant theorist of our generation, with these words: "A careful examination of the papers both on theory and on policy yields only the most oblique suggestion that neoclassical price theory is descriptive of the real world. Of course, there is no denial, but Samuelson's attitude is clearly guarded and agnostic" (*Journal of Political Economy*, October, 1967).

Why is it that modern economic theory presents the spectacle of superb intellectual achievement without much social relevance? To my mind there are two reasons. One lies in the difficulties of reducing the real world—both in its technical and in its behavioral aspects—to reliable patterns with which we can then construct dependable models. It is one thing to ascribe an underlying "lawlike" character to the processes of production and to the responses of the economic actors, and quite another to reduce these activities to mathematical functions. In the case of production, for example, we encounter enormous difficulties in devising mathematical functions that will accurately account for the constantly changing nature of technology. And this difficulty is compounded by the even more intractable problem of finding functional representations of human behavior. No doubt, for instance, men tend to buy less when prices rise and to buy more when prices fall. Yet, on occasion, they will do just the opposite, as when they expect a price rise or price fall to *continue*—in which case their self-interest bids them to buy more in a hurry in the first case, and to hold off in the second.

Hence the inherent complexities of the production process and the vagaries of human behavior may well set limits to the predictive possibilities of economic theorizing, and these limits may account for much of the gap that exists between economic theory and economic reality. Yet, however much these difficulties explain the inaccuracy of economic theorizing, they do not account for its irrelevance. I have already mentioned the failure of price theory to explain the behavior of the large corporation and the gap between the theory and the reality of international trade. Now I must point out other areas of economic life over which modern economic theory passes in virtual silence. The distribution of wealth, for example, is a central economic fact about which it is mute. The effects on the distribution of income attributable to the process of growth is another, so that economics give us no hint of the disturbances and frictions produced by long-run economic advance. The effect of a constantly improving technology on the level of employment is similarly ignored, so that today the theory of technological unemployment is in much the same shape as was the theory of mass unemployment in the days before Keynes. The nature of class interests in a capitalist system is not mentioned in any textbook, so that nothing in the nature of political or social constraints confines the free movement of the economic model.

In all of this, it will be noted, there is a common denominator. This is the systematic exclusion of matters that might connect the functional model with the pressures and resistances of the political world. This exclusion, which accounts for so much of the irrelevance of economics, is by no means accidental. Rather, it results from a fundamental failure of vision on the part of the modern model-builders, *who do not see that the social universe that they are attempting to reproduce in a set of equations is not and cannot be adequately described by functional relationships alone, but must also and simultaneously be described as a system of privilege.* In other words, if a model of economic reality is to be relevant, it must portray both the functional relationships peculiar to the provisioning process and those stemming from the clash of interests generated by this very functional process itself.

Is it possible to construct a system that is at one and the same time a portrayal of functional relationships and of privilege? There is one such system, Marxian economics—that vast *terra incognita* over which the average economics student flies while en route to the oral examination (where it may be mentioned as part of the History of Economic Doctrines) and at which he never again casts a glance. For what is unique about the Marxian system is that the categories, both of production and of behavior, into which it disaggregates the world are considerably different from those of the neoclassical system. On the production side, for example, Marxism lays great stress on the necessity for a "fit" between the output of the capital goods sector and that of the consumer goods sector, a relationship that is unnoticed in neoclassical economics where the aggregate output of *all* sectors is stressed rather than the relationship between them. Similarly, on the behavioral side, Marx approaches the problem of describing the great "human" functions by building up a picture of the actions of producers that is, workers and capitalists—rather than by analyzing the activities of *buyers*, i.e., of consumers and investors. In different words, the Marxian analysis breaks down the total flow of economic activity into layers of costs, wages, and profits rather than into the slices of consumption and investment characteristic of the Keynesian approach.

The result of the special categories of abstraction imposed by the Marxian view is to bring into the foreground a number of matters that fail to appear in neoclassical analysis, in particular the instability of the economy stemming from a failure of its productive components to interlock, and the changing division of the social product among the classes— profit receivers and wage earners—that compete for it. Now it should be said immediately that the manner in which classical Marxian analysis performs its task of constructing a model of society is very awkward and occasionally downright wrong. The "laws of motion" that it discerns within the capitalist system depend on rigid assumptions about the way in which technology permits labor to be combined with capital and loses sight of the central effect of productivity in changing the real shares of wage earners in the final product. Worse yet, as a means of explaining the price mechanism by which the system is coordinated, Marxian economics is hopelessly clumsy: if one examines the efforts of the more liberal Soviet or Czech economists to create a rational pricing system using Marxian concepts, and compares these efforts with the results obtained by nonMarxian price theory, the contrast is like that between a dull cleaver and a sharp scalpel.

Why then bother with Marxian economics when, as virtually every economist will tell you, it is "wrong"? The reason is that, unlike neoclassical analysis, which is "right," the Marxian model has in surfeit the quality of social relevance that is so egregiously lacking in the other. The neoclassical model has rigor, but, alas, also mortis. The Marxian model has relevance, but, alas, also mistakes. The answer, then, is clear. Marxian insights must be married to neoclassical techniques to produce an economic theory that is both elegant and consistent as a model and freighted with meaning as a theory of society.

29. The Environment of Accounting*

Maurice Moonitz**

ECONOMIC ACTIVITY

In virtually all the organized groups of which knowledge exists goods and services are produced by the interaction of human effort with the other elements in the environment. Elements in the environment include natural resources as well as the brain and muscle of human beings, and also imply their combination in all conceivable stages. Furthermore, the goods and services produced are, for the most part, distributed through exchange of some sort, and not consumed by the producers themselves.

QUANTITATIVE DATA

Given the general pattern sketched above, the necessity for decisions of various types becomes apparent. Decisions must be made as to the goods and services to be produced and the resources to be used in their production. In primitive or elementary or simple conditions, the alternatives available are few, and the results of decisions made usually become apparent at an early stage. But, as soon as the processes become complex or sophisticated, a means of calculation is necessary to weigh alternatives, to measure and check on the progress that is being made, and ultimately to measure and evaluate the results obtained. Accounting clearly furnishes one type of quantitative data that can be used as a basis for making some of the choices that have to be made from among the alternatives available, and for checking and evaluating progress and results. How well accounting has performed this function can be answered only in terms of specific problems and specific types of accounting. But the relationship of accounting, along with other forms of systematic calculation, to the economic environment is clear and direct.

PREDICTABILITY

Accounting seems to flourish in a stable environment, and to languish in an unstable one. Flux, change, and disorder are always unsettling,

* Reprinted from *The Basic Postulates of Accounting*, Accounting Research Study No. 1, copyrighted 1961 by the American Institute of CPAs, pages 8–15.
** Maurice Moonitz is Professor of Accounting at University of California, Berkeley.

requiring the adaptation of behavior to the changed circumstances. If the changes are small in magnitude or slow in pace, adaptations can be made smoothly. But if the changes are large and swift, as in war or revolution or in a rapid inflation or deep depression, the underpinnings of action become unstable and behavior becomes erratic.

Uncertainty of any type makes economic calculations difficult, perhaps even impossible. Some types of uncertainty may, however, be reduced, if not eliminated, by appropriate social arrangements. For example, a police system is of immense help to holders of property to assure them that they can continue in quiet possession in lawful uses. A system of courts to enforce commercial agreements acts to stimulate their use. Laws establishing property rights make for a firmer basis of accountability. The whole climate becomes one in which more and more formal consequences become almost indistinguishable from actual consequences.

This influence of the "orderly society" on accounting is so powerful that accounting principles, procedures, and rules often rest squarely on the formal relationships themselves, sometimes even to the point of overshadowing the real events that are occurring. For example, there may be a tendency to accept the salary of the president, who is also the principal stockholder, of a closely held corporation as the result of arm's-length bargaining simply because, in form, the amount was set in an agreement between the man and the corporation. In similar fashion, the acts of a wholly owned subsidiary are often treated as though they were independent of the parent company because they were performed by a separate corporation. Form and custom, rules, laws, and traditional patterns of action are all powerful forces. But a transaction among related interests, for example, must be more than form or custom or legal relationship in order to possess substance.

CHARACTERISTICS OF ECONOMIC ORGANIZATION

Three of the salient characteristics of our economic organization from the standpoint of accounting are as follows:

1. Private ownership of most productive resources. This characteristic, for example, accounts for the observed emphasis on "investors" as the group for whom financial statements are prepared, and the related tendency to restrict accounting to the needs of that group. But observation also reveals that accounting is used in cases where private ownership is not present. As a consequence, we can conclude that the problems of investors as a class, while undeniably important and worthy of close study and attention, do not encompass all the relevant or important problems of accounting.

2. Role of the market. In recent years, the market, as the agency or machinery by which the exchange of goods and services is effected, has clearly increased in importance. Two familiar examples will illustrate this assertion: (1) the housewife formerly baked her own bread; today she buys it from a retailer who in turn obtained it from a commercial baker; (2) farmers used to raise their own vegetables and chickens, and kept a cow to provide milk for the family; today many farmers buy these products in town, preferring to devote the farm's resources to the crops which can be sold for cash. The importance of production for exchange rather than for consumption by the producer himself is so great that later we formulate a proposition to indicate that the primary basis of accounting lies in records of exchange dealings or their equivalents.

Related to the function of a market as a method of effecting exchanges is its function in generating prices which act as guides to everyone concerned with economic activity. The influence of these market prices on the tremendous number of economic decisions that have to be made has, in relative terms, been declining. As industrialization increases, and with it the size and complexity of the most efficient productive unit, more and more decisions have to be made within the framework of the economic (business) unit. Ultimately, of course, the decisions made must stand the test of the market, but meanwhile management can and must exercise a considerable degree of control over the company's activities. One evident result has been an increased interest in "managerial accounting," where the emphasis is inward to assist management in making better decisions and in improving its control, through better "intelligence," over the activities going on inside the economic unit.

3. Free labor. A significant aspect of our form of economic organization is that the services of human beings are supplied by free and not by slave labor. From the vantage point of accounting, the significance is seen in the fact that labor services cannot be "inventoried" or "stockpiled" in advance. We can have accounts for materials on hand, awaiting usage, or for equipment available for use, but except for a few minor instances such as "prepaid wages," we can have no accounts for labor services stockpiled and awaiting usage. Even in the face of an agreement between an employer and an employee, specific performance cannot be enforced under our legal system, although damages in some limited amount might be recoverable in the event of a breach. A small business worth $5,000 can be sold, lock, stock, and barrel, and all the benefits transferred to the buyer who can hold the former owner to "specific

performance" as to the *business* transferred. An employment contract for ten times that amount cannot be sold with any assurance to the buyer that he will get any benefits at all in the form of specific performance. Contracts in professional sports and in the movie industry are apparent but not real exceptions, since the "owners" of those contracts (the employers) do not use the courts to enforce them, but instead rely on extra-legal means of insuring compliance.

The upshot of these considerations is that we can deal with greater confidence with agreements concerning property where both the property and the agreements are highly marketable, transferable, exchangeable than we can with agreements concerning the services of human beings. And this result flows not from any characteristic of accounting but of the environment. . . .

WEALTH AND WELFARE

The position occupied by the concept of wealth has undergone a transformation in recent years. The dominant voices of the early nineteenth century had no doubts on the score—wealth in the form of an abundance of goods and services became identified with happiness; wealth and welfare were almost interchangeable terms. In fact, one economist (J. B. Say) stated explicitly that the main task of the economist was to teach people the advantages of wealth, to make them want to be wealthy.

We of the twentieth century are somewhat more sophisticated, at least to the extent of distinguishing between wealth and welfare. The two concepts are clearly related, but they are not identical, and neither one equates necessarily with happiness. These observations are hardly profound, but they are significant for accounting. In its present and prospective stages of development, accounting is intimately and directly tied to the processes and institutions surrounding the production, safeguarding, distribution, and consumption of *wealth*, not of welfare or of happiness. Accounting can conceivably measure how "well off" some person or some organization is, provided that "well offness" is measured by wealth in one form or another. Criticisms of accounting which say in essence that it does not measure welfare or happiness can be rejected as irrelevant and unwarranted. By the same token, assertions by some that accounting can or should measure welfare or happiness should likewise be viewed with a critical eye.

WEALTH AND ASSETS

The preceding discussion referred to an interest in wealth with the term "wealth" used in a broad economic sense. From the vantage point of accounting, this interest in wealth is really an interest in assets. Furthermore, this interest in assets is the common thread which unites accounting, economics, business administration, industrial engineering, and other similar areas. Thus, an economist is concerned with "wealth," usually in a social sense, while the accountant, the administrator, and the engineer are concerned with "wealth" in particular forms, normally owned or in the possession of business concerns.

Economic analysis is usually not concerned with the specific person who owns the wealth or to whom the benefits run. The economist's apparent interest at times in units of activity turns out on closer examination to be an interest in these units as types or as examples. It is not an interest in the fate of the unit, as such, as distinct from any and all other similar units. The accountant, by contrast, is almost always concerned with specific units and must assign the "wealth" and its changes to *some specific entity* for a *specified time period.* Incidentally, this specific interest of the accountant makes him more conservative than the economist faced with the same problem—for example, the accountant typically hesitates to recognize a favorable change "too early" because it may never be "realized," and the party to whom the benefit flows may prematurely demand his share or act on the presumption that it is his.

THE ACCOUNTING ENTITY

In a preceding paragraph, we translated the "wealth" of economics into the "assets" of accounting. Let us now cross the bridge the other way by defining the accounting entity in economic terms. The purpose of the earlier translation of "wealth" into "assets" was to relate a general idea to a specific, more familiar, context. The purpose of the proposed explanation of the accounting entity in economic terms is to get the advantage of the more general attitude of the economist.

An accounting entity controls and transforms resources. It acquires them from some source and transforms them in order to produce goods and services.

The term "transforms" is used in the broadest possible sense to denote conversion or combination or rearrangement. It includes physical transformation, as in manufacturing, but also covers, for example, the activities of professional men in applying their knowledge and skill to the solution of a client's problems. In order to do this, the accounting entity incurs costs for the services of persons, for money borrowed, and for other property used in whatever form (e.g., materials, supplies, equipment) and acquired by whatever means (e.g., purchase, lease). Its revenues are "distributable" in the form of wages, rent, taxes, interest, and dividends, with the residue (if any) retained by the entity. (If the occasion demands, we can add "noneconomic" attributes, e.g., that an accounting entity is also a "communication network" or a "social institution.")

Another attribute of an accounting entity is that it is almost always an intermediary between natural resources on the one hand, and ultimate consumption of goods and services by human beings on the other. We observe that accounting has been applied most successfully to the affairs of those economic entities which are actually links in a chain connecting basic resources and ultimate consumption. On this point, F. Sewell Bray, the eminent English accounting theorist, has written in correspondence:

> *In a completely articulated economy, everyone assumed to be keeping accounts, we should find that apart from the generators of income most people's accounts would fall within the category of spending ones.* Enterprises *do not need to have spending or consumer accounts because they* are concerned with the generation of income and its transfer *either to owners or to governments. [Emphasis added.]*

In other words, entities produce, consume, spend; business or business-type entities concentrate mainly on producing goods and services. This distinction is widely recognized in the separation of business and personal affairs (e.g., the use of separate records for each distinctive venture under common ownership in proprietorships, partnerships, and other forms of unincorporated associations). We propose to use this distinction as the basis for suggesting that "income" is a term that should not be applied both to natural persons and to business entities. Mainly because the economic theory of income is primarily a theory of the income of natural persons and not of accounting entities, we should restrict the term "income" to personal income. The terms "earnings" or "profit" are then available to describe the related concept when applied to accounting entities.[1]

In Accounting Terminology Bulletin No. 2 (March 1955), the committee on terminology of the American Institute of Certified Public Accountants made the following recommendation with respect to "earnings":

> *The committee is hopeful that eventually there will be a single term, uniformly used to designate the net results of business operations. In recent years there has been a trend toward the term "earnings," although a majority of published financial statements employ the term "net income."*

---

[1] Professor C. A. Moyer, as a member of the project advisory committee, dissents to this proposal as to terminology. He states that: "The term 'income,' especially when used with appropriate adjectives or descriptive phrases, is a useful and meaningful term in business and in accounting. There seems to be no convincing reason for abandoning this word in accounting. It has been widely accepted, particularly in the income statement and in discussions of the income concept in accounting, and an extension of its use should be encouraged."

Until one or the other of these terms achieves pronounced preference, the committee makes no recommendation as between them. It approves the use of the term in accounting language in connection with the concept of ability to realize net income [e.g., "earning power"] (page 4).

The Institute of Chartered Accountants in England and Wales seems to favor "profit" and "loss," as does the Canadian Institute of Chartered Accountants.

THE NONPROFIT AREA

Limitation on the profit concept is found in cases where its relevance is not apparent from observation, that is to say, no earnings are generated that are subject to tax or to distribution as a dividend to investors or other beneficiaries.

The example of government comes to mind. But many governmental activities involve the management of economic resources and their conversion into goods and services. Examples of these activities are found in the case of roads, bridges, dams, postal service, recreational facilities, schools, hospitals, prisons, irrigation projects, etc. In some cases, government is carrying on activities (e.g., public utilities) which are also carried on by private enterprises. In other cases, government has simply acquired a monopoly (e.g., postal service) of services formerly carried on by private enterprises.

Many nongovernmental activities are also "nonprofit" and therefore seem at first glance to fall outside the "profit" area. But, as in the case of the governmental activities sketched above, many of these "nonprofit" enterprises also manage and convert economic resources.

To the extent, then, that the principal activities of a nonprofit entity involve the management and conversion of economic resources, it resembles an entity in the "profit" sector. Accordingly, propositions that bear directly on accounting for resources (assets) should be applicable equally to the "profit" and "nonprofit" areas. If there are distinctive differences between the two, they should emerge in connection with the analysis of or reports on equity interests and changes in resources (operations). What changes are relevant to the measurement of the progress of a nonprofit enterprise might be different from those relevant to a profit-oriented one. We anticipate no such difference, however, at the level of the broader or more basic propositions.

The Senate, the House of Representatives, the Office of the President of the United States, the U. S. Supreme Court, and the corresponding units at the state and local levels, illustrate types of activities whose primary or even major interest is definitely *not* the management of their own economic resources. These activities are political in nature, in the technical meaning of that term. Each of these activities, however, has some economic aspect. To the extent that it has, the operations should be accounted for in the same manner as any other economic activity.

30. Cost, Output and the Accountancy Student*

M. J. Mepham**

The study of economics has now been accepted in the English Institute's examination syllabus as a necessary feature in an accountant's education. This is a broadening of the educational base with which few will quarrel but there are, in economics, difficulties for accountancy students which perhaps are not encountered by other students. The overlapping terminology of economics and accountancy is one obvious source of difficulty. Other difficulties are latent in the conventional 'theory of the firm.'

The accountancy student warily picking his way through the 'theory of the firm' in an economic text, is frequently disturbed at the gulf which exists between this theoretical exposition of business activity and the real life business situations which he daily observes or in which he finds himself involved. An economist would point out that the theory is not 'descriptive' but 'prescriptive,' i.e. it is designed to give guidance to a hypothetical entrepreneur as to what he should do, rather than to describe what business executives actually do. The theory does, nevertheless, involve constructing a model and it is difficult to maintain this distinction —indeed, one wonders whether it is valid since to prescribe optimizing techniques (as the economist does) on the basis of a defective model, is surely a questionable procedure. This is especially so if these techniques are taken over into 'managerial economics,' a developing field which purports to advise, not a hypothetical, but the real business man.

Many economists are aware of this unsatisfactory situation. In his "Approaches to the Study of Decision-making relevant to the Firm" (*The Journal of Business*, April 1961), Martin Shubik has written:

* Reprinted from *The Accountant*, May 8, 1965, pages 605–611.
** M. J. Mepham is Senior Lecturer in Accountancy at Heriot Watt University, Edinburgh, Scotland.

Microeconomics has been, and to some extent remains, a jungle of special assumptions, special cases, unsatisfactory measurements and tenuous theorizing.

Attempts to improve the model are currently being made; a notable recent example being *A Behavioural Theory of the Firm*, by Cyert and March (Prentice Hall, 1963).

THE COST/OUTPUT RELATIONSHIP

At certain points in the theory, economists derive from the model conclusions which seem to contradict what the accountancy student will have learned elsewhere in his studies. One such point is the cost/output relationship. Cost varies with output and the accountant considers that he knows how it varies.

Many accountants in industry spend much time and energy in measuring cost in successive financial periods and in preparing budgets for various levels of production. Many will have had to explain to management variations in unit cost figures resulting from output changes. Those who have read the amusing book, *How to Run a Basoon Factory*, by Mark Spade, will remember the following passage:

Don't be surprised if your costing department tells you one day that a thing cost £20 and the next that it costs 4s 3d. Costing departments always do that, and they will certainly be able to produce figures which prove absolutely conclusively that they were right on both occasions.

From their accumulated experience accountants have developed a theory,[1] which seems to disagree with that used by economists in the theory of the firm. The two competing theories can best be studied by looking at the six accompanying graphs, three showing the cost behaviour assumed by the accountant, and three the economist's view of the position. The economist makes a distinction between the short-run and the long-run period[2] and to simplify matters the short-run only will be considered here. A short-run period is one in which the organization is assumed to be unable to alter its fixed plant and buildings. To expand its output the firm will thus use its existing equipment more intensively.

Although accountants do not use this terminology it is easy to assume that the graphs have been prepared for a budget period in which

---

[1] Perhaps it would be more correct to say that certain accounting procedures presuppose an underlying theory—accountants would be loath to formulate a cost/output theory as such.

[2] P. J. D. Wiles uses instead the terms 'partial adaptation' and 'total adaptation.'

no capital expenditure is envisaged. A further simplification is the assumption that a single type of product is being produced. Apart from these two assumptions there are others made unilaterally by both accountants and economists; these are built into their respective graphs and it is difficult to generalize them without destroying the distinctive approaches of the two disciplines. These further points will be considered later as factors which contribute to the differing conclusions reached.

These six graphs are typical of those that the student finds in his textbooks. Most books would acknowledge that the charts are greatly simplified and few writers would deny that there are special cases which do not fit into the theories, but the graphs do purport to show the general position.

TOTAL COST CURVES

The first pair of graphs, A1 and A2, illustrate competing views of the reaction of total cost to output changes. The differences might appear to be of minor importance but they have significant implications when unit costs are derived from them. Both graphs necessitate a distinction between fixed and variable costs. The student will already be familiar with this. Fixed costs are costs which tend to remain constant in total, irrespective of the level of production; they are the costs involved in providing and maintaining the firm's production potential, its organization and equipment.

The usual example of a fixed cost is factory rent, this will have to be paid at the agreed rate whatever output level is attained. Variable costs are those which tend to vary with the level of production such as the cost of content material, direct labour and certain types of supplies and services.

Figure 30.1-A1 is usually shown with the addition of a sales curve to indicate the firm's break-even point—it is then called a 'break-even chart.' Accountants would recognize that the relationship between total cost and output is not linear but they would claim that this is a useful approximation not too remote from the truth. Numerous empirical studies seem to support this contention but it is important to remember that usually the chart will be constructed from data derived from past experience over a limited range of production. The curve derived from this information will be extended down to nil output and up to full capacity. The curve is therefore more certainly substantiated over the range which corresponds to normal activity.

Figure 30.1-A2 The fixed costs in the economist's graph are shown at a higher level than those in A1, because of the inclusion of items that

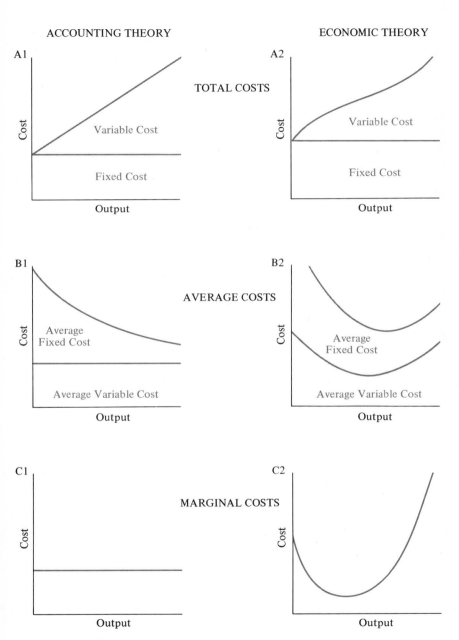

Figure 30.1
The Behaviour of Cost at Varying Levels of Output

the accountant generally excludes from the category of cost, e.g. normal profit, entrepreneurial salary, etc. The effect of these additional items may, however, be offset by differences in the treatment of depreciation. The accountant often treats this as a fixed cost (*vide* the English Institute's Recommendations) but the economist would segregate user cost and deal with this as a variable element of depreciation.

The curve itself is assumed to take the form of an inverted ogive. The reasoning substantiating this is as follows: with a given plant, production at low levels of output will be inefficient and variable costs will therefore increase quite rapidly (though at a decreasing rate); after a certain point the plant will be operating in the range for which it was designed and the curve will be much less steep. Eventually it will rise again at an increasing rate as the plant is overworked and the 'law of diminishing returns' comes into play. This 'law of diminishing returns' states that if the firm's output rate is increased beyond a certain level, the additional units of output will cost progressively more and more. Each additional input of a variable factor of production (e.g. an additional labourer hired) will have a lower productivity. This is partly because the firm's capital equipment is diluted (i.e. the labourer will have less mechanical power at his elbow), and partly because the firm's administrative staff will (after a certain point) experience managerial problems, e.g. difficulties in coordinating the work. As additional variable factors of production are added the productivity of the existing factors is also likely to diminish.

The law is essentially based on common-sense considerations but the reasoning lacks corroboration from econometric studies.

AVERAGE COST CURVES

From the total cost curves can be derived average unit cost curves. The distinction between fixed and variable costs is also important here but it will be obvious that the change in viewpoint, from total figures to average figures, results in a metamorphosis in the character of fixed costs. Costs which remain fixed in total, vary when expressed as an amount per unit of production at varying levels of output. Whether or not variable costs undergo a similar transformation into costs which are fixed per output unit·is the main point at dispute in the two theories that are under discussion.

Figure 30.1-B1 Average cost is depicted here as falling as output increases. Fixed costs are spread over a greater number of units of output and thus decline per unit of output whilst variable costs per unit are assumed to remain constant. This theory is built into the structure of costing procedures. Thus the preparation of budgets (and in particular flexible budgets) will be based on this model. Break-even analysis, variance analysis and the calculation of predetermined overhead rates also utilize the theory.

Figure 30.1-B2   The average cost curve is considered by economic theory to be U-shaped. Average fixed cost per unit falls as output increases; average variable cost also falls but after a certain point the 'law of diminishing returns' begins to operate, the rate of fall slows down and eventually the curve turns upwards. With some factors of production fixed (as plant is assumed to be in the short-run) the theory is that average costs will rise as production is pushed beyond the plant's most efficient level of output.

MARGINAL COST CURVES

From the above discussion it can be seen that the major point at issue is the behaviour of the variable cost element as output changes. Does variable cost increase in proportion to output increases or does it, at high output levels, increase at a greater rate? The last pair of charts segregate this aspect by comparing the marginal cost curves of accounting and economic theory.

'*Marginal cost is the amount at any given volume of output by which aggregate costs are changed if the volume of output is increased or decreased by one unit.*' (A Report on Marginal Costing. *The Institute of Cost and Works Accountants, 1961.*)

Figure 30.1-C1   The accountant's marginal cost curve coincides with his average variable cost curve. The additional cost of producing an extra unit of output is the additional variable cost incurred and the accountant assumes that this remains constant per unit of output. This is likely to confuse the student since it is easy to assume that marginal cost and average variable cost are the same thing. Here they are the same quantitatively but the concepts are clearly not the same and should be distinguished.[3]

Figure 30.1-C2   The economist's marginal cost curve is U-shaped but it does not coincide with the U-shaped average variable cost curve—the lower curve in 30.1-B2. The process of averaging in 30.1-B2 produces a shallower curve, whereas the marginal curve in 30.1-C2 is usually assumed to be markedly U-shaped. The marginal cost curve cuts the average variable cost curve at the latter's lowest point. Marginal cost is assumed to exceed average unit cost at high levels of production—accounting

---

[3] The earlier definition of marginal cost given by The Institute of Cost and Works Accountants in *Terminology of Cost Accountancy* did not help matters. Marginal cost was there defined as 'prime cost plus variable overhead.'

textbooks, by equating marginal cost and average variable cost, rule out this possibility.

DIFFERING VIEWPOINTS

The two viewpoints have been outlined and the differences between them are evident. Can they be reconciled—or must the student be reconciled to learning two sets of mutually conflicting theories? He may even fail consciously to realize that there is a contradiction present, as so often accountancy and economics are dispensed in separate packages as if there were no relationship between them. Several general points need to be considered before an attempt to effect the needed reconciliation is made.

The first point is the complex nature of business activity. This is too obvious to need stressing. There will inevitably be simplification and distortion in any manageable model of a representative firm. The importance of achieving a balance between the conflicting aims of accuracy of representation and the avoidance of unnecessary complication is apparent.

Secondly, there is the economic theory of a hypothetical firm's activities. This is built up from certain postulates using rigorous argument. Logically it is impeccable but it may not closely enough resemble reality because of unrealistic assumptions built into its foundations. This is particularly likely since the theory seems to have been constructed for a purpose differing from that for which it is currently being used.

The third consideration is the accountant's attempt to describe and interpret quantitatively the conditions obtaining in a particular firm. It is tempting to draw a contrast between the economist looking at reality through his theories and the accountant looking at reality directly. The accountancy student might well murmur, as he alternates between his economics textbook and Bigg's *Cost Accounts*, 'For now we see through a glass darkly but then face to face'; but this would be unfair. The accountant, too, has glasses through which he peers at reality. He approaches his task empirically but the established methods and conventions that he uses may well impart a bias to his work and any theories based on the results of his work may reflect this bias.

Some of the economist's less realistic assumptions and some of the accounting cost measurement conventions are points which need to be elaborated. The effect of these on the marginal cost curves will be examined.

FLEXIBILITY OF WORKING

Shift Working

The economist when considering the short-run period seems tacitly to exclude the possibility of shift working, overtime working, or short-time working in his model. This is because a fixed plant is envisaged in the short-run and to permit flexibility in the running time of a plant installation is essentially the same as allowing an alteration to the stock of plant. Accountants have no such overtime ban built into their graphs. They would recognize the possibility of shift working where the firm finds it economic to introduce such measures. Shift working and overtime are common in practice and the flexibility which they impart may result in a flatter marginal cost curve. This is so even though the advantages of flexibility are reduced by the premium which is invariably paid to compensate the work staff for the disadvantages of overtime and night shifts.

Similar reasoning also applies to short-time working at low levels of output; the management's room for manoeuvre is greater if sections of the plant can be shut down; the average and marginal cost curves in such circumstances are likely to be flatter.

The Production Process

If the economist's entrepreneur has no flexibility in altering the operating time of his plant, he also has an extremely inflexible type of plant. By implication, the firm's plant is treated as being a single indivisible unit which has to be operated as a whole or not at all. Although installations of this type may exist they are rare. Variations in production are achieved in the economist's model by varying the input of variable factors of production, such as the number of operators to each machine. The accountant's approach is more realistic in that it recognizes the possibility of shift work, overtime and short-time working and also the application of these measures to part of the plant.

Limiting Factors

The economist's assumptions are, in the main, simplifications which he considers assist in building a manageable model of the firm without rendering the model too unrealistic. These simplifications deprive the hypothetical entrepreneur of much of the flexibility which exists in practice. But in one respect the economist's model appears to be more flexible than that of the accountant.

Both disciplines recognize that limiting factors exist which restrict a firm's ability to produce. Thus the firm's opportunities are restricted by its financial resources. The economist's law of diminishing returns is linked with this concept and this law is the main reason for assuming that costs increase at a higher rate than production at high levels of production. In the short-run the manufacturing capacity of the plant will be a limiting factor; it constitutes, in economic terminology, a fixed factor of production. The economist reasons that production results from combining fixed factors of production (e.g. manufacturing plant) with variable factors of production (e.g. productive labour).

These variable factors of production can be used in varying proportions but there is an optimum mixture. Once this optimum is reached output can only be increased in the short-run by adding increasing measures of the variable factors; marginal cost increases as a result of this. The law of diminishing returns operates. Many economists, at least in elementary and intermediate texts, appear to suggest that output can be forced up to extremely high levels if enough units of the variable factors of production are added. (An exception is Professor C. F. Carter in his book *The Science of Wealth.*) This is unrealistic as most plant installations will have a maximum capacity above which it will be futile to increase the inputs of variable factors of production. The maximum may be higher than management often considers it to be but a ceiling will exist in the short-run. If the machine governs the rate of output it is useless to add more manpower once the machine's limit is reached. The accountant's output axis will range from nil output up to this maximum capacity but the economist's graph often appears to extend beyond this to levels of production which the firm would not attempt to reach and which it probably could never reach in the short-run.

COST MEASUREMENT

The Constant Marginal Cost Assumption

Certain assumptions of the economist have been examined and if the criticisms have substance it might well be that many businesses have marginal costs which change little (or even remain constant) for considerable ranges of output. Flat-bottomed marginal cost curves are feasible if some of the points made are valid. Such curves would still conflict, but not nearly so drastically, with the accountant's assumption that average variable cost and marginal cost are quantitatively identical and that they are constant at *all* levels of output. The curves now differ in shape only at the extreme ends of the output range. Experience of cost behaviour at both these extremes of the output axis will be rare and it has already been suggested that the economist's axis extends, without regard to any limit fixed by the firm's production capacity, to levels of production which may be incapable of attainment.

The accountant is uninterested in the behaviour of cost at ranges of output which are never experienced in practice. He would tend to agree with Mr F. Troughton that

if anything is not experienced and cannot be experienced (assuming ordinary, sensible, management) then no one is justified in saying categorically, what "would happen if . . .", because we should then be within the realm of the imaginary; and we cannot pretend that what allegedly happens in that realm is a sound basis for real management decisions. It is necessary to know *that certain things* can and do *happen in practice before we can produce graphs purporting to describe certain behaviours.* (Some Thoughts on the Theory of the Firm, *Management International, 1963/6.*)

The econometric studies, mentioned later, seem to confirm that, over the ranges of production actually experienced, marginal costs do not rise. A further relevant point may be that in the short-run, experience of cost behaviour at both extremes of the output axis may be rare because if production does tend to reach these levels it is likely that the firm will, in anticipation, have altered its fixed plant and this immediately excludes it from the short-run period discussion. To summarize: if the economist modifies his marginal cost graph into a flat-bottomed curve, the accountant would find such a revision acceptable, with the proviso that the extremities of the curve are at levels of production which are not reached in practice.

Depreciation

It is now necessary to examine a weakness in the measurement procedures used by accountants. Depreciation is part of cost and the accountant's treatment of it warrants attention. There is an enormous amount of written matter on the topic but his will be carefully skirted and depreciation will be defined briefly as the 'diminution in the value of an asset due to effluxion of time and wear and tear.'

The component part of depreciation which depends on effluxion of time is a fixed cost and it will not feature in any marginal cost calculation. Wear and tear depreciation, i.e. that part of depreciation which does vary with production and which was termed 'user cost' by Keynes, might well be part of marginal cost. The accountancy estimates of depreciation do not usually attempt to measure user cost and the English Institute, in its recommendation on depreciation, gives general approval to the 'straight-line' method of estimation; this method, which is widely used, treats depreciation as a fixed cost. Current methods of measuring depreciation may therefore impart a bias to the accounting results. The more mechanized or automated firms are, the more important does this factor become but, until some research is done on this topic, it is difficult to say whether the present methods falsify the position substantially. Although to leave the topic is unsatisfactory nothing further can usefully be said on the measurement of user cost.

STATISTICAL EVIDENCE

There has been a number of econometric studies to establish the cost/output relationship. Here it will suffice to quote from two major works. The American National Bureau of Economic Research state in their study *Cost Behaviour and Price Policy* (1943), 'a smooth U-shaped curve reflects a bias in economic theory.' In his *Statistical Cost Analysis* (McGraw-Hill, 1960), Professor Johnston summarizing some of the statistical studies made on the subject, says:

the various short-run studies more often than not indicate constant marginal cost and declining average cost as the pattern that best seems to describe the data that have been analysed.

Some economists would dispute the validity of these summaries on the grounds that the data utilized have been affected by the linear bias of accounting procedures. Professor Johnston deals with such doubts in some detail and, apart from the user cost problem, he meets the objections satisfactorily. For a wide range of output the econometric studies appear to be valid, constant marginal cost appears to be the rule and the accountant seems to be largely vindicated.

CONCLUSION

The suggested alterations to the graphs deal only with the effects of the gross assumptions made in the model of the business enterprise. The theory of the firm is currently the target of much criticism and many would agree that, unless the theory is to be restricted to giving advice to a fictitious business man in a make-believe environment, this model must be made more realistic. As Martin Shubik has observed:

'*The simplifications made to obtain the competitive model of the firm are too drastic to provide either a normative or descriptive microeconomic theory of more than limited use to the firm.*'

Until a new model is developed there is need for first-aid treatment if many accountancy students are not to succumb. Such books as *Managerial Economics*, by Joel Dean (Prentice Hall, 1961), can act as an antidote, but the real need is for some degree of integration in the teaching of the two disciplines which would prevent inconsistencies arising. Such co-operation would help in developing a more rigorous theoretical background for accountancy and would assist in making the model of the firm more realistic. Kenneth Boulding in 'Economics and Accounting: The Uncongenial Twins,' *Studies in Accounting Theory* (Sweet & Maxwell, 1962), says: 'The point where accounting and economics come closest together is in what the economists call the theory of the firm.' This may be true but it is not apparent in the textbooks at present.

Chapter VII

The Conventional Approach and Emphasis

31. Basic Concepts to Which Accepted Accounting Principles Are Oriented*

Paul Grady**

Accountants are generally agreed that accounting principles cannot be derived from or proven by the laws of nature. They are rather in the category of conventions or rules developed by man from experience to fulfill the essential and useful needs and purposes in establishing reliable financial and operating information control for business entities. In this respect they are similar to principles of commercial law and other social disciplines.

There is general agreement, also, among accounting teachers and practitioners that there are a number of concepts which underlie or permeate accepted accounting principles. The first comprehensive exposition of concepts in accounting literature was in *An Introduction to Corporate Accounting Standards*, by W. A. Paton and A. C. Littleton. This pioneering classic in accounting thought, published in 1940 by the American Accounting Association, discusses seven concepts. A lesser number of concepts had been discussed by Professor Paton in an account-

* Reprinted from *Inventory of Generally Accepted Accounting Principles for Business Enterprises*, Accounting Research Study No. 7, copyrighted 1965 by the American Institute of CPAs, pages 23–24.
** Paul Grady is retired. He is a former Director of the Accounting Research Division of the American Institute of CPAs, and is also a former partner of Price Waterhouse & Co. and Arthur Andersen & Co.

ing textbook written some twenty years earlier, and George O. May's monograph, *Business Income and Price Levels* in 1949 states that the "going concern" concept was adequately presented in Dicksee's *Advanced Accounting*, published in England at a still earlier date.

Concepts, as well as principles, are derived from experience in observing the conduct of business and the meeting of its accountabilities within our society whose objectives include: (a) the exercise of government power in a manner responsive to the will of the people, and (b) the maintenance of an economic system based upon individual incentives and opportunities for employment and investment in competitive business enterprise.

Different authors, on a basis of the analysis of their own experience, probably would select somewhat differing lists of concepts; and it is impossible to eliminate personal views from the discussion. Nevertheless, it is believed that each of the ten concepts listed below may be justified as providing qualities of usefulness and dependability to accounting information or as setting forth limitations inherent in financial statements produced by the accounting process:

1. A society and government structure honoring private property rights
2. Specific business entities
3. Going concern
4. Monetary expression in accounts
5. Consistency between periods for the same entity
6. Diversity in accounting among independent entities
7. Conservatism
8. Dependability of data through internal control
9. Materiality
10. Timeliness in financial reporting requires estimates

32. The Impact of Federal Income Tax Law and Regulations on Accounting Principles*

J. S. Seidman**

Accounting and taxes did mighty well by each other these last fifty years. Without accounting, taxes—certainly income taxes—would be on infirm foundation. Without taxes, accounting would be leading a quieter and less significant existence.

As with so many companionships, crosscurrents and irritants have come into the picture. In the encounter, accounting has been exposing its chin. Unless accounting puts up a darned sight better fight, it may go down for the count.

What causes a rupture between such good friends? The usual. The failure to understand one another's place.

The alliance between the *practice* of accounting and the practice of taxes is natural. But an alliance between accounting *principles* and tax principles is something else again.

It is true that they both use the same words. Both talk of net income. But they don't mean the same thing. Net income in accounting is entirely different from net income in taxes. This is desirably so, because their purposes are so different.

Accounting seeks to reflect a company's standing and results, and to do so fairly. Taxes are designed to raise revenue, and to do so expeditiously. While accounting tries to be objective, taxes are geared to the expedient. Taxes must also maintain an eye on politics, economics, and general welfare.

Accounting is guided by materiality, taxes aim at exactness. In short, accounting has an entirely different orbit from taxes.

I said that each has had considerable technical influence over the other. What has accounting contributed to taxes? Many things. Here are a few:

* Reprinted from Proceedings of the Third Annual Accounting Forum of Hayden, Stone, Incorporated, December 1964, pages 19–22.
** J. S. Seidman is the managing partner of Seidman & Seidman and is a former president of the American Institute of CPAs.

Accounting got taxes to break away from the old cash-coming-in and going-out way of figuring things, and to recognize the accrual method; that is, income earned and expenditures incurred.

Accounting got taxes to unglue itself from inventories figured only at cost, and to recognize inventories at the lower of cost or market. So also, accounting got taxes to recognize a reserve for bad debts.

The reverse has also taken place. While in the main, accounting resisted tax pressures, it was inevitable that growing out of the close association with taxes there would be some rub-off on accounting. I will cover part of that ground. Each single area on its own can make a significant difference in reported earnings—up or down. All areas taken together can make the difference huge.

Let us start with the marked effect taxes have had on accounting in arriving at the figure of inventory cost. One method of calculating the flow of goods, and therefore, what's left in inventory, is to assume that the item acquired last was sold first. This is popularly known as last-in-first-out, or lifo.

In accounting circles, lifo originally was regarded as appropriate in only a very limited area. That area was where, as in mining, tanning, and petroleum, the raw material factor was constant year in and year out, involving the same sort of items. That is, like so many tons of ore, sides of leather, or gallons of oil, the individual units within each item were uniform and unidentifiable one from the other. However, when tax law gave the lifo method its blessing, no such limitation was included. Now, inventory on lifo is found in financial statements even of department stores and specialty stores.

How come? This spectacular extension didn't develop from a sudden awakening to the accounting merits of lifo in the broader area. On its own, it probably never would have gotten accounting acceptance in the extended field. But taxes pressured accounting with tax advantage, and accounting buckled under.

Lifo is really old hat, and so let's take a brand new item just put into the tax law in 1964. It is called the imputed interest rule. It says that on sales—and even tax free exchanges—of property involving deferred payments, where little or no interest is provided for on the deferred payments in the arrangements made by the parties themselves, interest at 5% is to be imputed to both the buyer and the seller.

Watch the immediate impact of this on accounting. I am ready to give dollars to doughnut holes that this theoretical interest for tax purposes will now be reported as actual interest income or expense in financial statements.

Before this, accounting did not impute interest. Was accounting wrong last year, and made right now? Did it require taxes to wake accounting up? Or is accounting another John Q. Milquetoast, letting taxes push it around?

Let's consider some potential areas—things that have not happened but are in the wind. For this, let's go back to inventory again. Many accountants feel that inventory should be costed out only for material, labor, and direct expenses. They say that fixed charges like depreciation, rent, taxes, and so on, should not be considered as part of inventory cost, but rather taken in full as an expense of the year. This is known as direct costing.

So far, the tax rules don't permit direct costing, and neither do the accounting rules. What do you think will happen if the tax rules are changed? I predict that many companies will flock to direct costing, and accounting will meekly give way.

The second potential area has to do with capital erosion because of inflation. Neither accounting nor taxes today allows for the diminishing purchasing power of the dollar and resulting higher replacement prices. Were taxes to make the allowance, accounting would assuredly follow suit. This was established in a recent questionnaire to industry.

But if it is good accounting, it is good accounting without reference to taxes. Why should accounting wait for taxes to take the initiative? Doesn't waiting for taxes reflect on soundness and independence, the two things that should be at the very foundation of accounting principles?

What is behind all this amiability or deference to taxes shown by accounting? There are many factors. Taxation is eminently practical, and so is accounting. Taxpayers like to avoid two sets of books. Separate reconciliation between book and taxable income can be ponderous and costly, especially with things like inventories involving a huge number of items.

Besides, book figures that differ from tax figures can sometimes work against the taxpayer and result in higher taxes. It is natural for a taxpayer to resist following accounting if it means paying taxes at rates of 48% as corporations or 70% as individuals.

I recognize that accounting must be utilitarian to be of real value to business. But surely there is a point where utilitarianism ends and opportunism begins. Just such a test came in 1954, and accounting flunked.

The case involved expense reserves. Until 1954, taxes, except for bad debt reserves, did not allow a deduction against the current year's income for things that might happen in the future to the current year's income. In other words, taxes ignored the fundamental accounting principle of matching costs against revenues. The result was that costs for matters like product and service guarantees, cash discounts on sales, etc., were allowable only in the year actually experienced.

But in 1954 came the change in law to allow expense reserves. Then what happened? The fertility and nimbleness of the taxpayer mind, aided and abetted by accountants, trotted out reserves never dreamed of or appearing in financial statements before. Reserves were conjured up for things like major overhaul of plant, anticipated returns of merchandise sold, future collection costs of receivables, claims of all sorts.

Taxes took fright at all this, and in 1955—that is, one year later—the allowance for expense reserves was retroactively repealed. Now what happened? The same voices that were so vociferous that all these reserves were in order suddenly became mute. Accounting crept back into its old shell, and these reserves have never been heard from since.

This whole episode was not one of accounting's better performances. To the contrary, the cat-and-mouse approach exposed accounting to a bit of hypocrisy, in draping itself around the word "principles." Either these reserves belong in financial statements, or they don't. If they do, why aren't they shown now, taxes or no taxes? Why are earnings reported that do not take these reserves into consideration? If the reserves really don't belong in financial statements, didn't accounting dabble in a bit of prostitution to help grab off some tax dollars? The very least that can be said is that accounting certainly came off with a tarnished image on that one.

Other illustrations can be given of where accounting succumbed to taxes, as in stock options, pensions, etc., but I think enough has already been established to formulate conclusions.

Obviously, there have been times when the tax tail wagged the accounting dog. Shouldn't accounting say to taxes, "So far will I go, and no further?" Shouldn't accounting at least in its own bailiwick be leader, rather than led? Otherwise, doesn't accounting face the forfeit of its birthright?

Over 18 million investors look to accounting statements to help decide whether to buy, sell, or hold securities. Tax figures or earnings won't do this. It takes statements based on sound accounting principles.

We have seen that the marriage of accounting and taxes produces the wrong boss of the household. Let them part company in recognition that they really have nothing in common. As the youngsters say, accounting must stop playing footsie with taxes.

We must not let taxes blind us to the essential purpose of accounting, namely, to report what happened—not to do special pleading or produce special effects. To put this in dramatic terms, taxes have a lean and hungry look. Unless accounting exercises vigilance, it will fall prey to tax cannibalism. I hope accounting will not thus go to pot!

33. Generally Accepted Accounting Principles in the United States*

Weldon Powell**

The standard independent certified public accountant's opinion on financial statements issued in the United States reads as follows:

We have examined the balance sheet of X Company as of December 31, 19— and the related statements of income and retained earnings for the year then ended. Our examination was made in accordance with generally accepted auditing standards, and accordingly included such tests of the accounting records and such other auditing procedures as we considered necessary in the circumstances.

In our opinion, the accompanying balance sheet and statements of income and retained earnings present fairly the financial position of X Company at December 31, 19—, and the results of its operations for the year then ended, in conformity with generally accepted accounting principles applied on a basis consistent with that of the preceding year.

The first paragraph of the standard opinion deals with the nature and extent of the audit examination. The second paragraph contains the expression of the accountant's opinion on the financial statements examined. The essence of this opinion is that the financial statements are a fair presentation "in conformity with *generally accepted accounting principles.*"

The term "generally accepteed accounting principles" is required as the frame of reference in accountants' opinions by generally accepted auditing standards as set forth in a special report [1] by the Committee

---

* Reprinted by special permission from Weldon Powell, *Selected Papers—1963,* New York: Haskin & Sells, 1964, pages 13–29. First published in *Die Wirtschaft-sprufung,* the Journal of the German Institute of Certified Public Accountants, February 1964.

** Weldon Powell was a former Senior Partner of Haskin & Sells.

[1] Generally Accepted Auditing Standards, a special report by the Committee on Auditing Procedure, published in 1954, sets forth (1) General Standards, as to training, independence, and due care in the performance of work; (2) Standards of Field Work, which relate to planning the audit, evaluation of internal control, and the competence of evidential matter; and (3) Standards of Reporting which require that,

1. "The report shall state whether the financial statements are presented in accordance with generally accepted principles of accounting.
2. "The report shall state whether such principles have been consistently observed in the current period in relation to the preceding period.
3. "Informative disclosures in the financial statements are to be regarded as reasonably adequate unless otherwise stated in the report.
4. "The report shall either contain an expression of opinion regarding the financial statements, taken as a whole, or an assertion to the effect that an opinion cannot be expressed. When an over-all opinion cannot be expressed, the reasons therefor should be stated. In all cases where an auditor's name is associated with financial statements the report should contain a clear-cut indication of the character of the auditor's examination, if any, and the degree of responsibility he is taking."

on Auditing Procedure of the American Institute of Certified Public Accountants, the national professional organization of certified public accountants in the United States. Moreover, the Code of Professional Ethics of the Institute provides that a member or associate may be held guilty of an act discreditable to the profession if "he fails to direct attention to any material departure from generally accepted accounting principles. . . ."

In view of the significance attached to this term in the accountant's opinion, it may be surprising to the practitioner outside the United States to learn that "generally accepted accounting principles" have never been officially defined by any governmental authority or professional organization. Although the Director of Accounting Research of the American Institute of Certified Public Accountants has recently undertaken a project to prepare a catalogue of these principles, at present no such catalogue exists.

It should not be inferred from this that generally accepted accounting principles do not exist. Rather, it reflects the fact that they have evolved through years of practice, not unlike the evolution of the common law. The term "generally accepted accounting principles" first appeared as a frame of reference in the accountant's opinion in the 1930s (as accepted principles of accounting) as a result of the joint efforts of the New York Stock Exchange and the American Institute of Certified Public Accountants (then known as the American Institute of Accountants) to develop ways to educate the public concerning the significance, as well as limitations, of financial statements, and to make published corporate reports more informative and authoritative.

In this connection the Institute dealt with such matters as the nature and importance of financial statements, considered the nature of accounting principles underlying their preparation, and recommended that corporations be required to apply,

 . . . certain broad principles of accounting which have won fairly general acceptance, and within the limits of such broad principles to make no attempt to restrict the right of corporations to select detailed methods of accounting deemed by them to be best adapted to the requirements of their business. (Emphasis added.)

In addition, the Institute recommended and the Exchange agreed to a change in the form of the accountant's opinion so that the accountant would specifically report to the shareholders whether the accounts were presented in accordance with "accepted principles of accounting."

Thus, the desire to achieve more informative and authoritative reports led to the concept that accounting principles be judged by their general acceptance; hence the term "generally accepted accounting principles."

DEVELOPMENT OF GENERALLY ACCEPTED ACCOUNTING PRINCIPLES

"Generally accepted accounting principles" in the United States have evolved through years of practice, and their development has been influenced primarily by the business and financial communities and the accounting profession. As a principle has become commonly applied it has acquired the stamp of "general" acceptability and has been recognized as such by the various elements of the United States economy concerned with financial statements. It is important to stress that the development of principles and their application has been voluntary on the part of business, rather than enforced by law, regulation, or other fiat.

The development of generally accepted accounting principles has also been greatly influenced by the accounting requirements of the United States Securities and Exchange Commission and the stock exchanges, primarily the New York Stock Exchange. Furthermore, the influence of these organizations has resulted in greater adherence to generally accepted accounting principles.

New York Stock Exchange

The New York Stock Exchange was one of the first to call for financial reporting to stockholders in an era when few companies published financial data. Since about the year 1900, the Exchange has required that a company issue financial reports to stockholders in order to list its stock on the Exchange. Moreover these financial reports must comply with generally accepted accounting principles.

In the area of reporting financial data the Exchange has long required the publication of comparative consolidated financial statements, the disclosure of the method of inventory valuation and depreciation policy, and the segregation of operating costs in the income statement.

United States Securities and Exchange Commission

The Securities and Exchange Commission is an administrative agency of the United States Government, established by the Congress to administer various statutes relating to the issuance and sale of securities to the public. The SEC, however, is also quasi-legislative in nature: It promulgates rules and regulations and prescribes registration and report forms. It is also quasi-judicial in nature: It conducts investigations, holds hearings, and issues orders and opinions, some of which are of a disciplinary character. Many of the Commission's actions are subject to judicial review.

The Securities Act of 1933 and the Securities Exchange Act of 1934, two of the basic acts administered by the SEC, have had great influence on the widespread application of "generally accepted accounting principles."

These acts require, with some exceptions, that new offerings of securities be registered with the SEC by the issuing corporation. In addition, these corporations and corporations having securities listed for trading on national securities exchanges are required to file annual financial reports with the Commission.

The SEC has established accounting requirements that govern the form and content of financial statements and provide that dependable, informative financial statements that disclose fully and fairly the financial position and results of operations be filed with it and furnished to prospective investors. The acts contain civil and criminal penalties where untrue statements of a material fact are made, or where material facts necessary to make the statements not misleading are omitted.

The SEC generally has not asserted control over annual reports to stockholders. In practice, however, stockholder reports are essentially the same as those filed with the SEC except that some of the supplementary information required by the Commission is usually omitted in stockholder reports.

In establishing its accounting requirements, the SEC issued Regulation S-X in 1940 to deal primarily with the form and content of financial statements filed with it. In addition, from time to time the Commission has rendered decisions in cases before it and its staff has issued Accounting Series Releases expressing views and requirements as to specific applications of accounting principles.

In this manner the SEC has dealt with such matters as asset valuation, accounting for stockholders' equities, income determination, financial statement footnotes, all-inclusive versus current operating concept of the income statement, interaction of financial accounting and the income tax, consolidated statements, pension plans, depreciation and replacement cost, and price-level adjustments.

However, in the broad area of accounting principles, the Commission's reliance for full and fair disclosure in corporate reports has been on the application of generally accepted accounting principles. Moreover, the Commission stated in Accounting Series Release No. 4 in 1938 that reports prepared in accordance with accounting principles for which there is no authoritative support would be presumed misleading or inaccurate despite disclosures contained in the footnotes, or opinion, if the matters are material.

The influence of the SEC on the development of generally accepted accounting principles has for the most part been indirect. In setting high standards to obtain full and fair disclosure in reports filed with the Commission, and in insisting on compliance with generally accepted accounting principles, the Commission has influenced corporations to report to their stockholders in no less an informative manner.

Internal Revenue Service and the Federal Income Tax

Income-tax laws in the United States, with some exceptions, have not had a major influence on the development of generally accepted accounting principles. In fact, the gap between tax laws and accounting principles seems to be widening to the extent that the income tax is becoming more of an excise tax. In general, tax accounting and financial accounting need not be the same. The outstanding exception to this generalization, however, is the general acceptance of the LIFO (last-in, first-out) method of inventory valuation. The method has gained widespread adoption for tax purposes because it results in the postponement of income taxes. Its appearance in financial statements stems primarily from the requirement that it be used in the books of the taxpayer in order to be acceptable for tax purposes.

Depreciation accounting has also been greatly influenced by the income-tax laws and the majority of companies record the same depreciation they are allowed for tax purposes. This is not required by the income-tax laws, however, and many companies have substantial differences between tax and book depreciation. In general, where this difference results from tax depreciation's being greater than book depreciation, a provision for deferred taxes is recorded. Where book depreciation exceeds tax depreciation, no accounting recognition is given to the tax effect of the difference.

Of course, the income-tax laws have had a tremendous impact on the profession of accountancy through the expansion of the role of the accountant in the business and financial community. Nevertheless, the income-tax laws have not contributed substantially to the development of generally accepted accounting principles.

American Institute of Certified Public Accountants

Perhaps the greatest contribution to the development of accounting principles has come from the members of the profession through the American Institute of Certified Public Accountants.

The early interest of the AICPA, and the profession, in the development of generally accepted accounting principles is shown by the publication of "Approved Methods for the Preparation of Balance Sheet

Statements." Prepared by the Institute in 1917 at the request of the United States Federal Trade Commission for the purpose of achieving greater uniformity in accounting practices, especially with respect to financial statements submitted for bank credit purposes, the publication dealt with auditing procedures, financial statement presentation, and the application of principles to specific accounts and transactions. This work was revised and reissued in 1929 under the title, "Verification of Financial Statements."

The major contribution of the Institute during this early period was the 1934 publication, "Audits of Corporate Accounts." An outgrowth of the joint efforts of the AICPA and the New York Stock Exchange, discussed previously, this publication examined the nature and importance of financial statements, considered the nature of accounting principles underlying their preparation, recommended that corporations be required to apply certain broad principles of accounting which had gained general acceptance, advocated a change in the auditor's opinion, and set forth five principles which were later adopted by the membership of the Institute.

1. "Unrealized profit should not be credited to income account of the corporation either directly or indirectly, through the medium of charging against such unrealized profits amounts which would ordinarily fall to be charged against income account. Profit is deemed to be realized when a sale in the ordinary course of business is effected, unless the circumstances are such that the collection of the sale price is not reasonably assured. An exception to the general rule may be made in respect of inventories in industries (such as the packing-house industry) in which, owing to the impossibility of determining costs, it is a trade custom to take inventories at net selling prices, which may exceed cost.

2. "Capital surplus, however created, should not be used to relieve the income account of the current [or] future years of charges which would otherwise fall to be made thereagainst. This rule might be subject to the exception that where, upon reorganization, a reorganized company would be relieved of charges which would require to be made against income if the existing corporation were continued, it might be regarded as permissible to accomplish the same result without reorganization provided the facts were as fully revealed to and the action as formally approved by the shareholders as in reorganization.

3. "Earned surplus of a subsidiary company created prior to acquisition does not form a part of the consolidated earned surplus of the parent company and subsidiaries; nor can any dividend

declared out of such surplus properly be credited to the income account of the parent company.

4. "While it is perhaps in some circumstances permissible to show stock of a corporation held in its own treasury as an asset, if adequately disclosed, the dividends on stock so held should not be treated as a credit to the income account of the company.

5. "Notes or accounts receivable due from officers, employees or affiliated companies must be shown separately and not included under a general heading such as Notes Receivable or Accounts Receivable."

Accounting Research Bulletins

From 1938 to 1959, the principal voice of the public accounting profession concerned with the continued evolution of accounting principles was that of the Committee of Accounting Procedure of the AICPA. Formed in the Fall of 1938, the Committee in its first report concluded that it would not be practical or desirable to formulate comprehensive rules covering the whole field of accounting. Rather, the report stated that its plan was,

. . . *to consider specific topics, first of all in relation to the existing state of practice, and to recommend, wherever possible, one or more alternative procedures as being definitely superior in its opinion to other procedures which have received a certain measure of recognition and, at the same time, to express itself adversely in regard to procedures which should in its opinion be regarded as unacceptable.*

In considering each case, particularly where alternative methods seems to possess substantial merit, it will aim to consider the conflict of considerations which make such a situation possible and thus gradually to prepare the way for further narrowing of choices.

Issuance of an opinion required the approval of two-thirds of the twenty-one-member Committee.

The authority of the pronouncements issued by the Committee rested on their general acceptability, rather than on any compulsion. Indeed, each opinion reiterated that,

Except in cases in which formal adoption by the Institute membership has been asked and secured, the authority of opinions reached by the committee rests upon their general acceptability. The committee recognizes that in extraordinary cases fair presentation and justice to all parties at interest may require exceptional treatment. But the burden of justifying departure from accepted procedures, to the extent that they are evidenced in committee opinions, must be assumed by those who adopt another treatment.

From 1939 to 1959 the Committee issued 51 Accounting Research Bulletins dealing with such topics as:

Business combinations
Consolidated financial statements
Contingencies
Depreciation
Foreign operations
Intangibles
Income taxes
Inventory pricing
Leases
Presentation of income and retained earnings
Stock dividends
Stock options
Working capital

The influence of the Committee is evident in the fact that its Accounting Research Bulletins are generally regarded as authoritative statements on the application of accounting principles. The SEC has, with rare exceptions, accepted the Accounting Research Bulletins as guides to accepted accounting practices.

Accounting Principles Board

In 1959 the Committee on Accounting Procedure was superseded by the Accounting Principles Board. The formation of the Board reflected a change in emphasis of the AICPA from the issuance of pronouncements on specific accounting problems as they arose to the development and codification of accounting principles as a basis for dealing with such problems. The broad problems of financial accounting are visualized as requiring attention at four levels: first, postulates; second, principles; third, rules or other guides for the application of principles in specific situations; and fourth, research.

To carry out the research phase of the project, an accounting research staff was formed under a Director of Accounting Research. When a research project is undertaken, a project advisory committee, composed of Institute members and qualified individuals from industry and other sources, is formed under the chairmanship of a member of the Board to consult and work with the staff in the conduct of the project. Research studies published upon completion of research projects are intended to be informative, but tentative and not highly authoritative. Their function is to explore problems under review, giving pro and con arguments and offering conclusions and recommendations. Before the formulation of any conclusions by the APB, the research studies are widely distributed so that members of the profession, the business and financial communities, and others can have an opportunity to express their views. In this manner the APB hopes to obtain a consensus and be in a position to issue statements on generally accepted accounting principles. To date, five research studies have been published and seven other research projects are in progress.

Statements of the position of the AICPA concerning generally accepted accounting principles can be issued only by the Board and must be approved by two-thirds of its twenty-one members. To date, two statements, not related to research studies, have been issued. In the usual case, it is expected that statements of the Board will result from research studies. As was true with the former Committee on Accounting Procedure, the authority of the pronouncements of the Board in the absence of formal membership approval rests upon their general acceptability. It is expected, however, that these statements will be regarded as authoritative expressions of what constitutes generally accepted accounting principles.

Other Accounting Organizations

Among the other accounting organizations that have contributed to the development of generally accepted accounting principles, is the American Accounting Association, an organization consisting primarily of educators. Its publication, "Accounting and Reporting Standards for Corporate Financial Statements," sets forth the views of the organization on the framework of accounting principles underlying corporate reports.

In addition, important contributions have been made by individual practitioners and educators through personal contributions to accounting literature and text books.

DESCRIPTION OF GENERALLY ACCEPTED ACCOUNTING PRINCIPLES

Against the background of the foregoing discussion, and emphasizing again that generally accepted accounting principles in the United States have evolved through practice and have not been codified or catalogued, I shall describe what I consider some of these principles to be. In doing so, I shall use "principles" in a broad sense to include assumptions, doctrines and conventions, as well as postulates and practices.

Accounting entities Accounting is conducted for specific entities. An entity represents a group of assets subject to common control and may be legal (corporation, trust) or non-legal (single proprietorship, partnership). The entity is viewed as the owner of the assets and the recipient of the income.

Accrual accounting   Accounting under the accrual basis requires that income be recorded in the period earned or realized and that expenses be recorded in the period incurred.

Conservatism   Conservatism represents a policy of caution, a desire to avoid positive error and to lean to the safe side. Conservatism may be illustrated by the phrase "record no gains till realized, but record losses when recognized." Conservatism, however, does not countenance the accumulation of secret or hidden reserves.

Consistency   The principle requires the consistent application of accounting practices and methods by a given company through periods of time. An inconsistency must be disclosed in financial statements and in the accountant's opinion. For example, a change from the straight-line to an accelerated method of depreciation or from the FIFO to the LIFO method of inventory cost would be an inconsistency requiring disclosure.

A change in conditions necessitating an accounting change, such as a change in the estimated useful life of property, does not create an inconsistency in accounting principles.

Cost   In general, assets are accounted for on the basis of acquisition cost measured in cash or its equivalent. Whenever assets are acquired in exchange for non-cash assets, cost may be considered either the fair market value of the consideration given or the fair market value of the property received, whichever is more clearly evident.

Going concern   The accounting for the transactions of a going concern is conducted under the assumption that it will continue in operation indefinitely.

Informative disclosure   Financial statements should disclose all information necessary to make the statements not misleading. This doctrine relates to such things as form, content, parenthetical comments, and notes to the financial statements.

Matching cost against revenue   This principle requires that costs incurred (or to be incurred) to produce revenues be recorded as expenses in the same period that the revenues are recorded. The application of this principle can result in the accrual of costs in periods preceding that in which incurred (future expenses under a product warranty) or the deferral of costs to a period subsequent to that in which incurred (research and development expenditures).

Materiality Inherently a part of the application of accounting principles, the doctrine of materiality specifies that items of little or no consequence may be dealt with as expediency may suggest.

Objectivity To the extent practicable accounting should be based on facts as shown by completed transactions. When estimation is required (depreciation, bad debts, etc.), the accountant should be objective in the required determinations.

Realization Income should not be recorded until it is realized. In general, income is realized when a sale or exchange is made or when services are rendered and a collectible receivable (or equivalent) results.

Stable measuring unit The dollar, which is the unit of account, is assumed to be a stable measuring unit. This assumption and its questionable validity are discussed later.

Uniform accounting period Comparability in reporting requires that accounting reports be prepared for uniform periodic intervals.

The foregoing principles, assumptions, conventions or doctrines have served as the base from which accounting practices have grown. Many of the practices are self-evident from the description of the principles. Other practices and matters of interest are discussed under the following headings:

Financial statements
Inventories
Fixed assets
Intangible assets
Net income
Price-level adjustments

Financial Statements

The basic financial statements in the United States considered necessary for the fair presentation of financial position and results of operations are the statement of financial position (balance sheet), the statement of income and the statement of earnings retained in the business (earned surplus). Frequently, the last two statements are combined. The statement of funds is becoming increasingly popular and is included in many reports to stockholders; it is not, however, considered one of the basic financial statements.

In the statement of financial position, assets and liabilities are usually divided between current and non-current. One year is the normal dividing point between current and non-current although the time length of the normal operating cycle may be the dividing point if it is clearly defined and exceeds one year.

Reasonable detail is given under each balance sheet caption, including disclosure of receivables from officers, employees and affiliates. The valuation basis of assets is stated. Stockholders' equity is divided into its major components: capital stock, other paid-in capital, and earnings retained in the business.

The income statement generally reveals sales, cost of goods sold, selling and administrative expenses, operating profit, Federal income taxes, and net income. Depreciation and depletion charges are separately stated.

Notes to financial statements usually disclose such matters as:

Assets subject to lien
Changes in accounting practices
Consolidation practices
Contingent liabilities
Commitments
Long-term lease agreements
Pension and retirement plans
Post balance sheet disclosures
Preferred stock data—call, conversion, or preference features
Restrictions on the availability of retained earnings for dividends
Retroactive adjustments
Stock options and stock purchase plans

Inventories

The primary basis of accounting for inventory is cost, and the major objective thereof is to match costs with revenues for purposes of income determination.

Only those costs which are necessary in bringing an article to its final condition and location are included in the inventory. For example, normal manufacturing overhead is included but costs arising from idle capacity, excessive spoilage, and other abnormal costs may be excluded. General and administrative expenses may be included in inventory to the extent applicable to the manufacturing process; selling costs are not included.

Accounting for the flow of cost (expired vs. unexpired) may be accomplished by specific identification, or, as is more common, by an assumption as to cost flow—first-in, first-out; last-in, first-out; average. The objective under these methods is a reasonable assignment of costs to the physical inventory on hand without the need for specific identification.

With few exceptions, inventories are valued at the lower of cost or market value. As used in inventory valuation, market value means the current cost to replace the article by purchase or reproduction. There is, however, both a floor and a ceiling to the market value thus established; it should not exceed the net realizable value (normal selling price less costs of completion and disposal) and it should not be less than net realizable value reduced by a normal profit margin.

Fixed Assets

The common basis of accounting for fixed assets is acquisition cost. As in the case of inventories, accounting for the flow of cost may proceed under different methods, each of which will result in a different periodic cost allocation. The most frequently used depreciation method is the straight-line, age-life method although the so-called accelerated methods, double-declining balances and sum-of-the-years-digits methods have become increasingly popular since 1954 when they became allowable for income tax purposes (see page 219). The unit of production methods are also widely used by the sinking fund, annuity or other interest methods are used only rarely in special situations.

Over the last two decades the cost of replacing fixed assets in the United States has increased considerably. Because of this, consideration has been given from time to time to the desirability of writing up fixed assets to reflect these higher values on the balance sheet and in depreciation charges. The advocates of this procedure maintain that it would reflect periodic income on a more realistic basis and would result in accumulated depreciation provisions more nearly equal to the replacement values. The more conventional view that it is not the function of depreciation to provide for the replacement of property has prevailed, however, and depreciation based on the cost of property remains the generally accepted method.

Intangible Assets

Intangible assets are carried at cost or cost less amortization. Those intangible assets having a limited life, whether by law or by their nature, are amortized by systematic charges to income over the period of their useful lives. Intangibles falling within this category are patents, copyrights, leases, licenses, franchises, and some forms of goodwill.

Intangible assets that do not have a limited life, such as perpetual franchises, trade names, secret processes, and most goodwill, may be carried at cost or amortized by charges to income over a reasonable period of time. If it becomes evident that the benefit period of such intangibles has become limited, then the intangibles should be amortized by charges to income.

It is not considered acceptable to write-off intangibles in a lump sum immediately after acquisition.

Net Income

In reporting net income for the year, it is generally accepted that all items of profit and loss recognized during the year are to be included. The only exceptions to this practice relate to material items that are unrelated to the typical business operations of the period and that if included in the determination of net income might tend to impair the significance of net income and lead to misleading inferences.

According to Research Bulletin No. 43 issued by the Committee on Accounting Procedure of the AICPA, only the following items may be excluded from the determination of net income:

a. Material charges or credits related to operations of prior years.
b. Material charges or credits arising from unusual sales of assets not acquired for resale.
c. Material losses resulting from events not usually insured against.
d. Material charges arising from the write-off of intangible assets that have become worthless.
e. Material charges arising from the write-off of bond discount or premium and bond issue expenses at the time of the retirement or refunding of the debt before maturity.

The items excluded from the determination of net income may either be shown as charges or credits to surplus in a separate statement of retained earnings or be shown in the income statement below net income under the caption "special items" with the final figure in the income statement being designated "Net income and special items."

Price-level Adjustments

The assumption of a stable measuring unit, fundamental to accounting, has been subject to question over the past two decades because of the inflation the economy has experienced.[2] The position taken by the accounting profession over the years, and reflected in accounting practice, has been to adhere to historical cost and the stable dollar assumption. Despite suggestions that supplementary statements reflecting price-level adjustments would be valuable to users of financial statements, few companies have presented such information.

[2] U.S. Dept. of Labor Wholesale price index, 1947-1949 = 100, August 1963 = 119. U.S. Dept. of Labor Consumer price index, 1947-1949 = 100, July 1963 = 131. U.S. Dept. of Commerce, Construction cost index, 1947-1949 = 100, August 1963 = 152.

The accounting profession and the business community in the United States are well aware of the changes that have taken place in the purchasing power of the dollar. Moreover, the stable dollar assumption never envisioned a rigid inflexible price structure. Rather, it was assumed that fluctuations in the value of the dollar, such as they were, would not have a materially significant impact on the financial statements.

In recent years, members of the profession and the American Institute of Certified Public Accountants have expressed the opinion that with the prospect of a continued lack of price stability it would be unrealistic to ignore fluctuations in the value of the dollar.

Although the stable dollar assumption continued to underlie the preparation of conventional statements, the Accounting Principles Board expressed the opinion that it would be wise to explore ways and means of presenting separate financial statements in terms of "common dollars"; such common dollars would explicitly reveal gains and losses in purchasing power resulting from the monetary position of the firm, and reveal the composition of long-term assets in terms of current purchasing power.

To that end, there has been under way since 1961 a research project, the results of which may be published shortly [3] for purposes of exposure and comment by members of the profession and the business community. The ultimate goal is to achieve some acceptable methods for dealing with the problem.

SUMMARY

The objectives of this article have been to acquaint the practitioner outside the United States with the generally accepted accounting principles that provide the framework of accounting and reporting practice in the United States. To aid in an understanding of these principles, I have discussed the evolutionary and voluntary nature of their development and have described some of the major forces that have contributed to their development.

Generally accepted accounting principles are the basic frame of reference in the auditor's opinion; they have gained the respect and confidence of financial statement users. This development, however, is not complete; it likely never will be. Many difficult and controversial problems remain. The research studies and the research projects of the Director of Accounting Research of the American Institute of Certified Public Accountants deal with some of these problems, others will be dealt with in due course. It is my earnest hope that our accounting problems will continue to be resolved in the manner I have described in this paper.

[3] Since published as Accounting Research Study No. 6, "Reporting the Financial Effects of Price-Level Changes."

34. The Accounting Principles Dilemma*

John R. E. Parker**

Accounting is often called the 'language of business,' for it is by means of accounting that the financial effects of business transactions are reported to interested parties. To those outside a business, accounting is the principal 'language' of communication about its affairs. At the same time, accounting is also concerned with providing internal management with information for decision making. At times these two functions are sufficiently far apart to almost suggest an analogy with the Canadian problem of two languages; the language of the public accountant and that of the managerial accountant are at least two separate dialects.

The distinction between the internal (managerial) and external (financial) aspects of accounting has become much more pronounced in recent years. One writer suggests that the "distinction is so great that a serious question has been raised as to whether both sets of characteristics can be preserved practically within a single set of procedures." [1]

DIVERSE READERSHIP OF STATEMENTS

With respect to external reporting, a further complication exists because of the diverse readership of financial statements. Although financial statements serve the interests of shareholders, management, creditors, labour, customers, government agencies and the public, they are still essentially general purpose statements. It is of course obvious that general purpose statements cannot be expected to satisfy equally the requirements of every interested group. At the same time it must be recognized that neither management nor the accountant has control over those who may read or use published financial statements. This being so, financial reporting must seek to provide reliable information that can be used by, and not be misleading to, any interested group.

In recent years there have been strong pressures for more flexibility and pragmatism in accounting matters, and although tradition favours

* Reprinted from *The Canadian Chartered Accountant*, October 1964, pages 271–273.

** John R. E. Parker is Senior Lecturer in Accounting at Queen's University in Canada.

[1] Richard L. Smith, *Management through Accounting*: Prentice-Hall Inc., Englewood Cliffs, 1962; p. 29.

flexibility there also exists substantial evidence of a desire to minimize the areas of difference in accounting. This conflict between uniformity and flexibility is one of the most important problems facing the accounting profession today, and without intending to minimize its complexity, it is suggested that pragmatism and flexibility are consistent with the aims and objectives of managerial accounting. However, such is certainly not the case with respect to the external reporting function of financial accounting.

There is an urgent need for sound, objective criteria in accounting matters which will facilitate financial reporting that is fair to all segments of our complex society. This need is easily stated and is not likely to provoke the disagreement of readers. However, the nature of the accounting process and certain characteristics of the accounting profession, among other factors, severely limit the attainment of what is needed.

NATURE OF THE ACCOUNTING PROCESS

Although accounting is not a precisely definable process it nevertheless performs a vital service to a wide variety of interested parties. There is a significant utilitarian basis inherent in its techniques because it has evolved from the practical needs of business. Its dominant characteristics are rooted in *a priori* logic and in its own historical functions. It is interesting to note that accounting, paradoxically, is based on subtle and complex concepts, which are nevertheless given their outward expression in the form of simple arithmetic. It is therefore incorrectly assumed to be a simple and concise kind of craft.

THE ROOT OF THE PROBLEMS

The interests served by accounting, the data handled and the functions performed have in common the characteristic of diversity. In the performance of his functions the accountant, of necessity, operates within a context of uncertainty, in the sense that definite knowledge about an outcome or result is often lacking. The impact of these two characteristics, diversity and uncertainty, cannot be overemphasized. The major accounting problems, in both theory and practice, are largely rooted in these characteristics.

In a very real sense the cost of the accounting function is also intermingled with the characteristics of diversity and uncertainty. Modern computers may make it possible to achieve a degree of accounting accuracy not practical with other methods. However, in practice, regardless of the manner in which data is processed, it must still be determined whether the incremental information is worth its incremental cost. Provided the item in question is not material, a policy of expediency consistently applied is often adequate—and perhaps necessary—in practical accounting.

The external aspects of accounting necessitate objectivity and a significant degree of uniformity because, in effect, financial reporting is cast in the role of an umpire. However—largely because of diversity—objectivity and uniformity can only be achieved at the expense of utility to specific interested parties. The inevitable result is a constant pressure for flexibility in financial reporting.

Although accountants may strive for objectivity in financial reporting, because of uncertainty, accounting interpretations are in varying degrees subjective and arbitrary. A further problem, particularly with respect to subjectivity, arises from the neutrality inherent in the concept of professional independence.

In order to mitigate the impact of diversity and uncertainty, accounting methods emphasize the processing of events and transactions in ways that can command the confidence of interested parties. The audit function provides further assurance to those who use financial statements.

The adaptation of accounting to a world of uncertainty largely explains the emphasis placed on such basic tenets of financial reporting as consistency and conservatism. Other precepts of financial reporting, such as full disclosure and materiality, are perhaps more a function of diversity.

NEEDS OF MANAGEMENT

With the increasing growth and complexity of modern business, more and more accounting data is necessary to guide management in making decisions. From the point of view of the business, accounting is strictly a service function and not an end in itself; therefore the internal aspects of accounting, often referred to as managerial accounting, emphasize the specific needs of the business. To a certain extent it is necessary to anticipate the uses of accounting information and adapt the processing of data to suit the circumstances. Thus in managerial accounting, purpose largely dictates the accounting process.

Although diversity and uncertainty also constitute a dilemma in managerial accounting, these characteristics are secondary to the flexibility and usefulness of the accounting system. While managerial accounting involves adapting standard financial reporting to the needs of management, its value is directly related to the success of the system in providing the information necessary for policy purposes, business decisions and cost control. It is for this reason that flexibility and usefulness are the dominant characteristics of managerial accounting.

It is hardly necessary to state that a profession requires some provision for the regulation of its members. In part this is provided by the rules of professional conduct included in the bylaws of most professional organizations, and in part by regulatory legislation that limits professional practice to one or more specified groups, or that grants legal recognition to a specific designation and restricts the use of the designation to those who have met the established qualifications. However, the authority inherent in these forms of regulation does not directly involve the body of knowledge that is characteristic of a profession.

While slightly over 50% of the chartered accountants in Canada are engaged in something other than public accounting, it is not suggested that there is any clash or dichotomy between the occupational groups that comprise the accounting profession. However, the fact remains that there is a diversity of interests that rather closely parallels the previously noted dictinction between financial and managerial accounting.

Furthermore the public accounting segment of the profession also represents a wide range of interests. This problem has been pinpointed by Prof. Kenneth F. Byrd: "The tragedy of many a chartered accountant now engaged, on the face of it, in the accounting profession is that he is not doing professional work." [2]

Given the diverse nature of the accounting function together with the diverse composition of the accounting profession, there is valid reason to question the ability of the profession in Canada to cope with the accounting principles dilemma. The problem in Canada is further complicated by the limited resources available for basic research.

With the establishment of its Accounting Principles Board in September 1959, the American Institute of Certified Public Accountants embarked on a new phase in its continuing programme of research, which it is hoped will produce an authoritative and comprehensive statement of accounting principles. A case that can be made for action in this matter by the Securities and Exchange Commission in the United States is presented in a thought-provoking article in the *Harvard Business Review*.[3] Of course, even the possibility of having its principles prescribed by a government agency is generally unpalatable to a profession.

ACCOUNTING PRINCIPLES DILEMMA

The accounting principles dilemma is not new. Writing in 1939, Stephen Gilman expressed it as follows:

Accountants are in the unenviable position of having committed themselves in their certificates as to the existence of generally accepted

---

[2] Kenneth F. Byrd, "The University's Contribution to the Education of C.A.s.," *The Canadian Chartered Accountant*, January, 1964, p. 43.

[3] Robert N. Anthony, "Showdown on Accounting Principles," *Harvard Business Review*, May-June 1963, pp. 99–106.

accounting principles while between themselves they are quarrelling as to whether there are any accounting principles and, if there are, how many of them should be recognized and accepted.[4]

The dilemma with respect to accounting principles can be briefly stated in the form of three questions:

1. What are the accounting principles referred to in the auditor's report?
2. What constitutes general acceptance—by whom and to what extent?
3. How can improvements be made if such improvements are not permissible until generally accepted?

The problem is further complicated by the fact that no definitive list of generally accepted principles exists. As a result many practices have simply evolved on an ad hoc basis.

As they presently exist, generally accepted accounting principles are incomplete in terms of fulfilling the need for an integrated and comprehensive structure of accounting theory. The bulletins of the Committee on Accounting and Auditing Research of the Canadian Institute of Chartered Accountants, together with the various releases of other professional accounting organizations, probably represent the best evidence of general acceptance. However, such statements lack the absolute authority to be binding on all accountants under all conditions. Furthermore, these bulletins and other pronouncements have been directed more to accounting practices than to the underlying principles. Therefore they generally lag behind the problems they purport to solve.

EFFECT OF ALTERNATIVE ACCOUNTING TREATMENTS

In both theoretical and practical accounting, certain events and transactions are subject to a wide range of alternative accounting treatments. Moreover the majority of available alternatives are supported by the respectability that emanates from 'general acceptance.' If it were not for the reconciling virtues of consistency and full disclosure the effect of alternative accounting treatments would certainly be chaotic.

It should also be recognized that consistency is achieved at a cost in terms of innovation and improvement. This cost is particularly significant when it is necessary to adapt accounting methods to changing circumstances.

Since accounting is, in general, utilitarian by nature, accounting

[4] Stephen Gilman, *Accounting Concepts of Profit,* published by Ronald Press Company, New York, 1939; p. 171.

principles are closely related to how accountants do their work. This close relationship between usefulness and principles is largely responsible for the flexible limits of permissibility that exist within the framework of generally accepted accounting principles.

The differences between businesses with respect to purpose, operations, size, location, legal characteristics and so forth are often cited to justify flexibility in accounting principles. Furthermore, there is the fact that at least some of the differences in accounting result from policy decisions that are the prerogative of management.

Hypothetical cases can easily be built up illustrating what can and does happen in financial reporting as a result of alternative accounting treatments. Such illustrations involve two companies that are assumed to be identical except for variations in the application of accounting principles.[5] One company uses accounting methods that are conservative in terms of income determination, the other company reports a significantly higher income as a result of using alternative accounting treatments, all of which are generally accepted. These illustrations are not designed to suggest the desirability of rigid uniformity, but point out the effect on net income, earnings per share and, by application of a price earnings ratio, the effect on the aggregate market value of the business that can result from the application of alternative accounting practices now actually being followed in industry.

ACCOUNTING STANDARDS

At least for the purposes of external reporting, logic suggests that it is necessary to eliminate the wide range of alternative practices currently available under generally accepted accounting principles. Within the context of the profession's minimum requirements the auditor must be satisfied that the accounting practices followed by clients conform to what are judged to be generally accepted accounting principles applied on a basis consistent with that of the preceding year.

It is the responsibility of the professional accountant to prepare financial statements that are fair to all segments of our complex society. As a prerequisite, the criterion of fairness assumes in him the competence and integrity to ascertain the economic facts of business transactions, to evaluate these facts, and with professional independence to report the facts as found and evaluated. However, the concept of fairness is largely subjective, and herein lies a critical problem in financial reporting.

[5] Leonard Spacek, "Business Success Requires an Understanding of Unresolved Problems of Accounting and Financial Reporting," Davidson et al. (editors); *An Income Approach to Accounting Theory,* published by Prentice-Hall Inc., Englewood Cliffs, 1964; p. 539.

It is obvious that there is an urgent need for basic research in accounting. At the same time, hasty and ill-conceived changes in accounting principles must be avoided. The scope and range of the environment in which accounting operates is so varied that it is extremely difficult to visualize a solution to the accounting principles dilemma. It is also clear that continued reliance on the process of gradual evolution is inconsistent with the degree of urgency that currently prevails. The only reasonable conclusions are:

> The accounting principles dilemma is the most important problem facing the accounting profession.

> The solution thereto must lie in basic research. It must also be recognized that the aggressive leadership of the accounting profession is expected, both by its members and other interested parties.

35. TWA Shows Net in '68 by Changing Its Accounting*

Trans World Airlines reported a profit for 1968, but would have had a net loss if it hadn't changed accounting method features, a spokesman said.

The company changed from a "conservative" method of writing off the lives of many of its planes and adapted the same treatment used by other major airlines. Extending the depreciable life of about 60% of its aircraft from 12 or 14 years from the previous 11 years, raised TWA's 1968 net before taxes by about $20.6 million and earnings by about $14 million.

In addition, TWA took down more of its available investment tax credit in computing deferred income taxes in 1968 than in 1967. This had the effect of increasing 1968 net by about $18.4 million.

As a result of these accounting treatments, TWA reported preliminary 1968 net of $21.2 million, or $1.94 a share, compared with nearly $40.8 million, or $3.97 a share, in 1967.

Charles C. Tillinghast Jr., president, blamed "increasing costs," lower-than-expected growth in long-haul U.S. passenger traffic, and the depressing effects on its international flights resulting from the Govern-

* Reprinted from *The Wall Street Journal*, January 22, 1969.

ment's plea early in 1968 that citizens curb their foreign travel to relieve pressures on the dollar.

It was a "less-than-satisfactory year" for the airline industry, he said. Fewer passengers were carried on the average flight, meaning less profit was earned on each passenger than in 1967, he said.

Some relief may be on the way, however, industry sources believe. The Civil Aeronautics Board recently approved domestic fare boosts averaging 3.8% if the airlines apply for them. Several airlines had asked the agency for higher increases, but they are expected to go along with the CAB. The increased fares are slated to be effective March 1.

TWA's drop in 1968 earnings occurred despite a 8.2% rise in revenue to $947.2 million from $875.5 million in 1967.

Its 1968 figures are preliminary and subject to year-end audit. Net in 1968 includes $6.2 million earnings from its subsidiary, Hilton International Co., which had 1967 net of about $4.9 million. Profit from TWA's airline operations in 1968 declined to $15 million from nearly $35.9 million a year earlier.

Earnings from airline operations before income tax credit totaled about $9.1 million, or 78% below the $41.4 million in 1967.

36. FMC's Earnings in '68 Led Year Ago, Helped by Accounting Changes*

FMC Corp. earned $75.2 million, or $2.31 a share in 1968, up from $60.8 million, or $1.86 a share a year earlier. The company said the 1968 earnings were increased by $6.4 million, or 21 cents a share, due to two accounting changes, which computed depreciation on essentially all new fixed assets on the straight-line rather than accelerated methods used for additions in prior years. Also investment tax credits earnings in 1968 were reflected in income.

Sales in 1968 were $1.4 billion, up from $1.3 billion the year before. FMC said all major operating groups showed increases, except commercial machinery, which had a 6% sales decline due mostly to reduced freight car production.

Sales of fiber and film products and commercial chemicals reached highs, exceeding 1967 by 14% and 7% respectively. Defense billings increased 18%.

* Reprinted from *The Wall Street Journal*, February 6, 1969.

At year end, FMC said its backlog totaled $354 million, compared with $367 million a year earlier. Unfilled defense orders, which represented $193 million of the total, were down $39 million from the 1967 backlog.

Commercial machinery orders accounted for the $161 million balance and were up $26 million. Neither commercial chemicals nor fiber and film products are included in the company's backlog.

37. Wolverine Aluminum Auditors Are at Odds on '68 Net Per Share*

Don Smith, controversial president of Wolverine Aluminum Corp., is at odds with the company's auditors, Price Waterhouse & Co., over how 1968 earnings per share should be reported.

On Thursday Wolverine reported record 1968 earnings of $802,298, or $1.30 a share, on average outstanding shares of 615,459. However, the company noted that earnings per share didn't reflect a 25% stock distribution made to shareholders on Feb. 28, 1969.

A spokesman for Price Waterhouse in Detroit said that under accepted procedures "you should reflect the earnings per share after showing—in this case—the 25% stock dividend." The adjustment would show how much each present share earned in 1968.

Mr. Smith, who once fought for 2½ years to get Wolverine delisted from the American Stock Exchange because he wasn't happy with the volume of trading in the stock, contends that since the dividend was given in 1969 it should have nothing to do with the 1968 earnings report. Reached in Florida where he is vacationing, Mr. Smith said, "I refuse to allow Price Waterhouse or anyone to tell me what I should say to my stockholders."

He said restated 1969 earnings per share come to $1.04, but he added he didn't think "$1.04 is correct or clearly reflects the 1968 picture." The Price Waterhouse spokesman noted, despite Mr. Smith's objections, Wolverine's annual report, which is being prepared, will show earnings per share both ways.

Wolverine's 1968 earnings were 21.5% higher than 1967 net of $660,136. Originally reported earnings per share for 1967 was $1.12 a share. Mr. Smith didn't disclose adjusted 1967 earnings per share.

* Reprinted from The Wall Street Journal, March 10, 1969.

Wolverine, now traded over the counter, prefinishes and forms aluminum products for the building industry. Its shares were delisted by the American exchange on Dec. 11, 1967, after Mr. Smith repeatedly charged that specialists and floor traders weren't doing a good job for the stock. The following month he did a turnabout and blamed the company itself for the low trading volume because it didn't hire a public relations firm to promote itself.

Part
Four

Accounting
Entities

We began this book with some readings on the nature of the accounting function. Now it is time to recognize that no collection, recording, and reporting of information can take place until the entity has been identified for which "an accounting" is to be made. The need to identify an appropriate accounting entity has been basic to accounting throughout its history. There is no reason to expect a change in this regard.

The readings in Part Four illustrate a few of the large variety of accounting entities that are found in most social systems. For instance, individuals are often called upon to give an accounting of their affairs. Tax returns need to be submitted to the Internal Revenue Service every year, and statements of assets and liabilities are usually required to accompany loan applications. However, individuals are also involved with accounting matters as members of or interested parties in organizations, and individuals and organizations are in turn members of a larger socioeconomic system for which an accounting can also be made. The globe is the next logical entity, and is in fact the superordinate system of individual socioeconomic systems. The "fringe" of the global system is discussed by introducing the balance of payments concept as part of the accounting function.

As was pointed out earlier, the emphasis of traditional introductory accounting courses is usually one of financial accounting for profit oriented organizations. An inevitable result of this is the development of a financial accounting bias which hinders rather than assists when students are confronted with the accounting problems of other types of entities.

Accounting entities are goal-oriented, and it is natural that the members of these entities want to know how effective a given entity is in its endeavors to attain its goals. The goal of survival is basic to all entities. At a higher and more specific level, the goals of different entity-types tend to be different. It follows, therefore, that measures of effectiveness also need to be different. For this reason the relevant measure (profit) for profit-oriented entities does not have applicability to not-for-profit entities. Furthermore, if goals are different, problems are not necessarily similar. And different problems require different solutions. These are but a few illustrations to substantiate the argument that it is potentially detrimental for a student to be left with the impression that accounting "principles" for profit-oriented entities are generally suitable for all entity-types. Hence we proceed to the study of various entity-types immediately after a few basic orienting concepts have been identified (in earlier parts of this book).

Viewing accounting entities as systems and subsystems permits a logical approach to the study of accounting. The systems approach often makes explicit important issues, concepts, and problems which have hitherto been narrowly interpreted, overlooked, or regarded as not having anything to do with accounting. For an example one has to look no further than national income accounting, which, although clearly an accounting problem, is traditionally never discussed in accounting courses. Because of the trend to give specific recognition to the information needs of more and more interested parties, it might even be useful to change the use of terms, that is, from an accounting "entity" to an accounting "system." The entity concept tends to focus on only those parties who are the legal owners, while the systems concept requires an identification of all interested parties. The systems concept implies that *all* interested parties comprise the system, which in turn has direct implications for accounting's reporting function.

The first group of readings in Part Four describes some of the accounting problems of a variety of entity-types that may be found in a socioeconomic system. It is probable that these entity-types, with the possible exception of the profit-oriented type, may be found in most social systems—even though specific forms of entities will differ from system to system.

The American public has been exposed on numerous occasions to the cost-value problems surrounding the personal financial statements of presidential and vice-presidential candidates. In this age of affluency and credit transactions it is not unlikely that an increasing number of people are going to be constructing personal financial statements. Note is also made in the first group of readings of the fact that entities such as baseball's Minnesota Twins are enterprises which do not escape accounting problems, and that federal agencies such as the Office of Economic Opportunity are entities which pose new problems to accounting and accountants, for example cost-benefit measurements.

In addition to a look at the problems of not-for-profit and profit-oriented organizations, attention is given to the problem of international uniformity of accounting principles. This problem is becoming of increasing concern to Americans because of the ever increasing volume of private foreign investment along with the development of the multi-national corporation.

The second group of readings completes the study of accounting systems or entities by focusing on various national income concepts and related measurement problems. The global system is introduced only in the form of the balance of payments problem and its relationship to national income. If a uniform methodology were employed by all countries, and appropriate adjustments were made, one could conceivably construct a set of accounting statements for the world.

Chapter VIII

Accounting for Individuals and Organizations

38. *Audited Personal Financial Statements**

James F. Pitt and E. Palmer Tang**

Presidential Campaign 1968 is over and the votes tallied. Fading into history are the primaries, platforms, promises and platitudes. We wonder, however, how many noticed the conspicuous absence of the CPA's opinion on personal financial statements published in connection with this campaign.

Having been personally involved with the statements of one candidate in 1964 who ran for top honors in 1968, we waited anxiously to see how the profession would resolve the controversies generated in 1964 among professional and academic people. But in contrast to 1964, when it was the vogue to issue audited personal financial statements, the CPA's opinion did not accompany the candidates' financial statements published in 1968.

What happened? Was the audited personal statement a fleeting fancy, or has the accounting profession been so unrealistic in its pronouncements in this area that the disclaimer of opinion, now required in virtually every case, offers little appeal to the potential buyer of our services?

Accounting Research Bulletins issued by the American Institute of CPAs have been specifically directed to "accounting practices reflected in financial statements and representations of commercial and industrial

Reprinted by special permission from *Tempo*, published by Touche Ross & Co., December 1968, pages 4–7.
** James F. Pitt and E. Palmer Tang are partners of Touche Ross & Co.

245

Table 38.1

	President Johnson	Vice President Humphrey
Family members included in the financial statements	President and Mrs. Johnson and daughters	Vice President and Mrs. Humphrey
Titles of the financial statements	Statement of assets and liabilities; statement of capital	Statement of financial condition
Basis of reporting assets	Cost (stock in family corporation reported at cost plus share of retained earnings, reduced by applicable capital gains taxes)	Present market value (stock in family corporation reported at share of book net equity; deferred taxes reported as liability)
U.S. government pension fund	Not included	Included
Assets in trust	Included	Not included; disclosed by footnote
Household goods and personal effects	Not included	Included
Personal documents and memorabilia	Not included	Not included
Designation of excess of assets over liabilities	Capital	Net assets
Auditors' scope paragraph	Substantially standard	Substantially standard, with two additional sentences: "In this connection we have received and relied upon appraisals by real estate agents as to the present market value of real estate and upon representations from the princi-

Table 38.1 (continued)

	President Johnson	Vice President Humphrey
		pals as to the present market value of household goods and personal effects. We have also received and relied upon representations from the principals as to the completeness of the statements."
Auditors' middle paragraph	Explains basis of reporting stock in family corporations and real estate; specifically disclaims any representation that reported amounts are representative of present market values	Explains that assets are reported at present market values and recites auditors' approval of that method of reporting
Auditors' opinion paragraph	Substantially standard	Substantially standard except no reference to consistency

companies" and not to "accounting problems or procedures of religious, charitable, scientific, educational, and similar nonprofit institutions, municipalities, professional firms, and the like." [1] Until 1968 virtually no printers' ink had been consumed in defining the standards for personal financial statements.

Banks have long required personal balance sheets from their personal borrowers and from guarantors, but, since audited statements were hardly ever required, the certified public accountant has exerted little or no influence over their form and content or the method of reporting.

In most instances, the forms provided by banks to personal borrowers for reporting upon their financial position have provided specifically for reporting assets at fair market value, without regard to historical cost. While this method of reporting assets has long been considered unacceptable for commercial and industrial enterprises, it has been used almost exclusively by investment companies and stock brokers.

[1] *Accounting Research Bulletin No. 43*, American Institute of Certified Public Accountants, 1953, page 8.

Much like an individual, these companies emphasize financial condition in their reports rather than the matching of revenues and expenses. Market values, therefore, provide the most timely criteria of that condition. Market values also provide comparability for measurement of total investment performance by including the effect of realized gains (dividends on income stocks) and unrealized gains (appreciation on growth stocks).

The financial statements published by the 1964 candidates were not models of consistency—which is quite natural considering the previous lack of attention to this subject. Perhaps the greatest divergency existed between the statements of President Johnson, which were basically at cost, and those of Vice President Humphrey, which were basically at market.

At any rate these divergencies, particularly the basis of reporting, caused the greatest furor within professional and academic circles. Important differences in the form and content of these two reports and financial statements are shown [in Table 38.1].

In an attempt to clarify some of the more controversial questions posed by the inconsistencies enumerated, an ad hoc committee on personal financial statements was appointed by the American Institute of CPAs. In June 1968 this committee issued an audit guide entitled "Audits of Personal Financial Statements."

In summary, the guide sets forth the following recommendations:

1. Ordinarily a combined statement of assets and liabilities of both spouses, and possibly those of minor children, will be the most appropriate representation.
2. The title of personal financial statements should be "Statement of Assets and Liabilities," instead of the more traditional "Balance Sheet" or "Statement of Financial Condition," and "Statement of Changes in Net Assets," instead of other customary descriptions.
3. The accrual method of reporting should be employed.
4. Assets should be reported primarily on a cost basis, but preferably in columnar form with present market values shown also. Apparently, however, the committee takes the position that absence of the cost column would require an auditor's exception while absence of the present market value column would not.
5. Business interests of significant size, whether corporate shares, partnership interest, or single proprietorship, should be reported as a single line item. Stocks in corporations should be reported at cost and, except for corporations maintaining Subchapter S elections, should not reflect earnings retained since acquisition of the shares.
6. Cost is defined substantially the same as basis for federal income

tax purposes, except that property acquired by gift or by non-taxable exchange is regarded as having a cost equal to the value when received.

7. Vested rights in pension or profit sharing funds, deferred compensation plans and property residuals should be reported in the financial statements in the absence of unusual circumstances. Nonvested interests and those subject to indefinite restrictions should be disclosed by footnote but should not be reported as assets.

8. Household goods, personal effects, etc. may be omitted, or reported at a nominal amount, unless such items are material in relation to total assets.

9. The excess of assets over liabilities should be designated in just those words, and not as "capital" or "net assets."

10. Internal control is a prerequisite in the case of personal financial statements, no less than those of business enterprises, and the absence of reliable control requires the auditor to disclaim an opinion.

11. Formal representations from the principals should be procured but should not be regarded as satisfying any of the auditor's procedural responsibilities.

12. When the auditor is unable to satisfy himself as to the existence of unreported assets or liabilities, he should disclaim an opinion.

13. A separate expression should be given by the auditor with respect to the "present market value" column of the financial statements.

While this guide represents a valuable addition to accounting literature, we take issue with several major areas.

In the first place, we disagree strongly with the recommendation that the historical cost basis of reporting should be regarded as a primary reporting method. We feel that personal financial statements are more comparable with those of investment companies, where assets are customarily included at present market value, rather than with those of typical commercial and industrial enterprises, where assets are customarily included at historical cost.

We feel that the dual basis of reporting serves a sound transitional purpose, but we disagree that cost data, without present value data, should be regarded as being in conformity with generally accepted accounting principles. On the contrary, we feel that the generally accepted reporting practice today is the one bankers have established over a long period of time—namely present market values—and that the omission of cost data would be much less critical than the omission of present market values.

We feel the committee's approach to internal control is impractical, self-defeating and out of touch with reality. Few individuals, even with sophisticated records, maintain effective internal control as that term is defined in our literature. Therefore, if we are to follow the guide with integrity, we must disclaim an opinion in virtually every case. And this practice can only lead to the discontinuation of our services in this area. Could the absence of auditors' opinions on financial statements published by the 1968 Presidential and Vice Presidential candidates be the beginning of such a trend?

No system of internal controls, however elaborate, could prevent an individual from secretly acquiring valuable property on credit, thereby creating both a material asset and a material liability. Further, no practicable audit procedures can be devised which will disclose such a transaction in the face of an effort to suppress it. An auditor is not charged with procedures which are impossible or impractical to perform, and therefore it is an unfortunate fact of life that he must rely on representations from the principals as to the completeness of personal financial statements.

Yet this need not be fatal to the expression of an opinion. There are responsible ways in which to express the nature and results of an auditor's work in the examination of personal financial statements without resorting to stereotyped terminology which evolved from completely different facts and circumstances. We feel that the committee's energies would have been more fruitful if they had been pointed in that direction.

We also take issue with the committee's suggested language for the auditor's report on the present market value data in the statement of assets and liabilities. The committee suggests a sentence beginning: "We have also determined that the additional information set forth in the accompanying statements on the estimated value basis . . ."

Must we regress!

"We have determined" is only a whisper away from "We hereby certify," the phrase we abandoned long ago on advice of counsel. We would substitute simply: "Further, in our opinion, the additional information set forth . . ."

Last, and perhaps least important, we feel there is a confusing inconsistency in recommended reporting terminology. On the Statement of Assets and Liabilities, the committee uses the caption "Excess of Assets Over Liabilities." Yet the recommended title for the related statement which reconciles the beginning and ending amounts so reported is "Statement of Changes in Net Assets." Nowhere else is the term "net assets" suggested. We think there should be consistency here.

This item should be identified in the Statement of Assets and Liabilities as "net assets" or else the caption of the related statement should be

"Statement of Changes in Excess of Assets Over Liabilities." Our preference is rather obvious, although "net equity" also would be quite acceptable.

The many excellent recommendations made by the committee should not be obscured by our criticisms.

We believe, however, that corrective action should be taken in the areas discussed and a new committee appointed by the AICPA to restudy the entire area. Certainly the public interest would be served best by a realistic approach to reporting on personal financial statements.

Such an approach must recognize that internal controls for an individual cannot be measured against those of the behemoths of industry. Further, it must recognize that an individual thinks of his worldly goods in terms of today's market values, not historical costs.

Looking forward to Campaign 1972, as well as everyday service in an important field, we must be able to report on personal financial statements after performing realistic audit steps. We accomplish nothing for the profession or for those using our services by establishing artificial criteria which virtually negate the opportunity for service. We believe that there is a "place in the sun" for auditors' reports on personal financial statements. But in our opinion, the existing guide puts it many moons away.

39. The Wealth of Richard Nixon*

President Nixon's assets, as now officially disclosed, are approaching the million-dollar mark.

A report on the President's wealth, issued by the White House on May 12, said that assets of Mr. and Mrs. Nixon total $980,400. This compares with assets of $858,190 reported in a financial statement released on Oct. 8, 1968, during the presidential campaign.

Mr. Nixon's present net worth—subtracting debts from total assets—is estimated at $596,900. The figure given last October was $515,830.

SELLING AND BUYING

The White House said that the President wished to update the previous report to reflect these actions taken by the Nixons:

---

* Reprinted from *U.S. News & World Report*, May 26, 1969, copyright 1969 U.S. News & World Report, Inc., page 56.

1. Mr. and Mrs. Nixon have agreed to sell their co-operative apartment at 810 Fifth Avenue, New York City, to Mr. and Mrs. Lewis Lehrman for $326,000. The Nixons acquired the apartment for $166,860 in 1963, made improvements costing $95,000, according to White House counsel John D. Ehrlichman.

2. The President and the First Lady have sold their 185,891 shares of common stock in Fisher's Island, Inc., which owns an undeveloped island off the Florida coast, for $2 a share—totaling $371,782. The stock was sold back to the Fisher's Island corporation. Mr. Ehrlichman said the Nixons bought the stock for $1 to $1.50 a share.

Mr. Nixon, his counsel explained, decided to sell the Fisher's Island stock because "we could see the possibility of a conflict problem down the road." The island is now reachable only by boat. Mr. Ehrlichman said the President wanted to dispose of his holdings in it before any proposal arose for building a causeway, which might involve federal aid. Mr. Nixon's close friend and neighbor at Key Biscayne, Fla., C.G. ["Bebe"] Rebozo, is a "substantial" shareholder in Fisher's Island, Inc.

3. The Nixons have purchased, for a total price of $252,800, two houses in Key Biscayne. The purchases were financed with conventional mortgages at about 7 per cent. The President has an equity in the houses totaling $71,800.

4. The President and Mrs. Nixon are buying five acres of a 21-acre property at San Clemente, Calif., between Los Angeles and San Diego. The Nixon purchase includes a 10-room house overlooking the Pacific. The President will pay approximately $340,000, with $100,000 down and the balance to be paid in five years, with interest at 7½ per cent.

AIM: "COMPATIBLE" USE

The 21-acre tract, owned by Mrs. Henry Hamilton Cotton, is valued at 1.4 million dollars. To make sure that the 16 acres not purchased by the Nixons will be put to "compatible" use, that portion of the property will be held in trust by the Title Insurance and Trust Company of Los Angeles until a suitable buyer is found.

That buyer, Mr. Ehrlichman indicated, may turn out to be the Richard Nixon Foundation, which, the White House announced, is being set up for "educational and charitable purposes including the formation and construction of a Richard Nixon library and museum."

The Nixon retreat at San Clemente includes, besides the main house—which has five bedrooms, all opening on a central patio—a guest house, two gazebos, and a tennis court.

NET WORTH

Here is the new statement of the President's net worth:

Assets   Cash and receivables, $571,000; life insurance cash value, $44,000; houses at 500 and 516 Bay Lane, Key Biscayne, $252,800; Key Biscayne vacant lots, $37,600; property at Whittier, Calif., Mr. Nixon's home town, $75,000. Total: $980,400.

Liabilities   Notes and loans payable to banks and others, $126,000; mortgages or contracts payable, $54,400 on Whittier property, $181,000 on 500 and 516 Bay Lane, Key Biscayne, and $22,100 on Key Biscayne vacant lots. Total, $383,500.

Net worth: $596,900.

Observers say that Mr. Nixon's financial position should continue to improve during his years in the White House. Some previous Presidents found it hard to save anything, but on the day Mr. Nixon took office, the presidential salary was doubled, from $100,000 a year to $200,000. In addition, the President receives $50,000 a year for expenses and a $40,000 travel allowance.

Compared with his immediate predecessors, John F. Kennedy and Lyndon B. Johnson, who were multimillionaires, Mr. Nixon's personal fortune is small.

Even so, the President, who grew up in extremely modest circumstances, personifies an American success story, financially as well as politically.

40. Baseball Is a Business, Too*

When Harmon Killebrew strides up to home plate and takes a few practice swats this spring, the eyes of Minnesota Twins' fans will be focused on him. But the eyes of the baseball club's accounting staff will be watching the gate receipts. After all, even though for millions of dedicated fans, professional baseball is just fun to watch—it's also big business.

* Reprinted from *Management Accounting*, (U.S.A.), March 1969, pages 63–65.

Jack Alexander, member of the *Minneapolis* Chapter, will tell you that. He's assistant controller of the Minnesota Twins Baseball Club and, consequently, the team's RBI's represent more than an idle statistic to him. The team's scoring may mean the difference between staying in the black or going in the red.

Years ago, baseball owners did not worry very much about the accounting aspects. Ownership and management was largely a family affair with a provincial flavor. The owner of a club could complete his accounts in a couple of weeks after the season closed, sit back, contemplate the results of the year's operation and changes, if any, that might be made in the club's personnel for the coming season, use his hat for a filing cabinet, and await the coming season.

Those days, like the spit ball, are gone forever. The upsurge in the American economy after World War II launched the baseball industry into a new era, bringing in its wake new owners with fresh capital, professional business managers and a whole new concept of practices, procedures and methods. It was at this point that accounting began to take on a greater degree of importance in baseball operations.

But only within the last decade, due to the increased complexities of the business, has the industry began to move with the times—developing and adopting a uniform system of accounts, methods and procedures, which have formed a basis for consistency in statement and comparative study presentations. The fact that periodic conferences are scheduled within the industry to review and examine problems pertinent to financial reporting testifies to the importance that club owners now place on the accounting area.

Obviously, baseball is a season and cash business, operating for a period of five and one-half months—from the middle of April to about October 1. Thus, income over this period must be sufficient to carry not only the burden of the club's own operation, but also the cost of its affiliated clubs in the minor leagues. In addition, since all transactions are for cash, there is no elaborate accounts receivable system, nor a need for a credit or collection department.

According to Mr. Alexander, the business is extremely vulnerable to conditions over which management has little or no control, such as weather, injuries to players, and the play of the team on the field. Should a club run into bad weather in the spring—necessitating double-headers later in the season—receipts never fully compensate for the loss of the earlier rained-out games.

The Twins have been doing pretty well in recent years. Attendance at games in 1967 reached an all-time high of 1,483,421. This figure may be partly due to the team's excellent record that year—second in the American League. The Twins dropped to seventh place in 1968.

Although team members are off during the winter months, the Twins' accounting department is hard at work preparing the year-end audit. It produces tax reports for the major league team, as well as the subsidiary corporations. In February, the accounting staff begins to complete the arrangements for spring training and the coming season.

Another characteristic of the baseball business is that a club has fixed contractual commitments, represented in player contracts. Once a player is signed to a major league contract it becomes a firm obligation of the club, up to the player's release. Such commitments have far-reaching implications for the club as a business.

For accounting purposes the baseball club is organized around the natural division of its operations. Almost every identifiable function of the business is in a separate department, the objective being to provide a maximum of information for management control. The principal operating departments, all independently staffed and responsible to the board of directors through the president, are: Team, Grounds Operation and Maintenance, Game-Ticket Department, Concessions, Public Relations and Team Development.

A baseball club has four major sources of income. They are: games, radio and television proceeds, concessions and advertising. The success of a professional baseball club, of course, depends upon the revenue from home games and road games. After allowance for excise taxes on admissions, receipts are shared with the visiting team and the league— the visiting team receiving 20% and the league 40% of paid admissions—the home team picks up the remainder.

A rather comprehensive Daily Game Statement is prepared and audited. This statement reflects total number of tickets sold, admission taxes, turnstile count, visiting team and league shares, as well as a summary showing total number of tickets printed for each game and the total sold and unsold. The unsold tickets, so-called "deadwood," are tabulated and placed under lock and key in the vault for future audit by the Internal Revenue Service.

Expenses are allocated to the various departments, including team expense, grounds operation and maintenance, game expense-ticket department, administrative and general, publicity and advertising, and team development. (For those who collect baseball trivia, the approximate cost of baseballs and bats during a typical season is $23,000.)

Jack Alexander enjoys working for the Twins and although he is too busy to attend day games, he usually manages to take in the night games at home in the Metropolitan Stadium in Bloomington. Each year the team gives him a baseball signed by each member of the team; the souvenirs are proudly displayed in Mr. Alexander's den.

A national pastime, true, but professional baseball is a business like any other. Not many of its fans, however, are aware of the staff organization, including accountants, that supports the nine players on the diamond.

41. Financial Reporting for Nonprofit Organizations*

Howard A. Withey**

Proper financial reporting for voluntary nonprofit organizations is becoming more important than ever before, and the absence of appropriate reporting principles and standards is leading to increasing confusion and misunderstanding. The need for appropriate financial data by government agencies in connection with the poverty programs, the cost complications of the Medicare rules and regulations, and the use of financial statements of nonprofit organizations to support long-term borrowings, are only a few examples of the immediate importance of developing reporting standards in this highly critical area. The intensity of the need to develop standards of financial reporting for nonprofit organizations may be gauged by the seriousness of the questions which these organizations and their independent public accountants can raise in this context. Here are some pertinent samples:

The fact that appropriate accounting principles are different in certain areas of the nonprofit field (such as hospitals or educational institutions) may not preclude the use of the term "generally accepted accounting principles." What are the appropriate principles in other areas of the nonprofit field?

Must the independent accountant qualify his opinion if substantial unrestricted gifts are reflected as direct additions to any fund designated by management without passing through general funds?

What are the minimum requirements for appropriate disclosure of sources of income and for classification of expenditures?

What position should be taken in situations where expendable and nonexpendable resources are pooled for investment purposes on a basis

* Reprinted from *Management Controls*, January 1969, pages 7–13.
** Howard A. Withey is retired. He is a former partner of Peat, Marwick, Mitchell & Co.

which does not permit the determination of the equity of expendable and nonexpendable funds?

Is it proper for the entity to withhold investment income from general fund uses under the guise of "equalizing the annual income"?

Can the term "presents fairly" be used with respect to a balance sheet which excludes, or records at nominal or appraised value, substantial fixed assets?

Can financial position and results of operations be presented without recording depreciation? Must it be recorded through a company's general fund, or may it be recorded as a direct reduction in equity invested in fixed assets?

Is it appropriate to reflect investments in marketable securities at quoted market value?

Is the commercial basis of reporting adequate for setting forth the financial position or "results of operations" of a library, a foundation, or a health and welfare organization?

In this article the writer proposes to set forth the basic concepts which should underlie sound accounting practices and principles for nonprofit entities, and to make specific recommendations for reporting on their financial position and financial activities.

BASIC CONSIDERATIONS

The objective of financial reporting is to present financial data fairly in accordance with a given body of principles or standards of presentation. In commercial applications, these principles are those recognized as "generally accepted." For educational institutions, hospitals and municipalities it has been recognized that fairness of presentation may encompass practices differing from those in the commercial field.

Fairness of presentation relates to the purposes of reporting. In financial statements of commercial organizations, data are presented to reveal such elements as current ratios, capital ratios, borrowing ratios, owners' equity, sales, cost of sales, operating results, earnings per share and distributions. For nonprofit organizations, however, the statements should reflect stewardship accountability for resources requiring subdivisions such as general resources, restricted expendable resources, and nonexpendable resources, rather than current, fixed and deferred assets. Accountability for transactions of the reporting period requires reporting of stewardship of financial resources received and the use of such financial resources during the reporting period, as well as the resources remaining on hand at the close of the period. Resources acquired should be reflected by source, and expenditure by function. The principle of matching revenues and expenses in a charitable organization relates substantially to the matching of expenditures with available expendable resources.

Stewardship reporting would seem to require a reporting to the public on the use of specific resources in the event such resources were subject to external restriction. If a donor, for example, were to give a charitable organization a sum of money for the erection of a building, proper accountability would require not only that the funds be used for such purpose, but that the accounting to the public include a reporting of the expenditures of such resources for the specific purpose contributed. In a like manner, if a donor were to contribute a sum of money with the understanding that the principal was to be invested with only the income to be used for the legitimate purposes of the organization, proper accountability would require that expendable and nonexpendable resources be accounted for separately. The various types of resources should, therefore, be divided into classes and accounted for by fund or fund group.

In nonprofit accounting, the term *fund* is defined as "an accountability established for the purpose of carrying on specific activities or attaining certain objectives in accordance with specific regulations, restrictions or limitations. In institutional accounting, the term includes assets, liabilities, reserves, principal and balances" (College and University Business Administration, Vol. 1). Fund or fund groups and the reflection of such groups in financial reports should be descriptive of the character or purpose of the fund and should be distinguished so as to designate whether the source of the fund was donor-restricted or board-designated.

Stewardship reporting should embrace a fair presentation of all resources and obligations of the organization. The modified accrual basis and modified cash basis of reporting should be discarded in favor of the full accrual basis. Accruals in some cases would include pledges receivable since these are significant resources of the organization. Fixed assets should preferably be shown at cost.

ENDOWMENT FUNDS [1]

As previously indicated, it would seem appropriate to account separately for a capital fund contributed to a nonprofit organization with the understanding that only the income of the fund was to be used for general or special purposes of the organization. The organization, in a sense, is a trustee of the principal amount and should account for the

[1] The terms *endowment funds* and *endowment* are perhaps the most misused terms in the nonprofit field. It is suggested that (and as used in this article) the term be defined as "funds, the principal of which must be maintained inviolate to conform

principal fund in generally the same manner as a trust—by accounting for the principal separately from expendable resources of the organization. Investment gains are a part of principal and are nonexpendable as long as the principal is nonexpendable. Such funds or resources are called endowment funds. If an organization has received a number of such funds, it is customary (unless prohibited by law or the gift instrument) for the reporting to be made by group totals and to merge the investments of the various funds. Income from the principal of such funds can usually be expended for the general purposes of the organization but may be restricted to a specific expendable purpose (in which event the income would be treated as a restricted expendable fund).

The terms establishing an endowment fund may provide for the termination of the restriction against the expenditure of the principal at some future time or upon the happening of a specific event. Upon the release of the restriction, the principal should be transferred to another appropriate fund group. The term *endowment fund* should be limited to the principal of resources restricted by an outside donor or agency for investment, and should not be confused with funds set aside by a governing board for investment for which the terms *funds functioning as endowment* or *quasi endowment* are used. Descriptions such as "Smith Memorial Fund" or "Jones Foundation Fund" should be discarded as inappropriate terms for major classifications since the descriptions are so meaningless as to be uninformative.

The investments of endowment funds, funds functioning as endowment, and term endowment funds are often pooled. The propriety of commingling expendable and nonexpendable resources may be subject to some question although it appears to be a generally accepted practice. In the event of such commingling, it is recommended that each individual fund making up the total be assigned shares or participations so that the fund can be administered in a manner somewhat similar to an open-end mutual fund. In this way the present value of the equity of any specific fund is readily determinable. Commingling of expendable and nonexpendable resources on any other basis might be subject to criticism. The same considerations may be required if the income of some of the funds is restricted. Investment income should be distributed currently. The withholding of income from distribution for an equalization reserve may result in a distortion in distribution in future periods.

Proposals are made from time to time that the investments of

---

to restrictions placed thereon by the donor or other outside agency." (The foregoing definition is from *College and University Business Administration—Volume I*.)

Restricted endowment is endowment in which the income is restricted to a specific purpose, and unrestricted endowment funds are endowment funds in which the income is unrestricted. An organization cannot endow itself by setting aside surplus resources and calling such resources endowment.

pooled funds be reflected in periodic reports on the basis of current market value. This practice is said to facilitate accounting for pooled investments and to reflect more accurately the income-producing potential of the assets. It is suggested, however, that the reflection of true trusteeship responsibility relates to the cost or fair market value of assets at date of acquisition, and the disclosure of such responsibility is one of the purposes of financial reporting. Further, the relationship of proceeds from sales or disposals to acquisition values should be a matter of disclosure in reporting. Reflection of current market values by parenthetical or footnote references should fulfill the needs for adequate disclosure and provide sufficient data for supplemental needs. It would appear therefore that the same considerations which require cost to be the generally accepted basis of reporting in the commercial area should prevail in the nonprofit field.

OTHER FUNDS

In addition to endowment gifts, it is not uncommon for donors to transfer resources to a nonprofit organization under terms by which the organization will pay to the donor or to a designated person or persons (for the lifetime of such person or persons or for a specified period) either an annuity or the income earned by the organization on such principal. These life income or annuity funds should be maintained separate and apart from other resources of the organization, and should be reported upon separately in the financial reports. In some governmental jurisdictions the acceptance of annuity or life income funds is subject to the approval of the insurance department or its equivalent. Upon termination of the restrictions, these resources should be transferred to another appropriate fund group.

Substantial contributions are received by many nonprofit organizations which, by agreement with the donor are expendable only for a specific purpose. The purpose for which these resources may be expended may be a current operating one, or restricted to plant facilities or debt retirement. For clarity in financial presentation, the resources expendable for fixed assets are usually distinguished from resources expendable for restricted operating purposes. The first is usually shown in the fixed asset section of the financial statements while the latter is classified either as a separate fund or as a liability in the current section. If the amount of such current restricted resources is material, it would seem appropriate to provide a separate fund group so as to indicate to the reader of the financial statements that such expendable resources are maintained in liquid assets. Some take the position that restricted gifts expendable for current operating purposes and unexpended at the reporting date may be reflected in the statement of financial position as liabilities, in the belief that the reader by interpretation can determine whether resources representing such gifts have been expended. Others maintain that strict accountability and reporting of stewardship for such resources would seem to require that the assets comprising such resources be stated separately.

In certain instances, nonprofit organizations will create indebtedness which involves the establishment of sinking funds for the retirement of the debt. Usually, the additions to the principal of such funds come from pledged revenues, and the expenditures from such funds are limited to payments of interest, principal of the debt, the creation of maintenance reserves, etc. Adequate reporting requires that the transactions of such funds be reflected separately from other resources.

On occasion, charitable organizations may be the recipients of resources under the terms of which the organization agrees to lend such resources with the expectation of repayment, to provide pension allowances to employees or to accomplish some other purpose. Stewardship responsibility requires that such resources be separately maintained and reflected as specific funds in the financial reports.

The aforementioned specific funds or fund groups together with a general fund containing all unrestricted assets, liabilities and fund balances should constitute the basic requirements for reporting. Such reporting should include a statement of financial position by fund groups, and a statement of changes in funds.

DISCRETIONARY FUND GROUPINGS

It has been found practical by many nonprofit organizations to subdivide the fund groups further for the purpose of reflecting more clearly the use of resources designated by the governing board. These fund groups should also be descriptive of the character or purpose of the fund and should be distinguished from fund groups which are donor-restricted. This type of identification changes the character of the financial statements from statements reflecting "operating results" to statements reflecting use of resources by types of resources. The fund groups most commonly found in this discretionary area will now be discussed.

The management of many nonprofit organizations may wish to reflect a division of the general fund between resources available and used for appropriations or expenditures and the transactions affecting equity in fixed assets. This is accomplished by segregating from the general fund all of the fixed assets and the related liabilities and equity pertaining to fixed assets and establishing a separate fixed asset fund or plant fund group. The reflection of such assets in a separately balanced section, offset by the liabilities and the equity with respect to such assets, gives the reader some information regarding the importance of fixed assets in the operations of the organization. It also results as well in segregating the equity and the transactions affecting plant fund equity from current expendable resources remaining in the current fund.

There would appear to be no more reason to omit fixed assets from the balance sheet of a nonprofit organization than to omit any other asset of consequence. Such assets would usually be reflected at cost, at fair market value at date of receipt in the case of donations, or at appraisal or insurance values in the absence of cost records.

Additions to fixed asset resources through the expenditures by any of the other funds should be recorded as an addition to fixed assets and to the equity account. Similarly, the disposition of such assets would be reflected as a reduction in the asset account by a contra reduction in the equity. If there is a desire on the part of management to reflect shrinkage in value through use ratably over the life of the asset, an allowance for such shrinkage should be provided as a reduction of the asset valuation with a contra reduction in the equity account.

At various times organizations may receive contributions or accumulate other resources which, in the judgment of the governing board, best serve the organization in the form of investments to produce income, despite the fact that no restrictions on the use of the resources were established by the donor. Since these resources can be used for any legitimate purpose of the organization, they need to be distinguished from resources which must be invested by reason of the restrictions placed on contributions by donors. On the other hand, until the principal of such funds is to be used, the governing board may wish that these funds be included in a category similar to endowment funds.

In many cases the assets representing free funds are merged with the assets of endowment funds. Accounting for such funds should be sufficiently detailed so that the equity of expendable funds, as contrasted with nonexpendable funds, is readily determinable. Additions to funds functioning as endowment should result from appropriations from unrestricted funds. Unrestricted gifts and bequests should flow through unrestricted funds rather than be credited directly to funds functioning as endowment.

The managements of some nonprofit organizations, as a matter of good management, desire to make regular and consistent provision for the replacement of fixed assets out of other current contributions or unrestricted bequests, or the income which a particular asset might produce. Since the financial reports constitute an accounting for resources, such a provision can only be made by the setting aside of resources for purposes of replacement. This is accomplished by transferring resources from unrestricted funds to a subsection of the plant facilities fund.

Some nonprofit organizations hold substantial resources as agent or custodian for others. Where these resources are significant, many organizations account for them in a separate fund. Transactions of custodian funds are not reflected as transactions of any other fund group.

The use of the mandatory funds previously enumerated and some or all of the discretionary funds listed above make it expedient to change the caption of the general fund to indicate its current or expendable nature. The caption recommended for use is "current unrestricted funds" to indicate the resources segregated for current operating purposes and to reflect the balance of the current fund assets over current fund liabilities. Restricted expendable resources for current operating purposes are commonly labeled "current restricted funds." Resources set aside by the governing board for specific operating purposes should be entitled "appropriations for special purposes."

DEPRECIATION AND REPLACEMENT

One of the confusing areas of financial statement reporting for nonprofit organizations arises from the failure to distinguish between depreciation and replacement. This stems primarily from the mistaken conviction that depreciation provides for replacement. It is generally agreed that the purpose of charging depreciation is to distribute the cost of fixed assets over the estimated useful life of the property in a systematic and rational manner. If the fixed assets are presented as resources separate from general funds, then the reflection of the diminution of value in a rational and systematic manner would be reflected in this fund as changes in the fixed asset fund equity. The practice of some nonprofit organizations of charging depreciation as current general fund expense with a contra credit to current general fund balance would seem to serve no useful purpose in accounting for use of current general fund resources.

Use of resources for equipment acquisitions can be made by the expenditure of current unrestricted funds, current restricted funds, plant replacement funds and unexpended plant funds, since it may be appropriate to use the resources of any of these funds for fixed assets additions or replacements. The statement of change in equity of the fixed asset fund brings these various acquisitions together in one place by a contra entry increasing both the equity and the assets. Additions to replacement funds may result from specific gifts for this purpose plus appropriations from current unrestricted funds, from funds functioning as endowment, or from sinking funds.

If the financial program of the governing board is to provide for the replacement of assets (irrespective of whether these assets were contributed or are income-producing), resources must be accumulated and

264   *Accounting for Individuals and Organizations*

maintained for this purpose, preferably by the transfer of resources to a replacement fund. The recording of depreciation does not accomplish this purpose.

The term *funded depreciation* is sometimes used to indicate that the equivalent of the depreciation charge in the current general fund has been set aside as a replacement fund. Since the term is self-contradictory, a preferable description would be *provision for replacement*, with appropriate notation where necessary as to the basis upon which the replacement provision has been determined.

INTERFUND TRANSACTIONS

The transactions of funds should be self-balancing within themselves; that is, charges and credits should be balanced in each particular fund. Only in this way can the balances of the funds be appropriately offset with specific assets. Where the transactions of a fund involve a receivable from another fund, the reciprocal entry should be made in the specific fund affected indicating the indebtedness to the first fund, with the offsetting debit to another account or accounts within the fund. Liquidation of the interfund receivables and payables should take place periodically in order to avoid the financing of one fund's transactions with the assets of another fund.

Transfer of certain assets between funds should be reflected at the fair value of the assets. For example, if a particular security is to be transferred from current fund investments to endowment fund investments, the transaction should be recorded as a purchase by the endowment funds at the market value of the security at the date of transfer. Similarly, the transfer of an investment from endowment funds to any other fund should be reflected as though the security was sold by the endowment funds at the market value at the date of transfer.

Normally, interfund receivables and payables should be liquidated by the transfer of cash or other assets prior to the preparation of the annual financial reports. In the event that such liquidation has not taken place and the financial statements reflect receivables from other funds, such receivables must be considered in the light of their collectibility in the same manner as though it were a receivable from an independent debtor. For example, assume a donor contributes funds to carry out a particular purpose or project. By reason of failure to budget properly and control the expenditures for the project, it turns out that more money has been spent than was originally contributed by the donors. These overexpenditures are usually reflected through the interfund receivables and payables since the current fund usually finances the expenditures of funds of this nature. The collectibility of the interfund receivable from the standpoint of the current general fund depends on whether or not donors will make good the deficiency. If donors will not, the receivables would seem to be uncollectible since there are no available resources in the restricted fund with which to make the payment. Such a receivable must be written off as being uncollectible or otherwise shown as a deduction from general fund balance.

REPORTING PROBLEMS

There has been growing concern in recent years that reporting of expenditures on a natural or objective classification by nonprofit organizations does not present a meaningful statement of stewardship. Any substantial organization which reports to the public only in terms of salaries, rent, telephone, travel, supplies, and so on, is not informing its readers meaningfully of the real activities of the organization. It should be obligatory to report expenditures in terms of program, project and management functions.

The difficulty of presenting statements on this functional basis by small organizations and the possible lack of supporting documentation in some areas are admitted. Many organizations, however, are taking the lead in this respect by requiring time reporting by function and other such improvements in order to document their activities in terms which are more meaningful to the public.

The use of the fund basis of reporting or accounting for use of resources as contrasted with accounting for operating results must be determined as a matter of policy before the statements are prepared. It would seem appropriate to use the fund basis of accounting for social clubs or trade associations, etc., only in the areas previously termed mandatory funds, depending on the objective in reporting. For example, a social club which has received an endowment fund the income from which is to maintain the club building, might account for the principal of the endowment as the only separate fund group. This does not prevent all of the other transactions of the club from being reflected, if desired, in a general fund. In other words, the normal operations of the club could be presented on a commercial basis with separate accountability for the special fund. Social clubs in some cases also wish to account for resources set aside for pensions, for rehabilitation and perhaps other purposes. The segregation of such resources in separate fund groups can be readily accomplished. However, the nature of the designation by the governing board should be sufficiently explicit to indicate that these are self-imposed designations which can be retracted by appropriate action of the governing board.

A similar situation exists in the hospital area. The objective of financial reporting for hospitals, according to many authorities, is to account for operating results. Such being the case, operating results should include all normal and recurring transactions affecting the change in equity. The recording of normal and recurring transactions directly in the current general fund equity account would not appear to be appropriate or in accord with generally acceptable practice. To report on operating results (accepting the usual definition of this term) requires that depreciation be included in expenses. The only practical basis by which this may be accomplished is to include the equity in fixed assets as part of the general funds. It is therefore suggested that if the hospital or any other organization wishes to report on "operating results" as contrasted with the "changes in resources" basis appropriate to most non-profit organizations, it should adopt the principles of fund accounting only with respect to those funds previously indicated as mandatory funds.

When an organization undertakes to report on a stewardship or fund basis using one or more of the discretionary fund groups, the character of the financial statements has been changed from statements reflecting operating results to statements reflecting changes in funds or resources. In this event, the standard short-form opinion should be modified to indicate that the principles used are those appropriate to an organization reporting on a fund basis. Unless the basis is apparent, footnotes might be advantageously used to amplify the principles used.

Some AICPA Pronouncements

The introduction of *Restatement and Revision of Accounting Research Bulletins* issued by the Committee on Accounting Procedure of The American Institute of Certified Public Accountants contains the following disclaimer of applicability of the committee's opinions to the nonprofit field:

"The principal objective of the committee has been to narrow areas of difference and inconsistency . . ., and to further the development and recognition of generally accepted accounting principles, through the issuance of opinions and recommendations that would serve as criteria for determining the suitability of accounting practices reflected in financial statements and representations of commercial and industrial companies. . . . The committee has not directed its attention to accounting problems or procedures of religious, charitable, scientific, educational, and similar nonprofit institutions, municipalities, professional firms, and the like. Accordingly, except where there is a specific statement of a different intent by the committee, its opinions and recommendations are directed primarily to business enterprises organized for profit."

In Statement on Auditing Procedure No. 33, issued by the AICPA's

Committee on Auditing Procedure, we find the following statement on the question:

"If the statements are those of a nonprofit organization, they may reflect accounting practices differing in some respects from those followed by enterprises organized for profit. In many cases generally accepted accounting principles applicable to nonprofit organizations have not been clearly defined. In those areas where the independent auditor believes generally accepted accounting principles have been clearly defined, he may state his opinion as to the conformity of the financial statements either with *generally accepted accounting principles* or (less desirably) with *accounting practices* for nonprofit organizations in the particular field (e.g., hospitals and educational institutions), and in such circumstances he may refer to financial position and results of operations. In those areas where he believes generally accepted accounting principles have not been clearly defined, the provisions covering special reports as discussed under cash basis and modified accrual basis statements are applicable."

42. GAO Review of the Economic Opportunity Programs*

Gregory J. Ahart**

One of the most comprehensive, complex, and difficult examinations ever undertaken by GAO was that directed by the Congress when it enacted the Economic Opportunity Amendments of 1967. This act directed the Comptroller General to investigate the programs and activities financed under the Economic Opportunity Act to determine (1) the efficiency of their administration, and (2) the extent to which they achieve the objectives set forth in the authorizing legislation.

The Comptroller General's summary report on this examination was submitted to the Congress on March 18, 1969. This was followed by five related reports prepared by an independent contractor, Resource Management Corp., Bethesda, Md., on special aspects of the examination it

* Reprinted from *The GAO Review*, Summer 1969, pages 37–42.
** Gregory J. Ahart was Deputy Director of the Civil Division at the Conference on Federal Affairs Sponsored by the Tax Foundation, Inc. on March 25, 1969.

had been engaged to assist on. In addition, about 50 supplementary GAO reports are being prepared for submission to the Congress on the detailed examination work performed at specific locations.

This examination pertained to an important national program commonly referred to as the war on poverty. Because of the controversial nature of the program as well as the nature of the examination GAO was directed to make, the GAO summary report received widespread attention.

The *Review* includes in this issue a selection of excerpts of explanatory and evaluative commentary about this work.

About 15 months ago, in the 1967 Economic Opportunity Amendments, the Congress threw the Comptroller General two very tough questions. With reference to the various programs authorized by the Economic Opportunity Act, the Congress directed him to determine.

1. the efficiency of the administration of such programs and activities by the Office of Economic Opportunity and by local public and private agencies carrying out such programs and activities; and
2. the extent to which such programs and activities achieve the objectives set forth in the relevant part or title of the Economic Opportunity Act of 1964 authorizing such programs or activities.

If you are at all familiar with these programs, and particularly if you have read the excellent report on them which was published by the Tax Foundation in December, you will appreciate the enormity of the task we have been struggling with for the past 15 months.

As you know the actual operation of the war on poverty was carried out by several departments and agencies besides OEO. Programs were delegated to the Departments of Labor; Health, Education, and Welfare; and Agriculture. The Small Business Administration also played a part.

Our review was directed to each of the principal economic opportunity programs and included in-depth field examinations of the programs at selected locations, a survey of prior evaluations made by others, and to the extent possible, economic and statistical analyses of available data relating to the operations and results of the programs.

We were assisted in our work by three outside contractors in the areas of analyzing available data and previous evaluations, assessing information needs and information availability, and interviewing program participants and others to obtain information about the programs.

We were also assisted by individual consultants with expertise in manpower training and development, education, health, and other areas. These individuals helped us principally in developing criteria and standards by which program results might be measured and in critiquing the conclusions and recommendations which grew out of our work.

It was a massive and difficult undertaking. Our summary report was issued to the Congress on March 18, just a week ago today. This report will be followed by many supporting reports covering our field reviews of individual programs at specific locations. Also, reports prepared by our contractor on economic and statistical analyses and other aspects of the war on poverty will also be available.

Time today will not permit an adequate discussion of the findings, conclusions, and recommendations which grew out of our study. But I would like to mention some of the things we had to consider in evaluating the efficiency with which the programs were administered and in evaluating their effectiveness. I would also like to discuss briefly certain of our conclusions and recommendations concerning the planning, coordination, and evaluation of Federal antipoverty efforts.

The accomplishments achieved under the Economic Opportunity Act must be appraised in the light of certain difficulties encountered by OEO and the other agencies involved. These difficulties include:

The urgency of getting programs underway as quickly as possible.

Problems in the development of a new organization and in obtaining experienced personnel.

Problems involved in establishing new or modified organizational arrangements at the local level.

The delays and uncertainties in obtaining congressional authorizations and appropriations.

The problems of working out relationships with other agencies and with State and local governments.

Lack of consensus as to the meaning of poverty.

Achievements of the programs authorized by the act can be assessed only in judgmental terms. This is so for several reasons some of which I have already mentioned: The programs are new; they deal with such intangible concepts as the social levels of disadvantaged people; they impose requirements and are subject to conditions which are not amenable to reliable, and in some cases any, quantitative measurement. More specifically:

Criteria is lacking by which to determine at what level of accomplishment a program is to be considered acceptably successful.

The methods for determining program accomplishments have not yet been developed to the point of assured reliability.

The large volume and variety of pertinent data necessary to ascertain program results have been and still are either not available or not reliable.

Program results may not be fully perceptible for many programs within a relatively short time frame.

Other programs—Federal, State, local, and private—aimed at helping the poor, as well as changes in local conditions—employment, wage scales, local attitudes—have their effect upon the same people who receive assistance under the programs authorized by the act.

Amendments to the act and revisions in agency guidelines at various times have necessitated redirection of programs and other changes, which have affected the progress of programs in the short run.

A basic objective of the Economic Opportunity Act was to strengthen, supplement, and coordinate efforts to provide to everyone the opportunity for education and training, the opportunity to work, and the opportunity to live in decency and dignity.

Included in this basic objective was coordination of the programs authorized by the act with one another and with related programs administered by other agencies. This coordinating task was assigned to the Economic Opportunity Council created by the act and to the OEO, the former having the dominant role.

The Council has never functioned effectively and as recast by the 1967 amendments to the act has not been established.

OEO, preoccupied with setting up the machinery to get a new agency started and then with its responsibility for initiating and administering programs authorized by the act, was not able to devote as much effort to its coordinating function as that function demanded. This coordinating task was made difficult by the necessity of OEO's influencing the actions and policies of older established agencies; as a consequence, effective coordination has not been achieved. It was our conclusion that effective coordination cannot be achieved under the existing organizational machinery.

On the basis of our study and other experience with the antipoverty efforts of the Federal Government, we believe that a central staff agency is needed to carry out overall planning, coordination, and evaluation responsibilities with respect to antipoverty efforts. This agency, to be effective, would require the full support of the President.

Our report contains our recommendation that such an agency be created by the Congress.

Our report also contains many conclusions and recommendations concerning the various programs covered. I might mention that OEO is in agreement with many of these conclusions and recommendations.

FROM STATEMENT BY SENATOR WINSTON L. PROUTY OF VERMONT, CONGRESSIONAL RECORD, MAY 13, 1969

This is the most factual and in-depth study that has been made of OEO and of the Job Corps program. I remember our 1967 hearings on poverty programs when many of us on the Labor and Public Welfare Committee were frustrated over our inability to ascertain specifics and facts with respect to the operation and administration of many of these programs. Generally, the people who appeared before us as witnesses said, "Give us more money and we will do a better job."

This study by the General Accounting Office, which incidentally was undertaken as the result of an amendment I offered on the floor of the Senate, included not only personnel of the General Accounting Office but also numerous other individuals, as well. I shall not undertake to read all of their names, but they appear in the GAO report to Congress. To assist in this examination the General Accounting Office engaged the services of three firms under contract: Resource Management Corp., of Bethesda, Md., Peat, Marwick, Livingston & Co., of Washington, D.C., and TransCentury Corp., of Washington, D.C., and many individuals, all of whom had great expertise in various related fields.

FROM THE JOURNAL OF ACCOUNTANCY, MAY 1969

The accounting profession faces an awesome task in seeking to measure the effectiveness of social action programs. This became clear with the publication last month of the most massive study yet undertaken to evaluate the progress being made in the federal government's war on poverty, or, as it is known officially, the "Economic Opportunity Act of 1964."

Although the GAO made many far-reaching recommendations for sharpening the attack on the problems of poverty, the government auditors readily conceded that they were in uncharted seas when it came to making a precise management judgment about the cost effectiveness of the total federal expenditure for assistance to the poor. This total stood at $9.8 billion in 1961 and by 1968 had grown to $22.1 billion. However, the funds appropriated for programs administered by the Office of Economic Opportunity in fiscal 1969 amounted to only $1.9 billion.

With respect to the role it is playing in the evaluation, the GAO said that "we were directed to formulate judgments as to the extent to which the Office of Economic Opportunity's antipoverty programs are achieving the objectives set forth in the act."

The GAO said that the "task is an extremely complex and difficult one. The methods of evaluating social programs such as these and the indicators of progress or accomplishment are not well developed or understood."

Looking toward a future when the efforts to combat poverty will be expanded, the GAO added:

"We recognize that, as the scope of governmental activity broadens and as the complexity of governmental programs increases, the Congress is recurrently confronted with the necessity of appraising accomplishments that cannot be measured in terms of dollars expended or in terms of such tangible yardsticks as the number of miles of road built or pieces of mail delivered.

"We recognize that it is essential that efforts be made to develop new yardsticks of effectiveness to meet the needs of the Congress."

The GAO used the services of three nongovernment contractors in the study: Resource Management Corporation, of Bethesda, Md.; Peat, Marwick, Livingston & Co., of Washington; and TransCentury Corporation, also of Washington.

Resource Management was asked to conduct economic and statistical studies of antipoverty programs and in the process made assessments of the usefulness of national data banks, available evaluation criteria and methods, and the numerous evaluation studies that have been conducted.

Peat, Marwick, Livingston assisted in reviewing the information systems relating to the war on poverty and TransCentury conducted interviews among participants in the programs. The GAO also consulted with a number of educators and other specialists to advise on the programs under review.

The GAO said that its problem in evaluating the programs was made doubly difficult since Congress sought dual judgments, i.e., a determination of the efficiency of administration and the extent to which the programs are achieving the objectives of the legislation.

"These are not mutually exclusive," the GAO said. "The quality of performance of many administrative functions has a direct bearing on the extent to which the economic opportunity programs achieve their objectives."

Although there is an urgent demand for "timely and reliable quantitative data" from thousands of fund spending points throughout the nation, the GAO said that "for the most part, needed data were unavailable, incomplete, or of doubtful reliability at the local levels and/or at the regional and headquarters offices of the federal agencies responsible for the economic opportunity programs."

The Office of Economic Opportunity tried to remedy this shortcoming in 1967 by setting up machinery to supply data of the sort sought by the GAO. But, the GAO concluded, "this system has not been successful principally because of certain basic faults and because of failures in reporting by local bodies."

The failure stems partly from the fact that prior to the legislation in 1964, little had been done about developing criteria for judging the programs and there still exists "a serious lack of agreed-upon criteria."

The GAO pointed to an observation made by one of its consulting firms that "when one drops below the level of the overall goal of alleviating poverty one discovers that the objectives of poverty programs are mixed, embracing economic and noneconomic, specific and vague, and approximate and ultimate objectives. In fact, low income itself is only an indication of deeper problems that may have social, psychological, medical, legal, educational and political ramifications."

The major recommendations made by the GAO for reforming the antipoverty drive focus on management techniques. About the aims of the poverty war, there is broad agreement between the GAO and the Office of Economic Opportunity, although the GAO, observing that the Job Corps has not achieved success, said it doubted if "the resources now being applied to this program can be fully justified."

FROM THE GOVERNMENT EXECUTIVE, APRIL 1969

. . . the GAO report on OEO programs is a studied, evaluated report. It does not make sweeping condemnations any more than it makes acclamatory evaluations of the effect of the several programs that comprise OEO. It is a measuredly temperate document, damning seldom, condoning some and acclaiming selectively—based solely on dedicated detachment—which, in itself, by its very nature, is an impossibility, considering the emotional ingredients involved. It does point out weaknesses, as will others in subsequent (some 50) follow-on reports.

VIEWS OF THE NATIONAL ASSOCIATION FOR COMMUNITY DEVELOPMENT

Excerpts from Position Paper Adopted in May 1969 by Board of Directors of This Association

Our overall feeling is that although we may not agree with the entire report, it is a rather good job and shows a new level of competence and a new sense of social awareness on the part of the General Accounting Office which has not always characterized it in the past.

The National Association for Community Development originally viewed the Congressional mandate to the General Accounting Office to conduct an investigation of Economic Opportunity Act programs as a most important review. GAO reports have tended to be critical without sufficient understanding of the problems or to be somewhat calloused to social and human concerns. We recognized the great respect in which

274 Accounting for Individuals and Organizations

the Congress holds the GAO and thus knew that the conclusions reached by the GAO would have a great bearing on the future of the antipoverty program.

It is indeed unfortunate that early press leaks on the report gave it a somewhat unfair image. Although we obviously do not agree with all of the conclusions of the GAO, we did find it a reasonable and honest effort to review not only Economic Opportunity Programs but to assess in the process the tools available for evaluation. The report is relatively balanced and contains some justifiable praise as well as criticism of anti-poverty efforts. We agree that anti-poverty activities, for example, have been uncoordinated but we share GAO's point that OEO controls only a small percentage of anti-poverty program funds and thus, without active White House support and involvement, could not have been expected to master a challenge which has faced the Federal government in every program front for decades.

The report also recognizes—and wisely so—that some evaluation questions cannot yet be answered, and that there is a clear and continuing need for innovative exploration and new program approaches. We concur that some program approaches have been greatly handicapped by fund allocation, administrative and legislative procedures which are a part of our National and State grant-in-aid structure, and which do not offer a true test of program effectiveness.

In essence the report makes these major points:

The anti-poverty programs are dealing with very difficult problems—far more difficult than we have been aware of.

OEO is but a small part of the Federal government's total effort to cope with these problems.

This country has developed programs and services which serve certain needs but do not reach the fundamental causes of poverty. Many well-established programs play a helpful role, perhaps, but they will not be ultimately successful on their own.

In considering the areas in which the GAO recommends improvements, we must first note that a call for improvement is not in itself a criticism but rather the identification of an aspect of relative weakness. We, however, do not concur with the recommendation that income eligibility is a constructive program tool. Income eligibility becomes a new game or barrier to effective services to people which constantly diminished their dignity and reminds them of the "we" and "you" of local community action. Barriers are not needed. They exist already and must be diminished, not built upon.

Many of our members have long complained about the negative impact which unrealistic time frames and lack of continuity have had on program effectiveness. Many have argued with other evaluative institutions that more time is needed, and better data are required, and that new forms and areas of research must precede evaluation on which great significance or reliability can be based.

NACD particularly agrees with the need for stronger planning but notes that that planning must be realistic and relevant, particularly where the planning is taking place in the context of a social change institution. . . .

In conclusion the willingness of such a highly respected body as GAO in accepting and supporting the participation of the poor in anti-poverty efforts and in recognizing the valuable contributions being made by Community Action Agencies is encouraging to us as it should be to the President, the Congress, and the Nation.

Perhaps having demonstrated the ability to develop insight and restrain itself from a purely "audit" approach, the GAO, with Congressional blessing, should now extend its efforts and begin a similar review to other Federal programs which deal with problems of the disadvantaged such as Title I of the Elementary and Secondary Education Act.

43. Accounting Principles Generally Accepted in the United States Versus Those Generally Accepted Elsewhere*

Gerhard G. Mueller**

Substantial evidence exists to support the claim that material differences characterize generally-accepted accounting principles as applied in various countries.[1] While these differences are significant for a number of individual concepts and practices, they should not obscure the equally important observation that there are also a great many similari-

* Reprinted from *The International Journal of Accounting*, Spring 1968, pages 91–103.

** G. G. Mueller is Professor of Accounting at the University of Washington.

[1] For instance, *Professional Accounting in 25 Countries* (American Institute of Certified Public Accountants, 1964).

ties between the generally-accepted accounting principles of different countries. The differences, however, are the source of frequent and substantive problems in accounting practice.

With a steadily increasing volume of international business and investments, national differences in accounting principles have a growing impact. From a practical point of view, these national differences cause difficulties in at least these areas:

1. Reporting for international subsidiaries whose financial statements are to be consolidated or combined with United States parent-company statements.

2. Reporting for international subsidiaries which lie beyond the consolidation or combination requirements—separate reports being required by the United States parent company.

3. Reporting for independent companies located in countries other than the United States where the statements are for local use and a standard United States form of opinion is to be furnished.

4. Reporting for independent companies in countries outside the United States where the statements and the opinions are likely to be read and used in the United States, *e.g.*, for SEC filings, use by bankers, and possible acquisitions or general publication in English to stockholders residing in the United States.

This paper has as its main purpose the empirical evaluation of the complexities of varying accounting principles among different countries. While it is recognized that conceptual considerations are only one aspect of the over-all problem, a better perspective should be possible by limiting the focus of the discussion.

ECONOMIC AND BUSINESS ENVIRONMENTS DIFFER AMONG VARIOUS COUNTRIES

Experience and observation tell us that the business environment normally varies from one country to the next. Indeed, some parts of an over all business environment may well differ between individual regions of a single country. On the other hand, there are instances where two or more countries have essentially the same environmental conditions. This reduces to the proposition that the dimensions of a business environment are primarily economic in nature whereas borders of a country are drawn because of political factors. Thus, political boundaries are not necessarily the only or the best lines of distinction for differing business environments.

What separates one business environment from another? Primarily, there are four marks of separation:

1. States of economic development—A highly developed economy provides an environment different from an undeveloped economy. In an African country, workers at a plant had to walk three hours twice each day to get to and from work. An AID program provided them with bicycles, after which they quit work. Possession of a bicycle was the sole motive for their accepting employment in the first place.

2. Stages of business complexity—Business needs as well as business output are functions of business complexity. An example of this is that West Germany in a recent year imported approximately DM 600 million (net) of industrial know-how in the form of Research and Development services outside Germany.

3. Shades of political persuasion—Political tendencies clearly affect business environments. Among the better known international examples are the expropriations of private property by central governments in South America and the Near and Far East. Forms of social legislation also affect business environments directly.

4. Reliance on some particular system of law—Differences between common law and code law are widely known. There are other differences as well. Detailed companies legislation may inhibit or protect business, as the case may be. The United States has rather stringent unfair trade and antitrust laws. The legal systems of some European countries tolerate market share agreements and cartel arrangements.

Using principally these four elements of differentiation, a quick analysis of business environments existing in different countries can be undertaken. This yields, in the author's opinion, ten distinct sets of business environments. Each differs from all others in at least one important respect. The ten are:

1. United States/Canada/The Netherlands—There is a minimum of commercial or companies legislation in this environment. Industry is highly developed; currencies are relatively stable. A strong orientation to business innovation exists. Many companies with widespread international business interests are headquartered in these countries.

2. British Commonwealth (Excluding Canada)—Comparable companies legislation exists in all Commonwealth countries and administrative procedures and social order reflect strong ties to the mother country. There exists an intertwining of currencies through the so-called "sterling block" arrangement. Business is highly developed but often quite traditional.

3. Germany/Japan—Rapid economic growth has occurred since

278   *Accounting for Individuals and Organizations*

World War II. Influences stemming from various United States military and administrative operations have caused considerable imitation of many facets of the United States practices, often by grafting United States procedures to various local traditions. The appearance of a new class of professional business managers is observable. Relative political, social, and currency stability exists.

4. Continental Europe (Excluding Germany, The Netherlands and Scandinavia)—Private business lacks significant government support. Private property and the profit motive are not necessarily in the center of economic and business orientation. Some national economic planning exists. Political swings from far right to far left, and vice versa, have a long history in this environment. Limited reservoirs of economic resources are available.

5. Scandinavia—Here we have developed economies, but characteristically slow rates of economic and business growth. Governments tend toward social legislation. Companies acts regulate business. Relative stability of population numbers is the rule. Currencies are quite stable. Several business innovations (especially in consumer goods) originated in Scandinavia. Personal characteristics and outlooks are quite similar in all five Scandinavian countries.

6. Israel/Mexico—These are the only two countries with substantial success in fairly rapid economic development. Trends of a shift to more reliance on private enterprise are beginning to appear; however, there is still a significant government presence in business. Political and monetary stability seem to be increasing. Some specialization in business and the professions is taking place. The general population apparently has a strong desire for higher standards of living.

7. South America [2]—Many instances are present of significant economic underdevelopment along with social and educational underdevelopment. The business base is narrow. Agricultural and military interests are strong and often dominate governments. There is considerable reliance on export/import trade. Currencies are generally soft. Populations are increasing heavily.

8. The Developing Nations of the Near and Far East [3]—Modern concepts and ethics of business have predominantly Western origins. These concepts and ethics often clash with the basic oriental cultures. Business in the developing nations of the orient largely means trade only. There is severe underdevelopment on most measures, coupled with vast population numbers. Political scenes and curren-

[2] These areas are obviously treated very generally; exceptions exist for a few given countries.
[3] See footnote 2.

cies are most shaky. Major economic advances are probably impossible without substantial assistance from the industrialized countries.

9. Africa (Excluding South Africa)[4]—Most of the African continent is still in the early stages of independent civilization and thus little or no native business environment presently exists. There are significant natural and human resources. Business is likely to assume a major role and responsibility in the development of African nations.

10. Communist Nations—The complete control by central governments removes these countries from any further interest for the purpose of this article.

The above categorization suggests that each country does not necessarily have a separate and distinct environment for its business. It also suggests a manageable way of viewing the existing differences.

One additional general observation on business environments seems worthwhile. In the ten categories listed above, little likelihood of change may be expected in the near future. Of course, details and specifics constantly change in the economic surroundings of business. But the overall philosophy and character that distinguish the ten separate cases seem rather well established, perhaps for as long as a quarter of a century. Therefore, relative stability appears to be one of the properties of different business environments. This means two things: (1) business concepts and practices, including accounting concepts and practices, do not necessarily require rapid changes if they are based on environmental conditions, and (2) business environments are probably more difficult to change than is sometimes assumed.

ACCOUNTING AND THE ECONOMIC/ BUSINESS ENVIRONMENT

In society, accounting performs a service function. This function is put in jeopardy unless accounting remains, above all, practically useful. Thus, it must respond to the ever-changing needs of society and must reflect the social, political, legal, and economic conditions within which it operates. Its meaningfulness depends upon its ability to mirror these conditions.

The history of accounting and accountants reveals the changes which accounting consistently undergoes. At one time accounting was little more than a recording system for certain banking services and tax collection plans. Later it responded with double-entry bookkeeping procedures to meet the needs of trading ventures. The industrialization and division of labor made possible cost and management-type accounting.

[4] See footnote 2.

The advent of modern corporation stimulated periodic financial reporting and auditing. Most recently, accounting has revealed a greater social awareness by assuming public-interest responsibilities together with the providing of decision information for the larger public-securities markets and management-consulting functions. Accounting is clearly concerned with its environment. Its developmental processes are often compared with that of common law.

From an environmental point of view, various developments in society affect accounting. What else would have caused, for instance, the very serious preoccupation of United States accountants with the needs of United States security analysts? Similar influences are present in recent U.S. efforts concerning lessor and lessee accounting, accounting for business combinations, and the wholesale extension of accounting to international business problems.

But accounting also affects its environment. Many economic resources are allocated to specific business uses on the basis of relevant accounting information. In some measure, national economic policies are formulated on the contents or message of corporate financial statements, and unions often base wage demands on similar information. Rate cases of regulated companies are based primarily on accounting data, and so are most antitrust cases initiated by governmental agencies. Therefore, accounting both reflects environmental conditions and influences them.

Dudley E. Browne touches on the relationship of accounting to its environment in his review of *Corporate Financial Reporting in a Competitive Economy,* by Herman W. Bevis:

The financial accounting and reporting of any corporation are subject to a variety of external influences. A larger number of common approaches to accounting and reporting problems can be found in a given industry or other relatively homogeneous group of corporations than in all of industry, but the internal relationship of its operations and programs with external influences will continue to make each corporation different from every other.

The necessity that corporate financial accounting and reporting be sufficiently unrestricted to respond readily to change should be kept in mind . . . the principle of full and fair disclosure must remain the keystone of successful corporation-stockholder and corporate-society relationships.[5]

THE ISSUE OF DIFFERENT ACCOUNTING PRINCIPLES

If we accept that (1) economic and business environments are not the same in all countries, and (2) a close interrelationship exists between

[5] Dudley E. Browne, *Financial Executive,* January 1966, p. 50.

economic and business environments and accounting, it follows that a single set of generally-accepted accounting principles cannot be useful and meaningful in all situations. This conclusion admits the possibility of some honest and well-founded differences in accounting principles that find general acceptance in certain national or geographic-area circumstances.

Let us postulate for a moment that accounting principles generally accepted in the United States were enforced in all countries of the free world. This would create an international uniformity which would have some intellectual appeal and would ease many problems in international accounting practice and international financial reporting.

At the same time, such uniformity would lack meaning. It would have to assume that business conditions are the same in all parts of the free world and that the same stage of professional, social, and economic development has been reached everywhere. This is certainly not the case. In fact, enforced international uniformity on the basis of United States accounting principles alone would probably lead to misinformation or inaccurate results in many instances. The same types of calamity which have characterized so many U.S. foreign aid problems in the past would result.

Nevertheless, the issue of international differences in accounting principles does not resolve itself into a complete laissez-faire approach. A strong theoretical argument can be made for consistency of generally-accepted accounting principles between those countries or geographic areas where economic and business environments are substantially similar. In other words, from a theoretical viewpoint, generally-accepted principles in the United States should be the same as those in Canada, but may differ in some respects from those used in South America or Pakistan or India. The business and economic environments of the United States and Canada are very similar; the respective environments of the United States and India are very dissimilar.

ENVIRONMENTAL CIRCUMSTANCES AND APPROPRIATE ACCOUNTING PRINCIPLES

Reference to environmental conditions is subjective. It is not possible, therefore, to develop a conclusive list of those circumstances which permit or require differing accounting principles from one country or area to the next, but some of the circumstances affecting the determination of appropriate accounting principles in an international framework can be identified. Such circumstances include:

1. Relative stability of the currency of account—If a currency is quite stable over time, historical cost accounting is generally indicated. Significant currency instability calls for some form of price

index adjustment, with the form of adjustments depending largely on the type of indexes available and reliable.

2. Degree of legislative business interference—Tax legislation may require the application of certain accounting principles. This is the case in Sweden where some tax allowances must be entered in the accounts before they can be claimed for tax purposes; this is also the situation for LIFO inventory valuations in the United States. Furthermore, varying social security laws may affect accounting principles. Severance pay requirements in several South American countries illustrate this.

3. Nature of business ownership—Widespread public ownership of corporate securities generally requires different financial reporting and disclosure principles from those applicable to predominantly family or bank-owned corporate equities. This is in essence a difference because public and closely held companies do not need to capitalize small stock distributions at market value whereas publicly held companies do.

4. Level of sophistication of business management—Highly refined accounting principles have no place in an environment where they are misunderstood and misused. A technical report on cost variances is meaningless unless the reader understands cost accounting well. A sources and uses of funds statement should not be prepared unless it can be read competently.

5. Differences in size and complexity of business firms—Self-insurance may be acceptable for a very large firm where it is obviously not for a smaller firm. Similarly, a large firm mounting an extensive advertising campaign directed at a specific market or season may be justified in deferring part of the resultant expenditure, whereas smaller programs in smaller firms may need to be expensed directly.

Comparable conclusions apply to complexity. Heavy and regular Research and Development outlays by a United States corporation may require accounting recognition, especially when long-range projects are involved. Incidental development costs of a firm producing only oil additives in Mexico normally have no such requirement.

6. Speed of business innovations—Business combinations became popular in Europe only a few years ago. Before that, European countries had little need of accounting principles and practices for this type of business event. Very small stock distributions occur most generally in the United States. Again, this produces differences in accounting principles. Equipment leasing is not practiced in a number of countries with the consequent absence of a need for lease accounting principles.

7. Presence of specific accounting legislation—Companies acts containing accounting provisions are found in many countries. While these acts change over time (for example, there were new acts recently in both Germany and the United Kingdom), their stipulations must be observed when in force and legally binding. The German act requires setting aside certain earnings as a "legal reserve." It also stipulates when and how consolidated financial statements are to be prepared. The British act defines how the term "reserve" is to be used in accounting. Many other examples of this type exist.

8. Stage of economic development—A one-crop agricultural economy needs accounting principles different from a United States-type economy. In the former, for instance, there is probably relatively little dependence on credit and long-term business contracts. Thus, sophisticated accrual accounting is out of place and essentially cash accounting is needed.

9. Type of economy involved—National economies vary in nature. Some are purely agricultural, while others depend heavily on the exploitation of natural resources (oil in the Near East, gold and diamonds in South Africa, copper in Chile, *etc.*). Some economies rely mainly on trade and institutions (Switzerland, Lebanon), whereas still others are highly diversified and touch on a great variety of economic and business activities. These are reasons for different principles regarding consolidations, accretion or discovery of natural resources, and inventory methods, among others.

10. Growing pattern of an economy—Companies and industries grow, stabilize, or decline. The same applies to national economies. If growth and expansion are typical, the capitalization of certain deferred charges is more feasible than under stable or declining conditions. Stable conditions intensify competition for existing markets, requiring restrictive credit and inventory methods. Declining conditions may indicate write-offs and adjustments not warranted in other situations.

11. Status of professional education and organization—In the absence of organized accounting professionalism and native sources of accounting authority, principles from other areas or countries may be needed to fill existing voids. The process of adaptation, however, will be unsuccessful unless it allows for circumstantial factors of the type identified here.

12. General levels of education and tool processes facilitating accounting—Statistical methods in accounting and auditing cannot be used successfully where little or no knowledge of statistics and mathematics exists. Computer principles are not needed in the absence of working EDP installations. The French general account-

ing plan has enjoyed wide acceptance in France because it is easily understood and readily usable by those with average levels of education and without sophisticated accounting training.

The reader will recognize that several of the factors listed above may apply to a national situation as well as the international scene. This is not surprising since national variations in accounting concepts and practices are increasingly analyzed in terms of their respective environmental backgrounds, particularly in the United States. A relationship seems to exist between accounting flexibility within a country and among countries or areas. The topic of such a possible relationship, however, falls beyond the scope of this paper.

SOME EXAMPLES

As a limited test of the applicability of the list of environmental circumstances referred to in the preceding section, several different accounting principles are related to this list in order to evaluate at least some of the underlying environmental relationships. A complete diagnosis of this type would be a substantial undertaking and is not attempted here.

Different Circumstances Resulting in Different Accounting Principles

Investments in marketable securities are generally carried at the lower of cost or market, stock exchange quotations being used as indications of "market." A different principle needs application where no national stock exchange exists, for example, in Guatemala.

Severance payments are normally at the option of the employer and thus are customarily expensed at the time of payment. If severance payments of material amounts are required by law, however, they should be accrued in some fashion before actual severance occurs.

In the United States, owners' equity is recorded, classified, and reported as to source. Interest in dividend potential is one reason for this. It results in basic distinctions between contributed capital, retained earnings, and capital from other sources.

On the other hand, a single owner's equity principle of legal capital dominates accounting in some European countries, *e.g.*, Germany. This is based on a balance-sheet accounting orientation to creditor protection.

Similar Circumstances Resulting in (Largely Unexplained) Different Accounting Principles

The circumstances of inventory valuation are highly similar in the United States and the United Kingdom. In the lower of cost or market test, "market" means essentially replacement value in the United States and net realizable future sales value in the United Kingdom.

Despite close similarities of circumstances, deferred income tax "liabilities" are generally recognized in the United States and only sparingly recognized in Canada. Deferred tax accounting is not a generally-accepted accounting principle in Canada.

Accounting terminology varies internationally to a considerable degree without good reason. United States and United Kingdom usage of the terms "reserve" and "provision" differs, French use of the term "depreciation" differs from that in other European countries, and "goodwill" means nearly all things to all people. This is largely unexplainable.

CHANGE IN ACCOUNTING PRINCIPLES

For the time being, meaningful international uniformity of generally-accepted accounting principles should have full regard for differences existing in the environments in which accounting operates. While complete differentiation for each politically recognized country is undesirable and unwarranted, fundamentally different conditions between different countries or areas conceptually call for separate recognition.

Assuming that this can be achieved, a most important mandate of accounting is to respond to any changes in environmental conditions as soon as they occur. Accounting can actually further the cause of change since it has, as we have seen, some influence on its environment in addition to reacting to its environment. Therefore, identification with desirable efforts toward change, and quick and full response to accomplished change are probably the primary leverage factors available to accounting in resolving justifiable international differences in generally-accepted accounting principles.

Three practical examples illustrate the force of change in accounting. First, the revised German companies law enacted in 1965 contains several financial disclosure provisions which are definitely patterned after United States SEC requirements. As Germany moves closer to a corporate business society that has much in common with the United States business society, tested SEC-type legislation would seem to be a valid response to the changes occurring.

Second, more comprehensive general financial-disclosure requirements are in evidence in the United Kingdom via the widely discussed 1964 London Stock Exchange memorandum as well as the recent new companies legislation. For some time the Swiss business press has carried repeated strong appeals for greater disclosure in the financial statements of Swiss companies. These and similar admonitions for wider general disclosures seem to be a consequence of widening securities markets in the countries concerned. Here again, an environmental condition has changed and accounting should respond.

Third, there is a notable increase in consolidated financial reporting on the part of larger corporations in countries outside of North America. In many instances, consolidated financial statements are presented even though applicable laws do not require such presentations. The cause of this move toward greater use of consolidated financial reports undoubtedly lies in the ever growing extent of intercorporate investments and the steady growth of portfolio investments beyond the domicile countries of respective investors. The companies affected may have changed somewhat, but the far greater change has occurred in the environment of their operations.

In summary, a particular responsibility which accounting has in relation to change seems to exist. Awareness of this responsibility and concentrated efforts in connection with it are theoretically the most effective ways in which accounting principles between countries can be brought into greater harmony.

CONCLUSIONS

The three main conclusions of this paper are:

1. *United States generally-accepted accounting principles should not be enforced arbitrarily in other countries.* There is a theoretical incompatibility between the economic and business environments prevailing in different countries and an arbitrary imposition of any single set of generally-accepted accounting principles would run counter to environmental differences which exist.

Only where environments are alike or similar can meaningful results be achieved by the use of a particular single body of accounting principles. At the same time, the overall theoretical framework of accounting itself needs to be general and permit analysis in terms of applicable environmental circumstances.

2. *Complete international diversity of accounting principles is undesirable and unnecessary.* The author has attempted to define ten different areas in which comparable environmental conditions exist and which therefore would gain from a particular approach to generally-accepted accounting principles. The ten-fold classification is highly subjective; nevertheless, it demonstrates a frame of reference with regard to limited international diversity of accounting principles.

Free international exchange and cooperation with regard to accounting principles would avoid unnecessary duplications in accounting research and provide the latest accounting knowhow for application when conditions demand it.

3. *Accounting is dynamic and operates in an atmosphere of change.* Even though the basic character of a given business environment

seems slow to change, the continuing evolution of the accounting discipline affords means toward more international harmony in generally-accepted accounting principles. Efforts to change unnecessary international diversities in accounting in response to changing economic and business conditions appear to hold greater promise, in theory, than legislation or another form of enforcement of dictated international accounting uniformity.

Chapter IX

National Income and International Balance of Payments Accounting

44. The Accountant and Social Accounting*

Kenneth S. Most**

Since the last war, an entirely new branch of accounting has developed, widely known as "social accounting" but also referred to generally as "national income accounting" and more specially as "macro-accounting." Surprisingly, however, this branch of accountancy has developed outside the accountancy profession, and is virtually unknown within it. Some academic accountants have displayed interest in the work, and have commented upon it in more or less detail [1] and British accountants have honoured the leading British social accountant, Professor Richard Stone, as the Leake Professor of Accounting at Cambridge University.

* Reprinted from *Accountancy*, October 1967, pages 661–662.
** Kenneth S. Most is Professor and Chairman, Department of Accounting, Texas A. & M. University.

[1] For an exhaustive list of references, virtually all emanating from the U.S.A. and Australia, see "Micro-accounting and Macro-accounting," by S. C. Yu (*The Accounting Review*, January 1966, pp. 8–20). In Britain, F. Sewell Bray has examined national income accounting from the accountant's viewpoint. (See *Interpretation of Accounts*, Oxford University Press, 1957, pp. 199–215, and *Social Accounts and the Business Enterprise Sector of the National Economy*, Cambridge University Press, 1949.)

But the social accounting systems in use today have been produced entirely by economists and statisticians.

There are a number of features of this situation which are of importance to the accountancy profession. In the first place, it must be a matter of concern to accountants, and possibly to a wider public outside the profession, that important accountancy functions are being carried out by non-accountants. It is as though cancer research were to be conducted exclusively by bio-chemists and the medical profession took no active part. The training and experience of accountants should contribute to the development of social accounting, which presents accounting problems and may produce answers which would not have been chosen were this training and experience available.

In the second place, accountants have much to learn from the attempt to apply accounting principles and practice to the social entities or functions embraced by social accounting. Concerned as they are with problems of recognition, collection and utilisation of data, its classification and analysis and presentation in significant form, social accounting and the accounting of the accountancy profession are closely related at all points. The task of applying accounting principles to entities and functions different from those with which accountants are traditionally concerned can, and should, lead to the refinement and improvement of those principles, and even their transformation in course of time. It is already clear that the common problems of consolidated accounting, the use of imputed benefits and costs and adjustment for price-level changes can be illuminated by experience in the preparation and use of social accounts.

There is a third feature which cannot be neglected by the accountancy profession. Company laws in Europe, notably in France, Germany and Italy, already reveal the influence of social accounting on legislation governing disclosure in published accounts. As the legislation regulating commercial activities becomes more sophisticated, increasingly situations will arise where the requirements of social accounting underlie regulations concerning companies, taxation, national insurance and other areas in which the accountancy profession operates. It would seem to be of considerable importance to the profession to be in constant relation to work which will have a major impact on its activities.

DEVELOPMENTS IN SOCIAL ACCOUNTING

The expression "social accounting" is attributed to J. R. Hicks, whose book *The Social Framework, an Introduction to Economics*[2] marked a turning point in its development. Some interest in national income determination can be seen as far back as the seventeenth century,

[2] Oxford at the Clarendon Press, 1942.

but it was not until the economically turbulent years following the First World War that economists began to devote a major effort in this direction.

Work was being carried out during the 1930s in a number of countries, to which the Keynesian theories acted as a spur. Other factors contributing were a marked increase in government economic activity, the growth in size of certain business firms and the increase in the strength of trade unions, which variously stimulated and facilitated the collection of data. It may be noted that social accounting had been a major tool of the planned economy of the U.S.S.R. since 1917, although for obvious reasons the system developed there differs from those in use in the west. By 1947, national accounts had been produced by the U.K., U.S.A., Australia, Canada, Ireland and the Netherlands. In that year, the sub-committee on national income statistics of the League of Nations Committee of Statistical Experts met and reported on "Measurement of National Income and the Construction of Social Accounts." To this report was attached a memorandum submitted by Richard Stone, the sub-Committee's Chairman, on "definition and measurement of the national income and related totals." [3] Most of the work done subsequent to 1947 has been based upon this memorandum.

It is not difficult to see wherein lay the importance of the measurement of national income by accounting means. The benefits are similar to those which accrue to business through systematic profit determination—formulation of economic and financial policy, international comparisons of output and income, model-building for planning and programming and obtaining data which would not otherwise be collected for use by government, business and organised labour. It is also a means of testing and improving economic theories and eliminating biases and errors in separately obtained statistics. Current work in this field will certainly lead to its extension to national capital accounting, at present restricted to the preparation of financial balance sheets in a few countries, which opens up exciting prospects for planning and control at the regional, national and even world levels.

TYPES OF SOCIAL ACCOUNTS

There are three basic types of social accounts in use outside the U.S.S.R., where the system includes aspects of all three. We have mentioned national income accounting based upon concepts clarified by Professor Stone, which can be likened to a national profit and loss account and appropriation account, showing the increase or decrease in net worth

[3] See M. Yanovsky, *Anatomy of Social Accounting Systems* (Chapman and Hall, 1965, Ch. 1).

attributable to the period. Yanovsky [4] describes the United Nations (SNA) system in detail and points out the differences between it and the systems used by the U.K., U.S.A., France and the U.S.S.R. These differences are partly due to conceptual disagreements (particularly those of France and the U.S.S.R.) and partly due to defects in the statistical services of the countries concerned.

A different type of social accounting system is the "input-output" system, based upon the studies of Wassily W. Leontief in the U.S.A., which later became known as "the closed model of the input-output system." This model attempts to depict the flow of values through the economy, from one industry to another, the output of one being the input of the other. The household sector is here regarded as one of the industries, as is the government sector and foreign trade. The model is called "closed" because there is no final demand, following a tradition of economic analysis traceable to Quesnay and the Physiocrats of the eighteenth century. Input-output models bear some resemblance to process costing and aid in determining the structure of the economy; they are thus valuable supplements to national income accounting systems, particularly in the "open model" form which has been constructed in a number of countries.

The third type of social accounting system is the "flow of funds" system, which resembles the funds flow statement familiar to accountants. Developed in the U.S.A. by Wesley C. Mitchell and Morris A. Copeland, the work done on this system appears to have influenced French and Canadian national income accounting, but is not generally used. It requires a limited form of financial balance sheet and restricts the flow of values to "funds," i.e. means of payment.

If we add to these the potentially invaluable national balance sheet and take cognisance of the balance of payments account, which is an integral part of national income accounting, we can see on the horizon a complete and integrated system of national accounts similar to the integrated systems of financial and cost accounts which business entities find indispensable to good management. The relevance of this to the accountancy profession must be clear by now.

COMMON ACCOUNTING PROBLEMS

In preparing social accounts, there are numerous similarities between the work of the statistician and that of the accountant. Double-entry methods are fundamental, and the accounts are thus described as "interlocking." Account classifications by type and function are easily recog-

[4] *Op. cit.*, Chap. 2.

nisable by accountants, and the distinction between flows and stocks is maintained. Where a balance sheet is prepared, assets equal liabilities. The accrual basis is used, wherever the data can be obtained, and the division into accounting periods is basic. Consolidation procedures do not differ greatly in their effort to avoid double-counting, and there seems to be tacit agreement among statisticians to limit imputations to a minimum.

Nevertheless, there are also basic and important dissimilarities. First among them must come the difference between accounting and statistical methods of collecting data, which leads to the result that although national income accounts may be interlocking, they are not always integrated. Not only do the various systems "lead their independent lives," as Professor Yu puts it,[5] but balancing figures also make their appearance. There is no control exercised over the source of data, and in particular, no doctrine comparable to the realisation principle.

Secondly, whereas financial and management accounting have grown out of empirical studies of business activities and management needs, social accounting is heavily wedded to economic theory, modified by the practical difficulties involved in applying it to actual conditions. Valuation is a case in point. Economic theory leads to the use of market value for all items; nevertheless, national income is calculated both at market and at "factor cost," which is essentially market value less indirect taxes, plus subsidies. Nor is depreciation included at replacement value, and capital gains and losses are disregarded. On the other hand, the emphasis on "real" income (as distinct from monetary income) which underlies social accounting is already a major influence on management accounting, and the two-way flow of ideas will not stop at this point. The influence of social accounting on company legislation has already been noted.

Dr. Yanovsky concludes his study with a discussion of the integration of social accounting systems; Professor Yu points out the need in social accounting for a set of operational rules similar to, though not necessarily the same as "generally accepted accounting principles." Attempts to interest accountants in this important branch of accountancy have so far met with no success. It would appear urgent for the accountancy profession to demonstrate, at the highest level, a concern for the construction and interpretation of social accounts, before they develop into an esoteric branch of econometrics with which all contact has been lost. At this stage it should not be impossible to develop a procedural framework for social accounting which will be consistent with modern accounting theory and accord with the facts of present-day economic life.

[5] *Op. cit.*, p. 12.

45. Balance of Payments*

Poul Høst-Madsen**

In the course of the postwar period the term "balance of payments" has become thoroughly familiar to readers of newspapers in all countries. Even in the United States, where ten years ago the balance of payments, outside the circle of economists and financial experts, was either an unknown concept or associated with something distant and foreign, the public has since become painfully conscious of its existence.

In articles in the press the balance of payments is often defined in a very simple manner. It may be described, for instance, as a record of a country's money receipts and payments from and to abroad, the difference between receipts and payments being the surplus or deficit. Such simple explanations are useful in that they immediately provide a common-sense notion of what the balance of payments is all about, and even though it is in fact something much more complex, such language provides a good starting point for defining it in more precise terms.

WHAT IS A "COUNTRY"?

Leaving aside for the time being what is meant by receipts and payments, we may first discuss what is meant by a country. For purposes of the balance of payments, as for most other economic statistics, a country means those individuals and business enterprises, including financial institutions, that have a permanent association with a country's territory, together with that country's governmental authorities at all levels. All these in balance of payments terminology are called the country's "residents." Residents include all those economic units whose economic activity is subject to direction and control by the national authorities. By the same token, everybody else is nonresident. This is an immensely practical definition, and a good deal of what follows flows from it naturally.

Thus, all enterprises that are engaged in production in the domestic territory are regarded as residents even if they are owned by foreigners. It is the transactions of such an enterprise with other countries, including its transactions with its own home office, that are recorded in the balance

* Reprinted from *Finance and Development*, published by the International Monetary Fund in conjunction with the International Bank for Reconstruction and Development, March 1966, pp. 31–40.
** Poul Høst-Madsen is Assistant Director of the Research and Statistics Department of the International Monetary Fund.

of payments, and not those between the foreign-owned enterprise and the rest of the economy of the host country. The balance of payments records the exports and imports of such enterprises, the profits accruing to their foreign owners, and the net movement of foreign capital invested in them—rather than their domestic expenditures, including the taxes and royalties they pay. This is so even though it is their local transactions that directly result in foreign exchange receipts by the country in which they operate. However, as can readily be shown, the balance of such a company's international transactions is equivalent to that of its local transactions.

In drawing the line of the national economy so as to include foreign-controlled enterprises, the balance of payments concepts are in accordance with those of the national accounts; both are founded upon political and economic reality. Foreign-controlled enterprises—for example, oil companies—have, of course, sometimes been able to exercise a great deal of autonomy in the country where they have operated. They may even have been geographically isolated from the rest of that country's economy. Nevertheless, the fact that any enterprise is operating on the territory of a given country implies that it is, like other local enterprises, subject to that country's authority in carrying out its productive activity, and the ultimate demonstration of this has been on occasion expropriation of the foreign owner. This subjection to government authority makes it an integral part of the host country's economy.

This is obviously not so with embassies or military units and personnel of governments stationed in foreign countries. Their economic activity is not subject to the direction of the government of the country in which they are located; they can best be regarded as part of the home country's economy, and therefore as nonresidents of the country in which they happen to dwell. The transactions of foreign embassies and military installations, and of their personnel, with the country in which they are located, are therefore recorded in the balance of payments of their home country. Remittances by a government to an embassy or a military agency abroad are not per se part of the home country's balance of payments. It is the amounts spent abroad by the embassy or military agency that enter it. Thus, the salary paid to the Danish Ambassador in Washington is not an item in Denmark's balance of payments; but when he pays a bill in a local restaurant, that *is* an item.

With respect to individuals it is sometimes less obvious where the line should be drawn between residents and nonresidents. Fortunately it is usually much less important also, although in recent years the question has assumed somewhat greater importance with the large migrations of workers in Europe. The tendency has been to treat all those who work in a given country as residents of that country unless they are "border workers," moving back and forth every day. Tourists and other travelers are, of course, residents of their home country.

RECEIPTS AND PAYMENTS

We return now to the question of what is meant by receipts and payments. This side of the popular notion represents an oversimplification. The balance of payments in the first place includes all transactions which at some stage (whether sooner or later) give rise to a monetary settlement, such as exports and imports against credits of varying duration. The common sense of this is readily apparent since the financial position of a country, like that of a business, depends not only on its cash holdings but also on what it owes and what others owe to it.

But the balance of payments has an even broader coverage. It includes economic transactions even if they will never give rise to monetary settlements. Although most resident-nonresident transactions give rise to such settlements, there are some important categories that do not. These include, for instance, goods granted under a foreign aid program and the shipment by a parent company of equipment for investment in its foreign subsidiaries and branches. Such transactions are included as exports or imports with a matching entry for the foreign aid or capital movement involved. Similarly, if a company does not repatriate all the proceeds of its exports but invests part of them abroad, there will be an entry in the capital account partly offsetting the entry for exports. This is because the balance of payments is intended to record systematically all the flows of *real resources* between a country (i.e., residents) and the rest of the world, and all the changes in its foreign assets and liabilities.

This wide coverage relates the balance of payments systematically to the economic activity in the domestic economy, and it does not make it any less suited for the assessment of international payments problems. On the contrary, it permits the analysis of these problems to be carried out in a broader economic context than if the balance of payments had been confined to a mere statement of money receipts and payments.

ACCOUNTING CONVENTIONS

The balance of payments is a double entry accounting statement based on rules of debit and credit similar to those of business accounting. For instance, exports (like the sales of a business) are credits, and imports (like the purchases of a business) are debits. In one rather superficial respect, the accounting procedures of the balance of payments are different: by tradition credit entries are made in the left-hand column and debit entries in the right-hand column. This is a tradition that appears almost as difficult to change as it is to change traffic from the left side to the right side of the road in a country. A fairly common alternative convention is to give debits a minus sign and credits no sign. This permits entering the balance of payments in a single column—which can be practical, for instance, when a time series covering many years is to be presented.

As in business accounting the balance of payments records increases in assets (say, direct investment abroad) and decreases in liabilities (say, repayment of debt) as debits, and decreases in assets (say, a sale of foreign securities) and increases in liabilities (say, the utilization of foreign loans) as credits. An elementary rule that may assist in understanding these conventions is that in such transactions it is the movement of a document, not of the money, that is recorded. An investment made abroad involves the import of a documentary acknowledgment of the investment; it is therefore a debit. The balance of payments has one important category that has no counterpart, or at least no significant counterpart, in business accounting, i.e., international gifts and grants and other so-called transfer payments. Transfer payments refer to transactions which have no quid pro quo. Transfer payments received from abroad are credits, and transfer payments made abroad are debits.

In general, credits may be conceived as receipts and debits as payments. However, this is not always possible. In particular, the change in a country's international reserves in gold and foreign exchange is treated as a debit if it is an increase and a credit if it is a decrease. This is merely a convention, or accounting device, perfectly familiar to professionals, but undoubtedly puzzling, because seemingly anomalous, to others. This procedure is to offset changes in reserves against changes in the other items in the table so that the grand total is always zero (except for errors and omissions).

The transactions entering the balance of payments fall into three broad categories: transactions in goods and services, transfer payments, and capital transactions, or in more precise language transactions in capital and monetary gold. Capital transactions are transactions representing a change in a country's foreign assets and liabilities, and gold entering a country's reserves is treated like a foreign asset.

In fact, a transaction entering the balance of payments usually has two aspects, as have transactions entered in business accounting, and invariably gives rise to two entries, one a debit and the other a credit. Often the two aspects fall into different categories. For instance, an export against cash payment may result in an increase in the exporting country's official foreign exchange holdings. Such a transaction is entered in the balance of payments as a credit for exports and as a debit in the capital account. Both aspects of a transaction may sometimes be appropriate to the same account. For instance, the purchase of a foreign security (recorded as a debit in the capital account) may have as its counterpart a reduction in official foreign exchange holdings (a credit also in the capital account). For barter (not a common phenomenon in free enterprise economies) both entries are in the goods and services account. In the case of a foreign grant one entry will be for a transfer payment and the other in the goods and services account (grants in kind) or in the capital account (cash grants) . . .

Summarizing, balance of payments statistics are a tool for economic analysis which relates the economic activity in a country to its transactions with the rest of the world. The transactions summarized in the balance of payments are the mechanism through which economic impulses are transmitted between a country and the rest of the world. They constitute, therefore, a limiting factor that must be considered in framing policies aimed at stimulating domestic production and growth. Such policies express themselves in added demands for foreign goods and services, and hence may, if carried too far, give rise to a loss of reserves, or more precisely a deficit in the balance of payments, calling for corrective action. A surplus or deficit in the balance of payments may provisionally be defined as the balance of the autonomous transactions for which financing is provided by the monetary authorities; but since it is difficult to distinguish between autonomous transactions and such compensatory financing, and because more than one significant balance can be drawn in the balance of payments, the definition of surplus or deficit is a complex matter.

46. How to Interpret the Balance of Payments Accounts*

The Balance of Payments Accounts is a double entry record of real and financial transactions between U.S. and foreign residents. Because it is based on double entry bookkeeping principles, the balance of payments always balances in the sense that receipts always equal payments. The double entry nature of the Balance of Payments Accounts is shown on the left-hand side of the accompanying table. This strictly accounting balance must not be confused, however, with a meaningful economic

* Reprinted from *Federal Reserve Bank of St. Louis,* December 1968, pages 18–19.

balance, because the economic behavior underlying some of these transactions may not be sustainable. For example, the receipt of $1.2 billion in 1967 from the sale of the U.S. gold stock (IV.3.a) can only continue as long as our gold stock lasts. There are two officially accepted measures of our economic Balance of Payments, the *Liquidity Balance* and the *Official Settlements Balance*, which are shown on the right-hand side of the table.

To understand the bookkeeping aspect, it is convenient to divide the Balance of Payments Accounts into four categories: Goods and Services, Private Capital, Government, and Other. These accounts are, of course, linked to one another; an export could be financed by a private bank loan, by a Government grant, or by a private gift.

I. Goods and Services   Merchandise exports and imports are a measure of physical goods which cross national boundaries. Service exports and imports measure purchases and sales of services by U.S. residents to foreign residents. Sales of military equipment are included in service exports, and U.S. military purchases abroad are included in service imports (I.2.a). Investment income from the large volume of U.S. direct and portfolio investment abroad is the largest surplus item in the service category (I.2.b). Next to military, travel is the largest deficit item in the Goods and Services category (I.2.c).

II. Private Capital   For long-term capital, this records all changes in U.S. private assets and liabilities to foreigners. Net increases in U.S. assets are measured as payments of dollars abroad, and net increases in U.S. liabilities are measured as receipts of U.S. dollars from abroad. Direct investment (II.1.a) by Americans abroad is much larger than direct investment by foreigners in the United States. However, portfolio investment (II.1.b) is about evenly divided. For short-term capital, payments represent changes in all private U.S. assets, while receipts represent only changes in non-bank short-term liabilities. Changes in U.S. bank short-term liabilities are listed under IV.4 along with short-term liabilities of U.S. official monetary institutions.

III. Government   Gross outflow of loans, grants, and transfers for the Government were $5.6 billion, and the net outflow was $4.2 billion in 1967. A large share of Government loans and grants is tied to purchases in the United States. To the extent that tied purchases would not have been made without the Government loan or grant, this results in an increase in exports of U.S. Goods and Services. Thus, the $4.2 billion deficit somewhat overstates the Government's real impact on the overall Balance of Payments deficit.

Table 46.1   U.S. Balance of Payments, 1967
(In Billions of Dollars)

Transactions	Balance of Payments Accounts			Balance of Payments Measures			
				Liquidity Balance		Official Settlements Balance	
	Receipts	Pay-ments	Balance	Net Balance	Financing of Net Balance	Net Balance	Financing of Net Balance
I. Goods and Services	45.8	41.0	+ 4.8	+ 4.8	—	+ 4.8	—
1. Mdse. Trade (goods)	30.5	27.0	+ 3.5	—	—	—	—
2. Services	15.3	14.0	+ 1.3	—	—	—	—
a. military	1.2	4.3	− 3.1	—	—	—	—
b. investment income	6.9	2.3	+ 4.6	—	—	—	—
c. travel	1.7	3.2	− 1.5	—	—	—	—
d. other	5.5	4.2	+ 1.3	—	—	—	—
II. Private Capital	2.7	5.5	− 2.8	− 2.8	—	—	—
1. Long term	2.3	4.3	− 2.0	—	—	− 2.8	—
a. direct investment	.2	3.0	− 2.8	—	—	—	—
b. portfolio investment	1.0	1.3	− .3	—	—	− .3	—
c. bank and other loans (net)	1.1	.0	+ 1.1	—	—	+ .3	+ .8
2. Short term	.4	1.2	− .8	—	—	− .8	—

III. Government (non-military)	1.4	5.6	− 4.2	− 4.2			
1. Loans	1.4	3.4	− 2.0			− 2.5	+ .5
2. Grants and Transfers	—	2.2	− 2.2			− 2.2	
IV. Other							
1. Private Transfers	—	.8	− .8	− .8		− .8	
2. Errors and Omissions	—	.5	− .5	− .5		− .5	− .1
3. Changes in U.S. Reserve Assets	1.2	1.1	+ .1		− .1		
a. Gold (outflow is receipt)	1.2	—	+ 1.2		+		
b. Convertible Currencies	—	1.0	− 1.0				
c. I M F Gold Tranche Position	—	.1	− .1		− 3.5		
4. Changes in U.S. Liquid Liabilities	3.7	.2	+ 3.5	+ 3.5			
a. Foreign Official Holders	2.0	—	+ 2.0				+ 2.0
b. Foreign Prvt. Holders	1.7	—	+ 1.7			+ 1.7	
c. Int'l. Organizations other than I M F	—	.2	− .2			− .2	
Total	54.8	54.8	.0	− 3.6*	+ 3.6	− 3.4*	+ 3.4

* Figures do not add because of rounding.

IV. Other   Private Transfers represents gifts and similar payments by American residents to foreign residents. Errors and Omissions is the statistical discrepancy between all specifically identifiable receipts and payments. It is believed to be largely unrecorded short-term capital movements. Changes in U.S. Reserve Assets represent official transactions of the U.S. Government with foreign governments and the International Monetary Fund. Changes in U.S. Liquid Liabilities represent increased foreign holdings of liquid dollar liabilities of U.S. private and official monetary institutions (Banks, the U.S. Treasury and the Federal Reserve).

BALANCE OF PAYMENTS MEASURES

Two economic measures of the balance of payments are represented in the table. The Net Balance column shows the source and overall size of the deficit or surplus, while the Financing column shows how the deficit is financed or the surplus disposed.

The major difference between these two measures is the way foreign holdings of U.S. bank and Treasury liabilities are handled. The underlying assumption about economic behavior in *Liquidity Balance* is that all foreign holdings of dollar liabilities which mature in one year or less (Liquid Liabilities) are a real claim on the U.S. gold stock. As such, the Liquidity Balance measures the actual decline in the U.S. gold stock and other reserve assets of the U.S. Government and increases in all U.S. liquid liabilities to foreigners.

The underlying economic rationale of the *Official Settlements Balance* is that only foreign official holdings of dollars represent a real claim on the gold stock. Foreign private holders and international organizations have a demand for dollar balances as an international currency in the same way as they may have a demand for any U.S. services. Thus, an increase in foreign private holdings of dollars is treated in a manner similar to that of a capital inflow; i.e., included in the Net Balance column rather than in the Financing column. The Official Settlements Balance measures changes in U.S. reserve assets, and changes in foreign official holdings of dollars both liquid and non-liquid. Thus, long term U.S. bank liabilities of $.8 billion and U.S. Treasury liabilities of $.5 billion purchased by foreign governments are in the Financing column.

Part Five

Sources of Accounting Thought

Part Four drew attention to a variety of entity-types and suggested that each entity-type should be identified and studied on a separate basis. In this manner, it appears that appropriate accounting concepts and guidelines for practice might be developed for each type of entity.

The objective of Part Five is to identify (1) the organizations, institutions and individuals who influence and contribute to the development of accounting's theories and practices and the manner in which they do this, and (2) the nature of the research currently conducted by accountants and the needs for further research. The organizations, institutions and individuals referred to are divided into four sections. The nature of their respective influences on and contributions to accounting thought is discussed in each section. Some discussion follows on the justification for each of these sections and the order in which they appear.

Accounting is "practiced." This makes it somewhat different from many other disciplines which do not have a pressing need to develop theories as a basis for practice. Although it is possible for accounting theorists to construct theories for theory sake, it is important to keep in mind that the major element in the development of accounting thought continues to be the evolution of guidelines for accounting practice.

The first group of readings consists of statements by seven accounting organizations and institutions about their objectives and programs. Our listing is not exhaustive; for example, certain federal, state and other regulatory agencies not specifically mentioned also play important roles. Some of the organizations and institutions identified have a concern with only one part of the accounting function, for example, the Securities and Exchange Commission and financial accounting. Others relate to a specific type of entity, for instance, the Federal Government Accountants Association. Most are involved in cooperative programs and activities. Although it is clear that the concern of these organizations and institutions is with the information that is communicated for decision making, that is, the output from an accounting system, it should be equally clear that this immediately implies a concern with the information that is admitted to an accounting system, that is, the data input.

The individual groups of accountants identified in the three remaining sections of Part Five are likely to be comprised of members of one or more of the organizations and institutions identified above. It is often through the latters' programs and influence that these individuals make their contribution.

A separate set of readings describes the functions of corporate financial executives. Their great variety of duties together with the social and economic importance of the corporations they represent, puts them in a prime position to influence accounting practices. Contributions by financial executives are often made to many parts of the accounting function, that is, social, financial and managerial, and come about through cooperation with the organizations and institutions listed in the preceding section.

Although attention is given to the American Institute of Certified Public Accountants in the first section, the CPA is discussed more specifically in the third section because of his important role in our society. The wide range of his potential influence and contribution is conveyed from the description of his duties and ever-increasing services and problems (Peloubet). Since the CPA "audits the work of the corporate financial executive," significant reciprocal influence relationships exist between these two groups of accountants. The CPA makes his contribution mainly through the AICPA and the SEC. This fact cannot be overemphasized.

Contrary to the expectations of most non-accountants, the accounting discipline does have researchers and many specific areas and problems in need of research. The objective of the final section in this part of our book is to describe some problems facing accounting research. The AICPA (Storey and Heath), American Accounting Association, National Association of Accountants, and Financial Executives Institute are but a few of the institutions who sponsor research on a formal and/or semi-formal basis. Researchers include practitioners, university professors and graduate students. Most are involved in such research in conjunction with other activities, but some (see the AICPA's program) are involved in full-time research.

Since the accounting function is very broad in scope, its research problems are numerous and of great variety. They include, for instance, the need to (1) refine measurements and define effects of information being communicated, (2) quantify more information for specific decision-making purposes, and (3) attend to the many human problems involved in the accounting function. And these problem areas do not yet include the many practical, and still proliferating, problems of the practicing CPA, such as how to organize efficiently a tax practice or how to improve audit techniques! Hence we agree with our original authors that research is a "must" in accounting today because accounting progress and innovation depend on it.

Chapter X

Accounting Organizations and Institutions

47. American Institute of Certified Public Accountants*

The American Institute of CPAs (AICPA) is the national professional organization of Certified Public Accountants. On July 31, 1969, its membership stood at 68,860. This compares with the total number of CPAs in the United States estimated as of August 31, 1968 to be about 106,000. The Institute traces its origins to the founding, in 1887, of the American Association of Public Accountants by a handful of public accounting pioneers in the United States.

The governing body of the AICPA is its Council, made up of more than 200 members and representing every state and United States territory, and weighted according to state membership. To strengthen the bond between the Institute and the autonomous state societies of CPAs, each society has an ex officio member on the Council of the AICPA.

More than 50 committees carry on the Institute's activities, supported by a full-time staff of 210 headquartered in New York City. Among the major committees is the Accounting Principles Board, which has become an authoritative source for accepted accounting principles. The Committee on Auditing Procedure is the authority on CPA reporting standards. The formal statements of this Committee on acceptable auditing procedures are frequently referred to in SEC decisions and court opinions.

The Institute has promulgated a code of professional ethics which outlines members' responsibilities with regard to technical standards, promotional practices, operating practices, and relations with clients, the public, and other members. Complaints against Institute members are investigated by the Committee on Professional Ethics. If the Committee feels a member has violated the code, he is summoned before the Institute's Trial Board, which may acquit, admonish, suspend, or expel him.

* Reprinted from *The Institute at Midyear*, 1968/69.

Among a multitude of professional services, the Institute prepares the uniform CPA examination, which is administered by each state in a nation-wide qualifying test for CPA candidates. This rigorous, two-and-a-half day professional examination is given in May and November of each year at some 90 locations throughout the country.

OBJECTIVES

The main objectives of the Institute are (1) to serve the accounting profession in the United States through a broad program of services, and (2) to enable the accounting profession to make its fullest possible contribution to the public welfare through consultation and cooperation with other organizations active in the field of accounting.

A selection of additional objectives based on AICPA Council actions over the last decade follows:

> To perform in a manner which will persuade all parties at interest—government, financial institutions, the business community, universities and the public generally—to accept the organization as the authoritative source of principles and procedures in its field.
>
> To promote improvements in financial reporting by seeking to eliminate variations in reporting practices which are not justified by substantial differences in circumstances.
>
> To communicate effectively to the public, as well as to all levels of government, in regard to matters of concern to the profession.
>
> To produce valuable, new knowledge in its field through research and experimentation, the analysis and synthesis of experience, and the development and adaptation of new techniques.
>
> To identify those areas in society where the need for the CPA's attest function exists and to assist its members in equipping themselves to perform the attest function wherever a useful social purpose would be served.
>
> To maintain surveillance over practice in the interest of promoting high standards of performance by the profession and public confidence in its work.
>
> To promote the adoption of uniform, nationwide standards governing the issuance of CPA certificates, recognition of qualified accountants of other countries, and freedom of movement in interstate and international accounting practice.
>
> To serve as a constructive force in improving education for the profession and, ultimately, all business education.
>
> To cooperate fully with all organizations of accountants, both at home and abroad, to the end that the entire accounting function can make its maximum contribution to the public good.

48. United States Securities and Exchange Commission

SECURITIES AND EXCHANGE COMMISSION[1]

The Securities and Exchange Commission (SEC) was created by an act of Congress entitled the Securities Exchange Act of 1934. It is an independent, bipartisan, quasi-judicial agency of the United States Government.

The laws administered by the Commission relate in general to the field of securities and finance, and seek to provide protection for investors and the public in their securities transactions. They include (in addition to the Securities Exchange Act of 1934) the Securities Act of 1933 (administered by the Federal Trade Commission until September 1934), the Public Utility Holding Company Act of 1935, the Trust Indenture Act of 1939, the Investment Company Act of 1940, and the Investment Advisers Act of 1940. The Commission also serves as advisor to Federal courts in corporate reorganization proceedings under Chapter X of the National Bankruptcy Act.

Organized July 2, 1934, the Commission is composed of five members not more than three of whom may be members of the same political party. They are appointed by the President, with the advice and consent of the Senate, for 5-year terms, the terms being staggered so that one expires on June 5th of each year. The Chairman is designated by the President.

The Commission's staff is composed of lawyers, accountants, engineers, security analysts and examiners, together with administrative and clerical employees. The staff is divided into Divisions and Offices (including nine Regional Offices), each under charge of officials appointed by the Commission.

The Commission reports annually to the Congress. These reports contain a review of the Commission's administration of the several laws.

OFFICE OF THE CHIEF ACCOUNTANT

Much information filed with the Commission is in the form of financial statements. The value of these statements is directly dependent on the soundness of the accounting principles and practices observed in their preparation, and on the adequacy and reliability of the work done by public accountants who certify to their accuracy. Therefore, a major objective of the Commission has been to improve accounting and auditing

[1] Reprinted from *The Work of the Securities and Exchange Commission*, October 1968, pages 20–21.

standards and to assist in the establishment and maintenance of high standards of professional conduct by certifying accountants.

To this end, the Commission has adopted a basic accounting regulation (Regulation S–X) which, together with a number of opinions entitled "Accounting Series Releases," governs the form and content of most of the financial statements currently filed with it. It also has formulated a financial questionnaire and specified minimum audit requirements for certain brokers and dealers in securities; has adopted uniform systems of accounts for public utility holding companies and service companies; and has issued formal Commission decisions concerning accounting problems presented in particular cases. These accounting rules, decisions and opinions, in conjunction with authoritative pronouncements by professional accounting societies and by other governmental agencies, have achieved a substantial clarification and improvement in the accounting and auditing principles and practices generally followed in the preparation of financial statements. . .

The Chief Accountant has responsibility for the drafting of rules and regulations establishing the requirements as to the form and content of financial statements to be filed with the Commission. He has supervisory responsibility for the drafting of uniform systems of accounts for public utility holding companies, mutual service companies and subsidiary service companies (under the Holding Company Act), and the general administration of those systems.

COOPERATION WITH THE AICPA[2]

Accounting series release No. 96 contained the following statement in regard to the Commission's general policy on financial reporting and its development:

"In accounting series release No. 1, published April 1, 1937, the Commission announced a program for the purpose of contributing to the development of uniform standards and practice in major accounting questions. Accounting series release No. 4 recognizes that there may be sincere differences of opinion between the Commission and the registrant as to the proper principles of accounting to be followed in a given situation and indicates that, as a matter of policy, disclosure in the accountant's certificate and footnotes will be accepted in lieu of conformance to the Commission's views only if such disclosure is adequate and the points involved are such that there is substantial authoritative support for the practice followed by the registrant, and then only if the position of the Commission has not been expressed previously in rules, regulations, or other official releases of the Commission, including the published opinions of its Chief Accountant. This policy is intended to

[2] Reprinted from a memorandum which is included in Part 2, *Investor Protection*, Hearings before a Subcommittee of the Committee on Interstate and Foreign Commerce, House of Representatives, H.R. 6789, H.R. 6793, S. 1642.

support the development of accounting principles and methods of presentation by the profession but to leave the Commission free to obtain the information and disclosure contemplated by the securities laws and conformance with accounting principles which have gained general acceptance."

As stated previously, and alluded to in this release, the Commission has cooperated throughout the years of its existence with representatives of the American Institute of Certified Public Accountants, and others, in an endeavor to develop and promote better financial reporting, and a more general acceptance of sound accounting practices. Experience has borne out that the investor, and the public, are best served by this practice, and by the policy of requiring a certificate of independent accountants which expresses an opinion as to the overall fairness of the financial position and operating results reported upon, and the avoidance of prescribing detailed regulations as to accounting methods, practices, or principles. No legislative endorsement of this policy is considered necessary.

49. *American Accounting Association**

The American Accounting Association is a society for educators, practitioners, and students of accounting—for advancing knowledge, encouraging research, improving practices, developing standards, and promoting the exchange of ideas in the field of accounting.

Members are provided opportunities to contribute to or learn about important findings in the rapidly changing field of accounting. These opportunities are amplified by the publication of the quarterly *Accounting Review* and the activities of its committees, national conventions, and regional meetings.

BACKGROUND

In 1916, a group of accounting teachers recognized the need for a means by which they might stimulate the exchange of ideas pertinent to their field. This led to the organization of the American Association of University Instructors in Accounting. In 1926, the *Accounting Review* was started as the organization's quarterly journal.

Later, the Association decided that the time had arrived for a broadening of membership and objectives to include persons active in research and the practical applications of accounting. Therefore, in 1935, the name of the organization was changed to the American Accounting Association, and membership was opened to all persons interested in the advancement of the Association's objectives.

* Reprinted from the *American Accounting Association for Over Fifty Years*, 1969.

The roster of members includes managers, accountants, educators, government officials, and students—all interested in the field of accounting. Many of the approximately 12,500 members are affiliated with outstanding business firms and educational institutions.

The Association is administered by its Executive Committee, which is elected at the Annual Convention.

OBJECTIVES OF THE ASSOCIATION

1. To initiate, encourage, and sponsor research in accounting and to publish or aid in the publication of the results of research.
2. To advance accounting instruction and to encourage qualified individuals to enter careers in the teaching of accounting.
3. To advance the development and application of accounting concepts and standards and seek their adoption for financial statements prepared for external purposes.
4. To advance the development and uses of accounting for internal management purposes.
5. To advance a widespread knowledge of accounting among qualified students and the public generally.

Research and Study Committees

Accounting progress is encouraged through participation in research and study committees. Under the direction of these committees, the Association publishes statements of accounting concepts and standards, research monographs, and special studies.

50. *Financial Executives Institute**

The Financial Executives Institute (FEI) is a non-profit association of corporate financial officers. Its objectives are:

1. To serve as an effective spokesman for the business community by:
   a. isolating in advance those problems and issues which might in time affect business or the environment in which it operates;
   b. preparing and presenting forceful recommendations for actions by business and professional groups and governmental agencies.
2. To develop a superior body of knowledge of advanced financial management techniques, ethics and philosophy.
3. To aid all financial executives to broaden their knowledge of

* Reprinted from *This Is FEI*, 1969.

these techniques, ethics and philosophies and to participate actively and successfully in the full range of business activities.

4. To provide a medium for, and to stimulate, the healthy exchange of ideas and experience between the business, government and academic communities.

SUMMARY OF THE RULES OF MEMBERSHIP AND ADMISSION [1]

Membership is open to eligible Financial Executives on an individual basis; there are no company memberships. Educators meeting certain qualifications are also eligible.

All applicants to be eligible must have a specific responsibility for a major portion of the subcomponents of at least three of the chief components of the financial function as defined by the Institute.

Requirements for Active Membership

Active membership is open to those executives who perform some or all of the duties of a financial executive, as defined by the Institute and who serve companies of sufficient size to meet Institute qualifications.

Eligible Enterprise

An eligible enterprise is one which is owned by private capital, operated for profit and meets certain size criteria.

Size of Enterprise

An enterprise to be eligible must have a net worth of at least $2,000,000 for an individual performing the functions of a financial executive as defined by the Institute.

(In the case of enterprises whose tangible net worth is under $2,000,000 and whose assets are financed in large part by equipment trust certificates, bonds or other forms of long-term indebtedness, the minimum size requirements can be met with a combined tangible net worth and long-term debt of at least $6,000,000.)

Exceptions to Above Size Criteria

The above-mentioned size criteria are to be used in all cases except for the following types of business organizations whose specific requirements have been established:

Commercial and Savings Banks $10,000,000 of Capital Funds (capital stock, surplus, undivided profits, surplus reserves and subordinated debt).

---

[1] Editors' Note: Total FEI membership was approximately 6,700 at midyear 1969. From *Journal of Accountancy*, July 1969, p. 20.

Educational Institutions (privately endowed) $10,000,000 of Annual Operating Expenses.

Finance Companies $10,000,000 of Capital Funds (ownership equity and subordinated debt).

Hospitals $5,000,000 of Annual Operating Expenses (excluding expenditures for capital additions).

Hotels $5,000,000 of Annual Gross Revenue, from all sources.

Insurance $10,000,000 of Annual Premium Income.

Investment Banking Firms $2,500,000 of Annual Gross Revenue.

Investment Trusts $200,000,000 of Total Assets.

Trucking Companies $15,000,000 of Annual Revenues.

Utilities $7,500,000 of Annual Gross Revenue.

Note: For all other types of enterprises where inventories are not a major factor in producing income, an eligible enterprise must have annual gross income of $10 million. (For this purpose, annual gross income shall be that portion of income from sales of goods or services which is available for the operation of the business, payment of taxes and profits.)

Size Requirements for Sub-Divisions

The subsidiary and division size criteria for a financial executive shall be two-and-one-half times the requirement for a resident parent company and one and one-half times that size when the subsidiary or division is located in a country outside parent company headquarters.

Size Requirements for Assistant Financial Executives

To be eligible for membership, an assistant financial executive must be employed by an enterprise five times the size criteria applicable for a financial executive; sponsorship of the corporate financial executive to whom he reports is also required.

Requirements for Academic Membership

This class of membership is open to educators in the field of financial management. Applicants must be engaged primarily in educational work, have an active interest in the development of financial management and have academic rank of senior grade (Dean, Assistant Dean, Professor and Associate Professor).

Sponsorship

Applicants for Active and Academic membership must be sponsored in writing by two Active members of the Institute who shall not be affiliated or associated with the applicant's organization. Applications of assistant financial executives must, in addition, be signed by the official to whom the applicant reports.

Applications of candidates employed by subsidiaries and divisions of enterprises must also be signed by the corporate financial executive of the enterprise.

Non-Eligible Enterprises

Enterprises which are responsible to or are financed principally by any government unit or political sub-division thereof, or whose governing board of management personnel are appointed by a government official or body shall be ineligible.

Certain other types of organizations shall be ineligible because of lack of community of interest.

COOPERATION WITH THE APB*

It appears to me that the FEI and the APB each have certain separate, but very basic strengths and limitations that should be recognized in determining the part each should play in attaining the objective of narrowing unjustified or unwarranted areas of differences in accounting principles and in defining the relationship between the two organizations.

Let us consider first those of the FEI, acting as the voice of Industry.

It is financial management that first encounters new accounting problems, and the initiative to come forward with appropriate accounting solutions should therefore be a natural to reside in the FEI members.

Having the responsibility for the implementation of accounting policies and practices, financial management should be in the best position to make an assessment about the practicality of alternative solutions. It is, so to speak, on the firing line where the work in applying the principles will be carried out.

Next, FEI members have more opportunities to direct contact with shareholders and investment analysts and, as a result, should be more cognizant of their desires for certain types of information. In my opinion, this knowledge should be used to initiate new and changed concepts that will be constructive in supporting the reporting needs of both management and outsiders.

* Reprinted from a speech by J. O. Edwards at the FEI International Conference, October 25, 1968.

FEI members are in the best position to relate to corporate chief executive officers and top management and to promote understanding by them of accounting principles and changing concepts. They can, however, bring business leaderships along and make sense out of new requirements only when they have sufficiently asserted their role in formulation of principles. (This understanding is also vital in achieving satisfactory shareholders' relations.)

One of the greatest strengths of FEI members is their vast potential for conducting empirical research. In this respect, they can aid in the development of principles by (1) recommending areas that are in need of study and (2) in suggesting and testing possible solutions under actual business conditions. This, of course, means that the FEI membership offers a large resource of analysis and testing.

51. *National Association of Accountants**

The National Association of Accountants (NAA) is the "largest international organization in the management accounting profession." It is comprised of men and women from every professional and industrial group occupied or interested in some phase of accounting. Present members are found at every level in business, public accounting, government, education and in many other fields.

NAA membership is open to all persons who are interested in the aims and purposes of the Association. As of mid-year 1969, NAA had approximately 70,000 members.

Purposes of NAA are stated in Article II of the NAA Constitution (as revised effective July 1, 1969):

1. To develop through research, discussion and exchange of information a better understanding of the sources, types, purposes and uses of accounting and related data as applied to all types of economic endeavor; and to make this information available to Members and others;

2. To assist and encourage with respect to the role of accounting in the implementation and development of the socio-economic structure;

3. To stimulate worldwide acquaintance and fellowship among Members;

---

* Reprinted from *Facts about NAA Membership*, 1969.

4. To unite through membership in the Association persons interested in accounting;

5. To provide opportunities for Members to increase their knowledge of accounting practices and methods and to increase their individual capabilities.

The NAA Continuing Education Program is "perhaps the most comprehensive in the accounting field." NAA's professional monthly journal is entitled *Management Accounting* . . . [from which a number of articles are reprinted in this book]. . . .

The technical accounting literature published by NAA also includes:

1. *Research Studies.* Each study delineates the current practice, including analysis of the various approaches taken to solve the problems significant to the subject under discussion. The studies are largely on experience of leading companies, with emphasis on the applications of management accounting; and

2. *Research Monographs. Research Monographs* are based on doctoral dissertations in the field of management accounting, and are a valuable byproduct of NAA's educational grants-in-aid program which assists graduate students specializing in financial management.

52. Federal Government Accountants Association*

The Federal Government Accountants Association (FGAA) is a national, professional organization, of and for persons in the Federal service who have administrative and policy advisory responsibilities in areas of accounting, budgeting, auditing and similar financial control operations.

Activities of FGAA members are directed toward the following basic aims:

I. The advancement of accounting theories and practices in order to effect continued improvement in Federal financial management;

II. The conduct of research which will lead to improved financial management techniques;

* Reprinted from *FGAA, Its Purposes and Programs,* 1969.

III. The attainment of higher quality in the caliber of Federal Government financial managerial personnel;

—all to the end that resulting benefits will accrue to the American people as a whole.

FGAA endeavors to help the Federal accountant do a better job, for his own satisfaction and for the benefit of the Government. It provides members with opportunities to exchange information, tackle mutual problems and analyze professional approaches to their work. It fosters self-development by keeping members abreast of significant changes and trends in accountancy, budgeting, audit, comptrollership and allied fields.

The FGAA membership certificate opens the way to advantages in the form of information, committee activity and personal contacts; plus the opportunity for the member to render a better, more satisfying service to his agency in his daily work.

FGAA—THEN AND NOW

A small group of accountants, auditors and similar financial executives in various Federal agencies organized FGAA in 1950. They recognized that the Association would meet needs which no other society in the accounting and auditing field could fulfill.

In the spring of 1951, the Association was incorporated under laws of the District of Columbia as a non-profit, educational, membership organization. Interest in establishing chapters outside Washington led to reorganization of the Association on a national basis in 1956.

Over the years, FGAA has grown from the original Washington group of 40 members to nearly 7,000 today. The Washington Chapter alone numbers some 1,400 members and there are two additional chapters in the suburbs of the Nation's Capital. FGAA chapters exist in leading cities throughout the country plus the Panama Canal Zone. The Association is in fact international in character, with members throughout the world.

In addition to its broad geographical range, FGAA represents a wide spectrum of Federal departments, divisions, bureaus, independent agencies and regulatory commissions. Its membership is open to military as well as civilian personnel. Some 125 agencies and major divisions thereof are currently represented.

An increasing number of accounting firms, state and local governments, universities and individuals in industry are represented in the Association's membership roster through affiliate memberships.

53. *Institute of Internal Auditors**

The Institute of Internal Auditors is a business educational corporation. Its members (approximately 7200 at mid-year 1969) are men and women in the internal auditing profession associated with government and companies in diversified lines of business and industry. Associate Members include representatives of leading public accounting firms and private accountants. Educational Associate Members are educators and writers in fields relating to internal auditing. Student Members include students pursuing the study of internal auditing.

ITS FORMATION

The Institute is the outgrowth of the belief on the part of internal auditors that an organization was needed to develop the true professional status of internal auditing, and that a medium should be provided for interchange of ideas and information among those engaged in its practice.

Crystallizing this belief, a group of internal auditors met in September 1941 to form The Institute of Internal Auditors. This association was incorporated formally in November 1941 under the laws of the State of New York as The Institute of Internal Auditors, Inc. Since then its growth has been steady, and today it is the internationally recognized professional organization in the field of internal auditing.

In 1968, the Institute established The Cadmus Education Foundation to provide members of the Institute, and others who have a professional interest in internal auditing, with an expanded educational program. The immediate goal of the Foundation is to provide a comprehensive program of educational activities directed toward improving the competence of members of the Institute in all fields of their professional work. This will be accomplished by education research and the development and presentation of a series of seminars, workshops, lectures and other programs in various strategic locations throughout the world.

ITS OBJECTIVES

Educational   To create, disseminate and promote an interest in information concerning internal auditing and related subjects. To cause the publication of articles on practices and methods pertinent to the subject of internal auditing.

* The information in this article was provided by the IIA Executive Officer.

Ethical   To establish and maintain high standards of professional conduct, honor and character among internal auditors.

Social   To promote contact and exchange of information among members through meetings, conferences, and other group activities.

General   To do any and all things which shall be lawful and appropriate in furtherance of any of the foregoing purposes.

ITS ORGANIZATION

Since the inception of the Institute, it has been realized that one of the major values of membership is the contact which results from association with men holding positions of similar responsibility. This association is fostered through the creation of chapters in leading metropolitan and industrial centers.

Chapters operate under their own elected officers and boards of governors and direct their own activities, cooperating with the officers, directors and committees of the international organization in the planning, development and fulfillment of the various objectives of the Institute.

The international officers and directors act as a representative body to determine matters of general policy, to promote the welfare of the Institute and the membership, through activities such as annual conferences, publications, and research, and to assist and coordinate the activities of chapters and of members.

Chapter XI

Corporate Financial Executives

54. Duties and Responsibilities
of Chief Financial Executives*

Jeremy Bacon and Francis J. Walsh, Jr.**

The job of chief financial officer, as reported by the participants in this survey, entails a broad range of duties and consists of much more than merely getting and spending money. In analyzing what the top financial man does and how much time he devotes to various aspects of the job, several underlying factors need to be considered.

FACTORS AFFECTING FINANCIAL
EXECUTIVES' RESPONSIBILITIES

The range of duties assigned to individual financial executives can differ widely from one company to another, depending on such variable factors as the organizational relations within the firm, the capabilities and personalities of key executives, and the stage of the company's development. For example, some firms are organized in such a way that the controllership function reports directly to the chief executive of the company, rather than to the principal financial officer, with the result that the latter has no responsibility for the accounting system and much of the planning and controlling burden is removed from his shoulders. Another example is the case of a company whose growth is slow enough to permit meeting its needs for funds with cash throw-offs resulting from

---

* Reprinted from *Duties and Problems of Chief Financial Executives*, The National Industrial Conference Board, 1968, pages 3–12.
** Jeremy Bacon and Francis J. Walsh, Jr., are on the staff of the Division of Business Practices of The National Industrial Conference Board.

retention of earnings and from depreciation charges; in such a situation the chief financial executive does not need to devote much attention to obtaining outside funds. By contrast, the chief financial officer of a rapidly expanding organization might need to devote a major share of his efforts to developing new sources of funds for his firm.

The foregoing factors can also have a strong influence on the allocation of a financial executive's time. For example, in a company whose organization provides that the chief financial executive will have the title of vice president-finance, and that a treasurer will report to him, the principal financial officer may need to spend little, if any, time on such activities as managing company funds or providing insurance protection. On the other hand, the chief financial officer may have no treasurer to assist him, or the treasurer may need considerable assistance from his superior; in which case the functions of treasurership will require large amounts of the chief financial executive's time.

MEASURING AND DEFINING DUTIES

Very few survey respondents keep accurate records of how they spend their time on the job. Quite a few executives, in fact, state that it is impossible to determine exactly how much of their time is spent on their various duties each day, week, or other period. Nevertheless, in response to The Conference Board's request, most participants made an effort to estimate the allocation of their working time, and the information they gave is summarized in this report merely as a rough indication of the demands on financial executives' time and not as an accurate accounting of hours actually spent.

Financial management is much more of an art than a science and no two practitioners describe the components of their jobs in quite the same way. Consequently, in order to examine the duties of the chief financial executive in an orderly manner, it is necessary to develop a set of broad categories for classifying the components of the job reported by the respondents. These broad categories, listed in order of the number of responses to each, are as follows:

Administration of funds
Planning and controlling business operations
Acquisition of funds
Accounting
Protection of assets
Tax administration
Investor relations
Management of the company's financial organization

Consultation
Analysis of acquisitions
Government reporting
Appraising the economic outlook

ADMINISTRATION OF FUNDS

Three out of four survey respondents list administration of company funds as one of their principal concerns. While this responsibility is a basic part of financial management in every company, some chief financial executives are not directly involved in it because the work is assigned to other executives.

Management of the company's cash and banking arrangements (including cash forecasting, cash budgeting, and investment of surplus cash) is the activity most frequently reported in this category. Credit and collection management and supervision of payrolls are other forms of fund administration in which participating financial executives are commonly involved. And, in many firms, management of company pension funds is a growing area of responsibility.

The amount of time spent on these aspects of financial management by participating executives ranges from 5% to 65% of their total working time. The latter percentage is an estimate given by two executives who are vice presidents as well as treasurers of their firms. Most estimates are in the 10% to 35% range.

PLANNING AND CONTROLLING BUSINESS OPERATIONS

Planning and controlling business operations is reported as a primary area of responsibility by about two-thirds of the participants, the second largest group. As used in this survey, the term refers to long- and short-range planning, budgeting (for capital expenditures as well as for income and expenses), establishing and up-dating cost standards, and internal auditing. Some participating executives deal only with one aspect of planning and controlling, while others are involved in several or all. The smallest amount of time devoted to planning and controlling is 2%, reported by the treasurer of a metal products company, while the other extreme is represented by several respondents who estimate that at least half of their time is devoted to this area of responsibility. One vice president-finance of a steel company describes the situation that prevails in a large firm such as his:

In a company the size of ours, the chief financial executive has subordinates in charge of the principal financial functions—a treasurer and controller. Thus, in these major areas his activities can be limited to setting goals and objectives, future planning, review and control, etc. A substantial portion of time is spent in conjunction with the chief executive officer and other principal corporate executives in the functions of planning and control, both long-range and short-range.

In several cases the reporting executive exercises this function by means of his supervision of a particular department, such as the controller's department or a financial planning department.

Eleven of the executives who are involved in planning and controlling now spend more time on this activity than they did five years ago, while four men say they now give less time to it.

ACQUISITION OF FUNDS

Acquiring funds from outside sources is a basic responsibility of financial management in every company. Nevertheless, only three out of five respondents list it as one of their principal current duties. Most of those who do not list it work for companies that do not use outside financing at the present time, but depend entirely on funds generated internally.

For the purposes of this survey, acquisition of funds includes the sale of stock, long-term borrowing, and, in connection with these, the establishment and maintenance of a desired ratio between debt and equity. It also includes the arrangement of bank loans or other short-term financing, and entering into leasing agreements as a means of financing. It does not include the task of establishing and maintaining favorable relations with investors, which is often a function of the chief financial officer and is discussed separately below.

About half the executives who give estimates of the time they spend on acquiring funds place the figure at either 5% or 10%. Estimates by the remaining half are spread quite evenly up to a maximum of 50%. Seven respondents say that they spend more time now on the acquisition of funds than they did five years ago; three executives say they spend less time on this duty now.

Respondents involved in this function are about equally divided between those who are treasurers, those who are vice presidents as well as treasurers, and those who are vice presidents but not treasurers. In other words, about two-thirds of the respondents who have responsibility for acquisition of funds are their companies' treasurers.

ACCOUNTING

Nearly six out of ten executives participating in this survey are responsible, in one way or another, for their companies' accounting functions.

The accounting function includes the recording, classification, analysis, and reporting of accounting data, establishment of accounting policies, and development and use of electronic data processing facilities and other systems and procedures. The products of the accounting system serve not only the owners of the business, to whom management must account for its stewardship, but also the company's executives who depend on accounting reports and analyses as part of the planning and controlling apparatus. In carrying out their accounting responsibilities financial executives also maintain their companies' relations with independent public accountants and also with money lenders and government agencies to whom reports must be submitted.

Most estimates of the time spent on accounting fall into the range of 10% to 40%; one estimate of 50% and a few of 5% are reported. Mentioned most often are 10% and 40%. Of five respondents who say that they now spend more time on accounting matters than they did five years ago, four relate the increase directly to the introduction of electronic data processing.

PROTECTION OF ASSETS

Responsibility for protecting company assets is specified as a primary function by 44% of the participating financial executives. Although this duty is fairly often the concern of the chief financial officer, it is seldom a demanding one in terms of time. Only three of the respondents who give a time estimate for this function say that they devote more than 10% of their working hours to it; one of them reports spending 25% of his time, and the estimate of the other two is 20%. Five respondents say that the task requires less than 5% of their time. There are almost no reports of increases during the past five years of the share of executives' time required by this function.

As used in this survey, "safeguarding the assets of a corporation" is almost entirely a matter of providing insurance protection, since internal auditing is considered to be essentially a method of control. One financial vice president mentions that in addition to being responsible for maintaining an adequate insurance program he also oversees the protection of his company's trademarks. A few executives indicate that insurance responsibilities in their companies are carried out by a separate department whose head reports to the chief financial officer.

TAX ADMINISTRATION

Seeing that their companies' tax obligations are computed correctly and payments made on time, giving advice on the tax effects of contemplated actions, planning for the minimization of company tax liabilities, and negotiating with representatives of taxing agencies constitute important duties for four out of ten participating financial executives. Tax administration, however, does not ordinarily consume a major portion of the chief financial executive's time, because most of the work is delegated to subordinates who are usually highly trained specialists in taxation. Most estimates of time spent by the top financial officer on tax matters range from 5% to 10%. The highest reported time allowance is 25%, while, at the other extreme, three executives devote less than 5% of their working hours to tax problems.

INVESTOR RELATIONS

Responsibility for maintaining a market for the company's securities and for fostering good relations with the investment community, as well as with the company's individual stockholders, is reported by 38% of the survey respondents as being part of their job. Almost all estimates given of the time required to fulfill this duty are in the range of 5% to 15%, and most of this time is devoted to meetings and interviews with security analysts.

MANAGEMENT OF THE FINANCIAL ORGANIZATION

Accomplishment of the manifold tasks assigned to the chief financial executive often requires a sizable work force composed of professional workers, technicians, and clerical help. Furthermore, in many companies elements of the financial organization may be found in widely dispersed geographical areas, and even in foreign countries. Planning, organizing, motivating, and controlling the activities of, and the personnel assigned to, financial management can be a demanding job. About 30% of the responding executives report that they are directly involved in administrative matters connected with their own departments. In many companies much of this work is delegated to subordinates.

There is no predominating pattern as regards the percentage of time that the participating executives spend on administrative duties. Estimates range all the way from 3% to 80% of the executives' working hours.

CONSULTATION

One-fourth of the respondents report that it is a regular part of their job to consult with and advise others in the company on financial matters. Estimates of time spent in consultation are almost all in the range of 10% to 20%. Consultation frequently takes the form of committee meetings (one executive sits on six committees) or board of directors meetings. Conferences with individual officers and other employees are also included; the chief executive officer and division heads are mentioned most often in this connection. As one vice president-finance says, "policy and operating decision meetings occupy large amounts of time, which vary widely from period to period." Another survey participant, executive vice president of a communications and electronics equipment manufacturer, explains:

My time is in considerable measure consumed by long-range planning and monthly operations review meetings with the divisions, by reviews with my staff, by interviews with outsiders and by study of reports and plans. I haven't timed my working hours, but in the past five years there has been increasing demand from the meetings with division management.

ANALYSIS OF ACQUISITIONS

Evaluation of acquisition or merger possibilities is reported as a principal duty by about 25% of the respondents. Acquisition and merger activity takes as little as 1% of one man's time and as much as 65% of another's, with other estimates at various levels in between. Just over half of the estimates are in the range of 5% to 15%, however. One-fourth of the cooperating financial executives who are involved in this activity say that it requires more time now than it did five years ago.

GOVERNMENT REPORTING

Responsibility for complying with the reporting requirements of governments (Federal, state, local, and foreign) is assigned to 15% of the respondents, only one of whom estimates that this task occupies more than 5% of his time, his estimate being 10%.

ECONOMIC APPRAISAL

Seven per cent of the survey participants say they spend time keeping abreast of economic conditions and reporting the financial outlook to management and/or to the board of directors. Time estimates indicate that this responsibility seldom takes up more than 5% of a chief financial officer's time. One exception is the situation of a vice president of a large pipeline firm, whose primary task is maintaining liaison between the board of directors and the treasurer and controller functions; he estimates that 30% of his time is spent on advising the board of the financial outlook and its relation to the company's cash position, earnings, and securities. Another executive, the treasurer of a producer of chemicals and allied products, lists these among his principal duties:

Keep informed regarding the politics and economics of silver
Supervise predictions of business conditions and sales and other statistical work
Determine policy with respect to foreign exchange protective measures.

Corporate Financial Executives

OTHER DUTIES

The duties described so far cover the functions that are generally considered to be part of the job of financial management in the typical business enterprise. But quite a few survey participants report that they have other responsibilities as well. For example, 16 of the respondents are corporate secretaries in addition to being chief financial officers of their respective firms. Furthermore, about 10% of the respondents say that they spend time on special assignments; in a few cases such projects occupy large proportions, sometimes as much as half, of the respondents' working time. As one vice president explains, it is possible for him to devote a great amount of time to special assignments "because the department heads in the financial organization are quite capable," and therefore basic financial matters do not require his full attention.

Several executives hold general management responsibility for one or more subsidiary companies, divisions, or departments, in addition to their financial management duties. Among the non-financial departments reported are personnel (including salary administration), industrial relations, and company aircraft. Some also mention playing a role in negotiating contracts with outside firms.

Among the less common activities reported by individual executives as being part of their area of responsibility are export sales, joint ventures for raw materials, custody of company files, warehousing, and customer services. Perhaps the most unusual duty is that of the treasurer of a newspaper publishing firm, who writes a daily financial column in the newspaper in addition to performing his financial management duties.

CHANGING DIMENSIONS OF FINANCIAL MANAGEMENT

Many of the chief financial executives were unable to state whether or not their jobs have changed materially in recent years, either in scope or in terms of time spent, either because they have not been in their present positions long enough or because they keep no records that would make a comparison possible. However, a number of respondents did make such a comparison and two factors stand out as causing significant shifts in emphasis on the chief financial officer's various duties. One of these factors is the present trend toward business expansion by means of mergers and acquisitions. Quite a few executives who are involved in this activity now spend more time on it than they did five years ago.

The other factor affecting financial executives' duties is the introduction of electronic data processing facilities and the effort to make such installations work more effectively. One treasurer and controller, whose time is divided equally between his duties as treasurer, as controller, and as administrator of EDP and systems development, makes this point clearly:

> *When I came to this company approximately six years ago, the company had no electronic data processing establishment. I have since introduced a broad program beamed toward development of a completely integrated management information system. The first major phase of this program has just been completed. Five years ago there was no such function, nor was there any specific systems and procedures function as such. Since I have introduced these two functions as separate entities under the chief financial officer, they now take approximately one-third of my time.*

Several executives are in agreement in attributing shifts in emphasis among their various duties to an increased pressure on profits. In the words of a secretary-treasurer whose concern with product decisions, controls, and the use of working capital has become more intense: "Our efforts as a company are directed now toward maximizing return on investment, whereas five years ago the goal was simply more sales volume." And another executive adds this comment:

> *Five years ago the company, essentially an aerospace contractor, was in a period of rapid growth in sales, profits, and employment. In today's climate of more intensive competition, limited government spending for research and development, and the policy of fixed price rather than cost-plus procurement, the emphasis of the company is toward improved budgeting, cost reduction, and diversification efforts.*

Despite external influences, however, changes in the dimensions of the financial executives' job are often simply individual adjustments to the needs of particular firms. As the following statement points out, the personality and capabilities of the man who is chief financial officer can change the boundaries of the position:

> *Five years ago the controller's position was quite limited and consisted mainly of general accounting, taxes, and insurance. Since that time, the controller has evolved from a relatively minor position into his present position as a senior officer for this company. It should also be noted that most of this change has come within the last two years. In this particular corporation, the importance of the position will vary with the caliber of the person occupying the position.*

55. Personal Data on Financial Executives*

Maturity, long service with his present company, solid educational background, and attainment of professional status in accounting or law are characteristics of the financial executive today.

A survey conducted by the National Industrial Conference Board of 160 financial executives reveals that, in addition to these characteristics, the financial executive is often a director of his company or on the board of other organizations, and he holds memberships in a variety of professional, business, industry, and civic associations.

The study revealed that the median age for financial executives is 53. The breakdown by age of respondents to the survey is as follows:

Age	Number of Executives
Under 40	13
40-49	45
50-59	68
60-65	29
Over 65	2
Total	157

Seventy per cent of the financial executives responding to the survey have been with their present company ten years or longer, while 17 per cent have been employed by their present firms less than five years.

Years with Company	Number of Executives
Less than 5	27
5-9	21
10-14	19
15-19	23
20-24	19
25-29	20
30-34	15
35 and over	13
Total	157

* Reprinted from *Financial Executive*, April 1968, page 10.

More treasurers and assistant treasurers become chief financial executives in their companies than holders of any other office. One-third of the respondents had been treasurers or assistant treasurers before becoming chief financial officers, while one-fourth were promoted from controllership of their companies. One-fifth joined their present companies as chief financial officers. The remaining respondents were promoted from a variety of positions, including some not related to the financial function.

According to the survey, the majority of financial executives are established in an occupation before joining their present companies, and more than a fourth have had experience in public accounting practice. One-sixth of those who began their careers with other companies had attained the level of vice president before joining their present firms.

About one-half of the executives responding to the survey are members of their companies' boards of directors. A number who are not members of the board say they regularly attend board meetings, and several indicate that, although they are not on the board of the parent company, they are directors of one or more subsidiaries.

Just over half are directors of outside companies.

Nine out of ten financial executives hold at least one college degree, and about one-third have graduate degrees, most frequently MBA's.

Highest Educational Attainment	Number of Executives
Attended college or equivalent but no degree	14
Bachelor's degree	77
Graduate work but no degree	10
Graduate degree	50
Total	151

Just under half of the cooperating financial executives reported having achieved some recognition of professional attainment or proficiency. The majority are certified public accountants and a number are members of the bar.

All but 20 per cent of the respondents report membership in at least one technical or professional society, and three-fourths say they belong to one or more business, trade, or industry associations. Seventy are members of the Financial Executives Institute, and about half that number are members of the American Institute of Certified Public Accountants. Thirty belong to the National Association of Accountants. Among business, trade, or industry associations, the Chamber of Commerce and the American Management Association rank first and second in the number of respondents who are affiliated with them; the National Association of Manufacturers ranks third and is followed by a long and varied list of organizations.

56. GM's Key Executives, Directors Had a Gain in Pay of 19% in 1968*

General Motors Corp.'s top officers and directors received $17,-739,500 last year in salaries, fees, cash bonus awards and stock credits, a rise of 19% from $14,906,480 a year earlier.

The percentage increase in GM's top level pay was much sharper than the 6% rise in 1968 profit to $1.73 billion, or $6.02 a share.

The proxy statement for the annual meeting further disclosed that two GM directors—Henry C. Alexander and Edward F. Fisher—won't stand for reelection. GM didn't nominate any successors. Its 23-man slate includes 12 outsiders.

Between now and 1970, three of the outsiders may leave the GM board under provisions of an agreement last June with the Justice Department. After the Government threatened antitrust action, 16 companies including GM and three oil companies said they would end their interlocking directorships.

The existing GM interlocks are caused by Albert L. Williams, who is a Mobil Oil Corp. director; Howard J. Morgens, who is on the Standard Oil Co. (New Jersey) board and Richard K. Mellon, who is a director of Gulf Oil Corp. The GM proxy statement doesn't discuss their plans, but earlier it was disclosed that Mr. Mellon will continue as a GM director until the "expiration of his period of eligibility," which is June 1970.

Those three directors could end their interlocks by quitting their oil company directorships.

GM didn't say why Mr. Alexander and Mr. Fisher were leaving the GM board. However, it did note that Mr. Fisher is chairman of Gar Wood Industries Inc., which sold GM and its subsidiaries about $11.5 million of products last year, mainly hub assemblies and wheel discs. The sales accounted for an estimated 20% of Gar Wood's total sales. Gar Wood also bought $206,000 of products from GM.

Mr. Fisher, 78 years old, is the last of the Fisher brothers that

* Reprinted from *The Wall Street Journal*, April 21, 1969.

owned Fisher Body Co., which became affiliated with GM in 1918. Mr. Alexander, 67, is the retired chairman of Morgan Guaranty Trust Co. of New York.

TOP PAY GOES TO ROCHE

The top pay at GM last year went to James M. Roche, chairman, who got $794,934, up from $708,316 a year earlier, and reaffirming his position as the nation's top paid salaried industrialist.

Edward N. Cole, president, received $717,490, up from $618,291, the same amounts that were paid in both years to George Russell, vice chairman. Tied for third in the pay race were Edward D. Rollert and Roger M. Kyes, two of General Motors' four executive vice presidents, who received $669,926 each. The other two executive vice presidents and their pay: Harold G. Warner, $623,694, and Richard C. Gerstenberg, $617,444.

Under GM's complicated pay formula, top officers and directors received salaries and fees during the year, a cash bonus paid out over five years and a certain number of contingent credits equal to a number of shares with a fixed value. The contingent credits are tied to the exercise of stock options. As an executive exercises his options, the number of contingent credits are reduced by an equal number of shares.

GM made available an analysis of executive pay last Friday when it released the proxy statement for the annual meeting on May 23 in Detroit. The analysis breaks down figures that are spread across the 16-page proxy statement. A spokesman explained that the figures represent only "new money" earned during the year, and gave no weight to gains executives achieved by exercising options issued prior to 1968.

STOCK OPTIONS

The proxy statement shows that between Jan. 1, 1968 and Feb. 28 of this year GM directors and officers purchased 27,536 shares of GM stock through the exercise of options granted between 1960 and 1963. They paid $1,605,678, or an average of $58.30 for the shares, on days when the stock market values of those shares total $2,235,636, or $81.17 a share.

Mr. Roche alone picked up 1,200 shares at a cost of $68,184, or $56.81 a share, on days when their market value was $90,000, or $75 a share.

GM top officials weren't the only GM men to receive handsome bonuses last year. The statement disclosed that 15,447 employes, including directors and officers who earned $13,500 or more last year also got a total of $103,266,200 in cash and stock bonus awards. That's up from $99,112,577 in 1967.

Chapter XII

CPAs

57. *Accounting Services Today**

Maurice E. Peloubet**

When Rip Van Winkle returned to his little Catskill village after an absence of twenty years, he found a strange, but not incomprehensible, society. Children had grown up, his wife had died, his daughter had married, and George Washington's picture had taken the place of King George's, but people lived in much the same way they did before he played his fateful game of bowls with Henry Hudson's men.

If, however, his absence had extended another one hundred and fifty years, he would have come back to not merely a strange but indeed an incomprehensible society. Automobiles, air conditioning, airplanes, telephones, radio, and television are only a few of the things that not only would have been outside his experience but would have been beyond his comprehension.

If an experienced and well-qualified accountant had fallen into a deep slumber in 1935 and had awakened in 1965, he would have found himself, so far as the changes in his profession were concerned, not in Rip's position at the end of a twenty years' absence, but rather in the position Rip would have been in at the end of one hundred and seventy years of slumber. Many things in the development of the profession in those thirty years not only would have seemed very strange to him but would have been, to a considerable extent, incomprehensible.

For some of the developments, the very terminology would be new, for example, *cybernetics, binary,* and *PERT.* Other expressions using familiar words would be equally difficult: *operations research, critical path,* and *problem solving by simulation.*

* Reprinted from Maurice E. Peloubet, *The Financial Executive and the New Accounting.* Copyright © 1967, pages 3–14, The Ronald Press Company, New York.
** Maurice E. Peloubet is a former partner of Price Waterhouse & Co.

335

Although the accounting profession has developed rapidly, the pace was hardly quick enough and the innovations hardly radical enough for the process to be called anything but evolutionary, until sometime in the 1940's. From then on the pace quickened; technical, administrative and theoretical break-throughs were made, and evolution changed into revolution.

DEVELOPMENT OF TRADITIONAL SERVICES

One of the principal effects of the new accounting is the great development of the traditional services to be expected from an accounting firm: audit, the attestation of financial statements for third parties, the preparation of tax returns and contesting disputed assessments, the design and improvement of accounting and control systems, and the provision of expert witnesses on accounting theory and practice.

These have been the functions of the certified public accountant from the beginning of the profession, but as will be seen, they have expanded and developed tremendously in the past ten to twenty years.

DEVELOPMENT OF MANAGEMENT ADVISORY SERVICES

Even more significant than these developments are some services of the accounting firm now available to business and government that have been developed in the last few years. These services originate for the most part in the department or group of members of a firm usually called the management advisory services section or division. Many of the smaller C.P.A. firms do not have a formal management advisory services department, but almost every accountant now renders some of these services and has done so in the past.

From the earliest days of the profession, system work of one kind or another has been part of the accountant's work. In the early part of the century, accountants and engineers shared the work of developing cost systems. Henry Lawrence Gantt was an engineer; J. Lee Nicholson and G. Charter Harrison were accountants. Frederick Winslow Taylor, the father of scientific management, was an engineer. They and others of that period laid the foundations of cost accounting and were reaching for the beginnings of standard costs.[1]

Although the transition from system work as an adjunct to the audit over to the formal organization of management service departments was gradual and progressed at different rates in different firms, it was in the

[1] For a description of the work of Gantt, Nicholson, and Taylor, see Morton Backer (ed.), *Modern Accounting Theory* (Englewood Cliffs, N. J.: Prentice-Hall, Inc., 1966), p. 14; and for the work of Harrison, see Morton Backer (ed.), *Handbook of Modern Accounting Theory* (Englewood Cliffs, N. J.: Prentice-Hall, Inc., 1955), p. 311.

1930's and 1940's that the changes were taking effect. The newer types of service went far beyond the system and cost work that had formerly been done.

Even before the opening of broader fields made possible by the computer, the change could be seen in the type of personnel found in these departments. Mathematicians, marketing specialists, economists, industrial and mechanical engineers, personnel consultants, and cost specialists, as well as many men trained in other specialties who would have been quite out of place in the old-fashioned accounting office, were employed, and full use was made of their abilities.

With the advent of high-speed data processing equipment, the potentials of management services mushroomed almost overnight. No longer was useful information unavailable because the cost of obtaining it was prohibitive or because the time required to produce it was so great that it was no longer useful when it became available.

It is an oversimplification to say that computers alone were responsible for the rapid expansion of management service departments; it is nevertheless true that the computer was the greatest single influence in the growth of these services and that without the computer such a growth would have been slow, if indeed it had taken place at all.

Types of Services Offered

The following discussions are concerned with the scope of the services that a client may, under present conditions, expect from a firm of certified public accountants.[2] Few if any clients will require all the various services, but the financial executive should know what he can reasonably expect when need arises. These services fall into the following principal categories: Management Advisory Services, Tax Services, Audit Services, and Financial Reporting. . . .

MANAGEMENT ADVISORY SERVICES

The non-accountant may think that the C.P.A.'s chief contribution to the profitability of an enterprise is in the area of taxes, in taking advantage of every legitimate or unchallenged method of reducing taxable income. He would be quite mistaken. In preventing overpayment of tax, good tax advice is conserving profits already earned and realized. Even the best tax counsel, however, must first have the profits to work on. Management services work has for its purpose increasing and maximizing the profitability of the client enterprise.

---

[2] The scope and organization of the national accounting firm are indicated in "The Auditors Have Arrived," *Fortune*, October and December, 1960, and "The Very Private World of Peat, Marwick, Mitchell," *Fortune*, July, 1966.

. . . Management services . . . [can be] grouped under the following headings: General Management, Finance, Manufacturing, Marketing and Distribution, Electronic Data Processing, and Administrative Support. Such an oversimplified and unrefined outline cannot properly convey the scope and variety of the services that are available today. If we were to attempt a complete list of the services that might be expected from the large national or international C.P.A. firm, it would run to seventy or more items and include such items as: calculating return on investment; appraising key accounting personnel; suggesting methods of approach to capital markets; developing information in anticipation of acquisitions and mergers; and advising on executive compensation plans, inventory policy, intracompany transfer pricing, coordination of production planning with sales forecasts, preventive maintenance programs, and clerical and administrative procedures.

Smaller accounting firms specializing in certain industries can frequently render important management services. For example, in the garment and fur trades an accountant must be able to prepare statements, often monthly, that promptly give credit grantors the information they need; advise the client on organization and overhead matters; and prepare statements for labor unions and confer with union representatives on various provisions of labor contracts. There are many other examples of how a smaller, local firm, familiar with the region or the industry, can be of the greatest value, particularly to the smaller client.

If we should examine the individual items in the long list of available management services, we would see that they all relate in some way to profitability, and that they are also distinctly and definitely for the benefit of the enterprise itself. No liability to the government is considered, as in tax work, and nothing is done for the benefit of third parties; renegotiation of government contracts might appear to be an exception, but even here the purpose is to arrive at a cost on which the reasonableness of a profit is based rather than to determine a liability to the government. Instead, the emphasis is on management's own problems, some recurring and some arising infrequently. Members of the individual management team would be well advised to consider carefully whether the various problems affecting profitability have been satisfactorily solved or whether, in some cases, they have even been recognized.

ACCOUNTANTS' TAX SERVICES AND INCOME

The relation of tax work to income is obvious, and every businessman, from the gas-station proprietor to the president of a corporation of national scope, knows that he must have as good tax advice as is available to him or face either the risk of overpaying his taxes or the equally serious risk of dispute, litigation, and possible fraud charges if he underpays them.

The most basic of tax services is, of course, the preparation of returns so that the statutes and regulations will be properly complied with, thus reducing the chance of unnecessary audits, and so that proper advantage will be taken of all provisions for the computation of taxable income.

Even more valuable may be the contribution the accountant can make to tax planning in estimating the probable tax effect of entering into certain transactions and the effects of alternative methods of handling the same transaction, and in suggesting changes in the form and substance of the transaction where this would result in a legitimate tax advantage. Tax planning is essential, for example, in the purchase, sale, or merger of a business; in the initial organization of a new enterprise; and in the timing and treatment of security transactions for individuals or corporations. The estate planning of corporate officers is sometimes closely connected with corporate affairs, and this is often considered to be a responsibility of the financial executive. The accountant should be a member of the team, along with attorneys and insurance advisors, when questions of estate planning arise. He can also give helpful advice on the organization and administration of the client's own tax department.

Another important kind of tax planning arises when new legislation is proposed. Because of his day-to-day knowledge of client affairs, the accountant can initiate and give advice on appropriate changes in organization, transactions, etc., to put the client in the most advantageous position when and if the proposal becomes law.

In their contacts with taxing and judicial bodies, the accountant may serve clients by advising or representing them in conferences with the Internal Revenue Service and state taxing authorities and by appearing as a witness in the Tax Court or other courts to testify to the facts in a given situation. He may sometimes testify for a party not otherwise a client on the application of accounting principles or trade practices in an industry with which he is familiar. . . .

AUDIT AND INVESTIGATION

The regular annual audit should not be regarded by the financial executive as a mere routine requirement or a conventional safeguard. Apart from its basic external functions, it is in the course of the regular audit that possibilities for improvements in system and methods and, frequently, opportunities for minimizing various types of taxes are brought to light. There is thus an indirect but nevertheless important connection between the annual audit and profitability.

To some financial officers an audit is like Shakespeare's cat, harmless and necessary. To others, hopefully the majority, it is an objective and impartial review of operations, a source of suggestions for improvement, and a guidepost to those areas of the enterprise that may need more executive attention than they have been getting. It may often serve as a guide to the use of the other capabilities of the accounting firm, particularly in the management services and tax departments.

The basic external function of the annual audit and the auditor's opinion is to make it possible to fulfill the obligations of the enterprise to third parties—stockholders, bondholders, banks, insurance companies, and other credit grantors, as well as various government agencies such as the Securities and Exchange Commission, public utility commissions, and, not infrequently, the Internal Revenue Service. In some cases audited statements are needed in dealings with labor unions.

It is on these third parties that a corporation depends for both its legal existence and its financial nourishment. This is more obviously true of a large corporation listed on a registered stock exchange, but there are few if any small, closely held corporations, partnerships, or proprietorships that do not have some third-party obligations requiring the use of audited financial statements.

A subsidiary purpose of the audit, the detection of internal fraud and the safeguarding of the company's property, is accomplished if enough work is done by either the internal auditors or the independent C.P.A. to ensure that the property and income shown in the financial statements are substantially correct.

Audits are also undertaken in connection with the sale or purchase of a business or the determination of shares in a joint venture, and for such other special purposes as to determine product costs and support insurance claims for fire or other losses. The difference between special audit work and some features of management advisory services is sometimes hard to define. . . .

FINANCIAL REPORTING

To Whom Is the Corporation Responsible?   The publicly owned corporation and, to a very considerable extent, the closely held corporation, large or small, have a multitude of responsibilities and are under many obligations to people, organizations, and various government agencies. Although these demands are for the most part met by the delivery of goods, the payment of money, or the rendering of service, a financial statement of some sort is a necessary part of meeting the obligation. In some instances it is the financial statement only that is required.

If we assume that the responsible source of the financial statements is the management of the corporation, the directors and officers, then every other person or organization, including the stockholder and the employee of the corporation, is a third party. Although not all corporations are required to furnish statements to all third parties included in the following list, every corporation has an obligation to furnish statements to some of them. Broadly speaking, those to whom financial statements must or may be submitted are:

Owners—holders of common or preferred stocks or analogous equity securities.

Creditors—bond and debenture holders, insurance companies, banks, pension funds, other creditors for loans, and, in some cases, suppliers of materials or equipment or equipment lessors.

Government Agencies:
Internal Revenue Service
Taxing authorities of states or municipalities
Securities and Exchange Commission
Federal Trade Commission
Federal Communications Commission
Interstate Commerce Commission
State and federal public utility commissions
Other regulatory bodies
State security commissions

Employees and Unions:
Individual employees
Local and international unions

The Public:
Financial writers and editors of daily and weekly newspapers and general and financial magazines.
Financial analysts representing brokerage and investment houses, or organizations representing institutional or private investors. The management of mutual funds, pension funds, and other institutional investors.

Financial Statements for Third Parties While the statements to be submitted to various third parties are widely different in form and extent of detail, they have two characteristics in common: they are all based on one set of financial books, and these books have been audited by independent C.P.A.'s or will be subject to audit. Nevertheless, they are the statements of the management of the corporation, and the management is primarily responsible for them. This does not mean that the independent C.P.A. is not consulted about form and content even when the statements have not yet been completely audited. This is particularly true of

monthly or quarterly statements where the management quite properly
wishes to avoid any large adjustment or serious inconsistency between
published interim figures and a statement of the results for an entire
period.

Any financial statement, whether condensed for newspaper publication or distribution to employees, or elaborated for financial analysts,
should be based on and be capable of reconciliation with the corporation's basic accounting records.

Stockholders and Credit Grantors   The principal financial statement of
most corporations is contained in the annual report to stockholders, which
consists of a balance sheet and income account and now generally
includes a fund or cash-flow statement. In some, details are given of
particular items such as capital additions or changes in funded debt.
For corporations the securities of which are publicly held, the report is
a public document and is reproduced in whole or in part in financial
manuals and magazines and daily or weekly journals.

Annual statements to the Securities and Exchange Commission
include the financial statements published to stockholders, occasionally
with minor differences in form but none in substance, and certain supporting statements not usually included in the published reports. These,
too, are public documents open to public inspection, copies of which can
be obtained for a nominal duplicating fee.

When an issue of equity securities is made by an existing corporation, these must ordinarily be registered with the Securities and Exchange
Commission and the stockholders notified and permitted to subscribe to
the new securities. An initial issue of equity securities must be registered
in the same way. Here again, these are public documents.

In agreements with bond and debenture holders, insurance companies, banks, pension funds, and other credit grantors, provision is
usually made for the submission of periodic audited financial statements,
frequently in somewhat more detail than is required by the Securities
and Exchange Commission. Where there are covenants requiring the
maintenance of a fixed amount or percentage of working capital or
restrictions on the use of the borrowed money, statements showing
whether or not these requirements are met are included with the usual
financial statements. Sometimes financial statements for individual units
in a consolidation, not otherwise required, are prepared for the credit
grantor. Where securities of this type are publicly held they must be
registered with the Securities and Exchange Commission.

On all of these statements the independent C.P.A. must, if he can,
give an opinion as to whether they fairly present the financial condition
of the corporation on the basis of accepted accounting principles and a

statement that the auditor has carried out all the procedures and tests required by generally accepted auditing standards. . . .

Government Agencies   There is one government agency to which every corporation must submit annual financial statements—the Internal Revenue Service. A corporate tax return is essentially a set of financial statements and supporting schedules. They are different in form from the annual financial statements, but the basic data and content are the same. The taxpayer is required to reconcile his taxable income and surplus with his corporate results.

The requirements of the Securities and Exchange Commission have already been discussed, and those of the various state security commissions operating under what are sometimes known as the "blue sky" laws are essentially similar. The auditor must be prepared to show that he meets the specific requirements of the SEC so far as independence is concerned.

The various regulatory commissions and agencies have their own special requirements for information, but they are all based on the financial books, and they differ from the published financial statements in form, emphasis, and amount of detail rather than in substance. The independent C.P.A. must be familiar with the requirements of any government agency under whose jurisdiction his clients (the Interstate Commerce Commission or public utility commissions, for instance) operate and should be prepared to defend his statements and represent his clients before such agencies if need be.

Employees, Labor Unions, and Analysts   Many corporations prepare summarized and more or less informal statements of company affairs and financial statements for employees. These, of course, must be accurate in spite of their informality, and although the auditor does not ordinarily give an opinion on such statements, his advice on form and content may be valuable. Statements for employees sometimes are required. Benefit associations and pension plans generally provide for audits and statements on which the auditor gives his professional opinion.

Agreements with unions may call for audited statements, as do certain needle-trade agreements whereunder the employer pays a penalty for employing non-union help. Some, but of course not all, labor unions are audited by independent certified public accountants, and their financial statements distributed to members.

Financial editors and analysts, either working as journalists or in the employ of financial institutions, are without doubt both the most difficult and critical readers of financial statements and at the same time the most appreciative of full disclosures and explanations. They feel keenly their responsibility to those who rely on them and, although they wish the corporation and its officers well, feel no duty or even inclination to excuse past mistakes or to gloss over present unfavorable conditions or deficiencies.

A corporation may wish to give more detailed information to analysts representing present or potential credit grantors or to institutional investors in its securities, and here again the advice and experience of the independent accountant may be of great value.

58. Problems of the Profession in the United States*

John L. Carey**

Comments in the public press—both in the United States and the United Kingdom—may have created an impression that the accounting profession in my country is in a sad state. But actually it has never been stronger or sounder. How can the apparent contradiction be explained?

In my opinion the adverse comment stems mainly from the recent discovery by the public—and particularly by financial writers—of two basic truths: (1) accounting by its nature is not, and cannot be, an exact science; therefore, net income and earnings per share for a single year inevitably involve a good deal of estimate, including judgment as to the probable effect of future events; and (2) CPAs, being human, are not infallible, they do not check every transaction when they audit financial statements, and an audit is not a guarantee against loss by investors or creditors.

Of course, anyone who took the trouble to read accounting literature over the past twenty years, or listened to speeches by the profession's leaders, would have known all this. But until recently the public and the press showed little interest in accounting or accountants, and didn't take the trouble to inquire about these matters.

Meanwhile, however, the numbers of stockholders grew to over twenty million, and the emerging profession of financial analysts increased in numbers to some ten thousand. For years the stockholders and the analysts apparently assumed things about accounting and auditing which were not correct. When they discovered the actual facts, they had a sense

* Reprinted from *Accountancy*, February 1968, pages 77–80.
** John L. Carey is the former administrative vice-president of the American Institute of CPAs.

of disillusionment, and looked around for someone to blame. The accounting profession was a convenient target.

ACCOUNTING PRINCIPLES

One erroneous assumption apparently was that the income statements of different companies were comparable—that earnings per share of one company could be compared with those of another. It seemed to be a shock to the financial community to find out that this was not necessarily true. The result was angry attacks on the 'flexibility' of accounting principles.

But neither corporate management nor the accounting profession had ever maintained that their objective was comparability. As a matter of fact, until fairly recent times, the profession assumed that consistency in the accounting of *an individual company* was the important goal. In other words, it was thought that the investor could make more intelligent decisions by studying earnings trends of individual companies, developed on internally consistent bases, than by attempting to compare the net income of one company with that of another. As all accountants know, efforts at such comparison can be misleading.

Until a relatively few years ago, I think it can be fairly said, the profession itself assumed, as a matter of basic philosophy, that there was, and always would be, diversity in accounting principles. The objective of the American Institute of Certified Public Accountants was simply to narrow the areas of difference by eliminating less desirable practices through a process of gradual education and persuasion.

It is now generally agreed that the American Institute's objective is to make like things look alike and unlike things look different: that is to say, to establish criteria indicating when one accounting principle or practice is to be preferred over another. Thus, when the circumstances are the same, the accounting should be the same. Obviously, circumstances can be very different, and to apply blindly the same accounting method to different situations could produce highly uninformative results.

With this objective in view, the Accounting Principles Board of the American Institute has recently issued several opinions—on leases, pension costs, reporting results of operations, and several other matters—all of which will remove some unnecessary impediments to comparability. Expected in the relatively near future are opinions on accounting for income taxes, goodwill, research and development costs and others, which should further reduce alternative accounting practices in similar circumstances.

Some of the recent opinions have obtained favourable comment in *Fortune*, the *New York Times*, the *Wall Street Journal* and many other publications. The presidents of the New York and American stock exchanges and the Chairman of the Securities and Exchange Commission praised the Institute for the Opinions on pension costs and reporting results of operations.

Opinions of the Accounting Principles Board carry more weight than formerly, when education and persuasion alone were relied upon to make them effective. In 1964 the Council of the American Institute adopted a resolution stating that members should see to it that departures from Board opinions were disclosed, either in footnotes to financial statements or in the independent auditor's report. Since such a disclosure might raise questions in the minds of regulatory authorities, investors or credit grantors, it may be assumed that Board opinions will be followed except in unusual circumstances.

American CPAs hope that they are well on the way to silencing critics of 'flexibility' in accounting principles. As more alternative practices in similar circumstances are eliminated, thus removing unnecessary obstacles to comparability of net incomes, criticism on this score will become irrelevant.

THE AUDITOR'S REPORT

It now seems possible also that the standard short form of auditor's report used in the US may have contributed to the public's misunderstanding.

The standard form reads as follows:

We have examined the balance sheet of X Company as of ...., and the related statements of income and retained earnings for the year then ended. Our examination was made in accordance with generally accepted auditing standards, and accordingly included such tests of the accounting records and such other auditing procedures as we considered necessary in the circumstances.

In our opinion, the accompanying balance sheet and statements of income and retained earnings present fairly the financial position of X Company at ...., and the results of its operations for the year then ended, in conformity with generally accepted accounting principles applied on a basis consistent with that of the preceding year.

In 1932, when this form of report was created, it was a great step forward. Up to then every firm wrote its report in its own language; there was no reference to accounting principles or auditing standards, nor any requirement of consistency in accounting principles from year to year. But the form of the opinion has been altered very little since that time, and from the viewpoint of today's investing public it may seem cut-and-dried, or even ambiguous. The term 'generally accepted accounting principles' could be taken to mean a precise standard of measurement applied across the board to all companies. The term 'generally accepted auditing standards' could be construed by a layman to mean that everything has been checked in every area where significant irregularities could occur. The term 'fairly presents', in conjunction with the precise number in which net income appears, could be taken to mean that net income is exact to the penny. Nothing in the financial statements or in the auditor's opinion conveys the understanding that judgement and estimates regarding future events must enter into the determination of income for a single year.

(One is reminded of the late George O. May's often quoted remark, to the effect that a single figure of net income for a single year would be indefensible if it weren't indispensable.)

Accordingly, for a year or so the American Institute's committee on auditing procedure has been studying possible revision of the standard form of auditor's opinion.

AUDITOR'S LIABILITY

In conjunction with the criticism of diversity of accounting principles, and possible misunderstanding of the auditor's opinion, publicity about lawsuits against accounting firms has aroused increased public interest.

Certified public accountants have always been subject to legal liability, of course, but lawsuits against them were very rare until quite recently. Even now the number of cases of which the American Institute has knowledge is much smaller than estimated by some financial writers. However, a few cases involve prominent companies and large amounts of money, and these have received so much publicity that an impression of widespread litigation may have been created.

Actually, none of the heavily publicised suits has been tried, though one has begun. But as this article is written, none of the accounting firms involved has been proven guilty of any wrongdoing. It is easy to start a lawsuit in the United States, and the charges get front-page headlines, while all the facts in favour of the defence may not be known for years. And many people are inclined to think that 'where there is smoke there must be fire'. The defendants have little choice but to grin and bear it.

INDEPENDENCE

Perhaps because of the chain of circumstances discussed above questions have arisen in the press and elsewhere about the independence of auditors in expressing opinions on financial statements to stockholders. Some financial writers have questioned the arrangements for appointment and discharge of auditors. In some cases—mainly in smaller companies—auditors are appointed by the management. Occasionally, they are replaced for reasons which are not publicly explained.

For example, the *Wall Street Journal*, 20 April 1967, reported that a company had dismissed its auditors with the explanation that the board had decided to follow a policy of rotating auditors. But there was an indication that the termination actually was connected with disagreements as to accounting practices. The auditors ethically are prevented from violating the confidential relationship with their clients and, therefore, cannot tell their side of the story.

In order to clarify the relationship of the auditor to the management, the directors and the stockholders, the American Institute recommends nomination of auditors by an audit committee of the board of directors composed of outside directors who are not part of the management. The auditors so nominated would then be subject to election by the stockholders. Many prominent corporations have adopted this procedure. The Institute believes it is good for the public, good for the company, and good for the auditors.

Audit committees should discuss with the auditors the scope of their examination before it is undertaken, with particular attention to areas where either the committee or the accountants believe special attention to be desirable. After the audit, the committee should satisfy itself that no restrictions were placed on the scope of the auditor's examination, and that they received all the information and explanations they needed. The committee should review the financial statements with the auditors, and should invite their recommendations regarding organisation, internal control and related matters. The auditors should communicate with the audit committee whenever any question arises that has a bearing on the propriety of the company's financial statements—past or prospective.

In some cases audit committees of boards of directors meet with the auditors without the presence of representatives of management, and sometimes with representatives of management without the presence of anyone from the auditor's firm. This is to avoid the possible reluctance of either the management or the auditors to discuss some problems in the presence of the other. Separate discussions often make it possible to resolve such problems without embarrassment or tension for any of the parties concerned.

Questions have been raised also about the impact of management services on audit independence—mostly by professors of accounting at the universities. A dozen or so articles on this subject have been published in the past few years, and some of them have been echoed in the public press.

In 1966, moreover, in a speech before the annual meeting of the Institute, the Chairman of the Securities and Exchange Commission addressed himself to this question. He said, in effect, that aid in the preparation of tax returns, budgetary procedures, costing methods, inventory controls, incentive plans and pension schemes could be considered natural consequences of the auditor's developed skills, and contribute to a better background for succeeding audits, as well as to better management. So long as such services are directed toward these ends, they do not appear to pose a serious threat to the accountant's independent status, the Chairman said. However, he offered a word of caution with regard to consulting services which cannot be related logically either to the financial process or to broadly defined information and control systems—such services as market surveys, factory layouts, psychological testing or public opinion polls 'and, I am disposed to add, executive recruitment for a fee'. The Chairman said that an accountant who directs or assists in programmes of this kind raises serious questions concerning his independence when he renders his opinion on the results of the programmes.

In fact, relatively few firms offer services of the sort the Chairman seemed to disapprove, and even in these cases such services constitute an insignificant part of the firms' total volume.

However, in view of the increasing public interest in this subject, the Executive Committee of the Institute in the fall of 1966 appointed a high-level special committee to study all aspects of the matter. So far the inquiry has not disclosed any evidence that independence *in fact* is impaired by the performance of management services. No responsible observer directly challenges the integrity of CPAs. However, many of those who have been consulted do feel that there may be an 'image' problem if the management services offered by CPAs appear to be unrelated to the accounting and auditing functions, or if the volume of management services grows so large that the 'tail wags the dog'.

The question is complicated by lack of general understanding of the scope and nature of management-services by CPAs, and of the role of the CPA in rendering such services. One large firm estimates that 85 per cent of the work performed by its management-services division is of a type which the firm performed before it had a management-services division! In other words most of the work is closely related to accounting, auditing and systems. Where it is apparently not so related, as in an engagement labelled 'plant layout' or 'market survey', the role of the CPA normally would be limited, perhaps mainly to consideration of cost factors, and might actually be carried out in collaboration with engineers or other experts.

Independence in appearance, as well as in fact, is not a simple concept. The American Institute's committee on professional ethics has warned members to avoid any relationship with audit clients—not only relationships in management services—which might be regarded by a reasonable observer, who had knowledge of all the facts, as involving conflicts of interest which might impair the auditor's objectivity. These guidelines are necessarily broad and general, and can be tested only by application to specific factual situations.

An interim report by the special committee on the independence problem is expected soon.

THE STRENGTH OF THE PROFESSION

So much for some of the problems that have given rise to concern about the state of the profession in the United States. It will have been seen that the American Institute is doing something about all of them.

It remains to justify the statement at the opening of this article that the profession in the United States has never been stronger or sounder.

First, it has grown rapidly. From about 25,000 in 1945, the number of CPAs have increased to nearly 100,000, of whom 61,000 are members of the Institute of Certified Public Accountants.

University education in accounting has improved continually. Last year a book entitled *Horizons for a Profession*[1] reported the results of a three-year study designed to outline the common body of knowledge which all CPAs in the future should possess. Scores of seminars are being conducted for discussion of the findings with university professors of accounting. The impact on curricula will surely be constructive.

Staff training has also improved immeasurably. Larger CPA firms support elaborate training programmes. For smaller firms the American Institute offers some forty 'professional development' courses and staff training programmes, in which there were about 18,000 participants last year.

Vigorous recruiting efforts are attracting promising young people to the profession. Films, brochures, and advertisements in student publications are part of the American Institute's contribution to these efforts.

In the fields of accounting principles and auditing procedures, standards are constantly being improved by official pronouncements of the American Institute. Concern about legal liability and the curiosity of the financial press are stimuli to strict compliance with these standards.

Interpretation and enforcement of the Code of Ethics have attained a higher level of effectiveness than ever before.

The Uniform CPA Examination (two-and-a-half days), which is used in all states and other political subdivisions, is subject to constant scrutiny and improvement.

[1] Reviewed by Mr. T. A. Hamilton Baynes in the November issue of *Accountancy*, see page 718.

Research activities are being expanded.

Much more could be said along these lines, and each of these assertions could be supported by facts and figures, if space permitted.

Suffice it to say that there is every reason to believe that the quality of professional accounting service in the United States today is higher than it ever has been. It is not perfect by far, and it must continue to improve to meet rising public expectations. The profession has been criticised mainly, I believe, because the rapid increase in number of shareholders has created a public interest in accounting far greater than ever before. A public previously indifferent to the profession is now demanding results which are difficult, and in some respects impossible, to provide.

The newest challenge facing the profession in the United States is better communication with the public on an ever wider scale. And steps are also being taken to this end.

Perhaps what has happened in the US is a precursor of what may occur in other countries also. If the profession abroad can profit from the experiences, sometimes painful, of their American colleagues, the latter may take comfort from the thought that their tribulations have not been in vain.

59. Accountancy and the Onslaught of Case Law in North America*

Kenneth F. Byrd**

A graduating commerce student in a recent university examination wrote: 'The auditor's care must be that of the reasonable man not possessing any particular skills.' We all know what he meant, no doubt, but some of the plaintiffs in today's North American lawsuits might seem to take him literally.

At present in the United States, according to *The Wall Street Journal* of November 15th, 1966, some hundred lawsuits are pending against firms of certified public accountants. Strong criticism of financial reporting comes from the Securities and Exchange Commission through the public

* Reprinted from *The Accountant*, July 8, 1967, pages 34–41.
** Kenneth F. Byrd is Professor of Accountancy at McGill University at Montreal, Canada.

utterances of its chairman, Mr Manuel Cohen, and in the Courts investors and creditors are pressing vast claims against auditors who are supposed to have failed in their duty as watchdogs.

In the same article from *The Wall Street Journal* the senior partner of one large accounting firm is quoted as saying; 'Prior to 1965 we faced no suits involving major companies whose reports we audited.' Yet the firm is now said to have twenty-eight suits filed against it, claiming compensation for damages of over $20 million and involving 'hundreds of thousands' a year on legal fees.

NO CASE LAW TRADITION IN NORTH AMERICA

In Britain, as is well known to any accountancy student, case law has long been recognized by tradition as an essential part of education for the profession. In North America there has been no such tradition. Not for the North American student in training the many hours of poring over cases—page after page, large print and small print, in *Spicer and Pegler* or *Dicksee*—that the British student has accepted as normal for well over half a century. This is true in spite of all that *McKesson and Robbins*—not a legal case but a one-in-a-million spectacular fraud—did to change auditing practice throughout North America since 1938. Nor has there been any dearth of legal cases over the long period of years.

In an article by Mr. Robert Metz in the *New York Times* of November 20th, 1966, Mr Manuel Cohen, the S.E.C. chairman, is quoted as saying: 'Our investigations often leave us with the feeling that each generation of auditors learns only by its own sad experiences rather than from earlier cases.'

The truth probably is that though the legal existence of some professional accountancy bodies in North America may have been quite as long as in Great Britain—The Institute of Chartered Accountants of Quebec, for example, was founded in 1880—the real tradition of professional ethics is much younger on the western side of the North Atlantic. However, all the accounting bodies have their rules of professional ethics, and today these are under close scrutiny for adaptation to the changing times. The great concern of the profession in North America today is to strengthen the acceptance and practice of true professionalism by each individual member, to diminish the time spent on the routine of so-called 'write-ups,' and develop the watchdog and advisory capacities involving all the expert skills of the profession.

SIGNS OF CHANGE

For a decade or more there have been signs of change. In 1954 The American Institute of Certified Public Accountants published an excellent pioneer book, *Accountants' Legal Responsibility*, by Saul Levy, chairman of a special committee set up by the Institute to study the question of legal liability. This was probably the first publication suitable for study of the subject within the universities or other institutions entrusted with training students for the profession. It has for some years been out of print, which may indicate that it has not been widely adopted either as a textbook or for the guidance of practitioners for whom it was no doubt intended.

Much more recently, in 1966, The Canadian Institute of Chartered Accountants has published *Accountants and the Law of Negligence*, by R. W. V. Dickerson. It has for a year been successfully used as a textbook for advanced students by McGill University but there has apparently, in its first year, been a disappointing response to the opportunities it offers for the education of accounting students. Students may find it difficult to study case law without guidance, but a good lecturer can easily stimulate them by showing how a great profession grows and matures as it learns from the lessons of the Law Courts. The response of students is immediate and it is thus that they learn from the beginning the essential truth of the value of professional ethics.

LEGAL LANDMARKS TO GROWTH

A truly dynamic and live profession cannot be guided by a codified set of rules. It needs landmarks to chart out the course it has been following and ensure that the course ahead is always one of progress. Outstanding legal cases—*Rex v. Kylsant*, for example, as all British accountants are well aware—may thus be of inestimable value to the accountancy profession. North America has traditionally based its professional standards on 'general acceptance', a requirement which would seem to rule out those experimental innovations which may be—indeed, some of which are bound to be—harbingers of a new age.

The accountant knows only too well, when charged by his principal with negligence, that his best defence is to show that his own practice has been in line with that of the whole profession, outdated though it may be. There could be no better example of this than *The Royal Mail Steam Packet* case (*Rex v. Kylsant*), which must have done as much, in the early 1930s, to advance auditing practice in Great Britain as *McKesson and Robbins* has done in North America, since the end of that decade. In *The Royal Mail Steam Packet* case it was a question of revealing the use of secret reserves to hide current operating losses; in *McKesson and Robbins* it was verification of inventories and accounts receivable. The landmarks are there for all professional accountants and all accountant students in training to see.

The point is that the proof of conformity with what was 'generally accepted' only exonerated the auditors at the time that the unsatisfactory situation was publicly revealed. After that, professional practice simply had to advance; for auditors would have no second chance after the warning had been given. The true dilemma of the accountancy profession is how to give 'fair play' to what is not generally accepted, but what is truly in line with the needs of changing times.

SEEKING THE CAUSES OF THE ONSLAUGHT

What are the particular circumstances which would seem to account for the rising tide of legal cases against North American accountants in the last two or three years? In an article, 'Embattled C.P.A.s', in *The Wall Street Journal* of May 24th, 1965, Mr Lee Silberman wrote that The American Institute of Certified Public Accountants had recently appointed a special committee on accountants' liability to investigate the reasons for the rise in lawsuits and make recommendations for dealing with the problem. Mr T. D. Flynn, the President, was reported as having stated that the committee would establish whether or not the public generally misunderstood the accountant's role in society. He believed, apparently, that the C.P.A. was expected 'to play the role of an all-wise and all-knowing Solomon . . .'. In addition to the due care expected of the professional man in Britain, Mr Flynn was quoted as saying: 'In this country, on the other hand, the C.P.A. is expected to go much further—to make judgements that at times can be as conclusive as an umpire calling a runner out at home plate.'

Well it is certainly true that, even in the textbooks, emphasis on the auditor's main role is not the discovery of fraud but the giving of an expert opinion on the fairness of the financial position reflected in financial statements, seems to be accepted as a comparatively recent development in North America. Also, while for thirty years the profession in North America has carefully worded the opinion paragraph of the auditor's report on the financial statements, before that time it seems to have been possible to omit any such opinion, so that the auditor's certificate then amounted to a guarantee. This fact is evidence of the comparative youthfulness of the profession in North America.

MISAPPREHENSION OF BANKERS

There can be no doubt that in spite of all the efforts of the profession to clarify the position, bankers still fail to accept the limitations which the profession would place on the accountant's responsibility. Thus, a report in the *New York Times* of February 2nd, 1966, of an address by Mr J. Howard Laeri, vice-chairman of the First National City Bank and also of the American Bankers' Association, drew an editorial from *The Journal of Accountancy* of March 1966.

Mr Laeri challenged the value of the 'generally accepted accounting principles' phrase, the cornerstone of the accountant's certificate, stating that it had 'almost reached the status of a cliché'. He said: 'We bankers are going to have to face the fact that the audit is not the guarantee of the worthiness of a loan'. Nevertheless, he urged that bankers needed confidence 'that auditing procedures are correct for a particular situation, that there are adequate controls in effect for the day-to-day operation of a business, and that there are adequate disclosures of departures from an understandable, generally accepted norm'. The trouble is, he said, that the accounting profession itself 'cannot say precisely—or perhaps even approximately—what those "generally accepted principles" are'.

The editorial of the *Journal* commented that apparently bankers 'do not pay much attention to developments in the accounting world until something goes wrong'. It emphasized the apparent failure to realize that auditors are now required to call attention to changes in a company's accounting principles as between one year and the next, and to state their effects on the financial statements. However, it concluded that the important thing is the fact of the misunderstanding, that it should be thought by a banker of such stature that accounting and auditing are as undisciplined as he seems to think they are.

DIVISION WITHIN THE PROFESSION

The misunderstandings which have led to the present state of cases are reflected by division within the accountancy profession itself. One of the most outspoken critics from within the profession's standards is Mr Leonard Spacek, C.P.A., chairman of Messrs Arthur Andersen & Company, one of the largest of the 'big eight' firms of national professional accountants in the United States. *The Journal of Accountancy* of November 1964, reports him as accusing the profession, in an address to security analysts, of permitting 'double standard accounting which is nothing less than double dealing to the investor'. Another well-known certified public accountant who openly expresses his criticism is Mr J. S. Seidman, a Past President of the American Institute.

Mr Seidman would have auditors selected and their fees fixed by a committee of stockholders, according to *The Wall Street Journal* of November 15th, 1966, for though legally they are elected by stockholders they are in fact picked by management for election. Also he would have the Institute determine one 'preferred' method for any particular accounting treatment, and would require any departure therefrom to be clearly stated in the auditor's certificate. He suggests that firms auditing company accounts should be rotated at fixed intervals—an idea which was unanimously rejected by the Institute's executive board.

356   CPAs

As to Mr Seidman's recommendation of the committee of stockholders, it may be added that the report on the Securities and Exchange
Commission's investigation of the *McKesson and Robbins* fraud, in
December 1940, proposed establishment of a committee to be selected
from non-officer members of the board of directors, to make all company
or management nominations of auditors and arrange the details of their
engagement. It also suggested that auditors be required to attend stockholders' meetings at which their report is to be presented. There is clearly
nothing new in the wish to avoid any restriction of the independence of
auditors by the management.

WIDE RANGE OF 'GENERAL ACCEPTANCE'

It is quite certain that there are many areas of accounting in which
large public concerns in similar lines of business can consistently conform
with different accepted accounting principles, thus publishing financial
statements which are misleading for comparative purposes. The areas
of divergence are well known: valuation of inventories at first-in first-out
cost, or on a last-in first-out basis (the latter very general in the United
States through its acceptance for income tax and its elimination of inflation profits); different methods of depreciation; deferment of income tax
saved through generous capital cost allowances; varying treatment of
research costs, dry wells, amortization of goodwill, and pension costs;
alternative accounting for amalgamations by the traditional method
based on acquisition, or by the modern 'pooling of interests' method. The
opportunities for profit increase or decrease resulting from such alternative accepted methods may well be irresistible for managements.

The kind of shift in accounting methods which tends to increase
the public unrest is that reported by Mr Lee Berton in *The Wall Street
Journal* of November 15th, 1966, in the case of Chock Full o' Nuts
Corporation of New York. In each of 1961, 1962 and 1963, Mr Berton
states that this company consistently deferred the portion of advertising
and promotion costs applicable to the development of new products, while
earnings grew steadily to 68 cents per share. In 1964, however, a deliberate
change was made by which a large part of the deferred cost was carried
back to previous years on the grounds that it applied to products now
discontinued. As a result the 1964 earnings were shown as 62 cents per
share, compared with a restated 60 cents for 1963.

Professor Michael Schiff, chairman of the accounting department of
New York University's School of Business, was quoted as saying that the
increase was an illusion. On the former basis of advertising cost deferment the 1964 profits would have been 45 cents per share as against the
68 cents of 1963, and this would have been the first decline in the
company's history. Professor Schiff's reported comment was that 'it is

difficult to avoid the conclusion that a concerted effort on the part of management was made to examine various accounting methods and select the one which makes for happy, though confused, stockholders'. The company's vice-president is reported as having satisfied the S.E.C. and the independent auditors and announced that in future the company's accounting would be 'ultra-conservative in expensing product introduction costs immediately'.

ACCOUNTANTS' LIABILITY INSURANCE

One factor which seems to be playing an increasingly large part in bringing the accounting profession before the Courts is the hope that insurers can be made to pay for losses suffered by those who bring the charges. An editorial in *The Journal of Accountancy* for September 1965, entitled 'The spectre of auditors' liability', blames the hopes of banks and other financial institutions that accounting firms can be made a source of salvage for losses from unpaid loans or extended credit. It points out that it is an illusion to think that accountants' liability insurance can take care of the problem. For the cost of insurance includes the often high cost of successful defence against unjust claims, the premiums rising higher as the lawsuits increase. The cost has ultimately to be paid from auditors' fees so that it is indirectly a levy on the business community and could ultimately become prohibitive.

Mr Lee Berton stated, in *The Wall Street Journal* of November 15th, 1966, that of fifteen insurers who wrote coverage freely for professional accounting firms a year before, six now handled it only as an 'accommodation' for big accounts, or 'in a limited manner'. Also, Insurance Company of North America, Philadelphia, had only one such policy in force in its New York office, where five years earlier it had a hundred. Evaluation of the sources and limits of insurance coverage, the nature and source of claims and the amount to be carried is being studied by the American Institute's Committee on Accountants' Legal Liability.

AUDITORS' LIABILITY TO THIRD PARTIES

It is to be noted that the cases brought by banks and financial institutions are third party cases. If fraud can be proved the question of privity of contract and the 'duty of care' of an agent to his principal does not arise, but where the case is a civil claim of damages resulting from negligence, there are other considerations.

A great deal of interest was aroused in North America by the case of *Hedley Byrne v. Heller and Partners*, 1963. Here, the House of Lords unanimously held, contrary to the late nineteenth-century case of *Le Lievre v. Gould* and succeeding cases down to *Candler v. Crane Christmas & Co.*, 1951 (the dissenting minority judgment of Lord Denning was a straw in the wind), that without any breach of contract, fraud or fiduciary relationship, a duty of care may arise where negligent statements result in financial loss:

If, in the ordinary course of business or professional affairs, a person seeks information or advice from another, who is not under contractual or fiduciary obligation to give the information or advice, in circumstances in which a reasonable man so asked would know that he was being trusted, or that his skill or judgement was being relied on, and the person asked chooses to give the information or advice without clearly so qualifying his answer as to show that he does not accept responsibility, then the person replying accepts a legal duty to exercise such care as the circumstances require in making his reply.

The United States had had its share of undetermined cases on this particular question of third party liability—*Ultramares Corporation v. Touche Niven & Co*, 1931, *State Street Trust Co v. Ernst*, 1938, and *C.I.T. Financial Corporation v. Glover*, 1955, though the latter, given in favour of the accountant, seemed to indicate that clear evidence of the accountant's knowledge that his certificate is required primarily for the benefit of a particular third party may make the accountant liable for simple negligence (contrary to *Candler v. Crane Christmas & Co* in Great Britain four years earlier).

The *Hedley Byrne* decision has not yet been put to the test in North American Courts, though there are cases pending which might well test it. At any rate, the *C.I.T. Financial* dictum and the *Hedley Byrne* decision do not seem far apart. In the *Financial Executive* for June 1966, Mr Robert M. Trueblood, C.P.A., President of the American Institute, was reported as advising use of a disclaimer on accounting reports furnished to third parties, stating that responsibility is solely to the client who commissioned the report. Also the firm of Peat, Marwick, Mitchell & Co is said to require companies for which it performs audits to make a covering statement that such examination of accounting records 'would not necessarily disclose irregularities, should any exist'. A senior partner is said to have suggested that the extensive publicity given to cases pending against the firm stimulates other parties to press claims.

Otis, McAllister & Co

A case of third party liability was brought against Messrs Peat, Marwick, Mitchell & Co, in June 1965, by four banks, including Bank of American of San Francisco and Chase Manhattan of New York. The charges, as reported in the *New York Herald Tribune*, of November 11th, 1965, are that loans were advanced to Otis, McAllister & Co, coffee importers, on the strength of false and misleading financial statements; also that repayment of the loans was not made from the proceeds of sales of the specific lots of coffee financed, but from proceeds of collateral pledged to another lender. The accountants should have been aware of this, say the banks, but failed to give any warning in their financial reports. The accountants say that the banks had reason to know what was happening, but took no action. A spokesman for the firm was reported by the journal as stating that the banks offered to settle for about $1.3 million, but the insurers 'preferred to have the matter litigated on its merits'. The total sums claimed exceed $6 million.

A complicating factor of the case is that Messrs Peat, Marwick, Mitchell & Co were at the same time auditors of Chase Manhattan who, they say, appointed them for the specific purpose of reporting on the use of the borrowed funds.

They resisted firmly any pressure of the bank for information as to whether they considered the borrowers' position to be unsound, on the grounds of privileged client relationship. Situations such as this naturally lead to the question of what would be the position if the independent accounting firm also provided the management consultants who investigate the 'privileged client'. This is the ethically complicated kind of development which faces large accounting firms in the future, as their activities become more and more extensive and many-sided.

The Douglas Aircraft Co

In *The Wall Street Journal* of October 24th, 1966, a long account of the financial troubles of the Douglas Aircraft Co refers to a $75 million debenture offering of June 1966, when the prospectus showed a big first quarter earnings gain, although the five-month profit was down. After June it appeared that the decline in earnings had become a $4 million loss in the second quarter compared with a like profit a year earlier, net profits for the six months being only $645,000 as against $14 million a year before. Some of the purchasers of the debenture issue, sceptical as to the company's expressed ignorance of the true position before June, filed suit against the company and its underwriters and also against its auditors, Messrs Ernst & Ernst, another of the 'big eight' national firms. The charge is failure to disclose the true facts.

Here again is an attempt by third parties to recover through embracing the auditors in the wide sweep of charges in the hope of benefiting from insurance.

CIVIL NEGLIGENCE CHARGES BY STOCKHOLDERS
Yale Express System Inc.

By far the biggest pending case brought by stockholders against the auditors is the *Yale Express* case. *Fortune*, of November 1965, had a lengthy article on this case by Mr Richard J. Whalen. Late in 1964 this great trucking concern, Yale Express System Inc, reported nine months' earnings of $904,000. In March 1965, however, the company reported that the interim report on profits was incorrect 'in the light of errors discovered in the 1964 accounts'. A loss of $3,300,000 was estimated for the year, instead of what had been forecast as a profit of as high as $1,800,000. Then it was disclosed that a $1,140,000 profit in the 1963 financial statements, audited by Messrs Peat, Marwick, Mitchell & Co, should have been a loss of $1,200,000, and this was again later revised as $1,880,000.

It appeared that internal controls had completely failed. The company had expanded from what amounted to a cash basis, discarding multi-carbon forms and introducing the latest developments of electronic data processing. But the discarded records were later badly needed to substantiate ageing claims against customers. Yale Express had merged with Republic Carloading & Distributing Co, a leading freight forwarding company, but the two never worked well together and intercompany accounting was faulty. The auditors stated that they had warned against Yale's intention of adopting for Republic the fast cut-off used by itself instead of normal accrual accounting. But the change was made in 1964, and $575,000 was transferred into profits by reversing a Republic reserve for refunds of customers' overpayments. An error of $750,000, in the same direction, was made through omission of a reserve for interline payments, the result being an overstatement of 1963 income, before tax, by $1,325,000.

The president, suspecting fraud, asked for a special investigation by the auditors. The auditors emphasized 'that the auditor's present function does not embrace ensuring anyone against fraud or the consequences of bad judgement'. They were quoted as believing that 'Yale and Republic were handling the same freight over and over', huge piles of misdirected and lost freight accumulating, while Yale's claim ratio rose from a normal 1 per cent of revenues to 3 per cent. Yale even hired a force of college accounting students, under the auditors' direction, to reconstruct every transaction of 1964 and any 1963 payables not previously detected. From mid-August 1964, Yale had, in effect, parallel accounting operations—one carried on by its employees in the day, on the basis of which the president declared the regular dividend and announced earnings of $904,000, and the other revealed by the night investigation.

Here, again, the auditors are included, by the stockholders' suits, with officers and directors of Yale Express and also the underwriters. The auditors are reported to have felt that the confidential relationship with the client prevented them from making any of their misgivings known to the New York Stock Exchange or the creditors.

San Francisco National Bank

A former director of the San Francisco National Bank, which failed early in 1965, accused the bank's auditors, Messrs Peat, Marwick, Mitchell & Co, of not advising the directors as to the bank's precarious financial position. *The Wall Street Journal* of September 29th, 1966, reported that fourteen other former directors were being sued by the Federal Deposit Insurance Corporation, which estimated its damages as deposit insurer at $10 million and as receiver of the bank's assets at $30 million. The auditors were accused of having 'negligently failed to reveal the acts, errors, and omissions and unlawful transactions in the affairs of the bank of which the directors were legally required to be aware'. While 'unsatisfactory internal controls' were reported, at the same time the auditors were said to have stated that the 'bank's records, generally, are in satisfactory condition'. The auditors were charged with having 'stated those facts without reasonable ground for belief in their truth, thereby consciously misrepresenting such material facts and perpetrating a fraud upon the directors of the bank'. The auditors stated that the bank failed more than two years after they had made their last audit, for they were not retained as auditors after November 15th, 1963.

Westec Corporation

A much talked-of current case, involving flexible income determination strained to its limits, is that of Westec Corporation, in which the auditors are being sued for negligence by the stockholders.

An article in *Forbes* of May 15th, 1967, says that the company took into income non-recurring profits on sales of oil properties; it treated as current income payments by an insurance company for oil production that had not yet taken place; and it included in earnings for a given year profits of companies not acquired until the following year. Nine months after reporting 1965 earnings of $4.9 million and assets of $56 million, the company went into bankruptcy. Mr Leonard Spacek, c.p.a., is quoted as saying that it would seem, nevertheless, that management did not exceed the rules.

The *Forbes* article accuses management and auditors of going to great lengths to find precedents for accounting devices that will suit their purposes. The picture, however distorted, of auditors seeking such precedents and not needing to look further than the pages of the American Institute's annual *Accounting Trends and Techniques*, certainly does great harm to the accountant's image in the eyes of the investing public.

However, the article also quotes the managing partner of Messrs Ernst & Ernst, the Westec auditors, as saying that his firm had over a hundred cases in one year in which it had to say 'no' to management.

Significantly also Mr Andrew Barr, chief accountant of the Securities and Exchange Commission, says he sees many such cases where accountants have stood up to management. It is clearly all too easy to seek to make accountants the scapegoats for the irregularities of management.

OPINION OF THE ACCOUNTING RESEARCH BOARD

It is relevant, at this stage, to draw attention to the recent 'opinion' of the American Institute's Accounting Research Board, entitled 'Reporting the results of operation'.

This is a milestone in the American Institute's campaign for greater comparability in financial reporting, and the *Westec* case is an excellent background for its publication. By this formal caveat, managements of corporate concerns will be compelled, if they want unqualified audit certificates, for fiscal periods beginning after December 31st, 1966, to include in their income statements, in classified form, first ordinary current income and next all extraordinary gains, less income tax, and losses, arriving at a final figure for net income.

The clean surplus theory has won the day and extraordinary items may no longer be entered direct in retained earnings, with the single exception of adjustments for events of earlier periods. The earnings-per-share figure, so enticing to the shareholder, is to be included in the income statement, with proper distinction between the figure before and after extraordinary items, and attested by the auditor. The earnings-per-share for common stock is to be based on a weighted average of the number of shares outstanding during the period, not the number at the year-end. Supplementary per-share figures will show the effect of potential dilution, through convertible senior securities or stock options.

With this compelling fiat of his Institute the certified public accountant will have written authority to strengthen him when he takes his stand as the watchdog for shareholders. It remains to be seen to what extent this codification of the rules for income presentation gives the investing public the information it needs and whether the information will be heeded.

CRIMINAL INDICTMENT OF AUDITOR

Continental Vending Machine Corporation

In a class by itself comes the rare criminal indictment of auditors, and there is one such pending case of great importance.

On October 18th, 1966, *The World Journal Tribune* carried an announcement by its financial editor, Mr Leslie Gould, that for the first time the partners in a major accounting firm were being held criminally responsible for alleged false statements in a company's balance sheet.

Such cases are rare indeed and this was the first time in the United States that a Federal grand jury had brought such indictments.

The case in question involved Continental Vending Machine Corporation which went into receivership in 1963. Three members of the national accounting firm of Lybrand, Ross Bros & Montgomery were charged with collusion with Mr Roth, the head of the company, in issuing a false report to the shareholders that the company had over $250,000 in cash, when there was actually a cash deficit of more than $1 million. The accounting firm was named as co-conspirator.

The Government charged that there was a $1 million cheque kiting transaction, large sums being transferred by Continental to an affiliated company, Valley Commercial Corporation, which was used by Mr Roth as a conduit for transfer of the money to himself. A footnote to Continental accounts indicated that the debt from Valley was secured by the assignment to Continental of Valley's equity in certain marketable securities. The indictment is that the debt was not in fact fully secured, and the securities were not marketable, consisting largely of Continental's own stock and bonds owned by Mr Roth, subject to prior liens.

The Journal of Accountancy for December 1966, reported that in a statement to the Press the managing partner of the accounting firm called the indictment shocking and unwarranted. He said the firm had been advised by the Government that representatives of leading accounting firms, called by the Government before the grand jury, had unanimously upheld the position taken by the firm. The action taken had been precipitated by the firm's own withholding of certification from Continental's 1962 annual report, and the managing partner said that the firm was being accused of having failed to second-guess the Continental management, which was never the auditors' function.

This tendency to cite the auditor as a sort of backstop to the management, jointly responsible with management for decision-making and policy, undoubtedly derives from the wish to invoke the resources represented by the accountants' insurers. It is only too easy to blur the distinction between affirming the auditor's duty of ensuring that published accounts are not misleading, and making him responsible for their form. They are the accounts of management.

A NON-LEGAL CASE

A non-legal case in which the Securities and Exchange Commission made an investigation and issued its report, as in the case of the *McKesson and Robbins* fraud, is that of Olen Co Inc, a retail chain, and its successor, the Olen Division of H. L. Green Co Inc. The Commission, as reported in *The Journal of Accountancy* for September 1966, found the financial statements prepared and certified by a firm of certified public accountants, for the years to January 31st, 1958 and 1959, materially false and misleading. It stated that ordinary tests of the accounts would have disclosed an inordinate number of errors and omissions. The firm, said the Commission, not only failed to question the inflated inventory figure of $2,640,137 presented by Olen's employees, but included in the certified financial statements a figure further inflated by $603,000. The report concluded:

When an independent public accountant in the course of an examination gains knowledge of facts which are of material importance to investors, he is under a duty to report such facts to investors in his certificate or report, if they are not set forth in the financial statements themselves.

THE 'SALAD OIL' SWINDLE

Some mention must also be made of the incredible 'salad oil' swindle of the notorious Tino de Angelis [1], though it has not brought auditors into the Courts. It involved the American Express Company through transactions of its American Express Field Warehousing subsidiary. As early as 1960 the warehousing company, warned of a hoax by mysterious telephone calls, had sent inspectors to examine the tanks of de Angelis's Allied Crude Vegetable Oil Refining Corporation, a main customer.

Hoodwinked by false inner tanks and a maze of interconnecting pipes, which facilitated transfer of oil from tank to tank as it was counted, the inspectors apparently satisfactorily verified the inventories. Three years later, when the parent company arranged for a thorough investigation by their own auditors, Messrs Haskins & Sells, still nothing seriously wrong was reported. The auditors gave their opinion that the controls of the warehousing subsidiary were satisfactory. There was no suspicion that the kiting of warehouse receipts had been taking place on a huge scale!

Yet very shortly after that it was discovered that the purportedly vast quantities of oil in the Allied Crude Vegetable Oil tanks were virtually non-existent, being represented by salt water. With claims against it amounting to $144½ million by May 11th, 1965, according to Mr Leslie Gould in *The World Journal Tribune* of that date, the American Express Field Warehousing Company had about reached agreement for a settlement of some $60 million, plus another $25 or $30 million from insurance. Yet Mr Gould said that the American Express annual report of 1964 contained a footnote that no provision had been made in the financial statements for any losses which might result from the *Allied Crude Vegetable Oil* case, since the outcome could not then be determined.

[1] See *The Accountant*, October 1st, 1966, pages 416–417.

LEGAL CASES IN CANADA

On the whole things seem to be quieter in Canada as far as legal attacks on auditors are concerned. During the onslaught in the United States there have been no major cases brought against accountants in Canada. In the category of liability to third parties, however, there is one at present pending in the Superior Court at Montreal. Here a firm of accountants is accused of negligence by suppliers who claim to have extended credit on the strength of financial statements which they allege were misleading.

A significant feature of this case is that both the defendant accountants and the plaintiffs are calling as expert witnesses chartered accountants. At times like these the concern of every professional accountant must be the maintenance of the reputation of a great profession. It should not, therefore, be surprising that chartered accountants are ready to testify as to generally accepted accounting and auditing practice, not only in defence of a fellow member but also against him. Nothing could be more damaging to the profession than unwillingness of its members to give open testimony, if they feel that its standards have been jeopardized by other members.

In the area of audits of finance companies, the collapse of Atlantic Acceptance of Toronto in June 1965 and the difficulties of Laurentide Financial of Vancouver and Alliance Finance of Montreal have led to plenty of criticism of Canadian auditors. This is well evidenced by an article, 'Crisis of confidence', by Mr F. J. McDiarmid, vice-president for investments of Lincoln National Life Insurance Co, in *Barron's* of April 10, 1967.

The losses of investors in Atlantic Acceptance are likely to be as high as $70 million; Laurentide Financial was saved only by injection of over $9 million of new junior capital by Power Corporation of Canada, its parent company, and Alliance Finance of Montreal was similarly rescued. In the United States, Pioneer Finance of Detroit failed late in 1965. What worries Mr McDiarmid is the lack of any forewarning in the financial reports of any of these companies, or by their auditors.

The Atlantic Acceptance report for 1964 showed over $1 million of net profit on $16 million of stockholders' equity. Yet in July 1965, it appeared that all equity and subordinated debt—nearly $40 million in all—would be lost, and perhaps 75 cents in the dollar might ultimately be available for holders of $107 million of senior debt. The investigating Royal Commission has reported that financial reports long before the Atlantic collapse were wholly misleading, and that there had been a great deal of fraud in business dealings. A reported profit of $3,791,000 by Laurentide Financial for the year to June 30th, 1965, turned into a loss of $9,627,000 in the following fiscal year—a trend which seems hardly credible, though attested by auditors.

Mr McDiarmid criticizes the auditors, not for failing to discover fraud but for not reporting in clearer terms. 'It is worthless to say that a finance company reports its operations in an acceptable manner. Acceptable to whom—to management, the auditors, the stockholders or creditors?' He wants uniformity of financial reporting by finance companies on income, loss charge-offs and delinquencies, so that their results may be compared.

The trouble with Atlantic Acceptance was that interest on loans which never paid any interest was taken into account in profit determination on a huge scale. By the rewriting of delinquent loans, with the unpaid income on the old loans written into the new, the fact that interest was never collected and that loans were bad was obscured. Mr McDiarmid suggests that auditors should be required to report on the condition of outstanding loans at the time of their renewal.

It would seem also that the management of Atlantic Acceptance ignored such matters as provisions in loan agreements as to maximum ratios of debt to underlying equity, and the maximum loan for any single borrower, without any report of this by the auditors.

RELIANCE OF AUDITORS ON OTHER AUDITORS

In Canada, as in Great Britain, there is no Securities and Exchange Commission to intervene in cases such as these. A great responsibility clearly rests on the accountancy profession. In its recently published Bulletin No. 22, of August 1965, the Canadian Institute of Chartered Accountants has specifically dealt with the problem of reporting where auditors rely on the work of other auditors, as the auditors of Atlantic Acceptance did. It distinguishes cases where there is an agency relationship between the two auditors from those where there is no such relationship. In the former it is clear that the parent company auditor must take full responsibility so far as consolidated financial statements are concerned. In the latter, reasonable reliance on the subsidiary company auditor's work and opinion is permissible, provided reasonable care is taken to ensure that such reliance is justified. Everything will then depend on the auditor's care and integrity in deciding what is reasonable.

There have, in recent months, been suggestions that a United States Accounting Court of Appeals be set up. *The Journal of Accountancy* of January 1966, commented on one such suggestion put forward for study purposes by Messrs Arthur Andersen & Co, in a lengthy pamphlet issued in December 1965. The firm warns, however, that this matter should be considered at a time when there is no public pressure for a quick legislative solution to the problem.

The Court would have appellate jurisdiction over the accountancy rules and regulations of five Federal agencies, including the Securities and Exchange Commission. It would have powers not only of affirmation, modification or reversal of existing rules, but also, on petition, to initiate rules if such a request had been denied by a Federal agency. There would be five members appointed by the President with confirmation by Senate, at $25,000 a year. The Court would be in the executive, rather than the judiciary, branch of the Government. The proposed Court is seen as giving additional stature to the American Institute's Accounting Principles Board, not as in any way detracting from it.

CONCLUSION

The Accounting Principles Board is now working at great pressure to resolve the problems of differing 'generally accepted accounting principles', urged on by rumblings from the Securities and Exchange Commission. The directive on accounting for pensions, issued in 1966, still leaves two alternative acceptable courses as critics have been quick to observe. Is it possible to have everything codified and fixed, regardless of individual circumstances and without putting the accounting profession in a strait-jacket?

The solution must surely lie in the development among professional accountants of the highest professional competence and integrity. The accountant must himself have an intense belief in the validity of basic accounting principles to which lip service seems only too often to be paid. Expediency should not be able to bend accountancy to its will.

To the present writer it seems that the troubles of today are closely concerned with the kind of concession to expediency that seems to have led to the 'pooling of interest' method of accounting rejected by the Jenkins Committee in Britain. Certainly, let it be said that accountants should not allow profits to be pooled, in a merger of established concerns, unless they are completely satisfied that the continuance of the old concerns, with no material change of ownership, is an established fact. Managements see the advantage of the pooling treatment because it leaves assets in the merger at original values, with the effect of lower depreciation charges against the probably higher profits of the merged companies. But accountants should be swayed by no such considerations and should make this very clear to management.

In the end the status of the accountancy profession, and the recognition by management of its stature as an advisory, and not merely a confirmatory body, will be enhanced as never before, if it makes its vaunted independence a self-evident fact. Deeds speak more strongly than words:

This above all—to thine own self be true;
And it must follow, as the night the day,
Thou canst not then be false to any man.

60. Landmark Decision on Liability*

A court decision of unusual importance was handed down March 29, 1968 (*Escott, et al. v. BarChris Construction Corporation, et al.* United States District Court, Southern District of New York). It is one of the most comprehensive actions so far brought under Section 11 of the Securities Act of 1933, and will undoubtedly be widely discussed in law journals.

Defendants included not only the corporation and its auditors, but officers and directors, underwriters and legal counsel who was also a director.

Plaintiffs were sixty purchasers of debentures issued by the corporation, joining in a "class action."

The court ruled all defendants responsible to some extent, but reserved decision on the extent of liability attaching to each, which involved consideration of cross-claims filed among the defendants.

The case involved a number of accounting and auditing questions of significance to the accounting profession. For example the court held that the percentage-of-completion method of accounting for construction in progress was permissible. The adequacy of reserves for uncollectible receivables and the propriety of classifying certain items as current assets were also considered. The court dismissed a contention of plaintiffs that a certain contingent liability was incorrectly computed.

With respect to one specific reserve, the court said: "The amount of such reserve is a matter of accounting judgment. The evidence does not convince me that the accountant's judgment here was so clearly wrong that the balance sheet can be found to be false or misleading for lack of a higher reserve"; and later, significantly, ". . . these matters are always more clearly discerned in retrospect than they are at the time." On the other hand, one of the items upon which liability was based was a failure to set up a reserve for a partially secured receivable of doubtful collectibility.

---

* Reprinted from *The Journal of Accountancy,* June 1968, page 20. Copyrighted 1968 by the American Institute of CPAs.

Of special interest to accountants is the judge's decision on the question of materiality. He found, for example, that a difference in earnings-per-share between 75 cents and 65 cents, as compared with 33 cents the year before, was not material within the meaning of Section 11, in view of the fact that the debentures were of speculative quality. However, certain balance-sheet discrepancies were found to be material, including errors in current assets and current liabilities resulting in the balance sheet's showing a current ratio of 1.9 instead of 1.6.

The auditors were found in some respects not to have proved that they made a "reasonable investigation," but to have sustained that burden of proof in regard to other items which were challenged. The court appears to have regarded their most serious omissions as those occurring in the review of events subsequent to the date of the "certified balance sheet." In SEC terms this is known as the "S-1 review," prior to the filing of a registration statement. The court said, "The scope of such a review, under generally accepted auditing standards, is limited. It does not amount to a complete audit"; and later in the opinion, "Accountants should not be held to a standard higher than that recognized in their profession." Despite its finding that the written program for the S-1 review was in accord with generally accepted auditing standards, the court found that the review actually conducted was deficient in the circumstances.

The court found that there were a number of errors and omissions in the registration statement, some in the audited financials for the year prior to filing of the registration statement, some in the unaudited stub period financials, and some in textual portions of the prospectus. The errors found to be chargeable to the auditors were in the audited financials only.

The liability of the auditors as to each of these errors rested upon ordinary negligence alone: an error of judgment, or an insufficient degree of diligence. There is not, in the court's opinion, the slightest suggestion of collusion with management, of willful concealment or misstatement, or of gross negligence.

The decision is far too lengthy to be reprinted in *The Journal*, and far too complex to be summarized adequately. Legal counsel for the Institute is studying it, and no doubt the technical committees will consider its implications.

The case is reported in CCH Federal Securities Law Reporter P92, 179.

It is understood that copies are also available from the Ad Press, 21 Hudson Street, New York, N.Y. 10013.

Chapter XIII

Accounting Researchers

61. Some Comments on Accounting Research*

Robert K. Jaedicke**

About ten years ago Professor Sidney Davidson, speaking to the American Accounting Association, told the following story—which sums up very well the importance of research in accounting.

It seems that an old backwoods fundamentalist minister was lecturing his flock on the need for staying on the straight and narrow path to salvation. He warned them that if they strayed too far they would fall off the edge of the flat world into inky nothingness. This was too much for the local college student and, after the sermon, he told the minister that the world wasn't really flat, that it was round. To clinch his argument, he added, "If the world's flat, what holds it up?" The minister quickly replied, "There's four poles, one at each corner, to hold it up." The student thought for a moment and then asked, "But what do the poles rest on?" The minister looked him straight in the eye and said, "I've been waiting for some smart-aleck college kid to ask me that. The poles don't rest on nothing; they go all the way down." [1]

As is the case in this story, we often assume that our accounting concepts and principles "don't rest on nothing" but "go all the way down." This is, of course, a dangerous assumption not only for the prac-

* Reprinted from *The Journal of Accountancy*, April 1967, pages 86–88. Copyrighted 1967 by the American Institute of CPAs.
** Robert K. Jaedicke is Professor of Accounting at Stanford University.
[1] Sidney Davidson, "Research and Publication by Accounting Faculty," *The Accounting Review*, January 1957, p. 155.

titioners and users of accounting data but for the accounting teacher and student as well.

The purpose of this article is to discuss three aspects of the problem of research in accounting: (1) What is the fundamental relationship of accounting research to accounting education? (2) Who should undertake accounting research? (3) What are some areas in accounting that are badly in need of research?

ACCOUNTING EDUCATION AND RESEARCH

In recent years the role of research in universities has been characterized as "publish or perish." Actually, judging from the quality of some of our publications, a better prediction would be "publish *and* perish." However, regardless of the interpretation chosen, it is unfortunate that this dogma has come to describe the role of research. It does not even come close to describing the true role and importance of research.

As in any field, research in accounting lays the basis for innovation and improvements. I'm told that there is a saying in the natural sciences that in order to control nature, it is first necessary to obey it, and, in order to obey nature, it is first necessary to understand it. In other words, understanding is the first step toward control. I suggest that this is also true in accounting. Research paves the way for an increased understanding.

But why is research such an integral part of academic life? Actually, as I will argue later, research should not be restricted to academia, and neither academia nor research is likely to survive without the other.

To begin with, the academic researcher should have more freedom in the research which he undertakes than his nonacademic counterpart. It is much more likely that academic research can focus better on long-run theoretical problems than on short-run applied problems. To be sure, both efforts are needed but the former is not likely to prosper in nonacademic environments. Furthermore, the academic researcher is in a better position to investigate questions about which there is much controversy. Also, he can usually publish findings which support any alternatives, no matter how unpopular the point of view. This is important, for research is not likely to flourish in a field where the researcher has to be concerned about the "acceptability" of the outcome.

But what about the other side of the coin? What does the academic man gain from doing research other than, perhaps, personal satisfaction and fame? Actually, one may argue that anyone concerned with the accounting profession should make a strong personal commitment to improve it. However, this argument (which I feel is true) is no less applicable to the practitioner than to the teacher.

The more important point is that research is the only type of activity in which the teacher engages that replenishes his intellectual capital. It is true that research improves the field, but it also improves the teacher. Research is what gives the teacher a high degree of vitality. If he can make the subject matter spark in the classroom, the chances are good that the sparks came from research activities. Every other activity of the teacher—teaching, consulting, textbook writing, administration and the like—uses up his intellectual capital; but research does not. This is the one important capital replenishing activity. Without it the teacher has a limited life indeed. If classroom and other activities do not erode the teacher's vitality, the passage of time certainly will. So, research is not something which should be engaged in to meet the publish-or-perish criterion; its main purposes are to improve the field and to give the teacher a high degree of vitality for the 30 to 40 years he is in the classroom. Those students who complain that teachers are "off doing research and are not available" (and all of us have probably registered this type of complaint) should recognize that a good teacher can turn into nothing more than a good "entertainer" without research activities.

In recent years the attitudes toward accounting education seem to be changing to recognize the importance of research. The question now seems to be not whether to do research but how to do it best. This is a healthy attitude, and it is a change. Historically, accounting is a field which is much more teaching-oriented than research-oriented. For example, our Ph.D. programs are characterized by teaching assistantships and instructorships, not research assistantships. Furthermore, only in recent years have the American Institute of Certified Public Accountants, the National Association of Accountants, the major public accounting firms and others sponsored fellowships aimed at dissertation research. Prior to these efforts some fellowships existed, but they were rarely aimed at dissertation *research* activities. In order for research to flourish in a university, it is probably necessary for the Ph.D. program to have a heavy research orientation. Through this type of arrangement, faculty and graduate students are continually involved in research activities, and the graduates of the program (who are future teachers) are also enthusiastic about and trained for research activities.

One of the major problems in education today is how to teach students to do research. We would all feel more comfortable if we knew even part of the solution to this problem. It does seem reasonable, however, that the faculty must be interested and competent in research if this skill is to be taught to the students. Furthermore, it is probably necessary for the student to acquire certain research tools. In my opinion, these tools are likely to be drawn from mathematics, economics and the behavioral sciences.

I was interested to see the emphasis placed on these subject areas by the Common Body of Knowledge Study.[2] The authors of this study recognize the need for accounting research.[3] However, it is disappointing to me that the study did not make it clear that this need is probably the important reason for students' acquiring a knowledge of mathematics, economics and behavioral science. That is, why do accountants need to know more mathematics, for example? One reason is to keep up with developments in operations research. However, a far more important reason, in my opinion, is that mathematics (and related areas such as statistics) is likely to be a powerful tool of the accounting researcher. It provides an important means of formulating and analyzing problems and testing the consequences of the solution and conclusions. But why should all students study research tools and methods? This brings us to the second question.

WHO SHOULD UNDERTAKE ACCOUNTING RESEARCH?

My answer to this question is that everyone concerned with the field of accounting should take some responsibility for research. Certainly the mainstay of research activities should be the university and the divisions of research of the American Institute of Certified Public Accountants, the National Association of Accountants, etc. However, great strides will undoubtedly be realized only if the base can be broadened.

More sponsored research in the academic environment is needed. If an academic researcher is willing to propose a project, just where does he propose it? His own university may have some funds, but this is not the general situation. The AAA would welcome him, but the support would be more of a moral than a financial nature. The AAA research budget is not large enough to provide a salary that compensates for taking time off from teaching. What is needed if we are really to exploit the academic research environment is financial support for the academic researcher on a more extensive basis than the AICPA and a few other organizations now provide.

But the members of the profession must accept responsibility for research, too. It is difficult for the academic researcher to deal with applied problems and to implement research findings. He does not have the laboratory which is necessary to carry out this type of research. Hence, to make progress, the members of the profession must vigorously supplement academic research.

---

[2] Robert H. Roy and James H. MacNeill, "Horizons for a Profession: The Common Body of Knowledge for CPAs," *Journal of Accounting*, Sept. 66, pp. 46, 47.
[3] *Ibid.*, p. 41.

BASIC PRINCIPLES OF ACCOUNTING ARE A GOAL OF RESEARCH

It is clear that our quest for generally accepted accounting principles for external reporting should not be relaxed. Indeed, we are still a long way from a solution. As a matter of fact, we are still attempting to solve specific accounting problems (leases, pension costs, etc.) without having a set of generally accepted measurement principles to serve as a guide. This *ad hoc* "brush fire" type of solution to financial accounting problems probably will not be very effective unless we somehow evolve a set of fundamental principles.

In order to make progress toward establishing a set of generally accepted principles, it seems that at least two problems, virtually unexplored at this time, must be researched.

1. We must develop a precise set of criteria which can be used to distinguish "good" principles from "bad" principles. These criteria must be rigorously defined so that there is no confusion. For example, exactly what is meant by "comparability"? I suggest that even the definition is ambiguous. Consequently, even though we all may agree that a "good" set of principles should give comparable financial results, we have no way of knowing when we actually have such a set. The same may be said of "objectivity." What does this mean? Furthermore, what criteria other than objectivity and comparability should be involved in judging principles?

2. We must undertake research of an implementation nature. That is, we have had little experience with current cost, market value, and price-level adjusted measures, etc. Yet, many recent efforts have called for these types of measurements. A usual comment is, for example, that "market values lack objectivity." How do we know this to be true? We need to be able to experiment more than we do now so that we can learn more about what is involved in using measures other than historical cost. Much of this type of research will have to be carried out by the practitioner and his staff because university researchers lack the laboratory to be effective here.

OTHER AREAS FOR ACCOUNTING RESEARCH

Other areas requiring research are management accounting and information systems. At the moment, management accounting is not a well-developed field; it is more a collection of some interesting and useful concepts and methods. The basis of these concepts is not absolutely clear and their interrelationships have not been developed.

Questions of cost allocation still plague the management accountant just as alternative sets of accounting methods plague the financial accountant. The cost allocation question is not likely to be settled until the field of management accounting has some structure. I am not suggesting that there are necessarily generally accepted principles of management accounting. However, the field must have some structure so that guidelines can be developed for solving problems.

We also need to do more research in the area of management control and control systems. We need to develop methods for determining when the control system is consistent with the planning model. We also need to learn more about individual and group behavior so that our control systems rest on sound behavioral assumptions. In my opinion, a greater knowledge of the behavioral sciences would pay handsome rewards for the accountant.

Much of this type of research can be and is being done in the universities. However, much support is needed from members of the profession. All accountants, whether in public practice or not, should be more interested and active in research in management accounting than they have been in the past. Great strides could be made in this type of research if all co-operate. In fact, we may gain some new insights into external reporting through research in the management accounting area.

Two other important areas for research are (1) control and planning in a decentralized organization and (2) accounting for planning and control in nonprofit organizations. We still do not know enough about constructing transfer price systems. Neither have we perfected our internal profit reporting and control systems. Furthermore, we really have very little notion of what happens to the internal information needs of management when the objective function of the organization is something other than profit. Accounting in general would undoubtedly be greatly improved if more attention were paid to program budgeting, cost-benefit analysis, etc.

SUMMARY AND CONCLUSIONS

Progress and innovation in accounting will come through research, as is the case in most fields. Academic researchers can and should make a contribution to this effort. In fact, a failure to do so probably means that the teacher will gradually lose vitality in his field. So far as the university is concerned, there is little doubt that the graduate programs must become more research-oriented. So far as the profession at large is concerned, research activity must also be increased, and the scope and boundaries of accounting research must be made broader. Through this activity we can hope to specify what our concepts and methods "rest on" rather than having to assert that "they don't rest on nothing; they go all the way down."

62. Research in Accounting*

H. Justin Davidson**

In the postwar era our society has changed dramatically. New products have supplanted old ones, old products have been radically improved and new technologies have opened up whole new areas of activity. Billions of research dollars and hours have been spent to achieve these advances.

For one thing, there has been a radical increase in the information needs of our economic system, and in the instruments of information production. Since the accountant's principal function is the development, communication and use of information, it is clear that he is deeply involved in these changes. If the CPA profession is to maintain a position of leadership, it is essential that CPAs be alert and responsive to the information needs and uses of the changing world. Even to stand still, continuing research is required. To enhance the profession's position, a substantial investment in the development and codification of knowledge must be undertaken.

The potential rewards from accounting research are enormous. Research can help CPAs increase their understanding of how the information they present is perceived by users. Research can clarify the information needs of management and help CPAs to respond to them satisfactorily, rather than be bypassed by them. Research in the rapidly expanding usage of computers can make the CPA creatively aware of the information-production capacity of new equipment, and can also inform him of the implications of the computer for the audit function.

On a somewhat less general level, research in taxation can help practitioners to advise their clients, while at the same time providing the profession with information which will assist it in making policy recommendations to legislative and administrative authorities. Similarly, re-

* Reprinted from *The Journal of Accountancy*, September 1968, pages 45–46. Copyright 1968 by the American Institute of CPAs.
** H. Justin Davidson is the Dean of the Graduate School of Business and Public Administration at Cornell University.

search on the management of an accounting practice can give specific assistance to CPAs in their daily problems: it can also guide the Institute in attracting young people into the profession and in helping them maintain their competence.

The penalties of not undertaking research are sobering. Without knowledge enabling him to adapt to changing needs, the CPA could find himself in a backwater of society, while new professions emerge to meet new requirements.

Having appraised these benefits and penalties, the American Institute of Certified Public Accountants is committed to research as a matter of policy. In May 1966 the Council approved the following goal: "In its field, the Institute will be the prime source of research in the production of new knowledge, in the analysis and synthesis of experience and in the development and adaptation of new procedures and techniques." In October 1966 Council approved the Description of the Professional Practice of Certified Public Accountants, which includes the following statement: "Within this broad field of accounting certified public accountants are the identified professional accountants. They provide leadership in accounting research and education."

RESEARCH NEEDS OF THE CPA PROFESSION

First to be considered is what new knowledge the profession needs. Any effort to describe these needs in detail would require a major research effort in itself. However, illustrative examples come readily to mind.

The scope of accounting has been described as follows:

Accounting is a discipline which provides financial and other information essential to the efficient conduct and evaluation of the activities of any organization.

The information which accounting provides is essential for (1) effective planning, control and decision-making by management, and (2) discharging the accountability of organizations to investors, creditors, government agencies, tax authorities, association members, contributors to welfare institutions, and others.

Accounting includes the development and analysis of data, the testing of its validity and relevance, and the interpretation and communication of the resulting information to intended users. The data may be expressed in monetary or other quantitative terms, or in symbolic or verbal forms.[1]

---

[1] "Description of the Professional Practice of Certified Public Accountants," *Journal of Accountancy*, Dec. 66, p. 61.

Research in accounting, therefore, should at the minimum embrace financial accounting and auditing, tax accounting and management information systems for planning, control and decision-making.

The objective of accounting research is the production of knowledge about the development, communication and use of information in all these areas, and the translation of this knowledge into accounting practice.

For convenience, the needs of the profession can be illustrated in three broad categories: (1) basic research (development of new knowledge—no assured payoff); (2) applied research (solution of specific problems); (3) codification research (organization and interpretation of existing knowledge for practical use).

. . . Basic research, for example, might include:

1. In accounting principles, study of the needs of various classes of users of financial reports, and the extent to which present reports aid or hamper decision-making processes.
2. In auditing, a study of conceptual foundations, such as sufficient evidential matter for validation purposes, and the interaction of internal controls with the scope of direct auditing procedures.
3. In taxation, studies of the impact of various forms of taxation on business decisions and managerial behavior.
4. In information and decision systems, studies of the information aspects of actual planning, control and decision-making processes within organizations of all kinds and all sizes.
5. In the management of accounting practices, studies of the motivation and attitudes of young people CPA firms would like to attract and retain.

Applied research might include:

1. In accounting principles, the continued development of criteria to determine the circumstances in which specific accounting treatments are preferable to others.
2. In auditing, the development of more precise standards governing application of such concepts as materiality and full disclosure.
3. In taxation, continuing studies of specific situations designed to maximize consistency, simplicity and equity.
4. In information systems, studies looking to extension of standard-cost concepts to marketing and distribution systems; refining budgetary and control procedures; measuring cost-benefit relationships of nonprofit activities.
5. In management of a practice, studies of staff-training procedures in firms of different sizes; client relations; legal liability; and other problems.

As to codification research:

1. Standardization of applied technical approaches is needed in all areas of practice, along with more bibliographic and reference materials.

2. Codification of accounting principles, auditing standards, and procedures, responsibilities in tax practice, and ethical rules and interpretive opinions must be continued. Special attention should be given to standards in tax practice and advisory and consulting services.

3. Opportunities for extension of services or introduction of new services by accounting firms should be codified on the basis of successful experiences of individual firms. . . .

CONCLUSION

Effective research will lead to the development of new services and the improvement of old services by certified public accountants in firms of all sizes, as well as assisting members not in practice. It will protect the profession against failure to adapt to a changing environment and changing public needs. It will add to the prestige of the profession in business and financial circles, in government and in the academic community. It will help to secure the position of certified public accountants as professional leaders in the broad field of accounting.

The goal is high—to be the prime mover in producing new knowledge and translating it into the practice of accounting. With confidence and action, the profession can reach this goal.

63. AICPA's Research Program*

Reed K. Storey and Loyd C. Heath**

Most accounting students know something about the work of the Accounting Principles Board of the American Institute of Certified Public Accountants because they have used "APB" Opinions in their classroom work. A few students have been introduced to the Accounting Research Division of the Institute through its research studies, but there are prob-

* Reprinted from *Beta Alpha Psi Newsletter*, Spring 1968.

** Reed K. Storey is the Director of Accounting Research Division of the American Institute of CPAs; Loyd C. Heath is Associate Professor of Accounting at the University of Washington.

ably very few who understand how this Division operates and its relationship with the APB in their joint task of improving accounting principles.

The Accounting Research Division and the Accounting Principles
Board both were established on September 1, 1959. Prior to that time
pronouncements of the AICPA on accounting principles were called
Accounting Research Bulletins and were issued by a committee known
as the Committee on Accounting Procedure. The term "Accounting
Research Bulletin" applied to these pronouncements was somewhat misleading because they were not based upon research in any formal sense
of the term; they were statements of the consensus of opinions held by
members of that committee based upon their experience as prominent
accounting practitioners.

The 51 Bulletins (ARBs) issued during the period 1939–1959 undeniably helped raise the general level of financial reporting and contributed to the eradication of numerous undesirable accounting practices,
but they came under increasing attack in the 1950's. They were criticized
as a "piecemeal approach" to the solution of accounting problems and
as a "distillation of practice" rather than reasoned solutions to accounting
problems.

The Institute's new program for the formulation and promulgation
of accounting principles which started in 1959 was designed to avoid
some of these objections. Perhaps the most significant differences between
this program and the pre-1959 program lie in the relationship between
the Accounting Principles Board and the Accounting Research Division
of the Institute.

The new program represents the first serious attempt to unite the
practical experience of the practicing accountant and the research potential and preoccupation with logical methods and conceptual matters of
the university professor. The Board is composed primarily of prominent
and influential accountants in public practice whose knowledge and competence of the practical aspects of financial accounting and reporting are
unchallenged, with a minority of equally qualified members from industry
and from the universities.

The choice of research staff emphasizes expertise of a nature com-
plementary to, rather than the same as, that of the Board. Graduate
education, research capability, writing ability, and creative thinking are
the qualifications stressed, in addition to accounting experience.

The Accounting Principles Board normally does not act upon a
matter until it has been thoroughly studied by a competent researcher
who is advised and assisted in this task by the Director of Accounting
Research and a project advisory committee of five to seven recognized
authorities on the subject under consideration. The researcher is free to
come to any conclusions he feels justified but his conclusions are not, of

course, binding on the Accounting Principles Board, and his study does not represent an official position of the Institute.

Accounting research studies perform a number of functions. First, and most obviously, they are useful to Board members in their consideration of the problems discussed. Since large parts of research studies are typically devoted to a consideration of the nature of the problem and a weighing of the pros and cons of alternative solutions to the problem, a study may be useful to a Board member even though he specifically rejects the solution proposed by the author of the study.

Second, the research studies have an indirect effect on Board members by stimulating discussion of the subject, both oral discussion and written articles in the professional accounting literature. Third, research studies have an even more indirect and long-run effect on accounting thought through classroom use. They are widely used in graduate courses and seminars, and it is expected that this use will give future accountants a greater appreciation of the application of logical methods and deductive reasoning in solving accounting problems.

Nine studies have been published since the Accounting Research Division was organized in 1959. Three of these (*Accounting Research Study Nos. 1, 3, and 7*) are on the general subject of accounting "postulates and principles"; the remainder deal with more specific accounting problems. APB Opinions have already been issued on the subjects covered by four of these: (1) cash flow and funds statements, (2) leases, (3) pension plans, and (4) inter-period allocation of corporate income taxes.

The Board currently is working on an Opinion based on *ARS 6*, "Reporting the Financial Effects of Price-Level Changes," and an Opinion tentatively entitled, "Basic Concepts and Broad Principles Underlying Financial Statements of Business Enterprises," based in part on the three research studies—*ARS 1*, "The Basic Postulates of Accounting" by Maurice Moonitz; *ARS 3*, "A Tentative Set of Broad Accounting Principles for Business Enterprises" by Robert T. Sprouse and Maurice Moonitz; and *ARS 7*, "Inventory of Generally Accepted Accounting Principles for Business Enterprises" by Paul Grady. The APB Opinion on *ARS 5*, "A Critical Study of Accounting for Business Combinations," by Arthur Wyatt, has been delayed pending the completion later this year of a related study, entitled "Accounting for Goodwill," by George R. Catlett and Norman O. Olson.

Improvement of accounting principles is a difficult task. Many of the problems which face the accounting profession today have been with us for many years. They involve difficult theoretical and practical issues. The Institute program is, in our opinion, a realistic, soundly conceived program for facing these issues.

Part
Six

Education
and Careers

The readings in prior parts make it clear that the role of accounting in society is such that it can be expected that accountants are employed on a wide front throughout societal strata. The readings in Part Six confirm this. They also draw attention to the serious problems confronting the educators of future accountants.

Although business schools have been in existence in America and other countries for many years, the major part of business education, including accounting education, has a long tradition of relying on on-the-job training. Thus a mixture of education and training has characterized the professional preparation of businessmen and accountants. In some measure this continues today in most enterprises, including professional public accounting firms.

Professional public accountants have always had to satisfy certain professional examination requirements, but the formal educational prerequisites for such examinations have in the past been few and highly specialized. Similarly, accountants not associated with CPA aspects of the profession have in the past encountered few specific educational requirements as job prerequisites.

During the most recent decade many changes have taken place in business and accounting education. Because (1) the overall complexity of socioeconomic systems and their entities continues to grow, (2) transactions between entities tend to become more and more complex, and (3) accounting is related to so much of an entity's activity, there is an increasing demand that accountants be more formally educated than they were in the past. This demand issues from all types of enterprises in society, but especially from professional public accounting firms, where the concept of a graduate profession for public accounting is receiving increasing support.

A trend toward higher educational requirements for accountants has already emerged and is exemplified by the fact that as of mid-1969, about 35 states in the United States required a baccalaureate as a prerequisite for a CPA certificate. Some states are considering an MBA degree as a possible professional entrance condition. Similar conditions prevail in other countries. Most licensed German professional accountants hold doctoral degrees, and minimal requirements at the bachelor's degree level are about to be instituted in Australia and Canada.

One specific requirement of modern educational programs in accounting is that they must be as broad as possible. It is no longer desirable for accountants to limit themselves to accounting courses. The call for broader education emphasizes the need to study the humanities, behavioral sciences and quantitative methods in addition to accounting. This call for a wider education is not dictated by a superficial desire to "degree" accountants, but is intended to equip them more fully for the complex nature of their future jobs. Recruiters today seek accounting specialists who are also all-encompassing generalists.

Collegiate accounting curricula for accounting majors have responded to the forces described in the preceding paragraphs and presently reflect certain marked changes from the curricula of only a decade ago. These changes include (1) a reduction in the number of required accounting courses, (2) the teaching of accounting courses with less of a technical emphasis, and (3) a curriculum not oriented to any one type of accounting career. One justification for these changes is that on-the-job training will always be necessary to some extent, and that such training will compensate for some of the changes referred to.

The new accounting curriculum has brought in its wake a need for a new breed of accounting educators. The new educators must be less practice oriented than their predecessors, and should tend to emphasize more philosophical and conceptual approaches. There is now less collegiate teaching of what "is," and more of what "should be."

The evolution of the new educational program for accountants is not yet complete. The continually changing nature of our social system as well as the amazing knowledge explosion of the past decade are but two of the reasons why the question concerning the nature of optimal accounting education is still in a state of flux.

The first three readings of this part discuss the education and training of accountants. The first (Smyth) sets forth the general philosophy of the new educational requirements for accountants, while the second (Hart) develops these requirements more specifically. The article by Ball discusses the education and training of CPAs. Career opportunities for accountants are discussed in the remaining readings in Part Six (as well as intermittently elsewhere in the book). Aside from the information reproduced here, rather voluminous literature about careers in accounting is freely available.

Chapter XIV

Changing Educational Concepts and Professional Opportunities

64. *Accounting Education in the United States**

E. Bryan Smyth**

The attempts which have been made during the twentieth century to formulate a set of accounting principles which might achieve universal acceptance may well be idealistic and incapable of complete fulfilment. Nevertheless, the hard thinking and continual re-examination of concepts which underlie these attempts must, in the long run, produce beneficial results which should earn the gratitude of all concerned in the development and well-being of the profession.

I intend to comment on two of the significant controversial issues which are still exercising the minds of academics in the United States. These are the conflict between liberalization and specialization in business courses and the impact on management accounting of what may be termed "Management Science". . . .

CONFLICT BETWEEN LIBERALIZATION AND SPECIALIZATION

It is generally accepted that the functions of a university are to impart to the student—first, ability to think analytically and critically

* Reprinted from *The Australian Accountant*, November 1965, pages 576–577 and 581.
** E. Bryan Smyth is Professor of Accountancy at The University of New South Wales.

about problems; secondly, ability to communicate his thoughts effectively with regard to them; thirdly, a knowledge of human relations; and fourthly, an appreciation of his social environment, thereby helping him to lead a fuller and richer life. In the particular area of accounting there are some who would add a further function, namely, to give the student a technical competence in accounting and related fields.

There are many who think that if one is to make a career in accounting one must have a broader and more liberal background than is provided by a good training in accounting concepts and techniques.

On the other hand, there are those who hold that existing courses do not allow sufficient time "to train the student well" and for this reason the length of the course should be extended to five years or more.

For some time now the universities have been subjected to criticism by practitioners who expect commerce and economics students on graduation to be skilled in techniques and procedures. The practitioners express keen disappointment when they are not. The expectation that universities should develop such professional competence which only experience can provide, surely reveals an unreasonable attitude on the part of those members of the accounting profession. The universities for the most part will not accept this criticism on the ground that their main function is to develop analytical minds—something they cannot do efficiently if too much time is devoted to the teaching of routine procedures and techniques, skills which, it is claimed, can be adequately acquired from on-the-job training and to a limited extent by vacation experience where this is practicable.

Then there are the questions of "course content" and "teaching method". In the United States, there is a distinct cleavage between those universities which place emphasis on the theoretical aspects of accounting and on training the student to think analytically and critically and, on the other hand, those universities which consider that the student's training will be deficient unless he is introduced to the techniques associated with professional practice.

Space does not permit me to discuss this controversial issue further but in considering the functions of a university, I am reminded of John Stuart Mill who, in discussing the classic aims of a liberal education, stated:—

> . . . *men are men before they are lawyers or physicians or merchants or manufacturers, and if you make them capable and sensible men they will make themselves capable and sensible lawyers and physicians. What professional men should carry away from the university is not a professional knowledge but that which should direct the use of their professional knowledge and bring the light of general culture to illuminate the technicalities of a special pursuit—education makes a man a more*

intelligent shoemaker, if that be his occupation, not by teaching him how to make shoes but it does it by the mental exercise it gives and the habits it impresses.[1]

NEW APPROACHES TO ACCOUNTING

A new approach[2] to the teaching of business subjects, including accounting, is what is known collectively as "management science". Academics in the United States have for some time now been re-examining their courses in relation to the management accounting function in a changing technological environment so as to place more emphasis on the flow of information through the business enterprise.

This management science concept has four main strands. The first is the behavioral science approach to the study of the firm with stress being placed on the human motivation aspects of each area of responsibility. The second is the use of mathematical tools and techniques which until fairly recently have been conveniently ignored by accountants. The third approach is through electronic data processing, the computer and communication theory. The fourth is scientific method as applied to the study of the firm and business situations. I would like to make a brief comment on two of these.

The first is mathematics as a tool in accounting education and research. The demands for quantitative criteria of efficiency in decision-making and operations are placing pressures on the accounting profession which it cannot afford to ignore. It seems certain that anyone aspiring to become a top-level accountant of the future will require considerable mathematical knowledge.

Mathematics is being used as a tool in inventory control, equipment replacement decisions and statistical sampling for inventory valuation, cost control and variance analysis, to name a few areas. Mathematical techniques are also being applied to model building to depict operations in order to study the inter-relationship between variables.

New courses which are being introduced and extended in some American university business schools include organisation theory, responsibility accounting, information systems and control, decision theory and E.D.P. . .

CONCLUSION

These prerequisites for analytical thinking are still in the process of development and there is a golden opportunity for fruitful contribution

[1] John Stuart Mill, Inaugural Address as Rector delivered to the University of St. Andrews, February, 1867. People's Edition: Longmans, Green, Reader & Dyer, 1867, pp. 4–5.
[2] See also Thomas R. Prince, "Information Systems for Management Control," *The Accounting Review*, April 1964, pp. 467–472.

by academic accountants to this cause. It behoves us in the universities to train our students in such a way that they will be equipped with those attributes which will give them a secure foundation for approaching business problems not only of the present but of the future as well. There is danger in being complacent or ultra-conservative in a rapidly changing technological environment—in the short-term this attitude could lead to increasing criticism of accounting as a profession; and in the long-term it could result in accounting being eliminated from the list of accepted academic disciplines.

65. An Outsider Looks at the Accounting Curriculum*

Donald J. Hart**

It is always difficult for an "outsider" to look critically at someone else's field and generate observations that have not already been discussed at length within the field. If there is any merit to an outside view, therefore, it lies in fortifying the conclusions that the insiders may have begun to formulate.

As a means of shaping a perspective, it may be useful to look at what was *not* particularly significant to accountants thirty-five years ago. For all practical purposes, there were no computers available. Computers obviously are not cure-alls, nor are they the primary concern of accountants today any more than they are the province only of accountants. Nevertheless, they now do concern accountants infinitely more than they did a generation ago.

In 1933, there was practically no regard (on accountants' part) for human-behavior aspects of accounting functions. There was some, but minimal, attention to the economic implications of price changes—from a costing point of view—under conditions of inflation and deflation, despite the depression conditions then prevailing.

A generation ago, accountants were not much interested in the public policy implications of monetary policy for accounting theory or

* Reprinted from *The Journal of Accountancy*, March 1969, pages 87–89. Copyrighted 1969 by the American Institute of CPAs.
** Donald J. Hart is President of St. Andrews Presbyterian College at Laurinburg, North Carolina.

for accounting practice. Indeed, monetary policy was just emerging as a significant economic tool at the national level.

The dynamics of technological change were not particularly evident to accountants; nor were the resultant impacts on internal operations of the firm, and therefore on possible modifications in accounting functions.

The reason for looking backward for thirty-five years is to provide an excuse for looking *forward* thirty-five years, at which time we will be over the threshold of the twenty-first century. This is the arena in which your students will be at the height of their careers, or they will be winding up successful careers—or they will have been bounced out by obsolescence. If it is the latter situation that prevails, this will be a sad commentary on what you did (or did not) do for them while they were your students.

Regarding the next thirty-five years, there are some areas of concern that are beginning to emerge rather clearly. One is the speed and the magnitude of change both in business and in society. Especially does the speed of change have implications for information-flow requirements within the firm, and, therefore, for the accounting profession.

Information systems will be far more sophisticated in the twenty-first century than they are now. So will information-retrieval systems, and these may affect the whole conceptual base of accounting methodology, and particularly accounting structures and procedures.

There are both technological and behavioral implications in the increased interdependency that will be experienced both within the firm and in society at large. Moreover, the integration of total knowledge will be vastly more significant for accountants than it is now or than it has been in the past. This is true, also, for other areas of business administration, as well as for the fields of architecture, engineering, medicine, and others.

Because we are moving at a rapid pace toward the changing environment of the next century, it becomes increasingly imperative that accounting curriculums be under constant review, and that they be kept flexible.

Accounting educators cannot afford to be hogtied by certification requirements which tend to be imposed and sustained by institutional considerations rather than by logic or rationale. For example, one institutional constraint is the continuing attitude of a substantial (though diminishing) segment of CPAs who want to "keep the rascals out." That is, there persists a feeling that newcomers to the field should go through precisely the same type of academic preparation that current practitioners were exposed to. If this kind of perpetuated hurdle were retained in medicine, doctors would still be bleeding patients rather than using wholly new diagnostic and treatment procedures.

A second kind of institutional constraint on curricular change in accounting education is the myopia of legislative certification requirements—which tend to lag farther and farther behind the rapidly changing needs of practitioners as well as the needs of those who struggle to develop new concepts and theories in accounting.

In the light of this preamble, what are some of the areas that need attention within the context of necessary areas of competency in the accounting field?

One need is in the area of communication. Verbal capacity is tremendously important, and especially so as the complexity of organizational structures increases. Skill in quantitative analysis also is vital—not merely ability to understand and use quantitative tools, but the capacity to transmit the results of analysis to others with unmistakable clarity.

A closely related need is competency in symbolic logic. Accountants in the twenty-first century will be required to develop and use sophisticated information systems without being hobbled by the chains of traditional formats and practices. The objective of acquiring skill in complex logic is to improve both accounting tools and the process of management decision-making through the development and use of improved information systems.

Emphasis on logic forces attention to critical evaluation of relationships among data—especially data that were (a) *not available* in the past, or (b) *not manipulatable* on a timely basis in the past (that is, could not be handled for adequate potential use until the time frame for decisions had expired), or (c) *not conceptually interwoven* in past accounting theory or procedures. Future data-bank sources will open up fantastic possibilities for fruitful use of data relationships that have not yet even been contemplated.

Another area that will require the attention of future accountants is technological change that is not directly associated with accounting, but which does relate to the rate of growth of human knowledge generally. It is only by being aware of the total growth of knowledge that accountants will be perceptive of means by which they may be able to improve both the quality and the range of services which they might perform both for industry and for society at large.

Developments in the behavioral sciences are yet another broad area which will be far more important to accountants in the future than in the past. "People problems" affect not only those directly engaged in accounting functions, but they affect the availability, accuracy, and ultimate interpretation and use of the increasing range of operational data with which accountants will be working.

It seems reasonable to expect that accountants in the future will play an even more central role in management decisions than they do currently, for they will be engaged increasingly in information management and analysis rather than in the accumulation and recording of information. It is recognized, of course, that accountants do more than "accumulate and record" now, but the scope of accounting functions appears certain to expand further by the time the twenty-first century rolls around. At least this could be the trend if they take advantage of a potential "lock" on informational skills, thereby moving ahead more rapidly in this bailiwick than others who might otherwise fill this need before accountants gear up their own capacities to the task.

In the light of all of this, there emerge certain specific implications for accounting curriculums.

A necessary initial step appears to be the breaching of the constraints of traditional course labels and textbooks which lag behind conceptual changes. Even though much course content has been broadened and modified in recent years, these built-in constraints encourage lack of change. Unfortunately, this is a chicken-or-egg problem. A faculty which changes course titles to accommodate content modifications faces the problem of finding adaptable textbooks to mount a satisfactory teaching effort. An author who attempts an unorthodox approach to accounting content finds a market resistance—partly because faculty members are reluctant to change course content in individual courses, since this affects the existing sequence of an integrated curriculum in accounting. Herculean effort will be required to co-ordinate these two attacks on course (and curricular) content, or else sterility will rob the accounting field of needed progress.

Equally important is the emphasis which must be given to non-accounting areas of study which, for the most part, are now merely tolerated or given lip service. The accounting faculty must persist in demanding the availability of appropriate content coverage in mathematics and quantitative analysis. Nearly every accounting and business administration program now requires courses under titles which presumably indicate that students are acquiring all of the background and skill needed in these vital areas. What is essential, however, is not "a" mathematics course, or "a" statistics course, but rather selected tool concepts and applications which often are not encountered until a student has had three or four courses in each of these areas. A student doesn't have time to major in these areas plus accounting, yet he needs far more background than he normally could acquire in an introductory course in one or more of these fields.

A similar problem exists in the area of behavioral sciences. What the student needs is appropriate course coverage, not one introductory course each in psychology, sociology, and anthropology. Introductory courses in any field (including accounting, unfortunately—which suggest that attention may be needed here, too, for nonaccounting students) tend to be geared to a sequence of courses leading to major concentration in that field. The gut concepts in a field rarely are exposed in illuminating detail until one reaches the third or fourth course level in a "major" sequence. As a consequence, nonmajor students who pursue an academic field only to the extent of an introductory course generally get only a very rudimentary knowledge of what the basic content of that field might be able to contribute to making performance in his own field more effective. Note, however, that it is not a watered-down approach that is proposed (i.e., in the behavioral sciences, or in mathematics, or in quantitative analysis, or in other nonaccounting areas), but rather a beefed-up approach. Indeed, such an approach might be quite valid even for students majoring in such areas, particularly in view of the horrendous pace at which knowledge is expanding in virtually all fields.

Microeconomics is a field in which future accountants will need competency, also. Here, again, the appropriateness of coverage is the paramount problem. In recent years, economists seem to have given much less attention to updating the theory of the firm than to the continuing development of macro theory. As in the case of the other supporting academic areas, therefore, accounting faculties will need to use all of the persuasion and reason that they can bring to bear on their colleagues to induce substantive improvements in coverage and approach in the fields which must be incorporated in forward-looking accounting curriculums.

Similarly, in the area of logic much is needed. Most existing logic courses (typically offered by philosophy departments) have received little developmental attention. Typically, such courses are based upon a relatively low-level syllogism approach. Though this may be valuable, it is far from a complete revelation of the ramifications of logic that are inherent in the complexities of sophisticated information systems with which future accountants must cope.

Oral and written reports must receive substantially greater emphasis than customarily is given in accounting courses. Traditional accounting reports of a stylized sort are simply inadequate for the development of twenty-first century accountants.

Greater emphasis will be required on managerial structures and functions. The purpose is to give accountants a better perspective from which to aid and participate in the development, modification, and appraisal of company objectives. For example, is the reporting and analysis of financial information the only (or even the main) contribution that accountants can make to the management process? Or, should accountants broaden their view to other forms of information analysis? It would seem appropriate for accountants to be concerned partly with information which is external to the firm, as economy-wide information retrieval becomes more feasible.

Most of the discussion has centered around internal, or company, accounting thus far. Public accountants, however, will require much greater educational breadth, also. Wider backgrounds will be needed to meet the growing demand for management services to be provided by public accounting firms. Moreover, though the auditing and tax functions undoubtedly will continue, the contexts of these services will have to shift to the changing environment in which all accountants will find themselves thirty-five years hence.

The possibility and necessity of curricular change should be approached on a total basis, not a piecemeal one. Piecemeal, course-by-course change can only be haphazard when it is applied to a package-type curriculum such as has been common in accounting education. Essentially, accounting curriculums must reflect the dynamics of change, not the sterility of tradition.

The accounting field is not unique, so far as many of the observations made here regarding it. Because it is one of the older academic disciplines, however, change will be much more difficult to generate and assimilate than would be the case in most of the other closely related areas in higher education for business.

Perhaps the viewpoint that might be most helpful is one that would recognize that accounting should not be regarded as dependent upon a set of constraining tools which limit the user's potential, but a set of facilitative and creative tools which can continue to enhance and elevate his competency.

66. Changing Concepts in the Education and Training of Accountants*

J. T. Ball**

The education and training of accountants have received much attention in recent years in all parts of the world. Various reports have been issued after considerable periods of study. U.S. accountants and accounting educators are currently pondering the recently released Common Body of Knowledge Study, *Horizons for a Profession*, the most significant undertaking of its kind in this country since the *Report of the Commission on Standards of Education and Experience for Certified*

* Reprinted from *The Journal of Accountancy*, July 1967, pages 83–85. Copyrighted 1967 by the American Institute of CPAs.

** J. T. Ball is the Assistant Director of Examinations for the American Institute of CPAs.

Public Accountants in 1959. The Parker Committee rendered the *Report of the Committee on Education and Training* to the Institute of Chartered Accountants in England and Wales in 1961. The Vatter Report, *Survey of Accountancy Education in Australia,* issued in 1965, was another such major undertaking. And now the Council of the Institute of Chartered Accountants of Scotland has adopted a revised plan for the education and training of Scottish chartered accountant apprentices as a result of the "Report of the Special Committee on Education and Training of Apprentices" after a three-year study by the committee. The report was published in a supplement to the February 1967 issue of *The Accountants'* magazine.

MOST CPAs ATTEND COLLEGE

In the United States it is commonly assumed that a CPA candidate will have prepared for his career largely through a college education. Americans therefore tend to speculate on the need for professional schools of accountancy or the need for postgraduate study in accounting. Currently, of the 53 jurisdictions utilizing the Uniform CPA Examination, 23 require or will require by 1970 a college degree or the equivalent to sit for the CPA examination; 8 states require or will require by 1969 two years of college; and 22 jurisdictions do not at the present require any college attendance. The legislatures of 4 states, however, now have bills pending to require a college degree to sit for the CPA examination and 2 other states are currently making studies of such a proposal.[1]

Most of the states with large numbers of candidates sitting for the CPA examination are included among those that require a college education. In several of the smaller states only a high school diploma is required. The legal requirements to sit for the examination may be misleading, however. William C. Bruschi, Director of Examinations of the American Institute of CPAs, reported that an analysis of data obtained from questionnaires completed by candidates sitting for the November 1965 CPA examination indicated that 93% had attended college for two or more years, 87% were college graduates, 12% had postgraduate educations, and less than 1% were only high school graduates. In addition, others had attended proprietary business schools or had taken correspondence courses in accounting.[2]

---

[1] Education and experience requirements to sit for the CPA examination in the various jurisdictions are available in the *Accountancy Law Reporter,* published by Commerce Clearing House in cooperation with the American Institute of CPAs. Education and experience requirements for professional accountants in other countries are summarized in *Professional Accounting in 25 Countries,* published by the American Institute of CPAs in 1964.

[2] From a speech to the American Woman's Society of Certified Public Accountants and the American Society of Women Accountants at their joint annual meeting in Boston, September 29, 1966.

EXPERIENCE REQUIREMENTS

Although an experience requirement is generally prevalent in this country, many states waive all or part of the experience requirement if the candidate completes postgraduate study in accounting. The Council of the American Institute of CPAs in 1959 and 1960, acting on the Bailey Committee Report, resolved that two years of experience should be required to obtain the CPA certificate but that this could be reduced to a minimum of one year of experience in public accounting if balanced by an appropriate amount of postgraduate education. John L. Carey, Executive Director of the American Institute of CPAs, however, has suggested that the present experience requirements may eventually be abandoned and that specified types of post-university training (e.g., in-firm or on-the-job training) may be substituted as part of the requirements to obtain the CPA certificate.[3]

In other parts of the world a prospective professional accountant must often complete an extended apprenticeship and a series of examinations during a period of several years. The Institute of Chartered Accountants in England and Wales provides for a substitution of university education in "special" degree courses and a "University Scheme" to satisfy a portion of the apprenticeship and examinations, with the result that the five-year basic apprenticeship period in England is reduced to a minimum of three years for university graduates. The Vatter Report on education and experience for Australian accountants recommended that the emphasis on experience be diminished and the emphasis on education be increased as the most efficient means of imparting accounting knowledge to beginning accountants. The Canadian Institute of Chartered Accountants has set its sights on university graduation by all entrants by 1970, while a Canadian university graduate can currently have his five-year apprenticeship reduced by two to four years.

SCOTTISH REPORT

In November 1963, the Council of the Institute of Chartered Accountants of Scotland resolved that a special committee be constituted to consider and report to the Council upon the examination and training of candidates for membership in the Institute and to consider the following related questions: the common body of knowledge the Institute should require of candidates for membership; additional specialized knowledge that should be required of candidates; recruitment, qualification, training and examination of candidates; and the relations between the Institute and educational institutions in the future. A committee was

---

[3] The changing concepts for the education and training of CPAs are discussed by John L. Carey in pp. 258–83 of *The CPA Plans for the Future*, published by the American Institute of Certified Public Accountants in 1965.

appointed on March 25, 1964, and its report was acted upon by the Council of the Institute in meetings on December 20, 1966, and January 27, 1967. The principal results of the adoption of the recommendations by the Council will be: (1) after February 1968 the minimum preliminary qualification for entry into a chartered accountant apprenticeship will be raised to that of an attestation of academic fitness for admission to a Scottish university; (2) the recruitment of a larger proportion of graduates will be greatly encouraged; (3) apprentices will attend courses in bookkeeping and elementary accounting full time for four weeks at the outset of their apprenticeships; (4) apprentices will spend an academic year in the second year of their apprenticeship as full-time students at a Scottish university rather than in the third year as now required; and (5) a new examination syllabus will be introduced in 1969 to include new subjects such as automatic data processing, management mathematics and statistics, and greater depth in taxation and management accounting.

EDUCATION

A major consideration for the committee was whether or not the requirement should be retained that an apprentice spend an academic year of his apprenticeship as a student in a Scottish university. The requirement for full-time study rather than part-time study was introduced in the 1960–61 session and the committee felt that a return to part-time study would be regression. (Currently the Scottish Institute is the only accountancy body in the British Isles to require a year of academic study of its apprentices.)

The committee recommended that graduate apprentices be exempted from prescribed classes in law and economics and that apprentices who do not pass the prescribed classes in law and economics no longer be required to reattend those classes as required at present.

The Council of the Scottish Institute first published its intent to raise the minimum requirement for entry as an apprentice to that of the requirement for admission to a Scottish university in 1962. The committee agreed with this requirement because it found that approximately 25 per cent of the apprenticeship entrants did not succeed in gaining admission to the Institute. Also, the committee believed that the percentage of unsuccessful candidates would undoubtedly increase unless the preliminary qualifications were raised because examinations would in the future tend to become wider in scope and more difficult. The committee thought that the Institute must have a qualification for admission at least as high as that of the universities if the Institute was to compete successfully for the best products of the schools and that the Institute would get "second best" entrants unless the qualifications were raised. (It is interesting to note that this same logic was reported by the Vatter Report in Australia.) The committee anticipated that this requirement would result in fewer apprentices but also fewer failures.

RECRUITING

The committee found that graduates had comprised approximately 9 per cent of the total entrants into apprenticeships over recent years. It appears that there is no significant difference between the proportion of graduates who take their articles for entry into the Scottish Institute and those who aspire to become members of the Institute of Chartered Accountants in England and Wales. A 1964 report of the Conference of the Joint Standing Committee of the Universities and the Accountancy Profession indicated that fewer than 10 per cent of the articled clerks apprenticed to members of the Scottish Institute were graduates.[4]

Although the committee did not foresee a wholesale improvement in the proportion of entrants from graduates, it felt that the Institute should make every effort to recruit from university graduates. The committee thus recommended that entrants to the Institute should be from one of three categories: (a) graduates with study of accounting in depth, (b) other graduates and (c) nongraduates with the academic requirements for entry into a university.

In terms of the period of time to be spent on the apprenticeship, the committee recommended that the nongraduate entrant remain on the apprenticeship for five years, that the graduate who had studied accounting spend three years on the apprenticeship and that other graduate entrants spend three years and six months on the apprenticeship. Consideration was given to an industrial apprenticeship, but this was rejected in favor of the broader experience available in a practitioner's office.

CONCLUSION

It appears that the balance between the education and training of professional accountants is shifting in favor of education as a more efficient means of imparting the common body of knowledge required by the profession. Perhaps this is only part of the evolutionary process in the development of a profession, or perhaps it is being imposed as the result of the rapidly changing technology of today's society. An accountant no longer becomes an "expert" by memorizing all of the journal entries which might be made, and he is now being required earlier to under-

---

[4] See pages 703 and 704 of the May 30, 1964, issue and page 633 of the November 21, 1964, issue of *The Accountant* for a comparison of the educational backgrounds of apprentices in various professions in England as reported by the Robbins Committee Report on Higher Education.

stand "why" before he learns "how." It is also true that today the recent graduate may know more about the operation and requirements of the modern information system than does the experienced practitioner who has not been studying as much as the graduate.

There are many indications that not only is accounting education becoming increasingly important, but it is also rapidly shifting from a procedural approach to a conceptual approach in this country. The de-emphasizing of techniques, however, creates a need for training in procedures that were formerly taught in the classroom.

All accountants agree that both training and education are necessary. Only two questions remain unanswered: "How much?" and "What kind?"

67. *A Career in Business Accounting**

Lynn A. Townsend**

It is a special privilege to address the Fiftieth Anniversary meeting of the American Accounting Association. This is certainly a notable milestone in itself; but what is even more important in my estimation than the celebration of 50 years of activity is the fact that the Association has become an increasingly more valuable servant of its members. For that achievement we all owe a vote of thanks to Herbert E. Miller and his fellow officers, and to those who have served before them. We all appreciate the great contribution that they have made to the profession of accountancy.

Because so many of you are teachers of accounting in business schools or colleges, and because the rest of you are certainly interested in the education of future accountants, I would like to discuss a subject of special interest to us and to the future accountants of America. I would like to discuss the special challenges of a career in business accounting, what has happened to business to create those special challenges, and then the job we have of creating greater public understanding of what business is all about.

I think all of us here pretty well agree there are few things as exciting and rewarding as a career in accounting. Many of us know at

* Reprinted from *The Accounting Review*, January 1967, pages 1–6.
** Lynn A. Townsend is Chairman of the Board of Directors of the Chrysler Corporation.

first hand especially how the accountant is being called on by business to help it maintain the economic health and strength of the nation—to create the jobs, the new investments, and the new growth opportunities that keep us moving ahead.

All this is familiar and clear to us. But it seems to me it needs to be made clearer to others. I am sure that even among those young people who have decided on a business career, many still carry around in their heads a stereotype of what business—especially big business— is like. You have all heard the old cliches to the effect that "big business is bad business," and you have surely run up against the stereotype in the minds of some students to the effect that businessmen are "captains of industry," and all of that.

I don't pretend to know why those stereotypes keep on clinging so tightly. Perhaps the reason is that the great contributions of business often get buried on the back pages of the daily newspaper, or perhaps it is because most of the books that are written tend to attack rather than praise. Whatever the cause, the result is often an incomplete under-standing of what makes the businessman run, and of what makes our business system one of the modern wonders of the world. All of you here, by the nature of your responsibilities and your interests, are in an excellent position to destroy some of these myths and to inform the students of our universities about the true nature of business.

It has been my privilege to look at the profession of business ac-counting from two distinct and separate points of view. I have seen it from the point of view of a practicing accountant advising companies in Canada and the United States. And on the other hand I have seen it from the point of view of an industrial manager who needs and uses and depends upon the advice of the corporate accountant. And on the basis of my experience I am convinced that in a very real sense, no pro-fession I know of is more important than the broad and many-sided profession of financial management—because financial management is critically important in guiding the sound progress of individual compa-nies and in turn maintaining the forward thrust of the entire free-world economy.

Thirty or forty years ago no one could have made this statement with any expectation of being taken seriously. Back in those days the accountant was essentially a bright and highly-trained watchdog—hired theoretically to protect the shareholder's interest in a business or to inspire the confidence of banks and government agencies. He helped the company comptroller to maintain a sound set of books and to report accurate financial data for legal and tax purposes. But neither he nor the comptroller had much to do with establishing profit objectives or suggesting ways in which a company might move a little faster toward those objectives. In other words, a generation ago the accountant and the comptroller were closer to being financial statisticians than they were to being financial strategists.

Today all that is changed. *Today, the business accountant is a strategist and a planner—a custodian, if you will, of the profit mechanism that guides and controls our entire free enterprise system.* He makes sure that the measurement of a company's profitability is precise. He studies the trends of profitability in all the sub-systems of the over-all company system to spot signs of strength and weakness. And he can see quickly which operations are on target and which are not. Doing all this— keeping a company on course, filling a public need, making a profit— at a time when upward cost pressures on the one hand and downward price pressures on the other have put us in a squeeze, is one of the great challenges of our time. And the business accountant has the job of meeting that challenge.

I believe that the schools and colleges of this country, and especially the professors of accounting who have anticipated the needs of business, should be congratulated for having trained the men who could meet that challenge, and who have made accountancy the highly respected profession it is today in the world of business.

Along with that change in the attitude and the stature of the business accountant, and almost parallel with it, has come a change in business itself. The shape, or the character if you will, of the American corporation has undergone a drastic change in the past several years. Gone beyond recall are the early days of the white-vested, gold-watch-chained owner-manager who worked only for himself and managed pretty much by instinct. Today we have large corporations—many of them multinational in character—which are publicly held by hundreds of thousands of private citizens of many countries on different continents, all working towards the economic improvement of many nations. And incidentally, in that sense stockholders become participants in a major force for world development.

A modern business manager of such a multi-national corporation responds to a political constituency who own the stock. And he needs a combination of many talents. He needs accountants, for example, who, when they look at the world, see six continents instead of just one. He wants in one package—if he can get it—a diplomat who understands the ways of people from other countries, a scientific seer who can plan for the future development of bold new ideas, a world economist who understands balance-of-payments problems in all countries, who knows fiscal policy, and who understands the geopolitical relationships of all six continents and their many countries. It seems to me that this should be enough to challenge any man—to convince him that the modern American corporation has a place for the man with the broad view, with ideas and ideals, who wants in on some of the action.

Many young students of business continue to think that a modern company cramps the style of the employee and destroys his individuality and creativity. There are those who still write books about how a corporation presses its people into a company mold, tells them whom to marry, how to dress and talk, and where to live. And there are still those who read them. They might be compared to the people who think that all accountants wear a green eyeshade and sit in a dark corner under a naked light bulb with an adding machine on their desk.

Our young people should be brought to understand and appreciate the dynamics of group action—that a man by working with others can have his individual efforts multiplied far beyond what he could accomplish on his own. Of course any young man who wants to get lost in the crowd can do it anywhere, and he probably will. *But the corporations I know about are looking for people who don't want to get lost and who won't get lost*—who will work to find the most effective combination of group effort and their own individual effort that will produce results.

Peter Drucker has stated the ideal combination of these two kinds of effort in these words: "The more the individual in an organization grows as a person, the more the organization can accomplish. . . . But . . . the more the organization grows in seriousness and integrity, objectives and competence, the more scope there is for the individual to grow and develop as a person." To anyone who has known the excitement and the satisfaction of participating in a vital and growing business enterprise, these words say a lot.

Business also provides young men the opportunity to develop their capacity for leadership. Of course I know that many people today are suspicious of leaders, because leaders are in positions of power; and in many minds the exercise of power is in itself corrupting regardless of the result. John W. Gardner, now Secretary of Health, Education, and Welfare and previously head of the Carnegie Corporation, points out that many people, especially in the universities, hesitate even to work toward leadership positions. While they believe every person has a right to advise or criticize the leader, very few ever want to be the leader, either in business or in government. This is a dangerous attitude, because by abdicating their desire for leadership they could very well be drying up the supply of future leaders that our country depends upon for its success.

The future businessmen of this nation should know that every program and every idea needs a leader to make it work, and that business provides an opportunity for the development of the leadership our society demands and needs.

Now I have mentioned just a few points that might be of some use in discussing with the students of business the true nature and the challenge of a career in business accounting. I have pointed out that the profession has taken on a new breadth and has gained new stature. I have said that business needs accountants with a world view and an understanding of world needs. It wants people who can express their individuality through the dynamics of group action. And it needs men who are willing to have their talents for leadership developed and put to work. With that knowledge a young student should have a clearer idea of the place he can make for himself in a world that depends on business for its economic strength.

But that's the easy part. After all, most college students are already somewhat sympathetic with the general goals of business. Above and beyond that there is the considerably more difficult job of convincing the unbelievers. I do not have to remind you that not everyone on a college campus or in government agrees with us about the basic benefits of our free market system. All of us run into negative attitude quite frequently. And because, by the very nature of your profession, you are the ex officio ambassadors of the business point of view, let me say samething about the larger educational job facing you and all the rest of us in business, namely, the job of educating the general public about the system as we know it.

How can we make a better case for ourselves? Well, it seems to me we could begin by singing a different tune, or marching as Thoreau says to the sound of a different drum. I am convinced that all of us at one time or another have made the mistake of talking in cliches about our business system. We have relied too much on old terminology to describe new ideas. We should acknowledge the possibility that the old words "capitalism," "free enterprise," and "laissez faire" no longer mean exactly what they once did and no longer adequately describe our ever-changing business system. Some people have talked of "people's capitalism," and others have called it an "open society." I have often described it as a "profit-energized, profit-disciplined system." But I think we should keep looking for new and better ways to describe this system of ours, which is based on old and tested principles and yet is always new. In this way we can do a better job of selling the idea to others.

We could also do well to change some of our tactics in handling the social problems of the day. Too often in the past the business community has got itself a reputation for dragging its feet on social issues and being opposed to anything that looks like a new approach. This is somewhat ironic—because in reality the businessman at his desk is *for* innovation—*for* expansion—*for* improved quality—*for* better service to the public—*for* building a better civilization, if you will.

We might also talk just a little less about the evils of government and a little more about the many ways in which government can help business do its work more effectively. As we all know, a government that is genuinely on the side of the enterprise system can give enormous assistance to the businessman. This can take the form of tax reform and liberalization, of efforts to open up foreign markets through the breaking down of trade barriers, of help to states and cities in providing better transportation facilities such as freeways within the great interstate system, and so on almost indefinitely. I think we can all agree that what is needed is to speak plainly about specific ways in which the flexibility and creativity of our business system can be helped by government, and then also speak up loud and clear and in specific terms when business is being cramped by government. Then something specific can be done.

Next, we should make it clear that business provides a variety of social benefits that are a natural part of its method of operation. I know that among young people especially there is the idea that business is interested only in profit, that it has no sense of social responsibility, and that it provides far less opportunity than government agencies like the Peace Corps for the solution of large global problems.

They should learn that one of the most attractive things about private enterprise is that there are so many double benefits—so many business problems on the one hand and social problems on the other that can be solved *at the same time.* Let me give you a few examples from my own company. We recently opened a new assembly plant near Rockford, Illinois. Before we could build our first automobile in that plant we had to recruit and train more than a thousand employees. And we now have some 4500 employees on the payroll. Many of those people we have trained ourselves. Others we have trained through a joint program with the Manpower Training Division of the Illinois Department of Labor. Still others have been provided training under the Federal Manpower Development Training Act. The result is an efficient and productive automobile plant on the one hand and 4500 new jobs on the other.

We have also had the great satisfaction in recent years of seeing men who once farmed in Philippine rice paddies become supervisors in our new automobile plant in Manila. We have brought men from the Turkish government back to Detroit for training in such things as truck maintenance and repair. We have hired Peruvian Indians and sent them to our plant in Mexico for training before they return to Peru to help operate our new plant there. In Colombia we have established a school near our plant for the children of our employees. The company rents the school and pays the teachers, and the children attend classes while their fathers work.

In Michigan, and in other states where we have plants or a large concentration of dealerships, we have extensive training programs in skills running all the way from automobile mechanic to clay modeler to skilled tradesman.

The result of all these programs in this country and around the world is a double benefit—thousands of people are finding new dignity in creative and responsible positions, and we are developing skilled workers for employment in our plants. We are not there to take the place of the Peace Corps, and we would not want to. But the answers to human problems are not found just in agencies of the Federal government. Private business provides a more basic kind of opportunity for a concrete expression of the idealism our young people are blessed with today. And they should know that the opportunity is there.

They should also know that even beyond the obvious human contribution made by business there is another equally important job done by companies that make investments in foreign countries. We hear a good deal about the benefits of government foreign aid. But let me give you an interesting figure. In 1964, the last year for which we have figures, business investment in foreign countries, many of them as yet underdeveloped, was more than double that sent over by the government in economic foreign aid. As a result of these private investments, other countries are developing their own business systems, improving the living conditions of their own people, creating jobs, balancing their international accounts, and generally strengthening their economies to the point of self-sufficiency.

I might add that these investments overseas also contribute favorably to the United States' balance of payments. For example, in every one of the last ten years Chrysler has returned more money from its foreign investments than it has sent abroad. And over those years it has contributed a total of more than $1 billion to the favorable side of our balance of payments.

In a way this free-wheeling business system of ours is a revolutionary force without precedent. It certainly would never be recognized by Adam Smith or John Stuart Mill. And in the last twenty years we have been learning a few things about the economics of full employment that would surprise even John Maynard Keynes. What we now have is a system of private multi-national business organizations undertaking separately to explore all the possibilities of the world's economic future, and laying plans for making that future happen. I have often thought that the emergence of this privately planned economy—in which the businessman is the active agent of growth—might very well be called the "quiet revolution." By its efficiency in providing for the needs of free people everywhere our business system is forcing the destruction of the inefficient and tyrannical system of controls used by the communists. The people of the underdeveloped nations of the world are beginning to see the superiority of our system and are coming our way. And this quiet revolution is the kind of thing that is like an extra dividend to a businessman.

Now I have pointed out a few of the attributes of our free business system because I believe we have to do a more thorough and effective job of selling the basic concepts that have made our country the strength of the free world. And I have done it because I believe that all of us have the great opportunity to do that job most effectively—to define this great system of business, to explain how it works, to help others understand the incredible coming together of varied talents in a common direction of purpose that takes place in a modern corporation. And most important of all, every man here has the challenge of making it clear how business, which has the flexibility to move with change and not rely on assumptions that worked in another time, is a social force for good unequaled anywhere in the world.

I would like to issue that challenge here today. The measure of our success in communicating this message to others could well be the measure of the success of our business system in the years ahead. The greater the understanding of the social contribution of business, the easier the businessman's job will be. The young accountants and comptrollers of tomorrow need our counsel and our help; and business needs theirs.

68. *Career Opportunities in Accounting**

Richard G. Williams**

One of the most significant developments in private accounting in recent years I think has been the financial officers' rise in status and I think this rise can be attributed to the responsibilities these men have assumed in dealing with the complexities of modern business. The position of financial vice president is a rather new one, and many controllers and treasurers have been elevated to this position because of their participation in the management decisions of their companies. In 1949 there were no members of the Controllers Institute with the title of financial vice president but by the beginning of this year 266 members held this title.

* Reprinted from *Selected Papers—1962*, New York: Haskins & Sells, 1962, pages 48–50.
** Richard G. Williams is a partner of Haskins & Sells.

Furthermore, many accountants are being selected as presidents and chairmen of their companies. Mr. Frederic G. Donner, Chairman of the Board of General Motors Corporation is one accountant who has risen to the top. Mr. Donner, who was recommended to General Motors in 1926 as a young accountant with an analytical mind, has had this to say about the profession: "As accounting has matured and expanded in its scope, it has become an essential part of every end of the business. It concerns itself with what *has* happened, what *is* happening, and what may be *expected* to happen. In this way it has become indispensable to management in insuring that proper controls and planning will result in profitable operations."

Others with accounting backgrounds who now head some of our large corporations are Ernest R. Breech, former chairman of Ford Motor Company and now chairman of Trans World Airlines; Charles S. Jones, President of Richfield Oil Company, Joel E. Hunter, President of Crucible Steel Company of America, Harold Blancke, President of Celanese Corporation of America and Gerald L. Phillippe, President of General Electric Company.

These recent developments in the business world and in the accounting profession adequately indicate I think that the accounting field is a large and expanding one and that its outlook for continued growth is excellent.

69. Accountants Wanted: A Severe Shortage Spurs Recruiting, Drives Up Pay*

The need for more accountants is "desperate," says the American Institute of Certified Public Accountants. Chicago's Arthur Andersen & Co., a big accounting firm, seeks 1,500 college grads this year, up 50% from 1967. "It's a wild situation," exclaims a Marquette University official. At Bentley College in Waltham, Mass., a record 175 employers, one seeking 200 accountants, are competing for less than 350 grads.

Accounting firms say that while computerage demand for accountants grows, the stodgy image of the work keeps the number of students choosing the profession constant or declining. Result: Starting salaries are zooming up about 10% a year. One survey of 200 companies finds the average starting pay now $737 a month, up from $594 three years ago.

* Reprinted from *The Wall Street Journal*, February 4, 1969.

70. When the Tax Ax Fell...*

. . . last night, it probably caught a record number of taxpayers with returns still in hand. The IRS believes that requests for extensions will top last year's unprecedented 630,000 (out of some 75 million returns expected this year). Some say the surtax fueled procrastination. Another factor may have been a shortage of accountants. Robert Half Personnel Agencies Inc. says it polled firms in nine cities, found all crying for CPAs.

* Reprinted from *The Wall Street Journal*, April 16, 1969.

71. Salary Levels for Bachelor's Degree in Accounting*

Frank S. Endicott, the Director of Placement and Professor of Education at Northwestern University conducts an annual survey of salary levels by college degree. In 1957, the average monthly salary paid by industrial companies to accounting graduates was $402 per month. In 1967, it was $648 and for 1969, the indication was that $737 would be the average monthly starting salary. Experience has shown, and this might apply only to larger cities, that $737 per month is low and that $800 per month is probably a more realistic figure.

In the same study, whereas a Bachelor's degree candidate in accounting showed a monthly starting salary of $737, a Master's degree candidate, in accounting, showed an average monthly starting salary of $929. In ten years, the starting salaries have doubled and there is no indication that we have hit a plateau nor will we hit a plateau within the near future.

* "Salary Levels for Bachelor's Degree in Accountancy," by Norman Berlant, reprinted from *The New York Certified Public Accountant*, October 1969, page 82.

Part Seven

Epilogue— The Dynamism of Accounting

This part is not a summary of the book. It is related to all other parts and carries an important message. Simply stated, the message is that the accounting function is dynamic and must change in response to changes in its environment and the continuously evolving needs and demands of an environment's participants.

For those who perceive accounting as nothing but bookkeeping, this book presents evidence that should change their perception. For those who live only in worlds of either financial or management accounting, the book makes a case for a new breadth of accounting's horizons. Those who want a detailed definition of accounting might realize that such can be given only with reference to a particular period of time or a particular set of circumstances. Accounting, as it is known today, has evolved over many years. There is evidence of this evolution in our book, and the present part includes readings that suggest that this evolution is not yet complete.

The first reading (Heitger) conveys the message of Part Seven in the form of a fanciful tale about an imaginary king. The story moves slowly, and the message comes through quite subtly. The next three items are all relatively short. They describe examples of changes that could conceivably occur during the next few years. They also imply further expansion of the accounting function as it is known today. These examples are not exhaustive; they illustrate and serve to substantiate the contention that accounting is indeed dynamic.

The Yale Express item carries implications of a need to report more frequently to outside users. More frequent reporting would, in the language of the cybernetic systems theorist, shorten the feedback loop and thereby possibly reduce uncertainty. While this might mean an expansion of the financial accounting function, we should realize that the concept of daily, weekly, or monthly reports has long been regarded as important for management, that is, internal enterprise users of accounting information.

The item from *The Economist* draws attention to an often heard criticism regarding the lack of concern, by accountants, for information about the future. Students of behavioral systems are increasingly seeking to predict a system's behavior in the future. Investors, potential investors and creditors have the same concern about entities for which accountings are made. It is quite conceivable that accountants are going to have to give this matter specific attention in the future. In this respect it is interesting to note that the Institute of Chartered Accountants in England and Wales recently approved the attestation of profit forecasts by Chartered Accountants.

The third of these short items raises the concept of human asset accounting, a topic receiving attention from organization psychologists like Rensis Likert. One has only to recall the reported benefits derived by American Motors from George Romney's management abilities in order to concede that the recording of a "Romney Asset" might have served a useful purpose. It should be realized though that accounting for assets and liabilities per se need not necessarily yield the same results as accounting for assets and liabilities based on transaction costs. Again a change in the accounting function might be predicted for this area.

Office of Economic Opportunity programs referred to in Part Four (not specifically mentioned here) are a further example of dynamic environmental conditions to which accounting should be responsive and which seem likely to change the scope of the accounting function.

Finally, the article by Stettler makes some interesting predictions about the future of the public accounting profession. Professor Stettler's speculations on the expansion of the attest function seem particularly important. They underscore once more the continuing evolution of accounting, which is also included in the last short selection with reference to international harmony in accounting.

Chapter XV

Accounting Responses to Change

72. The Tale of the King Who Changed Radically*

Lester E. Heitger**

Once upon a time, in a far-distant land, there lived a wise old king named Adding. (That was his last name; his first name was Comparing, and his middle name was Posting.) King Comparing, Posting, and Adding ruled over the country of Bookkeeping, and was much revered by his subjects, whose sole occupation was recording, classifying, and summarizing data. There were some, it is true, who grumbled about the kingdom's narrow economy, but no one ever paid them any heed.

One day a band of gypsies, who were passing through those parts, gave the king a beautiful mirror with a golden frame. The king had it hung on the wall in the great entrance hall of his palace, where all who passed could admire it.

Before very long, the word got about that the mirror had magic powers. Whenever someone stood in front of it and asked it a question, the mirror would answer. It could predict the weather, give the latest baseball scores, and even tell what was going on in the neighboring kingdoms. Not wanting such an intelligent mirror to go nameless, the people called it Ambition.

* Reprinted by permission, from *The Arthur Young Journal*, Autumn 1967, pages 11–14. Copyright © 1967 by Arthur Young & Company.

** Lester E. Heitger was an auditor in the Denver office of Arthur Young & Company at the time this article was written. He is now at work on his Ph.D. at Michigan State University.

One day a subject of Bookkeeping walked up to the mirror and said: "Mirror, mirror, on the wall, who is the smartest of them all?" The mirror replied, "You of this kingdom are no longer the smartest of them all. In the neighboring kingdom of Businessmania there are those who can do all that you do and yet interpret and evaluate as well."

Thereupon all the subjects of Bookkeeping scurried about in a great frenzy to become proficient in the arts of interpreting and evaluating. King CPA frowned on all this commotion and told his subjects that they need not be in such a hurry, since the work they were presently doing was indispensable. "Learn the new skills if you must," the old king warned, "but beware of Radical Change!" This was a piece of advice that the king had received from his father, along with the scepter and crown, and although he did not know exactly what it meant (since, to his knowledge, there had never been any Radical Change in the kingdom of Bookkeeping) he felt it important to pass this wisdom along to his subjects at every appropriate opportunity.

In time, despite King CPA's lack of enthusiasm, the subjects of Bookkeeping became quite proficient at their new skills—so proficient, indeed, that they decided to change the name of their kingdom to Accounting, since Bookkeeping no longer seemed adequate to describe all the services they rendered. As the kingdom prospered, the magic mirror, Ambition, fell into disuse; and one day it was replaced by a portrait of the king in golf attire, and was carried off to a storeroom in the remotest part of the palace, where old working papers were kept.

The years went by, and no one gave another thought to the magic mirror, until one day a young lad who was cleaning out some of the palace storerooms happened upon it, and, remembering the stories he had heard, he thought he would try it out. "Mirror, mirror, on the wall," he asked, "who is the smartest of them all?" And the mirror replied, "You of the kingdom of Accounting cannot possibly be the smartest of them all, for just outside your borders there roams a fierce dragon named Exceptionally Devastating Power who threatens to devour half your kingdom, yet you do not seem to be aware that he exists."

When the young lad told what he had heard, a party was sent out in search of the dragon. After several days they came upon the beast in a thicket, devouring data and spitting them out in usable form before the average subject of Accounting could sharpen his quill, much less dip it in the inkwell.

When they got over their fright, the searchers hurried back to the palace to tell King CPA what they had seen. Each had his own idea of what to do about the dragon. One said they should attack it, and kill it if possible, but it was feared that, if they failed to kill it, the beast might escape to some other country and return one day to haunt the kingdom of Accounting. Another suggested that perhaps the dragon would eventually die of starvation, but it was pointed out that the way he was eating up Accounting citizens (he showed a particular preference for smaller ones) it was more likely he would die of indigestion. One subject even went so far as to suggest that perhaps they could train the dragon to obey them.

King CPA said that he would need time to study the problem. "But fear not," he added, "for I am certain that we are still quite safe." And he took the occasion to remind them all again of the danger of Radical Change.

Though they respected the authority and wisdom of their king, his subjects did not all share his feeling of security. So a few of them banded together and learned how to train the dragon. The king, seeing their success, suggested that others do the same. At times the king had insisted on people doing certain things in certain ways, and he was in the habit of giving rigorous tests to see that such decrees were carried out. And those who failed these tests were banished from the kingdom. This time, however, things were happening so fast that the king did not know what to do. He did not want his kingdom to fall, but on the other hand he was opposed to Radical Change. So the king issued no decrees, but merely offered suggestions.

After awhile, secure in the knowledge that some, at least, of his subjects had learned to train the dragon, the king decided to consult the magic mirror, Ambition, once again. But the mirror told him, "You are still not the smartest of them all, for the powerful kingdom of Businessmania demands more information. You must be able to answer all questions pertaining to business." This was a problem the king had scarcely thought about, though some of his subjects had been offering this service for years.

He knew that certain of his subjects were not qualified to give the kind of answers that Businessmania was demanding. Indeed, some of his subjects were even bringing foreigners into the kingdom under cover of darkness, and trying to pass them off as citizens of Accounting. These people came from such kingdoms as Marketing, Statistics, Mathematics, Engineering, and Law. The king did not really approve of this activity. He knew he should take the lead in retraining his people, but alas, he did not have the resources for such an undertaking. And then, too, he was opposed to Radical Change.

Once again the king turned to the mirror for help: "Mirror, mirror, great and wise, what can I do, I need replies?" But all that came back was bad news: "You ask for solutions before you know the problems. The function for which your kingdom has sole responsibility, auditing, is becoming outdated. Businessmania is now demanding much more. The attest function may be extended to management audits, labor-management information audits, government audits, and tax return audits."

The king retired to his royal chamber in tears. He had more problems than he could solve in a hundred years of his normal decision-making processes. He confided in his chief advisor, Special Committee, but Special Committee merely referred the matter to Subcommittee for further study.

The intelligent subjects of Accounting proposed what seemed to be some excellent solutions to the problems, but the king could not decide which was best. Many of his older advisors cautioned him against hasty action, reminding him of the good old days and the way things had always been done. "And remember, too," they warned, "what the king your father told you about the dangers of Radical Change!"

In despair and confusion, the king decided that the magic mirror was to blame for all his troubles. "Perhaps if I destroy the mirror," he thought, "peace and unity will be restored to my kingdom." But when he tried to destroy the mirror, it would not break. Ambition is indestructible.

The mirror spoke to the king: "You cannot destroy me, nor can you blame me for your own indecision. I warned you of your problems, but you did not take me seriously. Now your subjects no longer look to you for leadership, for you would not lead them when they needed you."

Then, little by little, King CPA began to disappear from the face of the earth, for whenever something fails to perform the function for which it was created, it ceases to be. And as the old king saw himself fading away, it occurred to him to wonder whether *this* might not be the Radical Change of which his father had warned him.

73. *Yale Express System Former President Sues Auditor**

A former president of Yale Express System Inc. filed a $20 million damage suit against Peat, Marwick, Mitchell & Co., a leading accounting firm.

The complaint was filed yesterday in a state court at Mineola, N.Y. It alleges "deliberate and willful fraudulent acts, concealments and conspiracy" by the defendants in connection with the preparation of Yale Express financial statements.

* Reprinted from *The Wall Street Journal*, August 23, 1968.

Peat-Marwick was the auditor for Yale Express and its subsidiaries before they entered Chapter 10 bankruptcy reorganization proceedings in 1965. Yale Express had reported earnings of about $1.1 million for 1963. It later restated that year's results as a loss of nearly $1.9 million.

Gerald W. Eskow, the former Yale Express president who filed the suit, and two other former officers were indicted in 1967 by a Federal grand jury on charges of filing false company financial statements. Their trial is scheduled to begin in Federal court here early this fall.

Also named in Mr. Eskow's complaint as defendants are three individuals presently or formerly associated with Peat-Marwick as well as Donald Palmer, comptroller of Republic Carloading & Distributing Co., freight forwarding subsidiary of Yale Express.

Peat-Marwick officials had no immediate comment. Mr. Palmer said there are "adequate defenses" for the allegations.

The troubles of Yale Express, a trucking concern, began shortly after it acquired the larger Republic Carloading in May 1963. Republic, which gathers small shipments for carload freight movements, has a reorganization plan that has been pending since January. Republic's unsecured creditors are currently voting on it. The poll will be tallied by Sept. 10.

In Mr. Eskow's 44-page complaint is an allegation that a Peat-Marwick staffer on about Aug. 21, 1964, prepared a "cash flow" work paper that "advised and alerted" Peat-Marwick and the other defendants that Yale Express's "alleged profit" of $717,000 in the 1964 first half, as published, "was false, misleading and fraudulent" and, instead, a loss of $1,615,000 had been sustained. But Peat-Marwick "did nothing to correct these errors or to advise (Mr. Eskow) or third parties thereof."

74. Burgeoning Facts (Company Accounts)*

The new act [U.K. Companies Act, 1967] will help the evolutionary process towards more informative accounts, but one big shortcoming is likely to be with us for some time. The annual accounts have not lost their static nature: they account for money spent in the year in question. The forecast should not be confined to some general observations by the chairman coupled with an affirmation of faith in the company's future. It should have some solid figuring, at least for the next financial year,

* Reprinted from *The Economist*, February 3, 1968, page 70.

which is, in any case, one-third to a half gone by the time the accounts are produced. (The delay could well be cut down, too.) On this point the Scottish accountants must have the last word in a recent booklet: One may look forward to financial reporting in the last quarter of this century when the annual accounts will consist first of forecasts for the future (perhaps in type that gets fainter for each year ahead) and secondly of a report on what went wrong with last year's forecast.

75. Financial Reports Minus Humans May Be Misleading*

Corporate financial reports often detail precisely the value of financial and physical assets, but seldom if ever do they even attempt to assess the worth of a company's human resources.

Because of this, a tiny minority of business professors and accountants are beginning to insist that the net income statements of corporations not only are inadequate but may be misleading. . . .

Dr. R. Lee Brummet, a certified public accountant and a professor at the University of Michigan, and now deeply involved in research on the problem, states it this way:

"High sales and profits can exist for a period during which there is an exodus of key people or when morale is deteriorating or when the organization may be going downhill in other ways."

The opposite effect can be hidden too. A company's executives may be spending, investing and building for the future and, because this is not measured statistically, be unable to prove it until many years later.

As an accountant, Brummet says, "I believe we cannot justify continuing to ignore so vital a matter as human resources and refuse to try to say whether they increase or decrease in value."

These resources include the value of a firm's human organization, the education and abilities and morale of employes, customer, shareholder and supplier loyalty, reputation in the financial and neighborhood communities.

* From an Associated Press release by John Cunniff, published in *The Seattle Times*, February 7, 1969.

The goal is to devise accounting tools to measure such assets. Brummet began his research about a year ago at the insistence of Dr. Rensis Likert, a psychologist, author and director of the University of Michigan Institute for Social Research.

Brummet concedes that a solution isn't coming in the next few years but maintains that a measurement of human resources will be generally accepted by accountants 10 or 20 years from now.

"You can't expect the Securities and Exchange Commission to get excited right away," he said, "but for the manager of an organization insuring performance,developments of skills,attitudes and work relations."

The research now under way, with the on-the-job cooperation of R. G. Barry Corp. of Columbus, Ohio, and a few other companies, seeks to place human resources under measurement techniques similar to those used to survey and record physical and financial resources.

"The problem," says Brummet, "is the extent to which we can succeed in getting reliable measures, because human resources have never been assessed in dollar terms."

The importance of doing so is seen in a typical situation related by Likert.

"Ruthless pressure in the form of budget cuts, personnel limitations, tightened work standards and similar steps may maintain or increase cash flow," he says, and "this is treated as earnings in the accounting reports."

But just wait a few years and this hidden deterioration comes to the surface like termites in the last stages of destroying a building. By then, however, the ruthless manager may be "excelling" at another company.

76. CPAs / Auditing / 2000± *

Howard F. Stettler**

The mathematical term included in the title of this paper is intended to indicate (1) the growing tendency to communicate in mathematical terms and (2) the approximate point in time (circa 2000 A.D.) that is the focal point of the discussion that follows. The discussion itself relates primarily to some changes the author anticipates in professional auditing

* Reprinted from *The Journal of Accountancy*, May 1968, pages 55–60. Copyrighted 1968 by the American Institute of CPAs.

** Howard F. Stettler is Professor of Business Administration at the University of Kansas.

practice and in the certified public accountants who are responsible for most independent audits in the United States.

Accountants and auditors are often subjected to the criticism that their approach to the services they render is not unlike that of the crawfish, who customarily backs out of places and hence sees only where he has been—not where he is going. Although at one time such criticism was perhaps justified, certainly the movement in recent years has been largely away from the rearview mirror approach. But even to the extent that it remains, the backward look should not be summarily dismissed. The history-oriented accountant should be regarded in the light of Shakespeare's observation in *The Tempest:* "What's past is prologue."

The prognostications that follow are the result of the author's effort to peer into the future, but like all such efforts the prognostications are thoroughly grounded in the past and in an interpretation of what has taken place in the past.

HOW MANY CPAs?

By the year 2000 (actually about 1990) CPAs will have "arrived" professionally, for they will have begun to exceed in numbers each of the other two leading professional groups: physicians and surgeons, and lawyers and judges. But CPAs have considerable ground to cover to attain such numbers, for the 1960 census showed:

Physicians and surgeons	230,000
Lawyers and judges	213,000

By contrast, the American Institute of Certified Public Accountants estimated the number of CPAs in 1960 at a mere 69,000. In other words, the other two professions each counted over three times more members than there were CPAs in 1960.

The key to the prognostication of equal numbers lies in relative growth rates, which compare as follows on a compounded basis from 1950 to 1960:

Physicians and surgeons	1¾ % per year
Lawyers and judges	1½ % per year
United States population	1¾ % per year
Certified public accountants	6 % per year

Extrapolation of these growth rates from a 1960 base indicates the expected crossing of the other two professions' census lines by the CPA census line about 1990. But the same approach extended further into the future suggests that the entire U. S. population will be CPAs by 2080! This absurdity highlights the weakest link in the projection: the period of time that a 6% compounded growth rate for CPAs can be sustained relative to a much slower growth rate for the population as a whole.

A more specific question is whether the growth rate can be maintained for another 22 years, and for this answer an unqualified "yes" is tendered for these reasons:

1. The 6% growth rate has been maintained since 1960, with about 98,000 CPAs in 1966, and it has been sustained since 1930, when there were only 13,600 CPAs.

2. Although the amount of services required from the medical and legal professions is closely tied to population growth, CPA services are more closely tied to the amount of economic activity, and the gross national product has grown at a rate ranging from 3% to 5% per year.

3. There has been a history of extensions of services by CPAs:

   a. The growth in management services work is still at an early stage and the expansion should continue rapidly for another 10 to 15 years.

   b. The federal government has a history of requiring additional auditing work by CPAs that is likely to extend into the future. Recently added audit requirements cover such areas as Medicare intermediaries and providers, Rural Electrification Administration co-operatives, federal savings and loan associations, and a substantial number of additional corporations (more than 500 stockholders and $1 million is assets) required to file audited financial statements with the Securities and Exchange Commission. For the future, there seems to be growing interest in audits of local government units. And it is probably only a matter of time until all national banks or all banks in the Federal Reserve System will find that independent audits have been made mandatory.

   c. A growing number of states have adopted so-called "regulatory" CPA laws that reserve opinion auditing to CPAs as the only fully qualified practitioners. Public accountants in practice at the time such laws are passed are permitted to continue to provide all public accounting services, but no additional public accountants are registered and, as their number decreases, the service needs supplied by them tend to be transferred to CPAs.

EDUCATIONAL PREPARATION FOR ENTRANCE TO THE ACCOUNTING PROFESSION

By the year 2000 most persons will enter the accounting field with the master's degree. The bachelor's degree became prominent as a requirement to qualify for accounting positions during the 1930's, and it is almost a universal requirement for an accounting position today. An analysis of statistical information supplied by CPA candidates writing the CPA examination for the first time in November 1965 showed that over 90% of these candidates held the bachelor's degree. This percentage reflects primarily the candidates' own recognition of the importance of the degree since only a handful of state laws required it for admission to the CPA examination. (By August 1967 a total of 24 states had laws requiring, at least by some stated future date, a minimum of a college baccalaureate degree for admission to the CPA examination. That figure compares with only 7 states having such a requirement in 1961, as reported by Clifford V. Heimbucher in the November 1961 issue of *The Journal of Accountancy*.)

It is reasonable to expect that the master's degree will supersede the bachelor's degree as a saturation is reached in the percentage of entrants to accounting holding the bachelor's degree. The bachelor's degree superseded the high school diploma in a similar manner during the period 1930–1945. Other factors pointing in the direction of additional education are the findings of the Commission on the Common Body of Knowledge for CPAs, the continued expansion of our total store of knowledge, and the natural inclination toward "product differentiation." Job-seeking accountants can achieve such differentiation by the simple addition in most instances of a single year of graduate study. The first-time candidates for the November 1965 CPA examination show how far the trend to graduate study had already progressed by that time. Of the total candidates, 6% held the master's degree, another 6% were attending graduate school and 8% had previously earned some credit in graduate accounting courses. Thus 20% of the candidates had some exposure to graduate study.

Some additional interesting figures on accounting education may be gleaned from *Statistical Abstract of the United States* (published by the Bureau of the Census), but they give little support for the stated expectation of the prevalence of the master's degree by the year 2000. In 1964 there were 13,772 accounting undergraduate degrees awarded, representing 23% of the total undergraduate degrees in business, but only 530 master's degrees in accounting were awarded that year and these represented only 9% of the business master's degrees. Also of interest: the accounting master's degrees were 5% of the accounting undergraduate degrees in 1956, but 4% of that figure in 1964.

The trend that seems to underlie the above figures, however, is for graduate study to be directed to the general area of business, rather than to the specializations within the broader area. Overall, the master's degree in business is becoming relatively more popular. In 1956, the first year in which the detailed information became available, total master's degrees in business were 7% of the bachelor's degrees awarded, but by 1964 the relationship had increased to 11%.

GREATER PROPORTION OF ACCOUNTING GRADUATES TO ENTER PUBLIC ACCOUNTING

No figures are available to indicate the relative flow of college accounting graduates into public accounting, industry and government, but it is the author's prediction that by the year 2000 the flow will be almost entirely to public accounting, with the electronic computer the catalyst for this change. This expectation is based on past experience that most accountants entering business or government are likely to be involved in some form of advanced "figurework"—as for instance special cost studies—or else to be supervising clerical employees who perform routine data processing activities.

But routine data processing activities are rapidly being shifted to computers, and even some of the more complex types of accounting analyses are being programed for computer handling. Examples of this type of activity include PERT/Cost planning and control, variance analysis, contract estimating, and statement preparation and analysis. It is possible, nevertheless, that the accounting positions being eliminated might be replaced, at least in part, by positions in systems analysis and computer programing. That possibility seems unlikely, however, in the light of present developments in computer applications, which have seen most of the positions in data processing being filled by a highly heterogeneous group of individuals, very few of whom have accounting orientation or background. Accountants will, of course, continue to prescribe to the data processing department the needed outputs of the system and the internal controls to be incorporated, but this function will require fewer accountants than in the past when accountants supervised the clerical employees.

Public accounting work, on the other hand, is unlikely to experience a similar type of evolution. This is a professional service activity that is not susceptible to computerization, and a constantly increasing demand for accounting graduates is anticipated in this field. Hence, the demand for accountants in public accounting will grow relative to the demand in industry and government.

These comments should not be interpreted as suggesting that computers are being ignored by public accounting, for practitioners in the field must be capable of reviewing and testing their clients' computerized accounting systems, using computers in some auditing work, and assisting clients in the installation and modification of computerized accounting and data processing systems.

CHANGES IN THE APPROACH TO INDEPENDENT AUDITS

Early audits of business enterprises were largely directed inward. Owner-managers frequently desired assurance that cash had been correctly accounted for and that record-keeping was handled properly and accurately. Expanded capital needs developing from the industrial revolution frequently led to the addition of partners or to incorporation, but in either case determination of profits became of increasing importance. Even under these circumstances, though, audit direction was still primarily inward. Auditors were concerned mainly with internal accounting records, documents and procedures.

Short-term credit needs, however, gradually brought the balance sheet to the fore as the source of important information about liquidity and financial position, and audit activity was expanded to include reference to external forms of evidence which occurred outside the accounting system itself.

Developing public ownership of corporate shares likewise focused attention on financial statements—especially the income statement. The importance of external evidence to support the accounting records and resulting financial statements reached a climax with the startling disclosure of fraud that had gone undetected for many years in the *McKesson & Robbins* case.[1]

Now the attention of auditors is once again being directed inward, and the change is being accelerated by the replacement of manual and mechanical data processing methods with electronic data processing that occurs largely within the confines of computer systems.

The concept of auditing "through" the computer is coming to the fore, and, with the excellent tests and controls that can be incorporated within a well-designed computer processing system, external evidence is decreasing in importance. Even the year 2000 will not, however, see a complete switch in emphasis from external evidence to contemplation of the internal machinations of computerized accounting systems. Auditors will still need some opportunity to gain contact with "reality," but the sampling of external evidence is likely to be more to confirm the operation of the accounting system than to verify directly the bona fides of the resulting account balances.

MANAGEMENT AUDITS

In terms of new or expanded CPA services to clients and third parties, little development of management audits which result in an

---

[1] See *Report on Investigation, United States of America before the Securities and Exchange Commission in the Matter of McKesson & Robbins, Inc.*, December 1940, 501 pp., published by the Securities and Exchange Commission.

expression of opinion on management is expected to occur. Investors in common stocks are interested primarily in expectations of future returns from their investment, and management capability seems to be the most important single factor bearing on the future results to be realized. But management capability, or whatever the characteristic of management may be that bears on future success, is qualitative rather than quantitative, and there is no objective way to deal with qualitative factors comparable to the objective treatment of quantitative results. Nevertheless, CPAs, when called upon to do so, will make management reviews and disclose weaknesses detected in the structure and functioning of management, but the results of such reviews will be largely for internal use, or perhaps in connection with acquisitions of operating companies. Furthermore, the reports will include only specific criticisms and suggestions; there will be no overall rating or evaluation of management of the type that would be useful to investors who want to make comparative studies.

EXTENDING THE ATTEST FUNCTION
TO FORWARD ACCOUNTING

By the year 2000 it is likely that CPAs will be expressing independent opinions on the fairness, or reasonableness, of projections of cash flow, financial position and operating results for at least the year following the date of accompanying audited financial statements. Management services engagements for assistance in budget preparation for smaller clients have been common for many years, but CPAs are currently restrained from expressing independent opinions on figures pertaining to the future. Rule 2.04 of the AICPA Code of Professional Ethics provides: "A member or associate shall not permit his name to be used in conjunction with any forecast of the results of future transactions in a manner which may lead to the belief that the member or associate vouches for the accuracy of the forecast." The basis for this rule is that the public interest is heavily involved in the CPA's performance of the attest function, and nothing should be done that would in any way detract from the acceptance of CPA opinions expressed on objectively determined historical accounting results.

Historical information is essentially factual and there is relatively little difficulty in formulating an opinion on the fairness of management representations concerning such information. Also, there is little likelihood that future events might alter the figures attested to, except for known contingencies which would be disclosed by footnote to the statements or in the auditor's report. Forecasts, on the other hand, may not be realized, and it is felt that if CPAs express opinions on forecasts which may later prove to be at variance with subsequent reality, third parties might tend to question the credibility of CPAs' opinions, not only on forecasts but on more factual statements as well.

Counterbalancing any possible loss of acceptance of the work of CPAs is the need of creditors and investors for the best possible indication of what lies in the future when making loan or investment decisions. CPAs, whose very existence is grounded in service to others, will better fulfill their function if they extend their examinations and the added support of their opinions to forward-looking statements of operations, cash flow and financial position for the succeeding year. In addition to the service consideration of a move toward expressing opinions on forward accounting, there is the fact that CPAs in their auditing work are no strangers to the problem of dealing with the future. The current asset and liability classifications on the conventional balance sheet are based on future expectations of realization and cash flow. The future must similarly be dealt with in the acceptance of such important items bearing on "historical" financial statements as economic and useful life of plant assets and certain intangibles, market value of inventories, provision for future expenses arising out of product guarantees, and estimation of the amount of outstanding coupons, trading stamps, container deposits and other items that will never be presented for redemption.

Forward accounting, even though involving many imponderables, is basically a quantitative problem and can thus be dealt with effectively from an auditing standpoint. The system for developing needed estimates can be reviewed in much the same manner as a system of internal control. Although the figures cannot be checked with reality before they are released, they can be related to commonly held projections of future economic conditions, extrapolation of past experience, anticipation of expected changes in material and labor costs, tax rates, etc., and the reasonableness of the relationships of expected figures.

One of the most intriguing aspects of the extension of auditing to forward accounting and the publication of those results will be the removal of some relatively artificial barriers that have developed over the years. These barriers may be compared with the rules of contract bridge which prohibit partners from conversing across the table about their resources or lack thereof. To counteract the rules, a whole system of messages has been developed within the bidding process to convey much of the essential information, but the player is faced with the necessity of mastering a whole new communication system. Much the same situation prevails with creditors' use of balance sheet information about short-term debt-paying ability. The current ratio is generally taken as the best indication of whether liabilities can be paid as they come due in the succeeding year, and hence the accounting approach to the current classification is based on normal expectations of cash receipts and disbursements. But, at best, the current ratio gives only a static picture of a dynamic situation that extends through a full year. One of the things statement users are seeking to determine is whether there will be sufficient cash available to liquidate liabilities as they come due. CPAs will eventually recognize the desirability of aiding users by making available the specific information needed rather than by continuing to force users to develop similar but less complete information themselves.

By the year 2000, audit attestations can be expected to encompass projected balance sheets, income statements, and sources and uses of cash statements for the coming year as well as the realized results for the past year. Attesting of past results will continue to be important to provide a bench mark for evaluating both past projections as well as new projections. Reporting will likely be on a three-column basis showing last year's projections, last year's actual results and next year's projections.

ATTESTATION OF INCOME TAX RETURNS

Another extension of the CPA's attest function is likely to occur in the area of income tax returns. For all but quite small businesses, a CPA will already have examined and attested to the fairness of reported net income, and it is but a simple matter for the CPA to extend his examination to the differences between the accounting definition of income and the tax definition of income. In fact, this work is currently being done, since in many cases the CPA's engagement includes the preparation of income tax returns. But even if tax return responsibility is not a part of the engagement, the CPA must still examine the differences between accounting and taxable income since they have a significant bearing on the amount of income tax deducted in the income statement in arriving at net income, and on the liability for income tax shown in the balance sheet.

Under these circumstances, independence is assured by generally accepted auditing standards and the profession's Code of Professional Ethics, and there is little justification for a review of CPA-prepared tax returns by the taxing authorities. True, there are instances where the taxability or deductibility of an item is not clear-cut and an interpretation of the applicability of tax laws and regulations becomes a factor. In these situations, as in the application of generally accepted accounting principles to accounting figures, the client is responsible for the basic decision and will decide on the basis of what is most favorable to the business entity.

When such borderline matters are involved, tax examiners can be expected to be successful in some proportion of the cases, thus protecting government tax revenues. But it is doubtful whether the added taxes justify the tax examination costs in situations where the return is prepared by a CPA after completion of an examination of financial statements. The duplicate examination effort is in no way productive for the economy as a whole, and additions to long-run tax revenues will be nominal because most tax controversies in the situations discussed tend to involve only timing differences, so that the ultimate gains in tax revenues and tax-payer equity are likely to be minimal.

In view of the benefits to be derived, it can be expected that taxing authorities will eventually operate in the examination area much as does the Comptroller of the Currency with respect to required circularization of bank depositors' accounts. If this important examination activity is not performed under a bank's direction, the national bank examiners step in and add that activity to their other examination work. The Securities and Exchange Commission has likewise delegated examination responsibility but, unlike the Comptroller of the Currency, does not give affected businesses the option of having the government agency conduct the necessary examination.

The taxing authorities would likely function similar to the SEC in determining who shall be privileged to practice before the taxing authority, in influencing the standards to be followed by those entitled to practice in the area of tax return certification and in reviewing returns for outward conformity much as registration statements are reviewed by the SEC before a registration is permitted to become effective. Returns not bearing the attestation of a CPA would be subject to audit by government tax examiners, as at present.

RECAPITULATION

Bill Vaughan, the *Kansas City Star's* paragrapher and observer of the current scene through his "Starbeams" column, has noted. "True, people have always worried about the future, but usually about *what* it would be, not *if*." Hopefully, we may be excused for having returned briefly to the supposedly passé pastime of speculating about *what* the future may hold. The speculations have been developed in the spirit of Francis Bacon's admonition: "They are ill discoverers that think there is no land when they see nothing but sea." In an effort to look beyond the mire of day-to-day activities, the following prognostications have been made about what may lie beyond the horizon (at roughly the year 2000):

1. CPAs will exceed in number both medical and legal practitioners.
2. The common academic degree for admission to the CPA profession and accounting in general will be a master's degree.
3. Most college graduates who choose careers in accounting will be entering public accounting.

4. Independent auditing will be heavily systems-oriented, with less use of external evidence.

5. The CPA's attest function will not be extended to audit of management performance and potential, but it will be extended to forward accounting and income tax returns.

77. *Accounting Is Dynamic**

Accounting is dynamic and operates in an atmosphere of change. Even though the basic character of a given business environment seems slow to change, the continuing evolution of the accounting discipline affords means toward more international harmony in generally-accepted accounting principles. Efforts to change unnecessary international diversities in accounting in response to changing economic and business conditions appear to hold greater promise, in theory, than legislation or another form of enforcement of dictated international accounting uniformity.

* Reprinted from *The International Journal of Accounting*, Spring 1968, page 103.